# CIVIL WAR AMERICA

As war raged on the battlefields of the Civil War, regular men and women all over the nation continued their daily routines. They celebrated holidays, ran households, wrote letters, read newspapers, joined unions, attended plays, and graduated from high school and college. *Civil War America* reveals how Americans, both Northern and Southern, lived during the Civil War—the ways they worked, expressed themselves artistically, organized their family lives, treated illness, and worshipped.

Written by a variety of specialists, the chapters in this book cover the war's impact on the economy, the role of the federal government, labor, welfare and reform efforts, the Indian nations, universities, healthcare and medicine, news coverage, photography, and a host of other topics that flesh out the lives of ordinary Americans who just happened to be living through the biggest conflict in American history. Along with the original material presented in the book chapters, the website accompanying the book is a treasure trove of primary sources, both textual and visual, matched to each chapter topic.

*Civil War America* uncovers seismic shifts in the cultural and social landscape of the United States, providing the perfect addition to any course on the American Civil War.

**Maggi M. Morehouse** is Associate Professor of Southern History and Director of the Burroughs Fund for Southern Studies at Coastal Carolina University.

**Zoe Trodd** is Professor and Chair of American Literature in the Department of American and Canadian Studies at University of Nottingham.

With contributions by: A.J. Angulo, Laura M. Ansley, Shannon Smith Bennett, Lauren Brandt, John Casey, Kimberly Cook, Suanna H. Davis, Nicole Keller Day, W. Craig Gaines, James Gillespie, Jack Hamilton, Brayton Harris, Guy R. Hasegawa, Sharon A. Roger Hepburn, Mark A. Lause, Thomas Lawrence Long, Maggi M. Morehouse, Megan Kate Nelson, Jennifer Raab, Daniel Rasmussen, Rachel Redfern, Mandy A. Reid, James R. Rohrer, James M. Schmidt, Renee M. Sentilles, John Stauffer, Vanessa Steinroetter, Jennifer Stollman, Ryan Swanson, Phyllis Thompson, David Williams, and Bradford A. Wineman.

For additional information and classroom resources, please visit the *Civil War America* companion website at www.routledge.com/cs/morehouse.

# CIVIL WAR AMERICA

## A Social and Cultural History

*Edited by*

*Maggi M. Morehouse and Zoe Trodd*

Routledge
Taylor & Francis Group

NEW YORK AND LONDON

Please visit the companion website for this title at:
www.routledge.com/cw/morehouse

First published 2013
by Routledge
711 Third Avenue, New York, NY 10017

Simultaneously published in the UK
by Routledge
2 Park Square, Milton Park, Abingdon, Oxon OX14 4RN

*Routledge is an imprint of the Taylor & Francis Group, an informa business*

*Library of Congress Cataloging in Publication Data*
Civil War America : a social and cultural history / edited by Maggi M. Morehouse and
    Zoe Trodd.
    p. cm.
    1. United States—History—Civil War, 1861–1865—Social aspects. I. Morehouse,
    Maggi M., 1953– II. Trodd, Zoe.
    E468.9.C474 2012
    973.7'1—dc23
    2012012014

ISBN: 978-0-415-89596-5 (hbk)
ISBN: 978-0-415-89600-9 (pbk)
ISBN: 978-0-203-09516-4 (ebk)

Typeset in Bembo and Stone Sans
by EvS Communication Networx, Inc.

Printed and bound in the United States of America
by Edwards Brothers, Inc.

# CONTENTS

*Acknowledgements*                                                    *ix*

*Foreword*                                                            *xi*
   *John Stauffer*

*Introduction*                                                        *xix*
   *Maggi M. Morehouse and Zoe Trodd*

**PART I**
## Dissent and Disobedience                                           **1**

1   Draft Resistance and Rioting                                      3
    *Shannon Smith Bennett*

2   Southern Dissent                                                  13
    *David Williams*

3   Women Soldiers                                                    24
    *Rachel Redfern*

**PART II**
## Labor and Land                                                     **31**

4   The Domestic Sphere                                               33
    *Phyllis Thompson*

5   Labor Organizations                                               45
    *Mark A. Lause*

6   Commerce and Industry                                              56
    *Daniel Rasmussen*

7   The Environment                                                    64
    *Megan Kate Nelson*

**PART III**
**Religion and Reform**                                                **77**

8   Religion in the South                                              79
    *Thomas Lawrence Long*

9   Religion in the North                                              88
    *James R. Rohrer*

10  Reform and Welfare Societies                                       99
    *Lauren Brandt*

**PART IV**
**Health and Education**                                              **109**

11  Higher Education                                                   111
    *A.J. Angulo and Kimberly Cook*

12  Military Schools                                                   121
    *Bradford A. Wineman*

13  Military Medicines                                                 131
    *Guy R. Hasegawa*

14  Civilian Healthcare                                                142
    *James M. Schmidt*

**PART V**
**Ethnic American Lives**                                             **151**

15  Slave Emancipation                                                 153
    *Sharon A. Roger Hepburn*

16  Black Troops                                                       163
    *Maggi M. Morehouse*

17  Immigrants                                                         173
    *Jennifer A. Stollman*

18  Native Americans                                                    181
    *W. Craig Gaines*

**PART VI**
**Literature and Visual Culture**                                     **191**

19  Newspapers                                                         193
    *Brayton Harris*

20  Literature                                                         203
    *Vanessa Steinroetter*

21  Photography                                                        213
    *Mandy A. Reid*

22  Painting and Illustration                                          221
    *Jennifer Raab*

**PART VII**
**Leisure and Performance**                                           **231**

23  Music                                                              233
    *Jack Hamilton*

24  Theater                                                            242
    *Laura M. Ansley and Renée M. Sentilles*

25  Baseball                                                           253
    *Ryan Swanson*

26  Sacred and Secular Holidays                                        262
    *Suanna H. Davis*

**PART VIII**
**Death and Aftermath**                                               **273**

27  Death and Dying                                                    275
    *Nicole Keller Day*

28  Veterans                                                           284
    *John Casey*

29  Competing Memories                                                 293
    *James M. Gillispie*

*About the Editors*                                      *303*
*Contributor Biographies*                                *305*
*Index*                                                  *309*

# ACKNOWLEDGMENTS

At Routledge, the editors would like to thank Kimberly Guinta, who is a superb editor, and also Rebecca Novack. Maggi M. Morehouse would like to thank David Weintraub and Zoe Trodd for their support throughout this project, Maurice Isserman for first introducing her to the joys of visiting Civil War sites, and Kay Oxner for uncovering digitized documents. Zoe Trodd would like to thank Maggi M. Morehouse, John Stauffer, Alex Kent Williamson and Blake Gilpin for their advice and ideas on this book, and Tom Rob Smith, Brian Norman, Celeste-Marie Bernier, Joe Lockard, Kevin Bales and all her colleagues at the Institute for Research in African American Studies at Columbia University for their support. Zoe is grateful for a year-long fellowship from the Center for the Study of the American South at the University of North Carolina Chapel Hill; two years of funding from the American Council of Learned Societies and the Andrew W. Mellon Foundation; and a short-term fellowship from the Beinecke Library at Yale University.

# FOREWORD

*John Stauffer*

The Civil War was the greatest transforming event in American culture. Its memories continue to haunt and inspire people, and it is impossible to imagine what the United States would look like today had it never happened. With some 620,000 deaths, more Americans died in the conflict than in all other wars combined until Vietnam. More than 10 percent of the population was directly involved, and almost every American had a close friend or family member who was killed or maimed in the war. One of the largest expenditures in a few southern states after the war was payment for prosthetic limbs to its veterans. The war brought a centralized nation-state, a national income tax, conscription, and the emergence of large bureaucratic and regimented organizations in the public and private sectors, as well as the numerous other social and cultural shifts described in this book.

Slavery was, of course, the root of the war. But from the nation's founding (when the process of gradual emancipation began in the North) until 1850, the North and South agreed on a series of compromises that prevented the powder keg of slavery from exploding. The first compromise followed the crisis in 1819 over Missouri entering the Union as a slave state, which erupted "like a firebell in the night," as Thomas Jefferson put it (698). It was the first major crisis over slavery, and it shattered a tacit agreement between the two regions that had been in place since the Constitution. Under the terms of the agreement, the North would not interfere with slavery in southern states, and the South would recognize slavery as an evil that should be discouraged and eventually abolished whenever it was safe and feasible to do so. The agreement reflected the belief, shared by most of the Founding Fathers and framers of the Constitution, that slavery was wrong, the equivalent of America's "original sin," according to James Madison (Mellon 158).

The Missouri Crisis established the basic debates over slavery that persisted until the Civil War. During the controversy, the New York congressman James Tallmadge included an amendment that provided for gradual emancipation of Missouri's slaves, much as other northern states had done. Northerners worried that if slavery became legally entrenched in Missouri, it would spread throughout the West. Rufus King, another New Yorker, was the first politician to apply a "higher law" to slavery; he stated that any law upholding slavery was "absolutely void, because [it is] contrary to the law of nature, which is the law of God" (Ernst 372). The higher-law thesis would become a central rhetorical weapon in the writings of immediate abolitionists (those advocating an immediate end to slavery), including *Freedom's Journal*, the nation's first black newspaper; David Walker's *Appeal to the Coloured Citizens of the World* (1829); William Lloyd Garrison's *Liberator*; and the organs of the American Anti-Slavery Society and the Liberty Party, the nation's first abolitionist party. Ralph Waldo Emerson, Henry David Thoreau, Frederick Douglass, and Harriet Beecher Stowe all based their antislavery arguments on a higher-law thesis.

Southerners responded to the Missouri crisis by saying that Congress had no power to exclude slavery even in unorganized territories. They worried about losing representation in Congress, and with cotton production and slave prices on the rise, they became much more belligerent in their quest for national power and their defense of slavery. Restricting slavery, they said, implied eventual emancipation and racial equality. By the 1830s most southern writers had abandoned the beliefs of their forefathers and viewed slavery as a positive good for masters, slaves, and society at large. Implicit in their proslavery rhetoric was their assumption that blacks were subhuman, more akin to domesticated animals than to humans.

The Missouri Crisis was in essence a battle over the western frontier, which each side sought to control. In the compromise, which averted disunion and war, Missouri entered the Union as a slave state; but slavery was excluded from the remaining, unsettled portions of the Louisiana Territory north of 36°30′ north latitude, the same latitude as the southern border of Missouri. The frontier became the imaginative site where the battle over slavery and the future of America was played out.

Political debates over slavery and the frontier were averted for more than 20 years after the Missouri Compromise, until 1845, when Texas entered the Union as a slave state. This period of illusory calm stemmed from two factors. First, from 1819 until 1845 there was no new territorial expansion, and under the terms of the Missouri Compromise, existing territories petitioned for statehood in pairs, with one free and one slave state entering the Union together. Second, from 1836 to 1844, the so-called gag rules automatically tabled all abolitionist petitions in Congress and effectively prevented explosive debates on the subject of slavery.

The annexation of Texas in early 1845 outraged Northerners. John Quincy Adams, the last living Founding Father and a staunch antislavery congressman, described it as a "calamity" in his diary: "the day passes, and leaves scarcely a distinct trace upon the memory of anything, and precisely because ... the heaviest calamity that ever befell myself and my country was this day consummated" (574). As Adams anticipated, the annexation of Texas provoked hostilities with Mexico, which led in 1846 to the Mexican-American War. The war was perpetrated by Southerners including President James K. Polk, and their sympathizers, in order to acquire more slave territory. It virtually doubled the size of the Union, bringing in California and the entire Southwest. Protests occurred throughout the North. Henry David Thoreau abandoned society for Walden Pond on July 4, 1845, partly in response to southern belligerence. And the Free-Soil Party emerged out of the Liberty Party, offering a more conservative and inclusive alternative to the Liberty Party's radical platform. Free-Soilers sought to prohibit the further spread of slavery, which they hoped would lead to its ultimate extinction. The Liberty Party advocated an immediate end to slavery and was the party of choice among northern blacks in the 1850s, including Frederick Douglass, James McCune Smith, and Henry Highland Garnet. But by the late 1840s, members also accepted violent resistance to slavery.

In the wake of the Mexican-American War, the nation was on the verge of civil war, which was averted only by the Compromise of 1850. The compromise consisted of five basic parts, the most onerous of which was a stringent fugitive slave law that denied suspected fugitives the right to a jury trial and virtually legitimated slave stealing. The Fugitive Slave Law converted countless Northerners to the antislavery cause. In their eyes the law put the federal government in the business of manhunting. And since all citizens could now be required to hunt down suspected fugitives, Northerners could no longer wash their hands of slavery. The Fugitive Slave law inspired Harriet Beecher Stowe to write *Uncle Tom's Cabin; or, Life among the Lowly* (1852); and these two pieces of writing—the legislation and the novel—greatly exacerbated sectional hostilities and led to secession and war.

The Compromise of 1850 achieved the opposite of its intentions. Americans were increasingly *unwilling* to compromise, or to accept limits, the rule of law, and traditional boundaries. In effect, civil war broke out even before the explosions shook Fort Sumter in April 1861. Small battles erupted when slave catchers attempted to arrest fugitives, and there were casualties at Boston and Christiana, Pennsylvania. In 1854 Congress passed the Kansas-Nebraska Act, which opened the northern territories of Kansas and Nebraska to slavery and repealed the Missouri Compromise, creating a battleground in Kansas. The Kansas Territory erupted in guerrilla-style civil war from 1855 to 1858 and led to the founding of the Republican Party, the demise of the Whig Party, and the destabilization of the two-party system. In 1857 the Supreme Court declared the Republican Party unconstitutional in the infamous *Dred Scott v. Sandford* case. In his opinion Chief Justice Roger Taney, a proslavery Southerner, argued that Congress had no power to legislate slavery in territories or states; that blacks were "beings of an inferior order ... so far inferior that they had no rights which the white man was bound to respect; and that the negro might justly and lawfully be reduced to slavery for his benefit" (Finkelman 61). In the wake of the *Dred Scott* decision, numerous black writers abandoned their faith in American ideals and advocated emigration.

The last spark leading to disunion was John Brown's raid on the federal arsenal at Harpers Ferry, Virginia, in October 1859, shortly before the 1860 presidential election. Brown's small army of 16 whites and five blacks, and his "provisional constitution" that would govern those areas he hoped to liberate from slavery, terrified the South. The insurgents were captured, convicted of treason and murder, and Brown was sentenced to hang. Although Abraham Lincoln and other Republicans sought to distance themselves from Brown, most Southerners believed that he symbolized the spirit of the Republican Party and the North in general. While Northerners considered Brown a mad-man and murderer, they also called him a martyr and respected his principled actions. During his imprisonment and trial, his prison writings (among the most powerful of the genre) were distributed throughout the North. The sympathetic outpouring for him, led by Lydia Maria Child, Thoreau, and Emerson, helped Lincoln get elected. And in the immediate wake of Lincoln's election, southern states began seceding.

Lincoln famously said in his second inaugural that the North and South "read the same Bible and pray to the same God, and each invokes His aid against the other" (450). Well before the war, each side believed in a vision, sanctioned by God, of what the good society looked like. For the South, this vision was the agrarian way of life, supported and upheld by slavery and governed by "natural aristocrats" who would create an eventual empire of slavery. Southern leaders borrowed from Aristotle, who articulated a natural slave ideal based on the premise that some men were born to rule and others to do the basic work of society. The North's visions of the good society was the free labor ideal, premised on the assumption that one could begin a career as an employee or apprentice, and through hard work and the acquisition of a craft eventually become an independent artisan or entrepreneur and employ the next generation. Each vision threatened the other: Northerners believed that Southerners sought to extend slavery into every territory and state. And Southerners thought that the North sought to abolish slavery throughout the nation.

What neither side understood was that the economic and industrial forces unleashed by the war not only helped to destroy slavery (through the manufacture of weapons, equipment, and railroads); they hastened the end of the free labor ideal. By waging total war to defend an older America, the North assured the demise of its own society as well as that of the agrarian and aristocratic South. Thus, one of the tragic ironies of the war, as the historian Eric Foner has noted, was that "each side fought to defend a distinct vision of the good society, but each vision was destroyed by the very struggle to preserve it" (33).

The transformation of culture by the war was reflected in the very language that Americans used to define themselves: before the war they referred to themselves in the plural case ("the United States of America *are* ..."); after the war they used the singular ("the United States of America *is* ..."). The change of case reflected a much greater cultural transformation, from a weak to powerful central government, from small shops to big business, and unrestricted capitalist expansion at levels that were previously unimaginable. Even the ways in which Americans understood and represented reality were profoundly changed by the war. This shift in the zeitgeist, or collective identity of America, included (1) the displacement of God and (2) the masculinization of society.

The war created a profound crisis of faith in the collective consciousness of Americans. This crisis can be seen in the shift of soldiers' attitudes from the beginning to the end of the war. As the historian Gerald Linderman has shown in his 1987 book, *Embattled Courage: The Experience of Combat in the American Civil War,* northern and southern soldiers believed at the beginning of the war that with faith in God, coupled with courage, they would survive and conquer the enemy. But as the war dragged on, soldiers became disillusioned and no longer believed that God would protect them. They increasingly felt like objects rather than actors in events; and by war's end many had become fatalists. Soldiers on both sides reenlisted in the last year of the war in order to gain a 30-day furlough, in which they could see loved ones before returning to battle and probable death. This displacement of God is understandable when one recognizes that most Americans in both the North and South defined the war in apocalyptic terms. With the end of the war, it was as though the apocalypse had come, but the new age was nowhere in sight.

Frederick Douglass, often referred to as a "representative American" because he transformed himself from the poorest of the poor (a slave) to an independent entrepreneur (newspaperman and orator), was representative in his attitudes toward God as well. From his first speeches in 1841 through the Civil War, he frequently called on God to help him and his nation, even though he rejected conventional doctrines and denominations. Like other black and white abolitionists, Douglass drew from scripture and sought to "come out" from corrupt institutions and churches. Throughout the 1850s he defined himself as a prophet and millennialist and treated the Declaration of Independence, Constitution, and Bible as sacred texts. The principles of the Declaration of Independence, if fulfilled, "would release every slave in the world and prepare the earth for a millennium of righteousness and peace," he argued, adding: "I believe in the millennium" (Blassingame 529, 553). He likened the war to Revelations 12, where Michael and his angels battle against Satan. But after the war he gradually abandoned his faith in God as immanent or indwelling. A heaven on earth increasingly seemed to him a dangerous illusion. He became more secular in his worldview and no longer believed that God could change the world or affect the laws of nature. In his third autobiography, *The Life and*

*Times of Frederick Douglass* (1881), he castigated blacks for believing that they could procure "help from the Almighty." By remaining true to their faith, blacks were "false to fact" and thus to history, he argued. Material facts and the laws of nature now trumped "all the prayers of Christendom" (480).

Alongside this displacement of God, the war brought a masculinization of American society. The Civil War was the nation's first "total war," and it penetrated the home as well as the battlefield. The mentality of war destroyed the status of the domestic sphere as a sacred site that would ennoble and nurture its inhabitants. Women increasingly sought to participate in the battles of life along with men, in part as a means to gain power and basic rights. As a result, a crisis of manhood occurred among northern white men from 1860 to 1870, which coincided with the dwindling output among New England men who had been prominent and prolific writers before the war. During the same decade, especially during the war years, women's writings burgeoned. "Woman has now taken to her pen … and is flourishing it with a vengeance," wrote a journalist in *Frank Leslie's Illustrated* on October 10, 1863.

The crisis came to a head in 1869, when Stowe published "The True Story of Lady Byron's Life" in the *Atlantic Monthly,* followed by *Lady Byron Vindicated: A History of the Byron Controversy* in 1870. In these works Stowe attacked Lord Byron, accusing him of incest with his half sister, among other sins, and championing her friend Lady Byron as one of Europe's great intellectuals and literary figures. The male backlash was virtually unprecedented in American literature. The *Atlantic,* which catered primarily to literary men, lost 15,000 subscribers in the immediate wake of Stowe's article. Throughout the country, newspaper and magazine editors excoriated Stowe. Lord Byron had long been viewed as a symbol of the male liberator and freedom fighter par excellence. For numerous male readers, to attack Byron was tantamount to attacking the mass of northern men who had fought in the war to save their nation.

The male backlash against Stowe reflected changes in literature and culture. The backlash was "a symptom of the polarization of literature along gender lines" that became especially prominent after the war, according to Stowe's biographer Joan Hedrick (370). Stowe's attack on Lord Byron occurred at the end of a decade in which concepts of manhood were in a state of flux and would ultimately become codified in the 1880s by proponents of American realism and an embrace of masculine virtue.

John William De Forest's Civil War novel, *Miss Ravenel's Conversion from Secession to Loyalty* (1867), a loosely autobiographical book based on his wartime experience, explored these new meanings of manhood. The novel attributed the war to a crisis of gender, while also lauding its effects on northern men. De Forest distinguished between northern and southern manhood; while the former is superior, it is not without its genteel, feminine qualities, which he viewed as problematic. But fortunately the war accelerated northern combativeness and martial vigor, resulting in a healthier mixture of physical strength and moral fortitude, coupled with virtue, that constituted the essential ingredients of the "redeemed" nation's manhood. "The old innocence of the peaceable New England farmer and mechanic had disappeared from these war-seared visages and had been succeeded by an expression of hardened combativeness, not a little brutal," the narrator says happily (248). And the novel's protagonist, Edward Colburne, has similarly been transformed: "He is a better and stronger man for having fought three years, out-facing death and suffering. Like the nation, he has developed and learned his powers" (468).

Louisa May Alcott brilliantly captured this emerging masculinization of culture in her two war novels, *Hospital Sketches* (1863) and *Little Women* (1868). In each book, her female protagonists become, in effect, men. More than virtually any other writer of her era, Alcott understood the crisis of manhood caused by the war; and she transformed herself and her leading characters into masculine women for profit, opportunity, and the good of society. While Lillie Ravenel, the female protagonist of *Miss Ravenel's Conversion,* learns to love and appreciate northern manhood, Alcott and her characters become like men in order to vanquish their enemies, redeem their nation, and assert their independence. And she acknowledges that sentimentality can be dangerous, even fatal, in war. In effect, a war mentality had invaded her domestic sphere, and Alcott responded as a man. Seeing the war as a means to reconcile men and women, North and South, she attacked the corrupt influences of masculinity, especially men's efforts to control, govern, and exploit women, by creating masculine men. In a sense, she borrowed from her war experiences and affirmed a battle-field code, becoming like the enemy in order to subdue him.

By 1870, affirmations of a martial ideal and an attack on sentimentalism were already in place. This new masculinist ethos became widespread in the 1880s as one of the defining aspects of literary realism. With the vast economic transformation after the Civil War and the ever-increasing exploitation of labor, war had become an apt metaphor for life.

More broadly, however, and in spite of the war's profound impact on the culture's understanding of God and masculinity, many Americans simply wanted to forget the conflict. As early as 1866, a subscription book publisher argued that people were "tired of being importuned to buy various Histories of the War" (Fahs 313). *Harper's Weekly*, which had published hundreds of Civil War stories and articles during the war, virtually abandoned the war as a topic or setting in the entire decade of the 1870s. As the publisher, James Henry Harper, noted, "the public was tired of reading about the war" (Fahs 313).

The desire—indeed the need—to forget the conflict manifested itself in a disdain for professional soldiers. The *Army and Navy Journal* complained in 1883 that since the war, the designation of "soldier" seemed "to be a synonym for all that is degrading and low, and whenever" people meet someone "bearing it they cannot forbear showing their contempt" (Linderman 272). Veterans themselves sought to forget, and a widespread disillusionment and disorientation set in after the war. The Civil War historian Bruce Catton explained the collective feeling of veterans in these terms: they "lost something; if not life itself, then the dreams or illusions of youth which once seemed to give life its meaning … Like Adam, they had been cast out of the enchanted garden, leaving innocence behind" (159). This sense of loss affected the entire generation that lived through the war.

The resurgence of interest in the war in the 1880s and 1890s came from a younger generation—Americans who understood the war through memories and stories rather than experience, but who understood and represented reality in ways that had been profoundly changed by the war. Reformers of the post-war generation increasingly concluded that "moral certainty" was something they "should sacrifice a little of in exchange for order," as Louis Menand has noted (59). With so many people having needlessly died in the conflict, irony and the abridgment of hope became an acceptable, even desirable, mode of telling stories for post-war writers. Herman Melville's line in *Battle-Pieces*, "what like a bullet can undeceive," foreshadows the shattering of illusion and the rise of irony as a way to understand the world (63). Irony replaced moral certainty in post-Civil War America, as Americans confronted the losses and transformations wrought by the war.

## Works Cited

Adams, John Quincy. *The Diary of John Quincy Adams, 1794–1845.* New York: Longmans, Green, 1928.

Blassingame, John W., ed. *The Frederick Douglass Papers, Series One: Speeches, Debates, and Interviews, Volume 3: 1855–63.* New Haven: Yale University Press, 1985.

Catton, Bruce. *Reflections on the Civil War.* Garden City: Doubleday, 1981.

De Forest, John William. *Miss Ravenel's Conversion from Secession to Loyalty.* 1867; New York: Penguin, 2000.

Douglass, Frederick. *Life and Times of Frederick Douglass.* 1881. Rev. ed. 1892. New York: Collier, 1962.

Ernst, Robert. *Rufus King: American Federalist.* Chapel Hill: University of North Carolina Press, 1968.

Fahs, Alice. *The Imagined Civil War: Popular Literature of the North and South, 1861–1865.* Chapel Hill: University of North Carolina Press, 2001.

Finkelman, Paul. *Dred Scott v. Sandford: A Brief History with Documents.* Boston: Bedford/St. Martins, 1997.

Foner, Eric. *Politics and Ideology in the Age of the Civil War.* New York: Oxford University Press, 1980.

Hedrick, Joan D. *Harriet Beecher Stowe: A Life.* New York: Oxford University Press, 1994.

Jefferson, Thomas. *The Life and Selected Writings of Thomas Jefferson.* Ed. Adrienne Koch and William Peden. New York: Modern Library, 1944.

Lincoln, Abraham. *Selected Speeches and Writings.* New York: Library of America, 1992.

Linderman, Gerald F. *Embattled Courage: The Experience of Combat in the American Civil War.* New York: Free Press, 1987.

Mellon, Matthew T. *Early American Views on Negro Slavery.* Boston: Meador, 1934.

Melville, Herman. *Battle-Pieces and Aspects of the War.* New York: Harper & Brothers, 1866.

Menand, Louis. "John Brown's Body." *Raritan* 22.2 (2002): 55–61.

# INTRODUCTION

*Maggi M. Morehouse and Zoe Trodd*

Between 2011 and 2015, the United States marks the sesquicentennial of the Civil War. Numerous commemorations, exhibitions, reenactments, and editorials mark this 150th anniversary of what Robert Penn Warren called—on the war's centennial in 1961—"the great single event of our history" (1). A mere union "became a nation" (4), and formed Americans' "most significant sense of identity" (6–7), Warren argued, going on to describe the war as a "mystic cloud from which emerged our modernity" (49). This book takes a close look inside that "mystic cloud" to watch modernity emerge. We trace the changes set in motion by the war and we analyze the war's lasting impact on the country's life and culture, its individuals and communities. Stepping back from the history of the war itself—its battles, generals, and military strategies—we explore the daily life and societal transformations of Civil War America.

In addition to the book's twenty-nine chapters, a companion website includes primary sources that illuminate each chapter's argument. These sources consist of oral histories, letters, diaries, newspapers, cartoons, songs, ephemera, posters, photographs, and autobiographical accounts, among numerous other sources. They contextualize the book's chapters and open a window directly onto American life during the Civil War.

Both the book's chapters and the website's primary sources reveal people's beliefs, attitudes and practices—the ways they worked, expressed themselves artistically, organized their family lives, treated illness, and worshipped. We ask throughout: how did people live, behave, and understand their world during the Civil War? Beyond the battlefields, we explore what Warren termed the Civil War's "'felt' history"—remembering that during this military conflict, as states seceded, Lincoln was re-elected, slaves were declared free, and 620,000 Americans died as members of the Union or Confederate armed forces (the equivalent of 6 million in terms of today's population), men and women still went about their daily routines. They celebrated Christmas and Thanksgiving, ran their households, wrote letters, read newspapers and books, joined unions, attended plays, and graduated from high school and college.

As well as its emphasis on daily life during the war, this book emphasizes how that daily life changed. We lay out the social and cultural transformations that the war began, completed or interrupted. Of course, the war brought an end to slavery and achieved the preservation of the Union. The book shows that it also had an economic impact, preparing the United States to boom during the late nineteenth-century Industrial Revolution. It marked an increase in bureaucratic efficiency and a swift growth in the federal government's size and scope. It radically reshaped the nature of labor in America and the potential of any labor movement. It transformed the size, scope, and pattern of American welfare and reform efforts. It left the Indian nations in ruins. It changed the purpose of southern university campuses and remodeled military education. It brought several watersheds in medicine. It transformed news coverage from limited and local to broad and national. It drove technological development in photography and changed the course of American music. It altered American theater and the ways in which Americans produced and consumed literature.

In the realm of belief-systems and identities, it gave the South a more coherent regional identity and altered Americans' sense of community and locality. It stymied immigrants' efforts to assimilate into American life and fostered distinct cultural identities among immigrant communities. It upended gendered conventions of behavior and notions of respectable work, shattering the pre-war ideology of separate spheres for men and women. It tested common American assumptions about divine providence and the role of the United States in God's redemptive plan for the world. It nurtured pragmatism and altered beliefs in free will and destiny. It marked a shift in how Americans mourned and interpreted death.

By the end of the war, the country had the national holiday of Thanksgiving, the modern version of Santa Claus, the first national currency, the machine gun, the beginnings of a modern pharmaceutical industry, the role of civilian war correspondent, and a codified national version of baseball. Charting all these transformations, large and small, this book asserts that the Civil War was—in the words of James McPherson—"America's Second Revolution" (x).

The book is structured in eight parts. Part I, Dissent and Disobedience, includes three chapters that explore unrest and rebellion during the war years. In "Draft Resistance and Rioting," Shannon Smith Bennett shows that home front rioting and draft resistance influenced the outcomes of the war and helped to create a centralized federal government that often used the military to restore order and suppress protests. Bennett links the experiences of soldiers and civilians to demonstrate that the war "unleashed social forces that threatened, and then altered, the status quo." In "Southern Dissent," David Williams demonstrates that a violent "inner Civil War" shaped the Confederacy's fate. The South was defeated, explains Williams, not only by Union forces but also by sustained and violent resistance on the home front. Finally, Rachel Redfern's "Women Soldiers" outlines the multitude of ways that women participated in the war effort, including those who defied the law and became soldiers. Engaged in a different act of defiance than the draft resistors, rioters and southern dissenters, these rebellious women donned male clothing and fought on the front lines.

Part II, Labor and Land, includes four chapters about the country's changing labor force and landscape. In "The Domestic Sphere," Phyllis Thompson identifies the antebellum cult of "true womanhood" that defined women's roles and shows that as women engaged in "previously inconceivable tasks" during the war, the gendered norms of work and domesticity were transformed. In "Labor Organizations," Mark A. Lause argues that the war "wrought complex economic changes that left the workers' movement forever transformed." For example, wartime conditions validated the solidarity impulse and workers won serious gains as a result. In "Commerce and Industry," Daniel Rasmussen depicts Southerners' concerns about their power in the national federation. As the country expanded, a slave-based agricultural system was slipping from its dominant position and Americans were asking "which form of political economy would define new American acquisitions." Finally, in "The Environment," Megan Kate Nelson shifts the book's focus to a different kind of labor: that of soldiers marching through, camping on, destroying, and rebuilding the country's landscape of routes, rivers, forests, hills, and farms. She shows that even as the natural landscape played an important role in shaping battle tactics, warfare "shaped southern landscapes and transformed their meanings."

Part III, Religion and Reform, includes three chapters that illuminate Americans' changing faith in God, participation in organized religion, and approach to religiously based reform. In "Religion in the South," Thomas Lawrence Long distinguishes between the religious practices of the South's slaves, Native Americans, planters, and white laboring classes, also discussing southern Catholics, Quakers, Jews, and the Presbyterian, Baptist, Episcopal, and Methodist communities. He argues that as a religiously diverse region, the South shaped "religious expression more than its theologies shaped the culture" and southern identity "provided social cohesion across lines of religious belief." In "Religion in the North," James Rohrer explains that the Civil War was a theological crisis that, on the one hand, pushed America toward secularism, and on the other developed a civil religion—the "unprecedented association of cross and flag, the sanctification of patriotism." Responding to secession, Northerners decided that the government needed to be grounded upon a formal covenant with God. Finally, Lauren Brandt's chapter, "Reform and Welfare Societies," shows that these questions of religious identity were at the heart of reformers' projects, but that the war highlighted anew for reformers the tension between moral suasion and political action. Brandt argues that reform societies were transformed in their objectives and methods by the war, when "those citizens who existed on the margins of American political power were able to generate power, influence and authority for themselves and for the improvement of the nation."

Part IV, Health and Education, includes four chapters that chart the impact of the war on the philosophies and practices of medicine and education in the North and South, for both civilian and military communities. In "Higher Education," A.J. Angulo and Kimberly Cook show that the purpose of southern universities changed during the war, as military leaders used campuses as war camps, thousands of students entered the army, university officials promoted the war effort, and faculty eased degree requirements for students who enlisted. In the North, however, conditions were very different and students and faculty "focused less on glory, pride, revenge, and defense; rather, they questioned, debated, and took [a] cool, sober approach" to the war. In "Military Schools," Bradford A. Wineman argues that the sectional conflict initially encouraged the establishment of even more military schools and prompted civilian institutions to being teaching courses in military studies, but then almost destroyed the military school tradition as the schools' boards of trustees "placed the needs of the Confederate army before the operation of their institutions." Continuing to focus on the military—and its intersections with civilian life—Guy R. Hasegawa in "Military Medicines" surveys the country's drug companies, military medical supply lists, and prescription systems. He depicts the war's impact on market prices for drugs and the "conflicting practices, beliefs, and attitudes" toward medication use. Finally, James M. Schmidt in "Civilian Healthcare" argues that the war had a profound impact on the healthcare of civilians, prompting a greater "professionalization of the medical and pharmaceutical ranks" and a greater "influence of politics and the law on medicine." The war also opened avenues for the marketing of patent medicines and brought to a head the competition between traditional and alternative medical practices.

Part V, Ethnic American Lives, includes four chapters about the relationship of marginalized Americans—former slaves, black soldiers, recent immigrants, and Native Americans—to the war. In "Slave Emancipation," Sharon A. Roger Hepburn explains that slaves, at times considered "contraband of war," freed themselves by escaping to Union lines even before the proclamation of emancipation. She illustrates the changing attitudes of President Lincoln and other government officials toward slavery throughout the war, and the responses of slaves themselves to the Emancipation Proclamation. In "Black Troops," Maggi M. Morehouse continues the focus on black Americans and identifies the goal of many free blacks and former slaves to achieve citizenship as an outcome of the war. She argues that the decision to mobilize black troops "served a severe blow to the Confederacy, and signaled a change in thinking about the use of black soldiers in warfare." Turning to another group of soldiers and civilians, Jennifer A. Stollman in "Immigrants" discusses the role of immigrant soldiers and the attitudes of immigrant civilian communities toward slavery and seces-sion, including communities of Germans, British, Irish, and Jews. Describ-ing northern and southern hostility to ethnic and religious differences during the war, Stollman argues that even as immigrants "endeavored to demonstrate their patriotism throughout the war" they also were politicized by the nativ-ist backlash and "developed a stronger ethnic consciousness" and "a distinct cultural identity." Finally, in "Native Americans," W. Craig Gaines contin-ues the theme of conflicting ideals about American citizenship. Outlining the complicated history of Native American participation in both the Union and Confederate Armies and the varied impact of the war on the Indian nations, he concludes that "by the end of the war, the Indian nations were in ruins and would not recover for more than a generation."

Part VI, Literature and Visual Culture, includes four chapters about the war's depiction and consumption in literary and visual texts. In "Newspapers," Brayton Harris lays out the range of northern and southern newspapers—from southern democrat papers to northern radical republican papers—and shows that during the Civil War, northern newspapers created a "new breed of jour-nalistic adventurers" in the form of civilian war correspondents. He also shows the impact of the war on the southern press, its papers shutting down one by one as the war progressed, and charts the debates on wartime freedoms of the press in both the North and South. In "Literature," Vanessa Steinroetter explores both the little-known poems and stories about the war in the periodi-cal press, and the well-known war writings of Emily Dickinson, Walt Whit-man, and Herman Melville. Explaining that for writers the war brought both "disruption, distraction and dwindling demand for books" and "literary inspi-ration," she reveals literature's repeating themes of the dying soldier, the inva-sion of the domestic sanctuary by war news, letter-writing, womanly sacrifice and masculine courage, and argues that the highly patriotic contributions of writers "constituted the beginnings of a new national literature." With "Photo-graphy," Mandy A. Reid turns from written expression to visual "texts." She explains the popularity of photography for Civil War America and shows that the war advanced the genre of photojournalism and pushed photographers to find new ways to "document the war's events as they happened." The war shaped philosophies and technologies of photography even as photography shaped how Americans viewed the war, she argues. Finally, in "Painting and Illustration," Jennifer Raab argues that the war "presented both an opportunity and a dilemma for artists," forcing them to abandon the conventions of history painting in search of a new means to represent the war's violence.

Part VII, Leisure and Performance, includes four chapters that continue the topic of creative expression and expand to investigate a broad range of Ameri-can leisure activities during the war. In "Music," Jack Hamilton explains that "musical practice and consumption was a crucial facet of life" for Civil War America, and explores the "parlor song" industry of sentimental ballads, the vast proliferation of songs written about the war itself, and the emergence of the African American spiritual into the national consciousness. He concludes that it was the war's facilitation of the collection and publication of the spirituals that left the greatest musical mark, for this music of African Americans "would go on to become one of the nineteenth-century's great cultural legacies; the spirituals nothing short of a foundational document." In their chapter on "Theater," Laura M. Ansley and Renée M. Sentilles open access to theater halls in the Northeast, West, and South, using the common thread of the Booth brothers—June, Edwin, and John Wilkes—to explore all three regions. They argue that the war transformed the expectations of audiences, the careers of actors, the content and style of plays, and the strategies of producers, so that by 1865, a theater previously determined "by a desire for clear class distinctions and segregated gender practices" had become a topsy-turvy reflection of the country's new race, gender and class dynamics. Shifting to a new set of spectators, Ryan Swanson with "Baseball" reveals how the game was played across America during the war. He debates whether the Civil War made baseball a national sport or stunted its growth, explains the role of baseball in soldiers' camps and as a celebration of holidays and wartime victories, describes the promotion of baseball games for health reasons by the U.S. Sanitary Commission, and shows the press using baseball as a "metaphor to describe the Civil War to its daily readers." Finally, in "Sacred and Secular Holidays," Suanna H. Davis shows the war's impact on how Americans celebrated Valentine's Day, George Washington's birthday, Independence Day, Thanksgiving, and Christmas, as well as its impact on what they believed was appropriate activity on Sundays. The Civil War accelerated the secularization of American holidays and Sundays, Davis concludes—aiding the transformation of American holy days into holidays. By 1865, Thanksgiving meant feasting, the new main character of Christmas was Santa, rather than Christ, and even the Sabbath "had been challenged by the fact that war did not stop for rest."

The last section, Part VIII, Death and Aftermath, includes three chapters about the immediate and long-term aftershocks of the war's deaths, violence and injuries. In "Death and Dying," Nicole Keller Day argues that the war dramatically changed "the ways in which individual deaths were realized, mourned, interpreted and finally symbolized." Americans in both the North and the South developed new systems of beliefs and practices in response to the sheer number of fatalities, the manner of these war deaths, the changing status of the corpse, and the complicated nature of killing "one's own countrymen." In "Veterans," John Casey turns from casualties to survivors, and depicts veterans' struggle with their new sense of identity as they tried to reintegrate into civilian life. He shows that many veterans felt a "subtle wall dividing them from the civilian populace" and argues that although this divide was largely masked by the more visible tensions of race and regionalism during and after the war, it was so large that veterans in the North and South had more in common with each other than they did with their civilian neighbors. Struggling to create a new ex-soldier identity, demobilized men created the identity of "veteran"—"an identity that assured them of the meaning and value of their sacrifice." Finally, in "Competing Memories," James M. Gillispie narrates the "beginning of a new cultural cold war between the regions" in 1865 that included a battle "over the divine meaning of the war" and arguments over the conduct of the war itself. As members of the war generation promoted their own versions of the conflict—whether Northerners' version of a war that redeemed the nation by eradicating slavery, or Southerners' version of a Lost Cause attempt to preserve the sacred principle of states' rights—they often used the war's military prisons as a key example of their cause's righteousness. For several decades after the war, northern veterans published accounts of prisons like Andersonville that made the whole southern cause and society "seem more repugnant in northern minds," while southern veterans published narratives about northern prisons that sought to cast Union war conduct as dishonorable, and therefore the Union cause as invalid.

Gillispie is right to highlight the ongoing battle between the regions over the conflict's meaning after the shooting was over. In the 150 years since Robert E. Lee surrendered to Ulysses S. Grant at Appomattox Court House on April 9, 1865, the Civil War has occupied a central place in American memory and has continued to exert a far-reaching impact on American understandings of national identity. Even in the immediate aftermath of war, commentators sensed that they had just lived through America's B.C./A.D. moment. Southerner Mark Twain observed that the war was "what A.D. is elsewhere"—Americans, especially in the South, "date from it" (129). Twain explained that this sense of a great historical turning-point was because the war "uprooted institutions that were centuries old, changed the politics of a people, transformed the social life of half the country, and wrought so profoundly upon the entire national character that the influence cannot be measured short of two or three generations" (129). Other commentators used a different Biblical narrative to convey the sense of a pivotal moment: not Christ's birth but the original sin and man's Fall. The war marked the end of American innocence, suggested Melville in 1866. It brought "man's latter fall" from grace (14) and Americans' eviction from their Eden, because "What like a bullet can undeceive!" (63). Now, Melville concluded, there was an "uncertainty which forever impends over men and nations" (268). A few years later, Henry James expanded on this idea of the war as a Fall and an eviction from the Edenic American garden. He explained that the war "introduced into the national consciousness a certain sense of proportion and relation, of the world being a more complicated place than it had hitherto seemed, the future more treacherous." Therefore, James concluded, the "good American, in days to come, will be a more critical person than his complacent and confident grandfather" because he has "eaten of the tree of knowledge" (48).

Seeking to explain exactly why the war felt so deeply transformative to Americans then and now—why it seems to divide the country's history into the eras of before and after—this book and its companion website go beyond battles to uncover seismic shifts in the cultural and social landscape of religious beliefs, racial attitudes, gender relations, immigrant identities, science and technology, labor and commerce, educational philosophies, creative expression and communication. Whether on the largest scale—how the country understood time and place, life and death, God and humanity, self and community—or on the smallest scale—how it advertised goods, distributed newspapers, and scored baseball games—Civil War America was not only a House Divided but a site of transformation.

## Works Cited

James, Henry. *Hawthorne*. New York: Harper's, 1879.

McPherson, James. *Abraham Lincoln and America's Second Revolution*. New York: Oxford University Press, 1992.

Melville, Herman. *Battle-Pieces and Aspects of the War*. New York: Harper & Brothers, 1866.

Twain, Mark. *The Gilded Age*. 1873, London: Routledge, 1883.

Warren, Robert Penn. *The Legacy of the Civil War: Meditations on the Centennial*. New York: Random House, 1961.

# PART I

# Dissent and Disobedience

# 1

# DRAFT RESISTANCE AND RIOTING

*Shannon Smith Bennett*

On Thursday, July 10, 1862, a group of Irish laborers on the Cincinnati docks argued with two black dockworkers. Tensions had been rising throughout the summer as boat captains hired black roustabouts at lower wages than white men. Rumors circulated that soon all white river workers would be replaced by African Americans. As the argument grew heated, one of the black workers hit an Irishman with a block of wood in his hand. The white men immediately chased the black men aboard a steamship, and white stevedores began attacking African Americans along the docks. Angry white workers believed that "employers along the wharves have taken the negro by the arm, and given him the place of the white man. The result has been a terrible riot" ("Right of White Labor over Black," n.p.). White dockworkers vowed that no black men should work on the levee.

Fist and knife fights between black and white stevedores continued over the next two days, but the conflict became more violent on Sunday, July 13. Large groups of white residents gathered on the fringes of the African American neighborhood of Bucktown and attacked any black people traveling alone. Black and white Cincinnatians fought back and forth over several days, resulting in damage to homes, businesses, and churches. On Tuesday, July 15, many African Americans left the city to avoid further violence. Remaining black residents barricaded their homes and armed themselves to defend against attacks.

The white social and political leaders of Cincinnati finally took measures to stop the rioting. Several hundred property holders met at the Merchant's Exchange and called for one thousand citizen volunteers to restore peace. The city's "better elements" acted not because they feared more African Americans would be killed or be forced out of the city, but because they wanted to avoid further property destruction or damage to the reputation of their city. The police force was in a depleted state; 120 policemen had gone south to defend the city from possible attack by Confederate raiders led by John Hunt Morgan. City leaders believed the rioters had taken advantage of the officers' absence. The mayor swore in 40 volunteers to supplement the weakened force. A group of 75 men, the Winfield Rifles, volunteered for guard duty. Those men, along with the remaining policemen and deputized citizens, finally put an end to the violence. Small working-class skirmishes continued through the end of the month, but the attention of most Cincinnati residents turned to defense against possible Confederate attacks.

The rioting in Cincinnati was just a hint of what was to come on the Civil War homefront. Disorder and violence characterized the wartime experience not just of soldiers, but of all Americans. Such conflicts were more than the work of the military or the result of political decisions. The war unleashed social forces that threatened, and then altered, the status quo. With the future of slavery being decided on the battlefield, homefront rioting attempted to resolve other social issues—job competition, especially between black and white workers; distrust of government intervention in local matters; the ability to provide for one's family; and the methods of maintaining civil order in a rapidly changing world. These types of riots—labor struggles, racial confrontations, draft resistance, and food conflicts—demonstrated just how far Americans were willing to go to secure a measure of control over their daily lives. By requiring political and military responses and by altering social arrangements at home, rioting and civil disorder influenced the outcomes of the war for citizens, for government authority, and in race relations.

In 1862, apprehensions of social chaos seemed to be coming true. White workers in Cincinnati had long feared economic competition from free African Americans. Citizens throughout the Union and Confederacy were concerned about the federal government exerting power over individual choices and local matters. Laborers resisted poor working conditions and unfair pay by employers, and were especially afraid of losing their right to unionize. Rumors of pending changes were rampant. The federal government, assuming greater wartime authority, was taking steps toward emancipating the slaves, arming black soldiers, and, in the eyes of northern white laborers, releasing a "horde" of freedpeople to move across the Ohio River. The looming draft, according to critics, would force men to fight for the government, regardless of their individual desires or beliefs. Workers feared that their employers would use military authority to extract the greatest profits from their employees. Yet, even with anger at federal intrusion into their daily lives, citizens demanded that the government provide basic needs to those who had sacrificed so much for the war effort. While many people feared the changes brought about by war, some saw an opportunity to better their social condition.

The 1862 riots in Cincinnati were the result of the contentious circumstances of the Civil War era. Early in the war, the city experienced a downturn in the previously thriving economy. Cincinnati workers competed for diminishing jobs, and the railroad slowly displaced steamboats as the prevailing method of transportation. Men who worked as wage laborers feared that former slaves would accept lower wages for work. Even if soldiers and their families supported the Union and free labor, they did not necessarily believe in the emancipation of the slaves or equality for African Americans. White men spoke out harshly against the possibility of working alongside black men as laborers or as soldiers. Like those in Cincinnati, free black workers and their families throughout the North faced violence in their homes and workplaces. There was ongoing anger against abolitionists, who were viewed as synonymous with the Union and Republican goals. When the reality of changes wrought by the war came home to Cincinnati, decades of conflict over racial and ethnic divisions, economic needs, and political differences came to a head in the waterfront brawls between black and white dockworkers.

In all types of homefront conflicts, rioters—women, men, black, white, dockworkers, homemakers, immigrants, coal miners, business owners—were not necessarily unpatriotic or trying to undermine the war efforts. They saw the war as an opportunity to assert their own interests and address longstanding problems in their daily lives. Soldiers and fathers, wives and mothers, and breadwinners maintained a moral code that was not always in agreement with the needs of the federal government. Soldiers who returned home to harvest crops or care for their families did not think they were deserting the army, and women who participated in bread riots to feed their families did not consider it stealing. Believing they were justified in their actions, they thought that the federal government owed them physical and moral support in return for their allegiance. Most rioters did not try to destroy the government or economic structure, but instead wanted to modify it to ensure equality and protection for themselves.

In a time of war, however, a strong central government demanded that citizens subjugate their own needs to those of the state. Using conscription and the draft, the Union and the Confederacy demonstrated their power to raise an army. Police forces and troops put down draft resistance, showing rioters that they were no match for the power of social order. The threat of force was sometimes enough to deter rioters, while in other cases official forces did not respond to protect African Americans or people deemed at odds with the goals of the government.

Some Americans and Confederates believed that the government had a responsibility to protect those who backed the goals and politics of each nation. Loyal and wealthy citizens, like the Cincinnati city leaders, expected the government to protect their lives and property against mobs or dissenters. They feared that civil unrest was a sign of the breakdown of society, and many patriotic citizens were astonished that others would riot during a time of war. Just as the white businessmen of Cincinnati demanded police intervention in the rioting against African Americans in 1862, other Confederate and Union supporters criticized police and military authorities if they did not use force immediately to contain rioters. Maintaining law and order, including the status of property holders and social elites, was more important than expressing dissent.

The Civil War ushered in a new level of government intrusion in the private lives of people. While people had resorted to violence to work out their differences at the personal and local level prior to the war, during wartime more citizens began to demand that the government get involved to police unruly behavior. Civil unrest often pitted women against soldiers and government leaders, soldiers against their superior officers, and elite leaders against impoverished workers. Riots and civil unrest brought those with different visions of society into direct contact and forced them to debate their goals face-to-face.

In the fall of 1862 and the spring of 1863, tensions between personal needs and government support erupted in bread riots throughout the South. Uprisings took place in Atlanta, Savannah, Milledgeville, Macon and Columbus in Georgia, and in Salisbury, North Carolina, and Mobile, Alabama. Although many citizens supported the Union and Confederacy initially, people faced personal hardships as the war progressed. Women and families bore the brunt of declining homefront conditions. With little prospect of raising crops by themselves, many rural women moved to cities seeking wage work. Others relied on their husbands' wages from military service or work in war industries. Burgeoning urban populations placed stress on food production and transport systems, especially in the South. Faced with food shortages and inflation, women turned to violence to express their dissatisfaction with the government and living conditions.

The press frequently portrayed the protests as women's riots, although men certainly participated. Women were not after government handouts, but they expected the government to help ease their burdens while their husbands served the Confederacy. They still wanted to be self-sufficient, but urged the government to make food available at fair prices. Even when a supply of food was available, government ineptitude and war profiteering kept provisions away from those who needed them. Confederate women wanted to purchase adequate amounts of food at reasonable prices, and were willing to break the law in order to feed their families and to demand that the government remedy the situation.

Reports of riots in Atlanta and North Carolina in March of 1863 prompted women in Richmond, Virginia, to organize the largest food riot of the Civil War. On April 2, 1863, women gathered to protest conditions in the city. At a meeting the evening before, the women decided: "they would demand food from the governor and would take it by force from the merchants if their requests were not satisfied" (Chesson 143). When the governor's response was unsatisfactory, they moved through the city taking food, clothing, and other goods from stores. The women were armed with axes, hatchets, pistols, knives, and bayonets. Men followed the crowd and participated in the looting. Some merchants resisted and the crowd moved on to other stores. Governor John Letcher and Confederate President Jefferson Davis both addressed the crowd, and a show of force by the Public Guard caused the crowd to disperse about two hours after the violence had begun.

Media coverage of bread riots often portrayed women as violent, unwomanly hags rather than as wives and mothers expressing their frustrations in an organized manner. By creating images of harsh, ugly women, newspapers could portray women as a small minority of unworthy citizens that did not pose a real threat to government control. It is impossible to know the exact composition of the crowd, but women came from all areas of the city and suburbs and from all income levels. Many of the women, and especially the leaders of the Richmond uprising, were well-dressed members of wealthy families. Young, stylish women were more likely to receive a light judicial sentence, while older women, those with less money, and men received harsher punishments.

The bread riots revealed debates about the role of government in the lives of individuals. Supporting the rights of merchants to set their own prices, the government did not enforce a system of food distribution. Citizens, however, felt wartime needs justified federal action to protect consumers from profiteering and shortages. As a result of the Richmond riot, the government tried to censor newspapers to prevent violence in other cities, and at the first hint of trouble sent out troops to head off potential riots. Government officials were alarmed at the breakdown of morale and the social order in southern cities, and moved swiftly to control future outbreaks.

Government officials also acted to quell any labor violence that they perceived as a threat to the war effort. Just as the Civil War helped to clarify the relationship of individuals to the federal government, it was also a moment when workers on the homefront could challenge their relationship to their employers. Increasing demands on laborers in support of the war effort were the catalyst for intensive labor riots in the coalfields of Pennsylvania. Long victims of an unequal system of wage labor, workers in the mines used the war and high demand for their products as an opportunity to claim concessions from their employers and to improve their working conditions. But workplace strikes threatened the steady supply of coal, and thus the Union war effort. Siding with the mine owners, government officials decided to intervene in the workplace conflict. The provost marshals and employers conflated labor organization with conscription resistance, and used the threat of unrest to place a standing army in the mining regions. The presence of a military force served as a deterrent to labor organization during and after the Civil War.

Prior to the war, mine workers had fought against unfair wages and poor working conditions by organizing within their communities. The ethnic concentration of Irish, Welsh, and German workers allowed residents to rely on each other for daily needs. Mine operators felt threatened by the unity of ethnic groups and feared the power of their voting bloc. When the workers would strike or riot against unfair conditions, the operators blamed their ethnicity for the violence rather than social and economic inequalities. Capitalists accused the workers of being sympathetic to the South and trying to undermine the Union cause, but did not recognize that the laborers had different priorities than fighting for or supplying the northern armies.

Historian Grace Palladino has argued that there were major differences between local and national conceptions of duty, patriotism, and legitimate authority: "The men who were called to fight, and the people who loved them, tended to view the great issues at stake—freedom, duty, and government authority—through a local lens, which meant that survival, family welfare, and local autonomy sometimes came first, war or no war" (xii). Workers, capitalists, and government officials had different definitions of patriotism and different visions of how their society should work. Laborers were willing to violently secure their economic rights and provide for their families, even if they had to resist Union troops to do so.

The Union army, however, found it increasingly difficult to secure a steady supply of recruits. As the war entered its second year, individual choice and the government's need for men to replenish the military clashed in draft riots. Volunteerism for the Union and Confederate armies was initially enthusiastic, but that quickly changed to discontent with increasing demands of the government. Both armies boasted many recruits in the immediate aftermath of the calls to raise troops. Within a year or so, however, enthusiasm waned and it became more difficult for states to raise military units. In July 1862, President Lincoln called for 300,000 more troops and Congress passed the Militia Act. States that were unable to meet their quota with volunteers either had to institute bounties, a payment to encourage enlistment, or implement a draft to fill their ranks. Congress passed a national Conscription Act in February 1863. The bill was contentious; opponents felt that the act went against American values of individualism and local control, while proponents favored the centralization of the drafting process. Others argued that the militias were supposed to be under control of the states, not consolidated into a federal army. The bill made provisions for the exemption of affluent citizens. The wealthy could hire a substitute for $300 to take their place in the army, but few poor farmers or workers could afford the fee. The exemption of the rich placed an unequal burden on the poor, giving rise to the phrase, "A rich man's war but a poor man's fight."

Draft resistance was widespread throughout the Union and in some areas of the Confederacy. Large urban riots occurred in New York and Boston, and there were smaller confrontations in many counties in Ohio, Indiana, Illinois, Wisconsin, Missouri, Maryland, Delaware, Kentucky, and Pennsylvania. Midwestern resistance was especially fierce in counties with workers who earned lower-than-average wages, a high percentage of foreign-born residents, and those areas with high Democratic voting populations in the predominantly Republican states. Historians have often blamed draft resistance and civil unrest in the North on Democrats who opposed the war, known as Copperheads, but it was more widespread and multifaceted than simply the political influence of some dissenters.

Northern men resisted the draft for a number of reasons. First, many Union citizens, especially in the Midwest, had close ties to the South. A larger percentage of midwesterners had migrated north from states such as Virginia and Kentucky, so they still had family connections and economic relationships with the upper South. Second, although numerous Union workers and farmers believed in keeping their states free of slavery, they did not necessarily agree with freedom or equality for African Americans. They feared potential job competition from freed slaves or believed in maintaining white supremacy. Third, workers and farmers often placed a higher priority on family and community obligations than on military service. Many resisted forced conscription to fight in a war that they did not support, for causes that they did not embrace, and continued working to provide food and financial support for their families. Finally, the draft was a new level of federal intrusion into the lives of ordinary citizens. Men resisted the idea that the government could force them to serve in the military if they refused. Individualism and personal authority were essential to the outlook of white men in the mid-nineteenth century.

Northern resistance to the draft took on a myriad of forms, some more violent than others. Some "skedaddled" to the West or hid out in the woods to avoid enrollment in the draft. With the help of family and friends, others stayed away from draft officers and continued to live and work in their hometowns. They relied on local civilians to protect them. Many civilians assisted deserters or resisters because they opposed the war, while others kept quiet because they feared repercussions from their neighbors if they reported draft-eligible men to the authorities. Civilians and potential draftees frequently heckled draft officers or forced them out of town. Women threw eggs or other household products at enrolling officers, and crowds of women and children often blocked the entrance to towns or households. A group of women in Pennsylvania entered a courtroom brandishing knives to try to stop the draft enrollment. The "Trials of an Enrolling Officer," according to the *Chicago Times,* were great:

> He found the job more difficult than he could have imagined. Doors were barricaded upon his approach, and raw-boned, ferocious looking curs, snapping furiously, jumped out from every direction to repel the invader. At the same time exasperated matrons flung open second story windows and, elongating their necks through the apertures, poured forth the most vile execrations.... Loving their husbands better than they did the law, they did not fail to make of this first enrolling officer a significant example to all who should come after. They beat their victim well, and rolled him in the mud, and then dismissed him with a half-dozen pails full of swill thrown lavishly over his body.
>
> *(Sterling 221)*

In some cases, however, resistance turned lethal. Fierce opposition to draft enrollment or conscription occurred in numerous communities in the North and Midwest. Provost marshals, charged with enrolling men into the draft and capturing deserters, were the targets of lethal violence, resulting in the deaths of as many as thirty-eight marshals. In October 1864, Captain Eli McCarty was killed near Washington, Indiana, when he was accosted by a party of resisters, shot, and his body thrown in the White River. Local citizens and a U.S. marshal tried to find the culprits, but the leaders fled to the West. Armed resistance in Holmes County, Ohio, almost led to the deaths of several Union officers, and a military squad was dispatched to put down the guerrilla force of nearly 1,000 men. The provost marshal reported that "the resisters of Holmes County reportedly resorted to arms because they viewed the conscription measure as an unconstitutional usurpation by Congress of a state's authority over the militia" (Sterling 205). Many Union citizens were angry at the intrusion of the federal government into their private lives.

Even in the face of violence, the Union army and government authorities were hard-pressed to punish resisters. Advocating for federal enforcement of the conscription act and stiff penalties for resisters, the *Chicago Tribune* reported on March 31, 1863, that "in Illinois and Indiana where the Copperheads are arming, and where in 500 localities a deserter could not be reclaimed without imposing demonstration of military force," the government should make an example of those who avoided military service. Although authorities made some attempts to punish deserters and resisters, there were no widespread arrests or sentences. Draft resistance was so common that it would have been impossible to punish all the offenders.

The Confederacy also experienced acts of resistance to military service. The Confederate Congress passed a conscription act in the spring of 1862, and many plotted to resist the provost marshals. Just as men in the North did not necessarily support Lincoln and his policies, men in southern states did not always support the Confederate government. Not all non-slaveholders wanted to fight to preserve the institution of slavery or the plantation economy, of which they were not a part. Many resisted the centralization of power in the Confederate government rather than the individual states. As the war wore on, Confederate soldiers experienced declining morale and deteriorating wartime conditions, so many returned home to care for their families.

Confederate loyalists met dissenters, deserters, and "peace plots" with violence. Throughout Texas, Alabama, Arkansas, and Tennessee, vigilantes jailed, deported and executed hundreds of men for avoiding service. In the most extreme case, Confederate troops arrested dozens of men in Cooke County, Texas, for failing to report for militia duty. An angry mob of Confederate loyalists formed an impromptu tribunal. Two men were shot while trying to escape and 40 men were hanged. While civilians resisted government involvement in their daily lives, they responded harshly to those who did not share the war's burden.

The most infamous rioting of the Civil War took place in New York during the week of July 13, 1863. The city had been filled with antiwar and antidraft sentiments for many weeks, and men's fears of the draft only intensified when they received reports from the battle at Gettysburg. When draft lottery drawings began on Saturday, July 11, the crowd grew hostile. The working-class poor of the city joined with Peace Democrats in declaring the draft a product of the "rich man's war" and refused to fight. Workers were angry that rich draftees could purchase a replacement and avoid military service, and they resisted the idea of fighting to free African Americans. The lottery continued on Monday, July 13, and the crowd of mostly Irish and German immigrants decided to shut it down. Workplaces were nearly empty as workers gathered to resist. The draft office was burned, and the mob moved on to destroy the homes of wealthy Republicans and abolitionists. They also targeted pro-Lincoln businesses and newspapers, such as the *New York Tribune*. Republican-owned factories were looted and workers' entry blocked.

Filled with rage against government interference in their lives, poor workers also feared that freed African Americans would take their jobs. The violence quickly became a bloody race riot, and African American homes, businesses, and individuals were common targets of the mob. The Colored Orphan Asylum in the Nineteenth Ward was burned. The children barely escaped as the mob tried to kill them. Black men and women were hanged from trees and lampposts, shot, and burned in their homes. The violence shifted from anger at the government to fear of racial mixing and economic competition.

The riots were widespread, and it was difficult for the city police force to gain control. It took the intervention of Union troops on Thursday, July 16, to return the city to order. Many of the troops came directly from the battlefield at Gettysburg where they had recently secured a major victory in the fight to maintain the Union and uphold the Emancipation Proclamation. Some soldiers were disappointed in their urban duty. Oliver Shepherd with the 27th Indiana Volunteers wrote upon his arrival, "The great riot was about over but the presence of 20,000 veterans had a quieting effect on the people generally so that recruits were drafted in great numbers and sent to the front. We did nothing except to perfect ourselves in the bayonet exercise" (Shepherd 22). A military display of force was necessary to preserve order.

More than 100 people, many of them African Americans, died during the week-long melee, and hundreds more were injured. But the working-class residents and Copperheads had achieved one goal. City leaders were afraid of future outbreaks of violence, so they allocated money to pay the commutation fee for those who were drafted. In July of 1864, the commutation fee was abolished, but draftees could still hire substitutes to fight in their place. Those with money had the ability to stay out of the army while poorer draftees had fewer choices.

The New York draft riots had an impact throughout the nation. Federal officials learned it was best to deter violence before it began rather than try to stop an active mob. Although midwesterners fought hard to avoid the draft, there was no violence at the four lottery drafts in the Midwest in the summer of 1863. Draft officials called out Union troops to maintain order during the lottery, and "most draft critics inclined to violent opposition apparently recognized the futility of forcefully resisting the draft at the time and place of the government's greatest strength" (Sterling 462). Government and social leaders learned that an immediate response was essential to maintaining social order, a lesson that would serve them well in the violent final decades of the nineteenth century.

The clashes between black and white workers, the government and laborers, women and police, and elite and working-class citizens were not a new phenomenon in the Civil War era. The tensions that led to riots had been brewing for many years, but the war provided the impetus for those hostilities to turn to action. White workers believed that their jobs were in danger, both from black competitors, as in the Cincinnati riots, and from the restrictive actions of employers in the Pennsylvania mine fields. In return for their loyalty, women in Richmond demanded government intervention in the food market. Draft resisters in the Midwest and New York protested the demands of the state over their own needs, teaching government officials that they must suppress protests before they turned violent. Civil War riots resulted in a stronger, more centralized federal government that often used the military to restore order. Racial violence continued after the war as free African Americans fought for justice in society and angry whites tried to suppress black freedoms. Labor riots during the war between black and white workers and between capitalists and employees signaled the beginning of an aggressive industrial warfare that would continue well into the twentieth century. Even a bloody Civil War could not bring an end to the civil unrest and rioting in the United States.

## Further Reading

Bernstein, Iver. *The New York City Draft Riots: Their Significance for American Society and Politics in the Age of the Civil War.* New York: Oxford University Press, 1990.

Chesson, Michael B. "Harlots or Heroines? A New Look at the Richmond Bread Riot." *Virginia Magazine of History* 92 (April 1984): 131–175.

Gilje, Paul. *Rioting in America.* Bloomington: Indiana University Press, 1996.

Palladino, Grace. *Another Civil War: Labor, Capital, and the State in the Anthracite Regions of Pennsylvania, 1840–1868.* New York: Fordham University Press, 2006.

"Right of White Labor over Black." *Liberator,* August 22, 1862.

Schecter, Barnet. *The Devil's Own Work: The Civil War Draft Riots and the Fight to Reconstruct America.* New York: Walker, 2005.

Shepherd, Oliver. *Diary,* SC2358, folder 1, Oliver Shepherd Papers. Indiana Historical Society.

Sterling, Robert E. "Civil War Draft Resistance in the Middle West." Ph.D. Dissertation. DeKalb: Northern Illinois University, 1974.

# 2

# SOUTHERN DISSENT

*David Williams*

In 1863, as battles raged on distant fields, a newspaper editor in the central Georgia town of Milledgeville was more concerned about the war at home. In an essay discussing the many ways in which white Southerners were working against the Confederacy, the editor wrote: "We are fighting each other harder than we ever fought the enemy" (Williams, Williams, and Carlson 164). Samuel Knight agreed. After touring southwest Georgia in the late fall and winter of 1863–64, he wrote to Governor Joe Brown of "strong Union feeling" in that part of the state. Knight concluded that white Southerners were "as bitterly divided against each other" as they ever had been against Northerners (Williams 1).

These two men saw clearly in their place and time what generations of historians have so often ignored or dismissed—that during its brief existence, the Confederacy fought a two-front war. There was, of course, the war it waged with the North, the war so familiar to almost every school child. But, though school children rarely hear of it, there was another war. Between 1861 and 1865, the South was torn apart by a violent inner civil war, a war no less significant to the Confederacy's fate than its more widely known struggle against the Yankees.

From its beginnings, the Confederacy suffered from a rising tide of intense domestic hostility, not only among southern blacks but also increasingly among southern whites. Ironically, it was a hostility brought on largely by those most responsible for the Confederacy's creation. Planters excused themselves from the draft in various ways, then grew far too much cotton and tobacco, and not nearly enough food. Soldiers went hungry, as did their families back home. Women defied Confederate authorities by staging food riots from Richmond, Virginia, to Galveston, Texas. Soldiers deserted by the tens of thousands, and draft evasion became commonplace. By 1864, the draft law was practically impossible to enforce, and two-thirds of the Confederate army was absent with or without leave. Many deserters and draft dodgers formed armed bands that controlled vast areas of the southern countryside.

Wartime disaffection among southern whites had solid roots in the early secession crisis. Most white Southerners, three-fourths of whom owned no slaves, made it clear in the winter 1860-61 elections for state convention delegates that they opposed immediate secession. Nevertheless, state conventions across the South, all of them dominated by slaveholders, ultimately ignored majority will and took their states out of the Union. One Texas politician conceded that ambitious colleagues had engineered secession without strong backing from "the mass of the people" (Escott 157). A staunch South Carolina secessionist admitted the same: "But whoever waited for the common people when a great move was to be made—We must make the move and force them to follow" (Kibler 358).

Despite their general reluctance to secede, there was considerable enthusiasm for the war among southern whites in the wake of Lincoln's call for volunteers to invade the South. Whatever their misgivings about secession, invasion was another matter. And, at the prodding of secessionist leaders despite Lincoln's promise to the contrary, "fear of Negro equality," as historian Georgia Lee Tatum put it, "caused some of the more ignorant to rally to the support of the Confederacy" (38). But southern enlistments declined rapidly after First Manassas, or Bull Run as Yankees called the battle. Men were reluctant to leave their families in the fall and winter of 1861–62, and many of those already in the army deserted to help theirs.

In October 1861, one worried Confederate wrote to his governor: "our people don't seem to be inclined to offer their services" (Williams et al. 22). That same month, a recruiter from Columbus, Georgia, reported to the war department that it was almost impossible to find volunteers. In February 1862, W.H. Byrd of Augusta, Georgia, wrote that he had been trying for two weeks to raise a company in what he called "this 'Yankee City,' but I regret to say every effort has failed." That failure did not result from a lack of potential recruits. The *Augusta Chronicle and Sentinel* had noted a week earlier that "one who walks Broad street and sees the number of young men, would come to the conclusion that no war ... was now waging" (Williams et al. 22).

The Confederacy's response to its recruitment problems served only to weaken its support among plain folk. In April 1862, the Confederate Congress passed the first general conscription act in American history. But men of wealth could avoid the draft by hiring a substitute or paying an exemption fee. For planters, Congress also exempted one white male of draft age for every twenty slaves owned. This twenty-slave law was the most widely hated act ever imposed by the Confederacy. Said Private Sam Watkins of Tennessee, "It gave us the blues; we wanted twenty negroes. Negro property suddenly became very valuable, and there was raised the howl of 'rich man's war, poor man's fight'" (Watkins 69).

To make matters worse, planters devoted much of their land to cotton and tobacco while soldiers and their families went hungry. In the spring of 1862, a southwest Georgia man wrote to Governor Joe Brown about planters growing too much cotton, begging him to "stop those internal enemies of the country, for they will whip us sooner than all Lincolndom combined could do it" (Formwalt 272–75). Thousands of planters and merchants defied the Confederacy's cotton export policy and smuggled it out by the ton. Most states passed laws limiting production of non-food items, but enforcement was lax. With prices on the rise, cotton producers and dealers were getting richer than ever. Some bragged openly that the longer the war went on the more money they made.

The inevitable result of cotton and tobacco over-production was a severe food shortage that hit soldiers' families especially hard. With their husbands and fathers at the front and impressment officers confiscating what little food they had, it was difficult for soldiers' wives to provide for themselves and their children. Planters had promised to keep soldiers' families fed, but they never grew enough food to meet the need. Much of what food they did produce was sold to speculators, who hoarded it or priced it far beyond the reach of most plain folk.

Desperate to avoid starvation, thousands of women took action. As early as 1862, food riots began breaking out all over the South. Gangs of hungry women, many of them armed, ransacked stores, depots, and supply wagons searching for anything edible. Major urban centers like Richmond, Atlanta, Mobile, and Galveston experienced the biggest riots. Even smaller towns, like Georgia's Valdosta and Marietta, and North Carolina's High Point and Salisbury, saw hungry women rioting for food.

In an open letter to the *Savannah Morning News*, one enraged Georgian was sure where the blame lay: "The crime is with the planters ... as a class, they have yielded their patriotism, if they ever had any, to covetousness ... for the sake of money, they are pursuing a course to destroy or demoralize our army—to starve out the other class dependent on them for provisions" (Williams et al. 4). The letter spoke for a great many plain folk. It seemed increasingly obvious to them that they were fighting a rich man's war, which made the problem of desertion that much worse. One Confederate officer wrote home to his wife that "discontent is growing rapidly in the ranks and I fear that unless something is done ... we will have no army. The laws that have been passed generally protect the rich, and the poor begin to say it is the rich man's war and the poor man's fight, and they will not stand it" (Blakey, Lainhart, and Bryant 307).

Deserters who made it home found plenty of neighbors willing to help them avoid further entanglements with the Confederacy. That was obvious even from distant Richmond. A disgusted head of the Bureau of Conscription complained that desertion had "in popular estimation, lost the stigma that justly pertains to it, and therefore the criminals are everywhere shielded by their families and by the sympathies of many communities" (Edwards 93). A resident of Bibb County, Georgia, wrote that the area around Macon was "full of deserters and almost every man in the community will feed them and keep them from being arrested" (Williams et al. 182). In Marshall County, Mississippi, a witness noted that "many deserters have been for months in this place without molestation…. Conscripts and deserters are daily seen on the streets of the town" (Lonn 69). When deserters were arrested in Alabama's Randolph County, an armed mob stormed the jail and set them free.

Desertion became so serious by the summer of 1863 that Jefferson Davis begged absentees to return. If only they would, he insisted, the Confederacy could match Union armies man for man. But they did not return. A year later, Davis publically admitted that two-thirds of Confederate soldiers were absent, most of them without leave. Many thousands of these men joined antiwar organizations that had been active in the South since the war's beginning. Others joined with draft dodgers and other anti-Confederates to form guerrilla bands, often called "tory" or "layout" gangs. They attacked government supply trains, burned bridges, raided local plantations, and harassed impressment agents and conscript officers.

As early as the summer of 1862, there were newspaper reports of layout gangs in Calhoun County, Florida, just west of Tallahassee, who had "armed and organized themselves to resist those who may attempt their arrest" (Reiger 288). They were already in contact with the Union blockading fleet and receiving arms from them. At one point, they even hatched a plot to kidnap Governor Milton and turn him over to the Federals. A pro-Confederate citizen learned of the scheme and warned Milton, who stayed in Tallahassee to avoid capture.

Just east of the state capital, deserter bands raided plantations in Jefferson, Madison, and Taylor counties. Along Florida's western Gulf coast, armed and organized deserters and layouts were abundant in Lafayette, Walton, Levy, and Washington counties. In southwestern Florida between Tampa and Fort Myers, they ranged virtually unchallenged. On Florida's Atlantic coast, the counties Volusia, Duval, Putnam, and St. John's saw running battles between anti-Confederate bands and soldiers trying to bring them in.

Bands of deserters also ranged over southern Mississippi's Simpson County. When the sheriff arrested several of them, their friends broke them out of jail. That entire area of Mississippi was, in fact, largely controlled by deserters and resisters who killed or drove off anyone connected with the Confederacy. In spring 1864 Major James Hamilton, quartermaster for taxation in Mississippi, wrote to his superiors that in the state's Seventh District, covering most of southern Mississippi, deserters had "overrun and taken possession of the country." Hamilton's agent in Jones County had been driven off, and Hamilton had heard nothing more from him. In Covington County, deserters made the tax collector cease operations and distribute what he had on hand to their families.

Deserters raided the quartermaster depot in Perry County and destroyed the stores there. Under the circumstances, Hamilton could no longer continue tax collection in that region.

One of the most effective layout gangs operated in southeast Mississippi's Jones County and was led by Newton Knight, a slaveless farmer who deserted the Confederate army soon after conscription began. Upset that wealthy men could avoid the draft, Knight deserted and took up with others of his community who had done the same. "We stayed out in the woods minding our own business," Knight said, "until the Confederate Army began sending raiders after us with bloodhounds.... Then we saw we had to fight" (Bynum 105). And fight they did. For the rest of the war Knight and his men, roughly five hundred strong, drove off Confederate agents, ambushed army patrols, looted government depots, and distributed the food stored there to the poor. So successfully did they subvert Confederate control of the county that some called it the "free state of Jones."

"Free state" was a phrase widely applied as well to north Alabama's Winston County. Soon after Alabama seceded from the Union, Winston seceded from the state. A December 1861 letter to Alabama's governor warned that "if they had to fight for anybody, they would fight for Lincoln" (Thompson 33). And they did. Twice as many Winston County men served in the Union army as did in the Confederate. Even many of those who initially signed on with the Confederacy soon had a change of heart. Frank and Jasper Ridge, two brothers from Jackson County, deserted after just fifteen days. By the summer of 1863, there were at least ten thousand deserters and conscripts in the Alabama hill country formed into armed bands. Some did so to fend off Confederate authorities, killing officers sent to arrest them. Others went on the offensive. In Randolph County, about four hundred deserters organized and carried out "a systematic warfare upon conscript officers" (McMillan 41–42).

Farther south, still others in or near the Alabama Black Belt targeted planters and their property. "Destroying Angels" and "Prowling Brigades" swept out of their piney wood strongholds to burn cotton, gin houses, and any supplies they could not carry away. Along the Florida line in southeast Alabama, a Confederate captain sent in to catch deserters called the region "one of the Greatest Dens for Tories and deserters from our army in the World" (Martin 52).

In Louisiana, James Madison Wells, though a man of means himself, denounced the Confederacy as a rich man's government and organized a guerrilla campaign against it. From his Bear Wallow stronghold in Rapides Parish, Wells led deserters and other resisters in raids against Confederate supply lines and depots. In the state's Cajun parishes, bands of anti-Confederates did the same. One group that ranged west of Washington Parish, known locally as the "Clan," numbered more than three hundred. Commanded by a Cajun named Carrier, it drove off home guards and forced plunder from all who opposed them. A woman from Bayou Chicot wrote to Governor Moore of local guerrillas there: "We could not fare worse were we surrounded by a band of Lincoln's mercenary hirelings" (Taylor 425). Confederate Lieutenant John Sibley wrote in his diary that one band of "marauders" had "declared vengeance against Confederate soldiers…. After killing five members of the Home Guard, they almost inhumanly beat their faces to pieces with the breach of their guns so no friend would know them again" (Taylor 426).

In Bandera County, Texas, just west of San Antonio, residents formed a pro-Union militia, refused to pay taxes to the Confederate-backed state government, and threatened to kill anyone who tried to make them do so. At the state's northern extreme near Bonham, several hundred anti-Confederates established three large camps close enough so that the entire force could assemble within two hours. They patrolled the region so effectively that no one could approach without their knowing of it. In the central Texas county of Bell, deserters led by Lige Bivens fortified themselves in a cave known as Camp Safety. From there they mounted raids against the area's pro-Confederates. According to an 1863 report, 2,000 other Texas deserters "fortified themselves near the Red River, and defied the Confederacy. At last account they had been established … eight months, and were constantly receiving accession of discontented rebels and desperadoes" (Tatum 51).

An Arkansas band of anti-Confederates operated out of Greasy Cove, a mountain pass at the head of the Little Missouri River. Made up of "deserters, disaffected, and turbulent characters," as one newspaper called them, they swept through the countryside harassing Confederate loyalists and challenging Confederate authority (Moneyhon 230). So did anti-Confederates in east Tennessee, a region where open rebellion against the Confederacy was common from the start. As early as the fall of 1861, bands of native Unionists disrupted Confederate operations by spying for the Federals, cutting telegraph lines, and burning railroad bridges. The next spring Unionists in Scott and Morgan counties staged a coup. They forcibly took control of all county offices, disbanded the Confederate home guard, and put in its place a force made up of local Union men.

After pro-Confederates from neighboring North Carolina mounted a series of raids against Unionists in and around the Smoky Mountain town of Cades Cove, Tennessee, the area's Union men formed their own militia. Led by Russell Gregory, pastor of a local Primitive Baptist church, they established a network of sentries along the roads to warn of approaching danger. In the spring of 1864, raiders invaded Cades Cove once again to steal livestock and provisions. They plundered several farms, taking all they could carry, but never made it back to North Carolina with their loot. Near the state line, Gregory's militiamen felled trees across the roads and ambushed the Rebel partisans, forcing them to scatter and leave their loot behind.

Anti-Confederates, deserters, and resisters alike in the North Carolina mountains also formed defensive militias and set up warning networks. Wilkes County was home to a band of five hundred deserters organized as a guerrilla force who openly challenged Confederates to come and take them. Wilkes County's Trap Hill gang was especially aggressive in harassing local pro-Confederates. In Cherokee County, about one hundred lay-outs formed a resistance force that disarmed Confederate soldiers and terrorized Confederate loyalists.

Though their motives were not always the same, the one thing nearly all armed resisters had in common was that they were men of modest means. In eastern Tennessee, for example, Unionist guerillas were mainly small farmers, artisans, and laborers. By contrast, their pro-Confederate counterparts held three times as much real estate and twice as much personal property. In the North Fork district of western North Carolina's Ashe County, a comparison of thirty-four Union and forty-two Confederate volunteers shows that holdings in real and personal property among Confederates was more than twice that of their Union counterparts. In eastern North Carolina, the difference was even more dramatic. In Washington County, which supplied nearly an equal number of troops to the Union and the Confederacy, Union soldiers were fourteen times poorer than those in the Confederate army. Such figures reflect a class-based Unionism felt all across the South.

The rise of such class warfare was the very thing that slaveholders had tried to avoid for so long and what had, in large part, led many to push for secession in the first place. "Ironically," as historian Charles Bolton points out, "by engineering disunion, slaveowners fostered the growth of the kind of organizations they had long feared: class-based groups that pitted nonslaveholders against the interests of slaveowners" (160).

Nowhere was that more evident than in the lowcountry of North Carolina. Planters in the region were terrified to learn that, as one wrote, Unionists among the lower classes had "gone so far as to declare [that they] will take the property from the rich men & divide it among the poor men" (Current 137). It was no idle threat. From near the war's beginning, bands of Unionists had been raiding coastal plantations. Formed initially to protect themselves from conscription and Confederate raiders, their objectives eventually expanded to include driving planters from their land and dividing it among themselves.

In the spring and summer of 1862, a pro-Union newspaper in the port town of New Bern reported the formation of Unionist militias in Washington, Tyrrell, Martin, Bertie, Hertford, Gates, Chowan, Perquimans, Pasquotank, and Camden counties "not only for self-protection against rebel guerilas, but for the purpose of expatriating all the rebel families from their limits" (Durrill 108-09). Further west in the central piedmont region of North Carolina, class antagonism was also a strong motive for resistance. Many members of the Heroes of America were poor men who, as one contemporary recalled, were "induced to join the organization by the promise of a division here after among them of the property of the loyal Southern citizens" (Auman and Scarboro 345).

South Carolina's hill country saw its share of resistance. Centered in

Greenville, Pickens, and Spartanburg counties, deserter bands had designated assembly areas and an organized system of signals to warn of trouble on the way. "Every woman and child," according to one report, was "a watch and a guard for them" (Tatum 138). Deserters commandeered and fortified an island in the Broad River. They also built fortified positions at Jones Gap, Hogback Mountain, Table Rock, Caesars Head, and Potts Camp. Near Gowensville, they built a heavy log fort, "loopholed and prepared for defense" (Poole 61). Deserter bands went on the offensive too. A force of more than five hundred controlled a region bordering North Carolina. Operating in groups of between ten and thirty, they chased off conscript companies, raided supply depots, and looted and burned the property of anyone who openly supported the Confederacy.

Much the same was true in southwestern Virginia, where J. E. Joyner noted large numbers of deserters with weapons, which they vowed to use "against the Confederacy if there is any attempt to arrest them" (Weitz 198–99). Montgomery, Floyd, and Giles counties especially were home to numerous bands of deserters. Local Unionists too, aroused by Confederate home guard depredations, formed armed militias. One such unit, headed by "Captain" Charles Huff of Floyd County, regularly backed up local deserters and ambushed home guard patrols. The job was made easier by Joseph Phares, a double agent who kept Huff informed of the guard's plans while feeding its officers disinformation.

The Confederacy's keystone state of Georgia was one of the most divided in the South. Anti-Confederate gangs operated in every part of the state. Some areas were so hostile to the Confederacy that army patrols dared not enter them. The pine barrens region of southeast Georgia was a favorite hideout for those trying to avoid Confederate entanglements. Soldier Camp Island in the Okefenokee Swamp was home to as many as a thousand deserters. In southwest Georgia, a Fort Gaines man begged Governor Brown to send cavalry for protection against deserters and layout gangs. So did pro-Confederates in northwest Georgia's Dade and Walker counties.

From the upland county of Fannin, a letter arrived on the governor's desk in July 1862 warning that "a very large majority of the people now here, perhaps two-thirds, are disloyal" (Sarris 89). Anti-Confederates became so aggressive in Fannin that one man called it a "general uprising among our Torys of this County." That same month came news from Gilmer County, just north of Fannin, of "tories and traitors who have taken up their abode in the mountains." September found neighboring Lumpkin County overrun by tories and deserters, robbing pro-Confederates of guns, money, clothes, and provisions. One Confederate sympathizer wrote that "the Union men—Tories—are very abusive indeed and says they will do as they please" (Williams et al. 164–65).

Resistance was just as fierce in the lower part of the state. In September 1862, forty men of southwest Georgia's Marion County "secured and provisioned a house and arranged it in the manner of a military castle." Armed and provisioned for the long haul, they swore not only to prevent their own capture but also to protect anyone who sought sanctuary in their fortress. Though Confederate and state military officials tried repeatedly to force them out, they had little success against these men, determined as they were to "resist to the last extremity." Captain Caleb Camfield, stationed at Bainbridge with a detachment of cavalrymen, had no better luck. He finally retreated after fierce battles with layout gangs in south Georgia and north Florida (Williams et al. 164).

Blacks could often be counted on to aid anti-Confederate whites. Deserters escaping the Confederate army could rely on slaves to give them food and shelter on the journey back home. Some blacks joined Tory gangs in their war against the Confederacy. Two slaves in Dale County, Alabama, helped John Ward, leader of a local deserter gang, kill their owner in his bed. Three white citizens of Calhoun County, Georgia, were arrested for supplying area slaves with firearms in preparation for a rebellion. Slaves in neighboring Brooks County conspired with a local white man, John Vickery, to take the county and hold it for the Union. Tens of thousands of blacks fled to federal lines and joined Union forces. Of about 200,000 blacks under federal arms, four out of five were native Southerners. Together with roughly 300,000 southern whites who did the same, Southerners who served in the Union military totaled nearly half a million, or about a quarter of all federal armed forces.

Confederate armies were outnumbered mainly because so many Southerners refused to serve—or served on the Union side. It was not only the North's greater population and industry that explains Union victory. Although the North had more people and factories, the South imported and produced arms enough to keep its troops supplied. Never was a Confederate army defeated in a major battle for lack of munitions. What the Confederacy lacked was sufficient food and consistently willing men to carry arms. Many Northerners refused to serve as well and their resistance to the draft, and northern dissent generally, goes a long way toward explaining how a Confederacy at war with itself was able to survive for as long as it did. But northern dissent pales in comparison to that in the South. The Confederacy could nearly have met the Union man for man had it not been for problems of desertion and draft dodging that were far greater for the Confederates than the Federals. Furthermore, if the nearly half-million Southerners who served in the Union military had been with the Confederates, the opposing forces would have been almost evenly matched.

It should be little wonder to us today that most southern whites eventually turned against the Confederacy. Many had never supported it in the first place. It stole their votes, conscripted their men, impressed their supplies, and starved them out. It favored the rich and oppressed the poor. It made war on those who withheld their support and made life miserable for the rest. That dawning reality led plain folk all across the South to oppose the Confederacy. Their actions and attitudes contributed in large part to the Confederacy's downfall, a fact that was well known to Southerners at the time. Some had even predicted it. In his November 1860 speech warning against secession, Georgia's Alexander

H. Stephens, ironically soon-to-be Confederate vice president, prophesied that should the South secede, Southerners would "at no distant day commence cutting one another's throats" (Freehling and Simpson 68). In the fall of 1862, an Atlanta newspaper put it just as bluntly: "If we are defeated, it will be by the people at home" (Williams 250). And so, the Confederacy was defeated, not only by the Union army—in which 300,000 southern whites served—but also by sustained and violent resistance on the home front.

## Further Reading

Auman, William T., and David D. Scarboro. "The Heroes of America in Civil War North Carolina." *North Carolina Historical Review* 58 (1981): 327–363.

Baggett, James Alex. *The Scalawags: Southern Dissenters in the Civil War and Reconstruction*. Baton Rouge: Louisiana State University Press, 2003.

Beringer, Richard E., Herman Hattaway, Archer Jones, and William N. Still. *Why the South Lost the Civil War*. Athens: University of Georgia Press, 1986.

Blakey, Arch Fredric, Ann Smith Lainhart, and Winston Bryant Stephens, Jr., eds. *Rose Cottage Chronicles: Civil War Letters of the Bryant-Stephens Families of North Florida*. Gainesville: University Press of Florida, 1998.

Bolton, Charles C. *Poor Whites of the Antebellum South: Tenants and Laborers in Central North Carolina and Northeast Mississippi*. Durham: Duke University Press, 1994.

Bynum, Victoria E. *The Free State of Jones: Mississippi's Longest Civil War*. Chapel Hill: University of North Carolina Press, 2001.

Current, Richard N. *Lincoln's Loyalists: Union Soldiers from the Confederacy*. New York: Oxford University Press, 1994.

Durrill, Wayne K. *War of Another Kind: A Southern Community in the Great Rebellion*. New York: Oxford University Press, 1990.

Edwards, Laura F. *Scarlett Doesn't Live Here Anymore: Southern Women in the Civil War Era*. Urbana: University of Illinois Press, 2000.

Escott, Paul D. "Southern Yeomen and the Confederacy." *South Atlantic Quarterly* 77 (1978): 146–158.

Freehling, William W. *The South vs. the South: How Anti-Confederate Southerners Shaped the Course of the Civil War*. New York: Oxford University Press, 2001.

Freehling, William W., and Craig M. Simpson, eds. *Secession Debated: Georgia's Showdown in 1860*. New York: Oxford University Press, 1992.

Formwalt, Lee W. "Planters and Cotton Production as a Cause of Confederate Defeat: The Evidence from Southwest Georgia." *Georgia Historical Quarterly* 74 (1990): 269–276.

Kibler, Lillian A. "Unionist Sentiment in South Carolina." *Journal of Southern History* 4 (1938): 346–366.

Lonn, Ella. *Desertion During the Civil War*. 1928, Lincoln: University of Nebraska Press, 1998.

Martin, Bessie. *A Rich Man's War, A Poor Man's Fight: Desertion of Alabama Troops from the Confederate Army*. 1932, Tuscaloosa: University of Alabama Press, 2003.

McMillan, Malcolm C. *The Disintegration of a Confederate State: Three Governors and Alabama's Wartime Home Front, 1861–1865*. Macon: Mercer University Press, 1986.

Moneyhon, Carl. "Disloyalty and Class Consciousness in Southwestern Arkansas, 1862–1865." *Arkansas Historical Quarterly* 52 (1993): 223–243.

Poole, W. Scott. *South Carolina's Civil War*. Macon: Mercer University Press, 2005.

Sarris, Jonathan Dean. *A Separate Civil War: Communities in Conflict in the Mountain South*. Charlottesville: University of Virginia Press, 2006.

Storey, Margaret M. *Loyalty and Loss: Alabama's Unionists in the Civil War and Reconstruction*. Baton Rouge: Louisiana State University Press, 2004.

Tatum, Georgia Lee. *Disloyalty in the Confederacy*. 1934, Lincoln: University of Nebraska Press, 2000.

Taylor, Ethel. "Discontent in Confederate Louisiana." *Louisiana History* 2 (1961): 410–428.

Thompson, Wesley S. *The Free State of Winston: A History of Winston County, Alabama*. Winfield: Pareil Press, 1968.

Watkins, Sam R. *Co. Aytch: Maury Grays, First Tennessee Regiment*. 1882, Wilmington: Broadfoot Publishing, 1987.

Weitz, Mark A. *More Damning than Slaughter: Desertion in the Confederate Army*. Lincoln: University of Nebraska Press, 2005.

Williams, David. *Bitterly Divided: The South's Inner Civil War*. New York: The New Press, 2008.

Williams, David, Teresa Crisp Williams, and David Carlson. *Plain Folk in a Rich Man's War: Class and Dissent in Confederate Georgia*. Gainesville: University Press of Florida, 2002.

# 3

# WOMEN SOLDIERS

*Rachel Redfern*

At the start of the Civil War, neither the Union nor the Confederacy was well prepared to clothe and feed armies or take care of wounded and sick soldiers. Women on both sides of the conflict created a workforce beyond their new domestic responsibilities that tried to outfit and care for soldiers. Aid societies for both the Union and the Confederacy made socks, gloves, pillowcases, sheets, undergarments and whole uniforms. Women organized supplies for the hospitals, which they packaged and sent on, and also prepared and packaged food for the armies.

As the war progressed, the southern aid societies remained state and local entities, but the North quickly developed a more centralized system. On April 29, 1861, a large group of women met in New York City and formed the Women's Central Association for Relief. Two weeks later, representatives from the Association visited President Lincoln to ask for his approval of a United States Sanitary Commission (USSC), which went on to coordinate the work of local aid societies. Ten headquarters assisted the USSC in effectively distributing clothing, bandages and food.

The aid societies also sent women out on fund-raising efforts. Women in both the North and the South canvassed as part of "begging committees," asking for money and donations of supplies (Culpepper 252). A particularly noteworthy fund-raising venue was the fair. The first large-scale effort was Chicago's Northwestern Sanitary Commission Fair. Held on October 28, 1863, and organized largely by women, it raised $100,000. Countless women secured donations, prepared food and handcrafts to be sold, worked on publicity and set up booths, games and exhibitions. Perhaps the most prestigious prize available was solicited from President Lincoln: the original draft of the Emancipation Proclamation, which netted $3,000. After this fair's success, other large northern cities hosted their own fairs, and "fair mania" swept the North (Culpepper 262).

The USSC trained nurses as well and more than three thousand women worked as paid nurses for the Union and Confederate armies. A select few also worked as military doctors. The first-ever female U.S. Army Surgeon was Dr. Mary Edwards Walker from New York, who gained her medical degree in 1855. After serving on the front lines as a nurse in 1861 and as an unpaid field surgeon in 1862, she was finally given a commission as a surgeon in September 1863. She was captured by the Confederate army as a spy while crossing battle lines to treat the wounded in April 1864 and was held in Richmond as a prisoner of war for five months.

Some women also wanted to support the cause in an even more direct way. Hundreds served as spies for both the North and the South. For example, Elizabeth Van Lew was a southern spy for the Union during the war. She was from Richmond but was educated at a Quaker school in Philadelphia. There she became an abolitionist. During the Civil War, she communicated information to northern generals. On numerous occasions, pretending to be an eccentric and harmless Union sympathizer, she took food to Union captives in a Confederate prison in Richmond and gathered information from prisoners and Confederate guards about troop movements. General Grant described her information as the most valuable he received from Richmond during the war, and when Richmond fell in 1865, Van Lew was the first person to raise the U.S. flag in the city.

Still other women wanted to be part of the war in the most direct way possible: by fighting. In diary entries and letters, many bemoaned their gender as a barrier to joining the army. Wrote Sarah Morgan of Louisiana: "O! If only I was a man! Then I could don the breeches, and slay them with a will! If some few Southern women were in the ranks, they could set the men an example they would not blush to follow" (Dawson 24). Lucy Breckinridge of Virginia observed in her journal: "I wish that women could fight. I would gladly soldier my pistol and shoot some Yankees if it were allowable" (Blanton and Cook 25). On the Union side, Mrs. Black of Boston was mistakenly put on the army's draft roles. She showed up as ordered, did not want anyone to fight in her place and said she wanted to "take position in line" (Blanton and Cook 26).

In fact, although women were not allowed to enlist in either army, approximately four hundred women on record defied the law and managed to become soldiers during the war. The actual number is likely higher. Not only present in camps as nurses, spies, cooks and laundresses, women disguised themselves and fought as soldiers. They held every rank from musician to major, and several received promotions. A Union woman soldier known only as Margaret was killed at the Battle of Second Bull Run while holding the rank of Sergeant. An unnamed woman from New Jersey was promoted from Private to Corporal, and would have been made a Sergeant if she had not given birth to a son. Women were also commissioned officers.

A variety of reasons compelled women to enlist in the military. Some women followed their husbands, brothers or fathers in order to avoid a separation they could not bear. For example, Martha Parks Lindley served with her husband in the 6th U.S. Cavalry Company D, as "Jim Smith." On the Confederate side, Lucy Thompson Gauss served with her husband, Bryant, in the 18th North Carolina Infantry from August 1861 until December 1862, when she left after becoming pregnant. And although the husbands of Martha Parks Lindley and Lucy Thompson Gauss knew their wives were in the military, some women enlisted and followed their husbands or family members without telling them.

Other women enlisted because they were bored and restless. They saw war as a chance for adventure and independence, and the military as a way to escape stifling families or intolerable marriages. Several women saw little choice but to enlist when the war killed their entire family. A few enlisted to escape the other option for making a living: prostitution. The majority of women soldiers had working-class, immigrant or farming backgrounds, and so money was one motive for enlistment. For these women, bounties and military pay brought more money than they could ever hope to earn as cooks, laundresses or chambermaids. The majority of women who enlisted, however, explained their desire to fight in terms of patriotism and regional identity: they believed in the Union or Confederate cause.

The military practices of the time enabled women to enlist with relative ease. Military officials on both sides decreed that recruits undergo a thorough physical exam, but this rarely took place in practice, especially as each side found it increasingly difficult to raise the required number of troops. Medical inspections prior to enlistment were extremely cursory, and a woman who cut her hair, put on men's clothes and adopted a male alias could pass such assessments. Until 1864, eighteen was the minimum age of enlistment for service in both the Union and the Confederacy, but teenagers routinely lied about their age and, since many male soldiers were young, women soldiers with no facial hair and higher pitched voices did not attract attention. Recruiters and medical personnel simply looked for reasonable height, a partial set of teeth (to rip open powder cartridges) and a trigger finger.

Enlistment procedures became increasingly informal as the war continued. When units were depleted, commanders were more likely to accept any volunteer. And since there was no standardized means of identification, recruiters often accepted whatever name, age and background information they were given by recruits. Some women were able to deceive recruiters and reenlist two or three or more times after being exposed as female for the first time. A few were even able to avoid the enlistment procedures altogether by joining up with units as they readied for a battle or a march when the chaos of preparation prevented anyone from inquiring about a newcomer. Other women tried telling recruiters they were female and begged to be admitted against protocol, or sought out commanders to ask for permission to enlist.

Once in the army, the realities of camp life enabled women to continue the masquerade of masculinity. Soldiers slept in their clothes and bathed in their underwear, practices which helped women avoid detection. As well, soldiers bathed and changed clothes infrequently, and since latrines were filthy, many male soldiers sought out private places to relieve themselves. So women soldiers who bathed or urinated in private, in order to avoid the detection of their true gender, did not call particular attention to themselves. Even menstrual cycles did not necessarily bring their identities to light. Many women soldiers ceased having their periods all together due to the poor diet and physical exertion of military life. If women did menstruate, they retreated to the privacy of woodland or bushes to change the rags they were wearing. Beyond these issues of bathing and personal hygiene, women managed to maintain their disguises on a daily basis thanks to the poorly-fitting uniforms issued by armies on both sides. To further hide their figures, they bound their breasts and padded their waists.

Many women soldiers also adopted male mannerisms and habits to avoid detection. Women drank, gambled, cursed and fought with other soldiers to blend in with the male soldiers. One Union soldier in the 2nd Iowa Infantry, Nellie Williams, was arrested for being under the influence, and several other women were only exposed as women because they were intoxicated. Ella Reno was put in jail for verbally insulting a superior officer and Rosetta Wakeman bragged in a letter home that she was the winner in a fistfight with a male soldier. Further playing the part, at least three distaff women soldiers are known to have actively courted civilian women.

While some women relied on the assistance of loved ones in the ranks to conceal their true identities, others managed alone to maintain their forbidden identities as soldiers for months. Several additional factors helped them. The fact that the United States did not have a standing army at the start of the Civil War meant that the majority of soldiers had never been in the military, and they had to learn how to soldier from scratch, just like the disguised female soldiers. Unfamiliarity with weaponry or military conventions did not betray a female identity. Then, as they familiarized themselves with battle and its tools, women found that Civil War era weapons were not so heavy that they could not use them. Some women soldiers were aided in this physical challenge by their background and experiences as factory laborers or farm hands before the war.

In fact, most often, women soldiers were only discovered when they were wounded badly enough that physicians had to remove their clothing to reach an injury. Wounded women soldiers were discovered after the Battles of Shiloh, Richmond, Perryville, Murfreesboro, Antietam, Fredericksburg, Gettysburg, Green River, Lookout Mountain, Peachtree Creek, Allatoona and the Wilderness. Others were exposed as women when they were hospitalized for illness, although several were able to successfully plead with their nurses or doctors not to reveal their gender.

More minor wounds to feet, hands, faces or calves did not require any removal of clothing, however, and so women soldiers could escape detection. Union soldier Rebecca "Georgianna" Petermen received a wound above her temple and her gender was not detected, while some women soldiers treated their own wounds so that they could maintain their disguises. Sarah Edmonds, "Private Franklin Thompson" in the 2nd Michigan Infantry, cared for her own injuries on three occasions rather than risk detection. She suffered multiple contusions to her leg after falling from a mule and then suffered a lung hemorrhage, which left her coughing up blood for more than a week. Her third injury resulted when her horse was shot out from under her and she broke a bone in the fall. Edmonds refused medical care for each of these injuries.

But Edmonds later fell ill with malaria, and although she refused to go to the hospital, her comrades were insistent. Realizing that she was in danger of being discovered, she left the army and her regiment listed Pvt. Franklin Thompson as having deserted on April 19, 1863. She later wrote about her decision: "I now became discouraged, and fearing that if I remained longer my sex might be discovered, I left the Army" (Blanton and Cook 98). Although she tried to receive an increase in her soldier's pension because of the effects of her untreated injures, the request was denied because there were no records of her ever being injured. Edmonds responded: "Had I been what I represented myself to be, I should have gone to the hospital..... But being a woman I felt compelled to suffer in silence ... in order to escape detection of my sex. I would have rather have been shot dead, than to have been known to be a woman and sent away from the army" (Blanton and Cook 98).

Depending on how thorough burial preparations were, death could be an unavoidable moment of gender unveiling. However, occasionally, a woman soldier was only discovered long after the battle was over. When bodies were being moved in 1886 from the battle area near Resaca, Georgia, for re-interment to a national cemetery, the body of "Charles Johehouse, Private 6th Missouri" appeared to have unusually small feet. An examination revealed that Johehouse was a woman in full uniform who had been shot through the head. Later still, in 1934, a gardener was working around the Shiloh battlefield and found some human remains. Nine bodies were exhumed, one of which was female.

If death unavoidably exposed a woman soldier's true identity, so too did birth. Six soldiers are known to have performed their duties while pregnant and were not discovered until they went into labor. Two Confederate soldiers gave birth while prisoners of war. An unidentified corporal from New Jersey gave birth to a baby boy during the winter campaign of 1862 on the Rappahannock. In response, male soldiers wrote home expressing joy and wonderment at the birth, and even set up a contribution fund to give the boy a military education. Since the woman and the child's father were apparently not married, several soldiers demanded to know the father's identity in order to remove money from his monthly salary that would support the women and her child. Several years later, on March 2, 1865, an unidentified African American Union soldier gave birth in Petersburg, Virginia. Less than a week later, a corporal in the 6th New York Heavy Artillery went into labor while doing picket duty and gave birth to a baby boy. Upon receiving this gossip in a letter from her husband, a wife replied to him: "What a woman she must have been. I can't contrive how she hid it" (Blanton and Cook 105).

Neither army had any established rules for how to deal with soldiers who were discovered to be women. Women were discharged, either honorably or dishonorably, with papers declaring the reason for discharge to be "sexual incompatibility." A few were arrested and jailed, while others were kept on as nurses, laundresses and spies. Very occasionally, and usually in the Confederate Army, a woman was allowed to continue to serve as a soldier after the revelation of her gender.

## Further Reading

Blanton, DeAnne, and Lauren M. Cook. *They Fought Like Demons: Women Soldiers in the American Civil War.* Baton Rouge: Louisiana State Press, 2002.

Clinton, Catherine, and Nina Silber, eds. *Battle Scars: Gender and Sexuality in the American Civil War.* Oxford: Oxford University Press, 2006.

Culpepper, Marilyn Mayer. *Trials and Triumphs: Women of the American Civil War.* East Lansing: Michigan State University Press, 1991.

Dawson, Sarah Morgan. *A Confederate Girl's Diary.* Boston: Houghton Mifflin, 1913.

Edwards, Laura F. *Scarlett Doesn't Live Here Anymore: Southern Women in the Civil War Era.* Urbana: University of Illinois Press, 2000.

Faust, Drew Gilpin. "Altars of Sacrifice: Confederate Women and the Narratives of War." In *Divided Houses: Gender and the Civil War.* Ed. Catherine Clinton and Nina Silber. New York: Oxford University Press, 1992. 171–199.

Leonard, Elizabeth D. *Yankee Women: Gender Battles in the Civil War.* New York: W.W. Norton, 1994.

Silber, Nina. *Daughters of the Union: Northern Women Fight the Civil War.* Cambridge: Harvard University Press, 2005.

# PART II
# Labor and Land

# 4

# THE DOMESTIC SPHERE

*Phyllis Thompson*

"True, women cannot fight," Union journalist Gail Hamilton conceded, yet "the issue of war depends quite as much upon American women as upon American men...." Their primary duty, she argued, lay in cultivating a fierce brand of patriotism: "this soul of fire is what I wish to see kindled in our women, burning white and strong and steady ... scorching, blasting, annihilating whatsoever loveth and maketh a lie...." (345–46). This militant vision of the female heart was a new one, and was in stark contrast to pre-war ideas about female delicacy. Women could scarce afford frailty during the Civil War. At the same time that the war fractured the polity, it wrenched families apart, disrupted household and social routines, upended both gendered conventions of behavior and notions of respectable work, and visited hardship upon legions of American families. Grief was everywhere; few were untouched by tragedy. And "home," widely idealized as a haven, proved a challenge to maintain, both literally and as an ideal. With men on the battlefield, women on both sides of the Mason-Dixon line found themselves responsible for previously inconceivable tasks—both physical and emotional.

Antebellum ideologies of womanhood had centered on a "cult of domesticity," which privileged women's work within the home and framed household duties as complementary to the market work required of men in a rapidly industrializing economy. In dividing private from public, this ideal helped account for women's exclusion from full citizenship in an era in which America was transitioning from a republic to a democracy. Yet, in exalting women's care of home and family, it helped bring some dignity to an unequal system. Women, in this pre-war cultural system, were, as Barbara Welter summarizes it, expected to exhibit qualities of "piety, purity, submissiveness, and domesticity" (152). A gendered form of moral superiority adhered to the women who lived within these guidelines, and lent them authority in familial and spiritual matters. Further, since the late eighteenth century, women had been defined as the protectors of public virtue, via the mechanism of providing both selfless moral examples and wholesome home lives for their families. While such ideas lent certain women stature, they limited their ability to behave assertively, and also made it near impossible to work outside the home once married, which had the effect of excluding African Americans and the working classes from respectable womanhood. The gulf between the sexes gaped even wider in the South, where chivalric ideals required even greater delicacy on the part of women and gallantry on the part of men.

Throughout North America, mid-nineteenth-century women's lives were primarily bounded by their domestic circles: home, church, and visiting. One effect of this conceptual, social, and spatial confinement was to elevate the idea of home to that of a civilizing force and a refuge. War, however, ravaged homes, and disrupted the fantasy that there was such a thing as a place apart from a world of violence and aggression. And, as women took on new tasks necessitated by the departure of men for the front—from running businesses to the backbreaking work of hoeing and planting—both domestic life and notions of womanhood were inevitably revised.

Throughout the war, gender relations helped anchor the meaning of the conflict and identify the goals and aims of each side. The North understood its gender system as functional and virtuous, and idealized its slave-free homes as icons of moral purity. Given that most of the battles were fought on southern soil, it was harder for the Union to claim—as the Confederacy did, to great effect—that the cause was a defense of hearth and home. Representations framed women's consent (and need for protection) as central to the war's meaning, and men's obligation to fight. This melding of the personal obligation with the national was even more marked, literal, and direct for Confederates, who fought for "home," even as Union soldiers fought for "country." But still, the image of a patriotic, benevolent woman helped construct the Union's claim to moral superiority.

While northern women's rights advocates had already chipped away at polarized understandings of gender roles, nineteenth-century feminist efforts had had little impact on the South, and notions of womanhood had remained intractably rooted in an idea of biological opposition to manhood. At the same time, southern ideas of gender were inseparable from the classed and raced notions of "ladyhood," which depended upon a racially hierarchical social structure. Women's public reputations were derived from domestic roles—including the management of slaves—and how those roles were extended into the community. Southern women, then, were threatened as women by the idea of black freedom, which they understood as dangerous to their very femininity. For many, this personalized the stakes of the war and increased loyalty to the Confederacy; for planter-class women, war threatened their social standing, husbands, slaves, and wealth. Many young women refracted the "Glorious Cause" through the lens of female continuity: they longed to continue in the lives and traditions—not to mention the luxuries and privileges—of their mothers and grandmothers. The result was a passionate commitment not only to the war effort, but also to antebellum gender ideals and racial hierarchies. "I thank Heaven that I was born a Southerner, that I belong to the noblest race on earth," one young woman wrote, "for this is a heritage that nothing can ever take from me" (Andrews 380). For poorer southern women with no status to lose, the direct danger of the war itself was the greatest threat.

Northern women were much less likely to come into direct contact with danger, but this did not shelter them from daily contact with the war's exigencies. Though "marked as noncombatants" (Giesberg 10), which in the national imaginary meant they were in a terrain separate from war, even those northern women who remained entirely at home were very much pulled into the war. They constructed its materials, took on new responsibilities while men fought, and in many cases had to relocate, take in relatives or boarders, and increase their domestic production; for every woman, not just the nurses and spies so frequently memorialized, the war was a part of daily life.

They also took on the war as a political cause—in many cases rechanneling political passions, such as that for women's rights or abolitionism, into the cause of supporting the troops. Louisa May Alcott lamented "I long to be a man; but as I can't fight, I will content myself with working for those who can," and Harriet Beecher Stowe was confident that the Union effort was a "cause to die for" (Cott 179). Some families were divided within themselves: Eliza Andrews noted that "Father sticks to the Union through thick and thin, and mother sticks to father, though I believe she is more than half a rebel at heart, on account of the boys. Fred and Garnett are good Confederates, but too considerate of father to say much, while all the rest of us are red-hot Rebs" (220). Convictions tended to the vehement: in arguing with a family member, one woman observed that "we might as well have tried to make her believe that the sun shines here in the night as to make a secessionist of her, and this is the way with all the Unionists" (Smiley, May 30, 1861).

No matter their allegiances, women everywhere hurled themselves into project of raising morale from the moment war had been declared. Housewives in both the North and South ran charity bazaars, organized parades, attended military rallies, and sewed flags, and uniforms. These activities, all construable as extensions of household work and affective labor, had the effect of including women in the conflict while at the same time reifying their feminine identities. Certain symbolic acts—most iconically, the wearing of homespun cloth, so as to spare good commercially woven goods for the war effort—became emblematic of patriotism, particularly among well-off young women.

More effectively, thousands of community-based soldiers' aid societies sprang up to bind together households in the production of uniforms, bedding, and foodstuffs. Essentially, the sewing bee was politicized. Groups of women produced goods according to word-of-mouth information, and their own ideas of suitable aid. Some early efforts went astray—memorably, the overproduction of havelocks to protect delicate necks from the sun—but these household efforts, decentralized as they were, nonetheless provided critical support, not to mention knit socks and bandages, to the front lines. Troops before the war had been custom-outfitted by seamstresses; during the Civil War the Union military studied men's sizes and aggregated some standardized data (which was soon adopted by the menswear industry for civilian clothing) for industrial production. The Confederacy, less well funded and operating without reliable supply chains, depended heavily upon housewives for the manufacture of uniforms on an ad hoc basis: "I can, by using my table covers, scraps of flannel, etc., manage to piece out six flannel shirts," one women noted (Conklin 165).

When not tending to their own homes and children, or manufacturing goods for soldiers, women wrote letters. They understood the dispensation of moral support to be one of their key wartime roles. They expressed care, and shared neighborhood gossip and details of home life. In other cases they buoyed battle-fever with their own partisanship. Letters were serious business: a northern woman journalist instructed her fellow women to "... follow the soldier to the battlefield with your spirit. The great army of letters that marches Southward with every morning sun is a powerful engine of war" (Hamilton 347).

There was a nationally inscribed role for women even in the writing of love letters—special edition pictorial envelopes often depicted women with patriotic paraphernalia, in some cases literally clothed in the flag. Letters went astray in inconsistent mails (even reports of casualties from battles were sometimes delayed for months) and were frequently opened and censored; an inviolate letter was sufficiently comforting as to be of note. But still, letter writing was the only form of communication for many couples, and they poured their hearts out onto the page. People of the Civil War era, unlike those a century earlier, did expect to marry for love, and the nineteenth-century romantic ideal of love threads throughout Civil War correspondence, which often anatomized the human heart, God's will, and the particulars of patriotic fervor in equal balance and interrelated terms. Letters were a crucial dip into the ideology of the past—a place to preserve the imagined self in a changing, harshening world.

Pre-war Confederate lives for gentry women had been focused on courtship and marriage. The daughters of the well-off married for love, but within their class; to do otherwise would put a family's reputation on the line. Southern honor codes were constrictive, and expulsion from polite society was a risk. But the war often made conventional behavior impractical. For many couples, the war sped up courtship; there was a rush of weddings as men enlisted. As the war ground on, up to a quarter of men of military age died and an equal number were wounded, with very real implications for marriage and thus for southern womanhood. Because individual identity was so fully predicated upon the particulars of heterosexual love, "war and its mounting death toll would prove devastating not just to their life plans but to their fundamental self-definition" (Faust 141). The dearth of men was keenly felt in less populous rural areas, and while southerners tried to stick to the customary arrangement of gallant male courtship of passive women, all conducted under the watchful eye of family and community, unconventional matches, age disparities, and both hasty and delayed marriages abounded.

Because communities were disrupted, courtship was somewhat liberalized. While people stayed home more, and there were fewer opportunities to meet others, the absence of beaux and husbands created anxiety about fidelity on top of the sense of loss caused by wartime separation. In some cases men tried to manage behavior at home from afar, and in others they encouraged visits to encampments, despite the strain on women who would then have to abandon duties at home. There was a particular cultural anxiety about the supposedly flirtatious behavior of Confederate widows—an anxiety exacerbated by the very real fact that any husband who died intestate left his wife only dower rights for her lifetime to a third of his real estate and property, which was often insufficient to the purpose of supporting a family. The new specter of women in public also raised alarm about sexual behavior, as did a small but noticeable increase in divorce rates.

In this topsy-turvy domestic world, small rituals and formalities provided a comforting link to a stable past. Women clung to the ceremonial rituals of social life. Parlors were common both North and South, and the elaborate culture of punctiliously reciprocal half-hour social calls persisted. The ideals of domestic grace and of hospitality survived every assault, if in modified form. Southern hospitality in particular had been famous before the war: food and drink were abundant and fine and hosts more generous than in other regions, according to numerous reports. Yet transportation systems throughout the South were poor even before the war; the blockade of southern ports made luxuries a thing of the past. But people did gather for fun, even if at smaller scales and with vastly less extravagant accouterments. Balls tended to exist only as fundraisers, and grand dinners were scarce. Some gatherings were practical: barn raisings, berry picking expeditions, maple sap collection, and quilting bees. Others were intellectual: spelling contests, music recitals, speeches, debates, and plays.

In the effort to preserve normalcy and grace, women on both sides clung to antebellum appearances as well as activities. Mid-nineteenth century fashion in clothing was quite consistent throughout North America. Catalogs and magazines at every level—crucially *Godey's Lady's Book, Peterson's,* and *The Demorest*—exported images of fashions in dress to every corner. Even general interest magazines, like *Atlantic Monthly* and *Scribner's,* commented on what was worn by prominent women. The trends held true across social classes: nearly every woman whose daily life did not involve hard physical labor wore a chemise, drawers or pantalets, then a corset, and a crinoline or hoop under her bell-shaped skirt. The containment offered by corsets (sold by waist measurement) was seen as key to morality and was non-negotiable for those who aspired to be thought of as ladies. Hoops were found at many levels of quality and in every class, but the precise shape and size of a skirt indicated varying degrees to which a woman's dress was *au courant*.

High fashion was, to many, a much-mourned thing of the past. Decreased fabric production and blockades meant that cloth was in very short supply, especially in the South, which had, pre-war, imported most of its clothing and shoes from the North and from Europe, limiting its own production to that of coarse cloth for slaves' clothing. In 1864 one Confederate woman noted ruefully, "In dress we are just where we were in 1860—for fashion, but rags and wrinkles are more plentiful" (Fisher, January 3, 1864). What new clothes there were might well be made of repurposed bed-ticking, or from the linings of more luxurious pre-war garments. During the war most women reworked old dresses, or at the least saved lace from one dress to re-use in another. Southern women wrote in their diaries about the embarrassment of wearing out their silk dresses and donning calico—a material formerly used for the dresses of slaves and servants. Many women lamented the loss of fine linen undergarments—clothing, after all, signaled caste, even to its wearer; this could mean the difference between feeling "decent" rather than "vulgar and common" (Andrews 111).

Food was another basic aspect of life to swiftly diminish in quality. Shortages were widespread by 1862, and many found themselves living on field peas or "pork and hominy" (Fisher, January 7, 1864). Things were particularly dire during occupations, such as that of Columbia: "Father left us with some moldy, spoiled flour that was turned over to him by the Bureau. We can only possibly eat it made into batter-cakes and then it is horrid. We draw rations from the town every day—a tiny bit of rancid salt pork and a pint of meal. We have the battercakes for breakfast, the bit of meat and cornbread for dinner—no supper" (LeConte, February 23, 1865). The limited availability of salt made it difficult to preserve beef and pork, even when they could be obtained. Even in the North, diets were restricted as prices were high, labor short, and both resources and energies directed toward the army. One northern woman observed, "Nowadays our cooking does not take much time—nowadays being we do all our eating by piecing" (Mohr and Winslow 337).

Decency, in its antebellum sense, was difficult for everyone to maintain, and not just culinarily. Women tried to keep to their established household routines, but this was a challenge. Not that household responsibilities had been light before the war: wood-burning and coal stoves existed, though in rural areas it was still common to cook upon the hearth; butter had to be churned; multiple cast-iron flat-irons must be warmed in the fire before tackling the weeks' linens; and laundry was still boiled and beaten by hand (domestic counselor Catharine Beecher identified this task as "the American housekeeper's hardest problem" [388]). Household manuals suggest that women were additionally responsible for tending to their family's physical health and moral rectitude, interior decor, cooking, cleaning, budget-making, flower and vegetable gardens, childcare and eldercare, managing servants (or, in some cases, slaves), and providing emotional support to their household members. Every one of these tasks became more burdensome for middle-class and gentry-class women during the war, either because it was less plausible to farm out labor either to men or lower-class (or enslaved) women, or because the materials were lacking.

Most American women had always done at least a portion of their own housework; slave-owners were a small proportion of the population, and the standards of middle-class housework were sufficiently onerous that even a woman who employed a housekeeper and maid expended daily physical effort. But the war, with its shortages of goods and manpower, exacerbated the situation. Indeed, once their slaves had departed, even upper-class southern women had to learn to cook and clean. Sarah Morgan was "astonished that she could empty a dirty hearth, dust, move heavy weights, make myself generally useful and dirty, and all this thanks to the Yankees!" (Hoy 47). Emma LeConte noted that she had "… washed the dinner things and put the room to rights," in her "first experience in work of this kind" (February 19, 1865). Eliza Andrews ruefully observed that she didn't "find doing housework quite so much of a joke as I imagined it was going to be" (376). While housework had been framed before the war as an uplifting activity for women—one that inculcated patience, and required clever economies and the exercise of good judgment—the kind of work thus idealized was relatively gentle. (As such it excluded working-class and black women from its penumbra of virtue.) The work that war brought on was frequently rough, exhausting, and repetitive. Some husbands expressed reasonable—but futile—concern that the hard labor would be too much for their wives.

The manual labor was truly hard. After the Confederate Army initiated a draft in the spring of 1862, men vacated agricultural work; more than three-quarters of eligible southern white men would serve the army by the end of the war. Their absence was searingly obvious at planting time, when women had to learn to plow. In the North, despite men going off to war (and historians have estimated that half of all the soldiers in the U.S. Army had been farmers or farm laborers), agricultural production remained high, which indicates increased female participation, but was also in part a function of the availability of machinery, an asset less prevalent in the slave-labor-dependent South. But for most women, at least some new tasks—perhaps shearing sheep, hauling wood, or yoking oxen—that had once been the province of others joined their roster of responsibilities.

In the meantime, while waiting for the return of men—and of their physical labor and salaries—women on both sides had little choice but to make do. While letters from early in the war often solicit male guidance, by the end of the war women tended to have grown increasingly self-reliant. Some women managed family property or businesses by means of a "deputy husband" role, by which they maintained a veneer of respectability while filling in for their husbands or fathers in their absence. Inevitably, given the length of the conflict and the spottiness of the mail service, let alone the vast number of deaths, women by themselves had to make decisions even in what had been understood as "male" arenas. Domestic coherence was exceptionally difficult to maintain; the pre-war system was in shreds.

While women's dependence was rhetorically celebrated, and women's work only scantily remunerated, even in the relatively organized North there was no comprehensive federal commitment to support the wives of soldiers. Relief boards, before offering payments to soldiers' wives, scrutinized their behavior and evaluated their virtue. Payments were also eliminated when husbands deserted or died. Delayed wages could mean indigence for wives already on the economic edge. In response, thousands of northern women wrote to President Lincoln or to the Secretary of War to petition for the release of their husbands or sons from military service, or merely to learn of their location. For their part, Confederate troops were paid irregularly, and there was no formal system for sending pay home to families. Their wives, too, protested. In one famous example from 1863, the Richmond Bread Riots, several hundred working-class women armed themselves with axes and horse pistols and marched to the city's commercial center to demand bread for their families.

In the face of privation, southern women either did without or improvised. Many ran out of candles, and there was little fuel for cooking. There was no way to replace bedding, or broken utensils. Nails, screws, snaps, and needles were scarce. Paper, shoes, and all kinds of tools were hard to come by, even before troops left home, as a result of the Union embargo. Journals variously note that women made soap from water, lye, and grease; they replaced their face powder with rice flour, made piecrust from potatoes, and sewed their own shoes. But there were limits to this ingenuity; southern households, as Drew Faust noted, "did not become factories" (51). Women were more likely to go without and to sacrifice comfort, in hopes of a swift end to the war, than to become entirely self-sufficient.

There was, regardless, a long list of necessary adaptations for genteel women. For example, they found themselves responsible for an increased portion of medical care as doctors enlisted and, in the South, influxes of medical supplies fell victim to the blockades. With the trained professionals focused on the battlefield, childbirth in particular fell under female purview, and many women (and virtually all enslaved women) found themselves completely without professional help, unless within range of a competent midwife who hadn't departed to serve as an army nurse. Infection was as major risk, and grave birth injuries were common, as was death in childbirth. Consequently, southern women in particular—rightly concerned as well about the problem of more mouths to feed—were more vigilant about birth control than before the war, and abortions, though dangerous, grew more common. Even in the North, women tried to limit pregnancies and were often frightened to give birth (and risk death) without their husbands' support.

But children, many of them, already existed or did arrive during the war. While most northern children never saw a Confederate soldier, they followed the news of the war, and shared in their families' anxieties. Many southern children also saw houses burn, shells explode, and had direct confrontations with violence or its threat. Childhood itself was newly politicized—as just one example, the Union ABC book instructed that "A is for America, land of the free" (Mintz 127)—and children on both sides attended rallies, played war games, raised funds, staged parades, and joined in patriotic songs.

The war came at an awkward moment in the history of American childhood. Children had recently come to be understood as innocent and in need of protection, and middle-class parents were committed to sheltering their young from the harsh adult world. That world, unfortunately, had become unavoidable. Further, in dividing parents, the war also shifted the burden of care—formerly shared with fathers, who had supervised education and discipline—entirely to mothers. Already overburdened, Civil War era women turned to those same children for assistance in household tasks. Before the war, children had played games using simple, homemade materials (jump rope, checkers, rag dolls, cards) but, as the war dragged on, they spent less time amusing themselves and more time sewing, sweeping, gardening, fetching drinking water, building fires, and tending to babies. The division of chores by sex began very early, and girls served as apprentices to their mothers. The situation was, like all other domestic matters, more extreme in the South. A Georgia woman noted that children as young as eight were cooking, washing, and ironing, and even younger girls scraped lint to make bandages and knit socks.

Amidst all the effort and privation, life seemed to lose its normal punctuation. Many churches closed or limited services, depriving women of what had been a crucial source of comfort and meaning. Other rituals, too, became impracticable. Holidays were diminished in glow. Dolly Lunt wrote on Christmas Eve, 1864: "We are all sad; no loud, jovial laugh from our boys is heard ... I have nothing even to put in [my daughter's] stocking, which hangs so invitingly for Santa Claus. How disappointed she will be in the morning, though I have explained to her why he cannot come. Poor children! Why must the innocent suffer with the guilty?" (43–44). Birthdays too, fell by the wayside. During the siege of Atlanta, Carrie Berry observed in her diary of her tenth birthday: "I did not have a cake times were too hard so I celebrated with ironing" (Marten 145). One teenager went further and lamented the loss of the whole world she had imagined would be hers as a young woman:

> The weather is intensely, fearfully cold.... How dreadfully sick I am of this war. Truly we girls, whose lot it is to grow up in these times, are

unfortunate! It commenced when I was thirteen, and I am now seventeen and no prospect yet of its ending. No pleasure, no enjoyment—nothing but rigid economy and hard work—nothing but the stern realities of life…. It is a hard school to be bred up in and I often wonder if I will ever have my share of fun and happiness…. Now that everything is lost, perhaps we will all have to work for a living before long. I would far rather do that and bear much more than submit to the Yankees.

(LeConte, January 28, 1864)

But despite this commonly held fierceness of attitude, many Confederate women had little choice but to submit, in the most basic of ways, even before the conclusion of the war. Farms and households were called upon to feed Confederate forces as they passed through; this was bad enough in light of the limited rations available, but made worse by the fact that the troops were legally entitled to appropriate livestock, or even slaves as labor force if they chose. In theory, the troops were to offer payment, but not all households were so lucky as to receive it. The unluckiest were ransacked later by Union soldiers, who scoured homes of everything edible, alongside much of what was useful or saleable. While Union General Order No. 100 allowed soldiers to seize property that might in their judgment help facilitate the end of the war, in reality they took valuables and destroyed objects with no military use, from memorabilia to pianos. In self-defense, when incursions were rumored (and inevitably false rumors abounded), women slept fully dressed, buried their provisions, and tried to hide their domestic animals. Some elites deserted their homes, taking or hiding their valuables, and headed for the homes of relatives or other connections. This had costs: "Those who left their houses fared worse than others, at least their houses did. The wife of a worthy miller living near us [in Virginia] became so much alarmed that she went with her little children to a neighbor's. They stripped her house completely, destroying everything, left nothing but a straw bed & one sheet" (Emerson, July 15, 1864). "It was dreadful," Emma LeConte recalled of the invasion of her home, "everything was burst open—all our silver and valuables stolen—articles of clothing slashed up by bayonets and burned …" (February 22, 1865). Dolly Lunt's house too was ransacked:

But like demons they rush in! My yards are full. To my smoke-house, my dairy, pantry, kitchen, and cellar, like famished wolves they come, breaking locks and whatever is in their way. The thousand pounds of meat in my smoke-house is gone in a twinkling…. My eighteen fat turkeys, my hens, chickens, and fowls, my young pigs, are shot down in my yard and hunted as if they were rebels themselves…. As I stood there, from my lot I saw driven, first, old Dutch, my dear old buggy horse, who has carried my beloved husband so many miles, and who would so quietly wait at the block for him to mount and dismount, and who at last drew him to his grave; then came old Mary, my brood mare, who for years had been too old and stiff for work, with her three-year-old colt, my two-year-old mule, and her last little baby colt. There they go! There go my mules, my sheep, and, worse than all, my boys [slaves]!

*(22–24)*

And, there, with the invaders, went a way of life.

In the South, war had unsettled the patriarchal white-male-dominated order and the many hierarchies that had been knit into the slaveholding system. Home, as it had been understood under what would be derisively memorialized as the reign of "moonlight and magnolias," had absorbed a profound blow. After the war, southern women took up the "Lost Cause" and raised funds for memorials and veteran's societies, as well as banding together to form the United Daughters of the Confederacy. But, while nostalgia for a romanticized version of the past would persist, domestic life had been irrevocably altered.

In the North, too, home life shifted as a consequence of the war. Because the discourse surrounding women's patriotism had made claims about its naturalness—its source in supposedly innate female altruism—women's labor for the war had been assumed to be without natural or necessary limit. But it wasn't, of course. All that privation and physical labor and emotional strain had real costs. And because of the costs, it had substantive effects on women's ideas of themselves, and to some extent, on the culture's ideas of what women could do and be: "souls of fire" indeed had been much in evidence. The pre-war ideology of separate spheres had cast women as distant from the coarse aggression and violence of the public, male world, but the war made clear how incomplete that distinction was. Women—whether they were rolling bandages, feeding soldiers, petitioning their governments, or comforting those in mourning—interacted purposefully, not just instinctually, with the very public world of war, and were in turn changed by it. Domestic life was a quiet front in a noisy conflict, but neither in the North nor the South was it innocent of war's rough hand.

## Further Reading

Andrews, Eliza Frances. *The War-Time Journal of a Georgia Girl, 1864–1865*. New York: D. Appleton and Company, 1908.

Attie, Jeanie. *Patriotic Toil: Northern Women and the American Civil War*. Ithaca: Cornell University Press, 1998.

Beecher, Catharine Esther and Harriet Beecher Stowe. *The American Woman's Home*. New Brunswick: Rutgers University Press, 2002.

Conklin, Eileen. *The Journal of Women's Civil War History: From the Home Front to the Front Lines*. Gettysburg: Thomas Publications, 2002.

Emerson, Nancy. *Diary*. Albert and Shirley Small Special Collections Library, University of Virginia, Charlottesville, Virginia.

Faust, Drew Gilpin. *Mothers of Invention: Women of the Slaveholding South in the American Civil War*. Chapel Hill: University of North Carolina Press, 1996.

Fisher, Julia Johnson. *Diary*. Southern Historical Collection, University of North Carolina at Chapel Hill.

Giesberg, Judith Ann. *Army at Home: Women and the Civil War on the Northern Home Front*. Chapel Hill: University of North Carolina Press, 2009.

Hamilton, Gail. "A Call to My Country-Women." *The Atlantic Monthly*, March 1863: 345–350.

Hoy, Suellen M. *Chasing Dirt: The American Pursuit of Cleanliness*. New York: Oxford University Press, 1995.

LeConte, Emma. *Diary*. Southern Historical Collection, University of North Carolina at Chapel Hill.

Lunt, Dolly Sumner. A *Woman's Wartime Journal: an Account of the Passage over a Georgia Plantation of Sherman's Army on the March to the Sea, as Recorded in the Diary of Dolly Sumner Lunt* (Mrs. Thomas Burge). New York: The Century Co., 1918.

Marten, James Alan. *The Children's Civil War*. Chapel Hill: University of North Carolina Press, 1998.

Mintz, Stephen. *Huck's Raft: A History of American Childhood*. Cambridge: Harvard University Press, 2004.

Mohr, James C. and Robert E. Winslow III, eds. *The Cormany Diaries: A Northern Family in the Civil War*. Pittsburgh: University of Pittsburgh Press, 1982.

Ott, Victoria E. *Confederate Daughters: Coming of Age During the Civil War*. Carbondale: Southern Illinois University Press, 2008.

Richard, Patricia L. *Busy Hands: Images of the Family in the Northern Civil War Effort*. New York: Fordham University Press, 2003.

Silber, Nina. *Gender and the Sectional Conflict*. Chapel Hill: University of North Carolina Press, 2008.

Smiley Family Papers, Accession #1807 Special Collections Department, University of Virginia Library, Charlottesville, Virginia.

Welter, Barbara. "The Cult of True Womanhood: 1820–1860." *American Quarterly* 18.2 (1966): 151–174.

# 5

# LABOR ORGANIZATIONS

*Mark A. Lause*

In the decades leading to the Civil War, significant numbers of workers organized as a self-conscious force united by what came to be called "solidarity." Workers' participation in the conflict was essential, even as the nature of the war radically reshaped the nature of labor in America and the potential of any labor movement. These changes raised essential questions about the meaning of solidarity in an American context and what this would mean for the future of any class movement in the United States.

Law and custom defined several categories of labor in mid-nineteenth century America and created a multi-faceted working class. The issue that hired workers generally faced was that federal policy permitted state laws acknowledging the legal ownership of several million workers of African descent, who labored in workshops as well as in plantation crews and household service. Similar numbers experienced the temporary servitude of apprenticeships. Wage labor supplied almost all the farm labor in the non-slaveholding states, the traditional skilled crafts and the new, more mechanized industries.

In the years leading to the Civil War, wage labor grew disproportionately, though exact figures for free nonagricultural workers remain elusive. The census divided the population by age, failed to distinguish employing mechanics from their workers, and provide little good information on female labor. Still, the skilled and semiskilled white workingmen who more regularly did organize themselves grew from around 200,000 in the 1820s to nearly 1,500,000 by 1860. The most free, privileged and well-paid category of the laboring classes created some notably energetic labor organizations and cultivated a distinctive tradition of working-class politics, often related to labor reform traditions emerging in Britain and the European nations.

Indeed, large sections of the American work force came directly out of those Old World conditions. While English-speaking workers formed the core of the labor force, the unprecedented growth of the American economy assimilated immigrants, though in such a way that often shaped ethnic division of labor. Large minorities—sometimes majorities—of the larger cities consisted of the foreign-born and their children, especially the Irish and Germans. Cities in the slaveholding states found themselves reliant particularly for skilled work on immigrants from Europe and the North.

Despite these divisions, American workers began forming their own associations as early as the colonial period, and hired men established early trade unions in the eighteenth century. In the largest early city, Philadelphia craft unions formed city-wide bodies briefly in 1796, 1827, and again in the middle 1830s. This last effort coincided with similar federations in over half a dozen cities, representing a combined membership estimated at over 30,000 workers. These bodies, in turn, formed a short-lived National Trades' Union. While conditions associated with the Panic of 1837 made the larger and more complex organizations untenable. The workers movements expanded once more at mid-century.

Labor historians have refined our understanding of "artisan republicanism." Workers couched their arguments in the republican ideology of the Enlightenment. This suggested that natural law established essential human needs for survival, that these needs implied the natural rights to meet those needs, that the emergence of civilization represented a social contract that translated at least some of these rights into civil rights while others remained "inalienable." The experience of the English, American, and French revolutions established the ideas that the social contract had to ensure liberty and represent the consent of the governed; that civilizations which failed to fill its obligations under the social contract essentially nullified its claims upon the people; and that participants in the social contract could subsequently alter, abolish or remake the social contract.

American workers saw the workplace as an integral part of this view. Half a century before, New York City carpenters explicitly defined the workplace as a "social compact" that required respect for workers' inalienable natural rights. Among those rights, they enumerated the length of the workday, a wage sufficient to raise a family and sustain themselves in their old age, and other already familiar trade unionist themes. As the imperative of the market tended to nullify such a social contract of the workplace, the survival of labor's freedom seemed increasingly to require trade unions, the strike, even the establishment of cooperatives. From the 1840s, political activism around land reform, the shorter workday, and cooperation became central to working-class thought. At times, these provided issues that mobilized thousands in their communities, and nationally coordinated petition drives to Congress in 1850–52 collected tens of thousands of signatures asking for a Homestead Act.

The 1850s saw the organization of around 120,000 American workers in over a hundred kinds of trades or crafts, which also formed city-wide federations. Although often described as "the new unionism," bodies affiliated with groups such as the "New York City Industrial Congress" organized around concerns that did not necessarily center on wages, working conditions and hours—those later defined as "pure and simple" trade unionism—to the exclusion of fraternal or cooperative interests. Within weeks of its founding, the NYCIC sponsored a bilingual mass meeting to support the cooperative founded by striking Germans in the needle trades, and it regularly discussed the merits of various reform proposals including William B. Greene's *Mutual Banking* and Edward N. Kellogg's *Labor and Other Capital*. Workers involved in labor reform advocated ideas as radical as any articulated in the century.

However, most characteristic of the upsurge of the 1850s were the new national craft organizations. These included: the National Typographical Union (1853); Upholsterers National Union (1853); National Union of Building Trades (1854); Hat Finishers National Association (1854); National Protective Association of the United States—railroad engineers—(1855); Journeymen Stone Cutters Association of the United States and Canada 1855); Lithographers National Union (1856); Cigar Makers National Union (1856); and the National Convention of Silver Platers (1857). Shortly before the Civil War, the Panic of 1857 collapsed these organizations and their numbers, leaving the United States with perhaps 30,000 to 40,000 union members with twice as many more experienced with membership and its standards.

Still, the survival of the national unions of printers, hat finishers, and stonecutters marked the first time such bodies had actually survived hard times. In the case of the National Typographical Union, membership fell to only 1,286, but bounced back to 2,362 by 1859 and reached 3,592 members in 1860. The thirteen founding locals of 1853 would reach eighty-five by the war's end, not counting the unaffiliated unions at Toronto, the Columbia Typographical Union at Washington, and that at Richmond, Virginia. Not surprisingly, of the eighty locals reporting through the New York trade journal, *The Printer*, some fifty-four of the largest and most active locals functioned in states and territories that had no slavery. By then, the two large locals at Philadelphia and New York had six hundred and four hundred members respectively.

Moreover, new national organizations firmly committed to trade unionism appeared. The National Union of Machinists and Blacksmiths began with a Philadelphia local that started with fourteen members in April 1858 and grew to three hundred by late summer 1858; inspired by leaders like Jonathan C. Fincher, they launched the national union in March 1859. After holding its own in a four-month strike against the Baldwin Locomotive Works, it expanded by November 1860, to a membership of 2,828 in 57 locals. The National Union of Iron Moulders also grew from its Philadelphia local with the energetic William H. Sylvis; 11 other locals helped launch the national union in July 1859 and, by

1860, it had 44 locals with a membership of 2,744. In addition, the new national unions included: the National Cotton Mule Spinners' Association (1858); the Cordwainers' National Union (1859); the Painters National Union (1859); and the American Miners Association (1861).

Like the printers, shoemakers had unionized on the local level episodically since the eighteenth century. Shoemakers established a loose national organization briefly in the 1830s, and faced a large-scale introduction of children and half-trained adult men into the craft. By the 1850s, the industry combined dependence on a vast number of underpaid contract workers with major strides towards a factory system.

In February 1860, a strong regional network of New England shoemakers began a walkout of some 17,000 workers, several thousand of which were women. Its leaders included Alonzo Granville Draper, an ambitious and well-educated young man who edited the *New England Mechanic* for the local Mechanics' Association, formed a few years earlier during the "hard times" of the panic. The largest strike in antebellum American history to date, the shoemakers' effort became embittered and hard-fought, lasting in some communities well into the early summer and had very mixed results.

The strike entered the increasingly sectional debate over the nation's future. A Congressional Democrat ascribed the 1860 shoe strike to declining shoe orders from the South, "the result of the unfortunate warfare brought about by this sectional controversy." Then visiting New England, Abraham Lincoln responded by confessing his ignorance of the shoe markets, but continued, "I know one thing: there is a strike! And I am glad to know that there is a system of labor where the laborer can strike if he wants to! I would to God that such a system prevailed all over the world" (Basler 7). His stance reflected the compelling power of this "free labor" dimension of the sectional conflict.

When the Democratic political machines of the southern states opted to secede from the United States, free labor provided a genuine problem. They may have argued that slavery was the natural condition of a laboring class, but they needed skilled workers who often came from Europe and the North. Never as popular as southern politicians, press and pulpit claimed, workers were particularly discontented with secession and numbers of them began to leave, a partial explanation for the draconian imposition of what amounted to martial law in much of the South.

The thought of civil war horrified workers. Many participated in a short-lived peace movement that originated in Louisville and seemed to be the tool of political leaders eager to promote the Crittenden Compromise, reassuring the South that the North would not act against slavery. Nevertheless, the example detonated a series of often large meetings of "mechanics and workingmen" protesting the course of the nation towards war and a spectrum of concerns. Many, such as Fred Oberklein of the Cincinnati Moulders used them to protest the secession of the Southern political machines and clearly hoped the public expression of Unionist sentiment would deter such action by Kentucky and other states of the lower South. These meetings spread through the Ohio valley and back east, culminating in a demonstration and convention at Philadelphia on Washington's birthday.

Similar meetings took place in southern cities. There, local political leaders and newspaper editors cast these protests as made against northern attempts at "coercion." However, the northern and foreign born comprised much of the skilled work force in the South. The published accounts of the assemblies at Richmond, for example, reveal a deep Unionist sentiment and a deep discontent with the rhetoric of secessionism.

With the outbreak of war in April 1861, a wave of volunteer enlistments swept off most of those members without wives and children. Given that Americans started with a relatively small military, an extraordinarily high proportion of hired craftsmen—particularly those with antebellum militia associations—entered the army as officers. A.G. Draper, the leader of the shoemakers strike at Lynn also commanded a company of militia, largely shoemakers and veterans of the strike, who marched off with similar companies to form the 14th Massachusetts, the command given to Colonel William B. Greene, the labor reformer veteran of the Brook Farm socialist community and translator of Pierre Joseph Proudhon's works. Veterans of the shoe strike clustered in this "Essex County regiment," which became the 1st Massachusetts Heavy Artillery, assigned to protect the nation's capital. So, too, miners from the organized coal districts filled the ranks of the 48th Pennsylvania, later famous for digging the shaft under the Confederate trenches at Petersburg. *The Printer* reports ceremonies in newspaper offices across the North where coworkers presented their departing comrades a sword, belt and sash.

In the case of the well-documented National Typographical Union, something like a quarter to a third of the membership eventually went to war, and the proportions were surely higher in trades not exempt from later conscription. Service records for some 535 union printers can be identified, of which well over 120 survived the rigors of the war to attain an officer's commission. Almost two dozen reached the rank of Major or higher, and one becoming a brigadier general, as did Draper of the shoemakers. Three members of the Typographical Union won the Congressional Medal of Honor, including John M. Tobin, Amos Jay Cummings, and the president of the NTU John M. Farquhar. Many died, including the union's Vice President William Madigan, the larger locals noting losses in virtually every major battle or campaign.

Printers in uniform played a particularly important role, since military headquarters acquired presses to print orders, but dozens of times, union printers occupied secessionist workplaces, and made the types sing a different tune. William R. Creighton of the Cleveland NTU commanded a company that descended on a "defunct rebel paper office in western Virginia, on the 4th of July," and launched the *Ohio Seventh*. Union members were among the 1st

Iowa, which took over *The Register* at Macon, Missouri, and printed "a spicy loyal journal, called *Our Whole Union*." Before moving on, the Iowa typos addressed the absent secessionist editor: "We sat at your table; we stole from your 'Dictionary of Latin Quotations;' we wrote Union articles with your pen, your ink, on your paper. We printed them on your press. Our boys set 'em up with your types, and your galleys, your 'shooting-sticks,' your 'chases,' your 'quads,' your 'spaces,' your 'rules,' your every thing. We even drank some poor whisky out of your bottle" (Richardson 154–55). Such impromptu confiscations represented more than a kind of boyish prank.

Most immediately, perhaps, the experience of war fostered a rethinking on questions of race. On a national level, such rethinking was important but ultimately proved to be not essential to the country's survival. Among workers, however, the future of labor organizations required it.

The Civil War wrought complex economic changes that left the workers' movement forever transformed. By June 1862, two-thirds of the 4.5 million cotton spindles in the northeastern states had gone idle and the remaining did not work to their 1860 capacity. However, wartime demand spurred other kinds of industries. Due in part to military uses, wool production soared to an annual peak of 208 million pounds. Then, too, the demand for shoes sped the application of sewing machinery pioneered in textiles to leather work. Demand for such goods grew so much that contractors relied on sweepings and scraps to produce "shoddy".

Most strikingly, war fostered all sorts of new manufacturing. America, at the war's onset, had no real capacity for producing ironclads, cannon, and the other materiel of war on anything like the scale they would be needed. Iron foundries and machine shops faced such greater demand for their products that newer companies formed alongside expanding older ones. Jonathan C. Fincher recalled the radical changes in his industry. Living machinists recalled when their employers had worked alongside them in a job that represented "a compound of handiwork, a kind of cross between a millwright and a whitesmith, a fitter, finisher, locksmith and so forth" (Commons 8).

The government itself forged these productive capacities. Federal arsenals like that at Springfield, Massachusetts, employed several thousand workers who fed a thousand new rifles daily to the war. The government operation at Cold Springs, New York opposite West Point became a military research site of unprecedented scale.

The production of uniforms and equipage of all sorts opened new industries, partly government operations but largely run by private contractors, who, in turn, commissioned most of the actual work to be done by women. While the former never paid that well, the latter paid as little as they could and get the work done. Management in government works avoided any discussions with workers about the terms and payment of labor, referring them generally to the authorities at the capital. Where government did respond to appeals over such issues, it pursued a strict policy of non-interference with what the contractors did, which created different levels of incomes for the same kind of work. That women, often the mothers, wives, sisters, and daughters of the men fighting the war bore the burden of these inequalities moved reformers and trade unionists, but not policy makers. The impact of these tensions had only a subtle influence on the reshaping of the wartime city.

However, the nature of industrialized naval warfare transformed the waterfront radically. Particularly after the successful introduction of ironclads into the war, the navy yards took on thousands more employees and government contracts to build ironclads led to similarly explosive growth in the private shipyards nearby. The construction of these complex new vessels involved dozens of distinct crafts, as well as legions of unskilled laborers. From the fall of 1862, labor troubles and strikes became endemic in the navy yards from Maine to Washington, with the massive Brooklyn Navy Yard as the epicenter.

In the fall of 1863, according to the local press, an estimated seven thousand workers went on strike there. The private contractors demanded help from the government in breaking the strike, and the local authorities seemed inclined to give it. Thereafter, a delegation of strikers visited Washington for an unprecedented meeting with the president. Lincoln famously responded with a statement of his general sympathies for the strikers and a promise that the government would not interfere but permit "the best blood" to prevail between the workers and the bosses. Lincoln's interpretation of this neutrality was to send instructions to the Navy Department that it should not grant extensions to the contractors on the date due for the delivery of the ships, which essentially made it impossible for the employers not to negotiate with the unions.

War dramatically transformed the railroad network. Because logistical necessity required the rapid construction, repair and replacement of the rails, it permitted standardization. In late 1863, to hasten the movement of two corps near Washington to the beleaguered forces in Chattanooga, the War Department and railroad officials used the labor of displaced persons to replace the damaged narrow-gauge track through Kentucky and Tennessee with standard gauge. In a mere 11 days, they moved the 20,000 men almost 1,300 miles by rail. Once acquired, this kind of managerial expertise would not be forgotten.

Explicit blacklisting of unionists on the railroads did not prevent the organization of engineers and the other crafts. A number of regional strikes swept the industry across central Pennsylvania and on those lines operating in the upper Midwest. By the summer of 1863, telegraph operators established a national union, despite the threat of government action against them. Within a year, a new national Brotherhood of the Footboard was established, which soon changed its name to the Brotherhood of Locomotive Engineers.

In addition to the navy yards and the railroads, miners established a sufficient level of organization to wage regional strikes from Pennsylvania coal country into Illinois. In the former locations, conscription provided a particularly political dimension to the strikes. Workers already suffering in low-paying jobs resented being drafted out of their families and communities into military service that paid even less.

The introduction of conscription in the war created a backlash against the administrations in both the Union and the Confederacy. The latter needed men more, instituted forced military service earlier, and experienced what became massive levels of desertions and armed resistance to officials in the backcountry that essentially assured Federal victory. The Union forces also experienced desertions on a large scale and short-lived rioting over the draft, the most notable in New York City and Boston.

In the Union, where the government struggled to continue holding regular elections, disaffection opened partisan opportunities that part of the old Democratic Party sought to exploit. Steeped in the Jacksonian rhetoric of hostility to big government and to monopoly, the Democrats had always enjoyed broad support among many working-class voters, particularly the Irish, German and other immigrants. Democratic politics in the years leading directly to the war had alienated many such voters, but wartime conditions encouraged a swing back to those old allegiances. "War Democrats" supported the Union cause, but critics of the Lincoln administration, the draft, and the policy of slave emancipation appealed to antebellum white notions of freedom and adopted the figure of Liberty on the copper penny as their symbol. These "Copperheads" not only opposed Unionists at the polls, but also provided articulate criticisms of the draft and urged active resistance to it.

So, too, the antebellum Democratic use of race and the alleged threat of black emancipation to the jobs of white workers resurfaced in the course of the war. This exaggerated the real threat of black labor and exacerbated white fears, particularly among the Irish in some of the lowest-paid unskilled labor. Some whites had been and remained vulnerable to racial appeals.

The labor movement's experience of race relations remained complex and uneven. In a world where work had long been ethnically stratified, it was probably unnecessary for unions to bar African Americans from membership, though several did so, claiming that they would break strikes. In fact, instances of blacks actually breaking strikes by white workers were rare, and, on at least one occasion, white scabs broke a strike at Washington, D.C., by black workers. From any perspective, though, emancipation created a more mixed wage-earning work force that would face deeper ethnic and racial tensions in the war's aftermath.

However, no racial or ethnic appeals could address the essential dilemma of wartime wage labor. While a very active economy stimulated prices, wages never kept up. A reasonable account estimated that the cost of living rose 76 percent during the war while wages increased only 50 percent. Urban conditions radically exacerbated this gap. A New York City milliner made 17½ cents a shirt at the war's onset, but made only 8 cents by 1864. When the printers there requested an advance amounting to 72½ percent since 1861, a spokesman offered a budget demonstrating a 257 percent increase in the cost of living.

Wage earners drew decisive conclusions from their common experience of the wartime economy and its exigencies. Vastly larger groups of workers formed unions and those unions grew much larger and more quickly than any of their predecessors. Before the Civil War, big cities had stable labor organizations in a few trades, but they remained relatively unknown in most American communities. After the war began, unions cropped up in smaller cities like Terre Haute or Chattanooga, and even a relatively small city like Boston had a union membership that reached towards 10,000.

For people already living largely hand to mouth, this growing gap inspired even more desperate measures. The mothers, wives, sisters, and daughters of men fighting the war faced shameless exploitation by government arsenals and, worse, by private contractors, especially in the needle trades. Philanthropists and labor reformers helped them organize groups such as the Working Women's Protective Association at New York, but employers also began introducing women desperate for decent wages into the traditional crafts in an effort to break the unions.

Whether from desperation or militancy, new trade unions of unprecedented size and power reshaped labor relations in the big cities. New York sources describe strikes taking place almost daily in the city. At times, these represented thousands of workers going on strike in a society where hundreds would have been rare before the war. The contemporary press contains many examples of various unions combining their resources and numbers to assist an organization or workplace on strike. Before the war, labor reformers and radicals talked about issues of "class," but wartime conditions diffused a rudimentary class sensibility reflected in strikes where workers of different crafts supported each other or even acted in concert, as in the navy yards.

Some strong national unions emerged from the war. Printers, silk and fur hatters, molders, machinists and blacksmiths held conventions. In addition to those new organizations mentioned, the cigar makers, curriers, coach makers, carpenters and joiners formed a national union in 1864. War did not dissipate the antebellum working-class predilection for fraternal organizations. Indeed, harsh conditions fostered mutual aid in associations other than unions. These often reflected cooperative projects that mediated the necessity of unionism. The "League of Friendship, Supreme Mechanical Order of the Sun" spread across the Mid-Atlantic into the Midwest, but Philadelphia needle trades created the foundations of what became the Knights of Labor, which emerged after the war and rallied three quarters of a million members.

Employers repeatedly sought to involve the local military authorities in the repression of strike activities, and conservative Democratic generals complied in several cases. Generals William S. Rosecrans and Stephen G. Burbridge issued heavy-handed orders, respectively at St. Louis and Louisville. While

ultimately unsupported in Washington, the initiatives pushed local labor organizations into strong city-wide coalitions in those cities and elsewhere.

*Fincher's Trade Review* reported that the Workingmen's Assembly of Boston
and Rochester's Workingman's Assembly of Monroe County appeared in June
1863. The Trades' Assembly of Pittsburgh and the Trades' Assembly of Buffalo followed in September. Louisville workers formed a Trades' Assembly and
League of Friendship near the close of the year. The Trades' Assembly of Philadelphia appeared in March 1864, followed by Troy in July, Detroit in August,
Albany and Cincinnati in September; workers at New York City launched the
Workingmen's Union and those at St. Louis a Trades' Union League. Labor
papers reappeared. These included: *Fincher's Trade Review*, the *Weekly Miner*
(later the *Miner and Artisan*), and cooperative papers launched by printers in the
strike wave of 1864 at Chicago, St. Louis and Boston—the *Workingman's Advo-
cate*, the *Daily Press*, and the *Daily Evening Voice*.

Towards the close of 1864, Louisville hosted a pioneering convention that
established an International Industrial Assembly of North America that never
actually functioned. A few months later, in February 1865, representatives
of labor organizations on the eastern seaboard conferred at New York City's
Cooper Union. This conference foreshadowed the emergence of the postwar
National Labor Union. The government became increasingly concerned. New
York took up the Folger Anti-Trade Union Strike Bill to bar labor organizations from the use of "force, menace or threat of personal or pecuniary injury"
to prevent any workers from crossing a picket line; employers always imposed
their unilateral decisions about wages and working conditions upon their workers with the threat of "pecuniary injury." At times employers convinced the
army to break strikes. Organized labor, however, became important in changing government policies. The authorities in New York chose not to push the
draft during the massive strike wave in May 1864. More importantly, though,
Lincoln and the wartime Republicans serious about "free labor" did not believe
the government should involve itself in struggles between labor and capital.

Periodic clashes with local and military authorities acting on behalf of the
employers resurrected the desire in some quarters for an independent working-class political movement. The elimination or modification of the property
requirement for voting in many northern states a generation before the Civil
War had inspired the appearance of Workingmen's parties in some communities, notably New York, Philadelphia and Boston. Persistent token labor tickets
resurfaced regularly around issues like land reform through the 1840s, and the
shoe strikers of 1860 elected a city government at Lynn in 1860. That same
year, a mass meeting of émigré German socialists had called for a national convention to establish an independent party on the eve of the war. Shortly after,
the moderate spiritualist reformer Emma Hardinge predicted a new, popularly-
based republican party.

Wartime conditions resurrected the idea of independent politics. Although unsanctioned and sometimes directly repudiated by the Lincoln administration, local Republican officials and the military created vast new fields of contention by taking active roles on behalf of the employers in labor disputes. Extending the antebellum tradition and foreshadowing the class politics that would periodically resurface for a generation, independent "labor reform" tickets took the field in the municipal elections at Boston in December 1863 and Portland, Maine, in March 1865. By the war's end, the Boston Labor Reform Association and other groups pressed for government action on such issues as the hours of labor and the need to compile official labor statistics. They won a state legislation on those issues, and provided an inspiration for the national eight-hour law in 1868. While American workingmen had cultivated an idea of "solidarity" over generations, wartime conditions validated this impulse and won serious gains as a result. Wartime developments also raised questions that dwarfed the considerable ethnic differences that had separated native born white workers from European immigrants.

The Civil War's transformation of the work force included the further reduction of labor to mere "hired hands," with minimal requirements in terms of gender or ethnic identity. The white "workingmen" who had previously seen themselves exclusively as society's industrious producers would have to rethink their idea of "solidarity," and do so with workers who were female or non-whites. Their deliberations would be reflected in the course of their organizations as they coalesced into a postwar movement for the eight-hour workday, and a national labor movement.

## Further Reading

Basler, Roy P., ed. *Collected Works of Abraham Lincoln, Volume 4*. New Brunswick: Rutgers University Press, 1953–55.

Commons, John R., et al. *History of Labour in the United States, Volume II*. New York: The Macmillan Company, 1947.

Montgomery, David. *Beyond Equality: Labor and the Radical Republicans, 1862–1872*. New York: Alfred A. Knopf, 1967.

Richardson, Albert D. *The Secret Service, the Field, the Dungeon, and the Escape*. Hartford: American Publishing Company, 1866.

Roediger, David R. *The Wages of Whiteness: Race and the Making of the American Working Class*. Rev. ed. London: Verso Books, 1999.

Stevens, George A. *New York Typographical Union No. 6: Study of a Modern Trade Union and its Predecessors*. Albany: J.B. Lyon Company, 1913.

# 6

# COMMERCE AND INDUSTRY

*Daniel Rasmussen*

In 1860, the United States had reached an unprecedented level of interconnectedness. The Canal Era of the 1830s and 1840s had bound together New York and the Great Lakes, forming a dense network of waterways that connected the Empire State with the expanding northwest. The steam revolution had brought fast water travel to the Mississippi, Missouri, and Ohio Rivers, linking Pittsburgh, Cincinnati, Louisville, St. Louis, and New Orleans. Thirty thousand miles of railroad track created a truly national transportation system. Primarily, these new railroad tracks connected the big Atlantic ports of Boston, New York, Philadelphia, and Baltimore with the new commercial centers of the American West. A less dense string of railroad lines connected the agricultural and shipping centers of the southern agricultural states. By 1860, the transportation revolution bound the nation so closely together that the entire country's population was within six days' travel of New York City or Philadelphia.

These linkages formed the arteries of a thriving, unified, American commercial system. With business unrestricted by internal tariffs or trade barriers, steam engines pumped agricultural staples and manufactured goods from regional and national hubs to the outer reaches of the American nation. This internal commerce allowed for specialization, as different regions developed profitable niches and traded for goods produced more cheaply elsewhere. In turn, regional specialization made American products more competitive in Atlantic markets and allowed for a diversification of the economy, turning America into one of the most powerful economic engines in the world.

The seeds of this economic prosperity were planted in the rich cotton-growing soil of the Deep South. For most of the nineteenth century, slave-harvested cotton was the economic lifeblood of the United States, the prime driver for growth in all sectors of the economy. Cotton constituted the majority of American exports—the prime revenue source of the new nation. Though cotton production centered on a specific region of the country, the profits of cotton exports diffused broadly. The planters of the Deep South demanded food to feed their enslaved workers, agricultural tools for these workers to use, financing for the development of new land, and transportation services to bring their goods to market. And so in these early days of the Republic, western farmers and northeastern manufacturers depended on demand from southern cotton planters.

Slave workers of African descent—reaching a population of almost four million by 1860—planted, tended, and harvested this white gold. Most slaves lived on large plantations, controlled by a small minority of the white elite. These enslaved men and women lived lives circumscribed by a condition of chattel slavery and the intense regimen of cotton production. The planters, and their hired overseers, attempted to control every aspect of their slaves' existences in an effort to turn their slaves into cotton producing machines. "Besides directing the minute-by-minute performance of agricultural operations—shifting slaves from job to job to ensure that not a moment of daylight was lost to productive activity, establishing and maintaining (by force, if necessary) the pace at which they labored, selecting the tools to be used—planters and their agents strove to keep tabs on the clothes their slaves wore, the foods they consumed, the language they used, the conversations they held (and whom they held them with) and the conditions of their cabins (in and out)," explains historian Susan O'Donovan (26–27). In the frosty cold of January, slaves cleared the fields of debris, demarcated the land with fences, and broke new ground. After spreading fertilizer over these prepared fields, the slaves began the early spring rush to plant the cottonseed. A first wave of slaves used drills to open furrows in the ground, while a second wave followed to put the seed into the ground. In late spring and early summer, the slaves performed the laborious work of tending the crop, thinning the rows of cotton, and weeding the fields. In mid–August, the slaves began picking cotton. The planters needed to get the entire crop in before the first frost damaged the product, and so many of the slaves labored in 18-hour days to collect the bales of cotton prior to the first frost.

Planters and slaves constantly struggled over the terms of enslavement. Slaves fought with every means available. At the very minimum, they demanded certain privileges, free time, visitation rights, and rights to economic activity. At the maximum, the slaves of the American South had a history of violent resistance against the authority of the planters. As W.E.B. Du Bois noted, "They might be made to work continuously, but no power could make them work well" (40). To keep their slaves working well, the planters used confinement, whippings, and torture devices. They also threatened to sell slaves or separate them from their families, a less spectacular but highly effective method of coercion.

This system of chattel slavery for the purpose of cotton production for export and sale necessitated both a large supply of new workers and an expanding supply of new soil. With the African slave trade closed off, the cotton masters found a new source of slaves in the diminishingly-profitable slave economies of the Upper South—now a land neatly fenced into verdant pastures full of expensive livestock, all tended by black laborers. Between the signing of the Constitution and the first cannons fired at Fort Sumter, an internal slave trade brought close to one million enslaved people from the Upper South to the Lower South to provide the labor supply for the Lower South's cotton plantations. America acquired new land through war, first against the Native American tribes and then against the Spanish and Mexicans. By 1860, a flourishing cotton belt extended from the northern reaches of Florida to the eastern sections of Texas. Here, a vast majority of America's black enslaved population lived and labored.

While the production of cotton was regionally bounded, the profits from its sale spread far and wide. In the farmland of the upper Midwest, and across the Upper South, farmers, whether slave owners or not, grew staple crops and raised livestock to provide a food supply to the Lower South's enslaved workers. Merchants on the East Coast shipped the cotton from the Lower South to hubs like New York, for transshipment to newly emerging textile mills in New England or established ones in Liverpool, England. On the return trip, these merchant ships brought manufactured goods and luxury items for sale to the southern planters. This rich flow of trade provided the basis for the American national economy, but it did not represent its boundary.

By the 1840s, the economic engines of the West and Northeast were developing in capacity and efficiency, and beginning to move beyond complete dependence on southern cotton. After the War of 1812, the first signs of industrialization had emerged along the plentiful rivers of New England. Entrepreneurs built textile mills and weapons factories in order to provide more security for America's domestic economy. With the spread of railroads and canals, and increases in the urban population, the manufacturing of goods for the sale on the domestic market flourished. Quite simply, producers could market their products to a much larger number of customers—a simple fact that encouraged a trend towards mass production. While textile and arms manufacturing had been the seed industries, manufacturers began to develop new factories and manufacturing processes to produce less capital-intensive goods, like cheap shoes, furniture and clothing. The spread of these new industries was further enabled by the development of steam power, which enabled more productive and non-potamic factory development. The majority of this new manufacturing took place in the Northeast, from the rivers of New England to the coal deposits in the mountains of Pennsylvania.

This industrial and manufacturing economy, however, had yet to prove itself superior to the slave-based agricultural economy of the lower South, either in terms of profitability or in terms of material standards of living. Economic historians Stanley Engerman and Robert Fogel, conclude in their famous book *Time on the Cross: The Economics of American Negro Slavery* (1974) that the per capita income of the American South increased faster than that of the rest of the country between 1840 and 1860 and that the material standard of living of slaves in the South compared favorably with that of free workers in industry. And free adult males in the South held greater wealth on average than in the North. From the textile mills of Lowell, Massachusetts, to the iron mills in the Mid-Atlantic, free industrial workers faced working conditions not all that different from their enslaved fellows further south. Strict command strictures, prison-like discipline, dangerous working conditions, long hours, and low compensation were the common features of labor before and during the Civil War.

New England became the first great American manufacturing region. Starting in 1798, the inventor Eli Whitney worked to perfect the manufacture of interchangeable, standardized parts for muskets for supply to the federal government. Arial Bragg developed a process for the mass-production of ready-made shoes. And, perhaps most importantly, Francis Cabot Lowell, Patrick T. Jackson, and Nathan Appleton constructed America's first water-powered loom for the manufacture of cotton textiles in 1814. In Waltham, Massachusetts, these men created a mill-town and industrial center to turn the South's raw cotton into marketable textiles for sale on the mass-market. Textile manufacturing spread rapidly, and, by 1832, textile companies represented over 80 percent of the largest corporations in the country. The Lowell Mills began with an innovative employment strategy: they would employ primarily women, who were less engaged in agricultural work. The Lowell Mill Girls, as they were called, lived in boarding houses owned by the mill owners and worked six days a week, more than ten hours per day. Obeying the bells that marked the time and the overseers who supervised them, the mill workers labored in unventilated, humid, air thick with lint and lamp oil fumes. As the century progressed, labor conditions deteriorated, sparking some of the first industrial labor conflicts in American history.

The manufacturing of cloth led to the creation of America's heavy goods industry, providing a template for a variety of machine tools and locomotive industries. As the textile mills of Lowell spread to the mill cities on the major rivers of New England, the region began to take the shape of a powerful industrial engine, "employing tens of thousands of workers of every necessary skill to turn out a great diversity of products; with dozens of machine shops building every piece of equipment; inventors and tinkerers working continuously to enlarge and improve on machine designs; buyers, brokers, and agents of various kinds monitoring every aspect of production and marketing; and competing corporations and adventurous capitalist alert to every possible advantage" (Meinig 377). The textile industry formed the core of this industrial region, but other forms of manufacturing were also exploding. Factories produced a wide variety of goods, from clocks and silverware to guns and engines. In 1860, the top manufactured goods were (1) flour and meal, (2) cotton goods, (3) lumber,

(4) boots and shoes, (5) men's clothing, (6) iron, (7) leather, (8) woolen goods, (9) liquors, and (10) machinery.

With the spread of railroads, steamships, and other types of steam engines, the center of industrializing America shifted south. From New Jersey to Pennsylvania, across the Adirondacks to the western stretches of Virginia and eastern Tennessee, lay rich natural deposits of coal and iron, which provided the transportation systems and factories of America with fuel and raw materials. Pennsylvania, with its plentiful coal and iron deposits, formed the central hub of this new mining zone. Miners, many of them immigrants from Europe, dug the coal and iron out of the ground with axes and explosives. Workers transported the iron to mills, where it would be melted in a blast furnace and impurities removed with a blast of air. Workers, known as puddlers, would stir the molten iron until it was cast into molds made of sand mixed with clay, a process known as founding. Rates of death and injury were high. With a large supply of immigrants, owners had little financial incentive to take care of their workforce. The iron these men produced would be used for everything from railroad tracks to boilers to nails to complicated engines.

As in the Lower South, the few men with capital reaped the lion's share of the profits. "Most historians believe that the early industrial revolution widened inequalities in the standard of living; that is, while average per capita income doubled between 1820 and 1860, property owners and the rich benefited more than wage earners and the poor," observes historian Daniel Howe (538). Industrialists in the North grew rich from the wage labor of an increasingly foreign workforce, derived from the lower classes of Europe who flocked to American cities in search of opportunity. By 1860, the Northeast's population was overwhelmingly urban, with one million residents of New York City and Philadelphia's population at around 600,000, numbers largely reached by the flood of immigrants from Europe. The new industrial classes, working in an industrial landscape born out of the cotton South, were growing increasingly less dependent on southern cotton and southern consumers.

Yet, though these new tycoons found wealth outside of the traditional economic scheme, the merchant classes of the urban centers still relied heavily on the South for their economic well-being. Nowhere exemplified the growing conflict between industrialist wealth and merchant wealth better than New York City—the center of American manufacturing and commerce. The third richest city in the world after London and Paris, New York was the hub for two-thirds of American imports and one-third of American exports. By 1856, 20 percent of New York's wealthy elite was made up of industrialists. Yet, the other 80 percent remained dependent on commerce—and especially on southern cotton. The city was built around the trading houses that linked British industry to the cotton plantations of the American South. Exporting cotton to Liverpool in ships owned by New England shippers, New York merchants brought back farming goods, clothes, and commercial products for sale to

American consumers. Cotton, and the slave-labor that produced it, served as the prime driver of the northern merchant economy. The majority of bourgeois New Yorkers supported the cotton South, for they relied on it for their incomes. But by 1860, southern consumers no longer represented the main purchasers of the vast imports of New York City, nor of the manufactured implements produced in neighboring states. In the decade leading up the Civil War, western commerce began to rival that of the South, as commercial farmers rich from wheat, corn, and livestock flocked to New York to buy goods.

A growing interregional trade between the newly settled American West and the commercial and industrializing Northeast marked a seismic shift in the American economy. The expanding rail and water links between the urban hubs of the eastern seaboard and the new trading cities of the West created a new pattern of interregional trade in which the South was no longer either the prime consumer of western foodstuffs nor the prime consumer of northeastern imports and manufactures. The new trade between the West and the Northeast centered on domestic industrialization, trade in agricultural commodities produced by free farmers, and the substitution of domestic goods for European ones.

The pattern of western economic growth was distinctive. Across the later famous American Corn Belt of Iowa, Indiana, Illinois, and Ohio, free family farmers raised wheat and corn, as well as specialized breeds of hogs and cattle, to sell in the towns and cities that formed the hubs of the new American West—Kentucky, Chicago, Cincinnati, and Buffalo. The development of these cities was a central part of the development of the region, processing agricultural goods for shipment south and east and developing manufactured items for sale to the farmers. In Cincinnati, for example, large factories turned hogs into lard, bone, bristles, skins, and saleable meat, earning the city the name "Porkopolis." Chicago became the great lumber marketing city in the West, churning out furniture and other woodworks, while also producing thousands of McCormick reapers for sale to western grain farmers. St. Louis became a major market for iron ore, while smaller towns in Ohio produced high-grade steel. With no slave labor, the region pioneered the development and adoption of new agricultural technology in the twenty years before the Civil War. The concomitant expansion of rural commercial agriculture and urban manufacturing—all produced without the use of slave labor and increasingly exported to the non-slave owning states of the Northeast—created a new and distinctive form of political economy. The transportation networks that made this commerce possible also brought scores of immigrants from Europe, who settled in the highest proportions in the new Northwest. Immigrants from Britain, Germany, and Ireland especially flooded to these new frontier lands. These immigration patterns added to the distinctive nature of the region's political economy.

The settlement of the West and the progress of urbanization and industrialization in the Northeast functioned to remake the U.S. economy in the

1840s and 1850s. Once an export economy almost entirely dependent on cotton, the American economic system of 1860 was far more diversified with a strong internal supply of and demand for manufactured goods and agricultural products alike. The nation's interregional transportation links created a tightly cohesive, regionally specialized, economic system that functioned as one vast market. The Civil War would merely mark a pause in the progress of American economic growth.

The Civil War did not cause a fundamental transformation in America's political economy: the nation's economic course was set in the twenty years prior to the war. The war was not, as many suppose, a simple and inevitable clash between an industrial North and a slave South. In fact, the political economy of America served as a glue between the states, not a driver for separation. Those looking to explain the reasons behind the Civil War must look further than a simple story about industrialization and agriculture as two conflicting political economies—further towards the true dividing line between the states that seceded from and those that remained in the Union. While the flow of goods proceeded unobstructed across newly developed transportation infrastructure, there existed one barrier between the free economic intercourse of the northern and southern regions.

The transportation of one form of property across state lines was problematic: slaves. The increasing trade between the Northeast and the Northwest and the rise of manufacturing, increased the percentage of Americans who did not depend on slavery and southern cotton. "Industrial capitalism established itself in the Northeast and formed links with a society based on farming with family labor in the West," writes historian Barrington Moore. "With the West, the North created a society and culture whose values increasingly conflicted with those of the South. The focal point of the difference was slavery" (136). The power of this commercial alliance was expressed in the increasing unwillingness of northern states to enforce the Fugitive Slave Law and provide the southern economy with the security necessary to manage its captive population. As historian D.W. Meinig explains, "this lack of mutual respect for laws reflecting provincial mores imposed a serious restriction on Southern security, mobility, and participation in national life, undercutting the benefits of association in a federal structure" (425). While the merchant commercial interests of Boston and New York still strongly supported the South's political interests, the new free commercial agriculturalists and the new industrialists—and their immigrant workforces—did not. And so, as the country expanded and Americans asked which form of political economy would define new American acquisitions, southerners felt increasingly concerned about their power in the national federation. Questions of commerce and industry became increasingly important to a slave-based agricultural system that was slipping from its dominant and decisive position within the American national economy.

## Further Reading

Du Bois, W.E.B. *Black Reconstruction in America 1860–1880*. New York: Simon & Schuster, 1999.

Fogel, Robert William, and Stanley L. Engerman. *Time on the Cross: the Economics of American Negro Slavery*. Boston, Little: Brown, 1974.

Howe, Daniel Walker. *What Hath God Wrought: The Transformation of America, 1815–1848*. New York: Oxford University Press, 2007.

Meinig, D. W. *The Shaping of America: A Geographical Perspective on 500 Years of History*. New Haven: Yale University Press, 1986.

Moore, Barrington. *Social Origins of Dictatorship and Democracy: Lord and Peasant in the Making of the Modern World*. Boston: Beacon Press, 1967.

O'Donovan, Susan E. *Becoming Free in the Cotton South*. Cambridge: Harvard University Press, 2007.

# 7

# THE ENVIRONMENT

*Megan Kate Nelson*

Union and Confederate soldiers may have had unequal numbers but they all faced the same conditions while they were on the march, in camp, and in battle. They all shivered in the rain and snow, trudged through dust and mud, and saw their regiments' fortunes change when they suddenly came upon a mucky slough or a ravine in the middle of a battlefield. Northern and southern soldiers, in every theater of the war, sought to gain the environmental advantage by making sure they had shelter, and by taking high ground and securing waterways. In order to combat the elements, soldiers turned to the fields and forests of the South, seeking to remake their relationship with nature in order to prevail in their struggle with one another. Nature's resources moved armies, housed them, gave them a sense of place and camaraderie, and protected them during battles. Domesticated and wild animals provided entertainment and valuable food sources for tired, ailing troops. The forces of nature made them cold, wet, hot, and sick. The hills, valleys, ravines, rivers, and swamps of the South dictated their movements and played an important role in shaping battle tactics. And the stumps and ghost forests left in the wake of these armies during the Civil War suggest the many ways that the technologies of warfare shaped southern landscapes and transformed their meanings. Almost every wartime activity consumed natural resources and, for the most part, soldiers and civilians saw this as a wartime necessity.

Union officer Henry Spooner of the 4th Rhode Island Volunteers summarized this process of destruction and creation in his letters home. Soon after enlisting in September 1862, he wrote to his mother that while he was not very impressed by the log houses he passed on his march southward, he did think that "this is a splendid country about here, abounding in hills & mountains." However, Spooner came to change his views about Maryland's hills after fighting in the battle of Antietam on September 17, 1862. "No language... can carry to your mind a perfect picture of a battle field," he wrote to his father. "The mere presence of a hill here, a creek there & a gully yonder must influence your course in the presence of an enemy watchful of every opportunity." More than a month later, Spooner wrote with a sense of weariness from farther south: "This is a part of Virginia [which] has not yet suffered as that portion further east has." Spooner found the landscape pleasant to look at, but worried that "future campaigns & battles & campings may render this region too a scene of desolation. Perhaps the work of devastation has now commenced" (n.p.). Spooner's letters to his parents over the course of two months in the fall of 1862 point to the fact that both Union and Confederate soldiers marched, camped, and fought in the South with an interest in and awareness of its natural and built environments. Troops took pleasure in looking out across valleys from hills and mountaintops, meandering through forests, and swimming in rivers. They used all of nature's resources to survive during battles and downtime— cutting down trees for protection from artillery and from the elements, clogging and diverting streams, gathering flora and shooting fauna for meals. They wreaked havoc on plantations, in woodlots, and in towns across the South (and in some parts of the North), creating "scenes of desolation" while waging hard war against civilians. Topography, hydrology, and meteorology shaped their wartime experiences and battle strategies; soldiers in turn transformed the landscapes around them.

Between 1861 and 1865 soldiers marched, fought, and slept out in the open country, in forests, in towns, along rivers and through swamps, and on mountaintops. Many soldiers thought of their service as the "outdoor life" and they understood that nature and its processes influenced every aspect of their experiences. For Confederate soldier Josiah Moore, this outdoor life took some getting used to. During his first night in camp, Moore could not sleep due to the "awful hooting of an owl who made nights horrible ... the piercing cry of the whipporwil [sic], and the incessant croaking of a family of frogs in the neighboring pond." He was not able to catch up on his sleep, however, because the next night the clouds opened up and "it rained the whole night incessantly, verily, the windows of heaven seemed to have been thrown open for a second deluge." Moore and his compatriots slept fitfully, waking up groggy and "quite wet this morning" (n.p.).

Weather, in all of its great variety—rain, hail, snow, wind, heat, cold, humidity—was a source of constant comment and complaint in soldiers' diaries and letters. Even men from rural areas who were used to outdoor work suffered; their exposure to inclement weather, the inability to get their clothes fully dry, and the nature of an army camp (large numbers of strangers brought together for the first time in crowded spaces) meant that disease was rampant. Prolonged exposure to the elements weakened soldiers' immune systems; fevers and rheumatism resulted.

Soldiers got some rest and built themselves shelters during the off-season in "winter quarters," but the rates of illness were still high. As the days became warmer in the early spring, soldiers set out on the roads of the South, happy to feel the warm sun on their faces but irritated to find their feet mired in mud. "The soil is of the nastiest kind," wrote Union soldier Watson Hitchcock, "being a mixture of sand & clay, so far it has been dry but now it threatens to rain, then there will be mud enough. Oh! the sacred soil of Virginia!" (n.p.). Arthur O'Connor looked with a similar sense of despair upon the muck of the Virginia Peninsula in February 1862: "nothing can be done here owing to the depth of the mud. A hot sun may bake a crust on it but according to present appearances it will take years to dry it up" (n.p.). The mud did dry but, once it did, it turned to dust. To some soldiers, this was even worse. Henry Spooner was amazed at the difficulty of moving the Union army on roads "deep in dust & the air completely impregnated with it. Imagine … the thick smoke of a fire of green wood." There was no relief from it, Spooner lamented: "on we must go—the sun blazing overhead & the rough, dusty roads under foot" (n.p.). The seeming ubiquity of the mud in spring and the dust in summer and fall tortured soldiers on the march. It also suggests that the pace of soil erosion during the war was accelerated. Especially in Virginia, where soldiers marched and camped and fought over the same roads and fields again and again between 1861 and 1865, the movements of armies created even more mud and dust, rapidly depleting the topsoil.

Many soldiers were astounded that they were able to endure such conditions. "How did we stand these long, tiresome marches," one Confederate soldier remembered, "through the rain and the mud of spring, through the dust and heat of summer, and midst snow and ice of winter, often poorly shod, scantily clothed, and on short, very short rations, often none at all?" (Meier 100). Most soldiers tolerated these conditions only through "seasoning," a process of physical and mental adaptation to the outdoor life. This did happen—and it was a crucial element in the transformation of "green" soldiers into veterans—but it was a long process. For more than a year after they joined the army, soldiers were constantly exposed to the elements and became sick after trudging through shin-deep mud, breathing in dust, and sleeping out in the rain. As a result, roughly 25 percent of each army's manpower was unavailable at any given moment during the war.

Soldiers were not the only miserable creatures on the road and in camp. As Confederate surgeon George Caperton noted in January 1862, "Our poor horses suffer a great deal from the rigor of the winter, as they stand tied to the pines with ice and snow whitening their backs they look disconsolate. If they could speak would not their voices be for peace?" (n.p.). Both armies used hundreds of thousands of horses and mules for transportation and other forms of labor between 1861 and 1865. These domesticated animals had a profound impact on the southern landscape: their hooves churned the dirt into mud and kicked up huge dust plumes; they consumed millions of pounds of corn and wheat taken from both northern and southern fields, and when they died of disease, battle wounds, starvation or old age, their corpses presented a sanitation problem. Their enlistment in the war effort also impacted the northern and southern farms, plantations and city streets from which they came. Their absence was felt especially in agricultural fields across the nation, which often lay fallow without the horses and mules to pull plows and haul crops and other materials. This abandonment of fields often resulted in erosion (rainstorms washed topsoil down the unsown crop rows) and the rapid growth of shortleaf, loblolly, or slash pines encroaching on fallow areas from their forest margins.

Just as horses and mules disappeared from the landscape, so did other domesticated and wild animals. Soldiers purchased or stole cattle, pigs, turkeys, and chickens to supplement their meager rations. These animals came mostly from southern farms and plantations; the Union army also imported cattle from the Midwest and both armies bought beef from Mexico. Cattle drives, like the massive wagon trains that accompanied Union and Confederate armies, trampled vegetation along roadsides.

Union and Confederate soldiers consumed hundreds of thousands of cattle between 1861 and 1865. Soldiers' hunger and boredom also took a toll on the South's wild animals. James Barr, a captain in South Carolina, noted his regiment "killed [a] turkey yesterday evening and shot a buck but did not get him, though they kill one or two a week" (116). For Union soldier Charles Morse, hunting game provided not only fresh meat to roast over his campfire but also a respite from the dreary monotony of camp life in Tennessee. He acquired a double-barreled shotgun and went riding out every day to shoot quail, ducks, and gray squirrels. He wished for the luxuries of home: "If I had a good setter or pointer I could have some great shooting" (n.p.). In many cases, however, the decreasing numbers of birds and other game animals in some parts of the South corresponded with profusion in other parts. In the sand hills of South Carolina, for example, because "every man was in the war except doctors, ministers, school teachers, and old men ... game seemed to increase, partridges, mocking birds, robins, doves, rabbits, squirrels, turkeys and even deer" (Woodruff 20).

While they often roamed the woods in search of game, some soldiers did appreciate the South's fauna and flora in a less deadly way. Charles Morse, for example, enjoyed looking at birds as much as shooting them. In May of 1862, Morse threw down his pack at the end of a long march in the Shenandoah Valley and did not bother to erect his shelter tent. "It was pleasant enough just to lie 'round on the grass," he told his mother, to "hear the birds sing, and enjoy the beautiful prospect" (n.p.). He smiled as he watched scarlet tanagers, cardinal grosbeaks, and mockingbirds flit among the trees. "I never have got over my interest in birdology," he confessed later, "and I think if ever I became a man of leisure, which looks probable now, I shall go in to study strong again" (n.p.). Like Morse, many soldiers had an aesthetic appreciation of the southern landscape and its denizens. When their marches and campsites took them to hilltops and riverbanks, they sat outside and looked around. One morning "at sunrise or before" Connecticut soldier Watson Hitchcock "took a little stroll out into the open country" around the Union camp in Loudon County, Virginia. "I tell you the scenery was splendid," he wrote to his parents. "Off to the S.W. was a beautiful valley & fields of grain, up just enough to look green a log cabin here & there, patches of wood land" (n.p.). Looking at nature improved soldiers' morale; it took their minds off of marches and battles and allowed them to drift into pleasant reveries.

But soldiers knew that the valleys and hills were not just for viewing; they were also of paramount military importance. During battles, each army maneuvered in order to take the high ground; it was vital for artillery batteries to have a clear view of the field of battle and steep hillsides gave a distinct advantage to those defending them from rifle pits or behind stone-heaped walls. Union soldiers fended off Confederates at Malvern Hill in July 1862 from the top of the 100-foot incline; the steep pitch of the hills at Marye's Heights behind Fredericksburg effectively slowed successive Union charges later that year. Hills obstructed all kinds of movement and often prevented one army corps from knowing what other corps were doing. In the fall of 1862, Union soldiers under General Don Carlos Buell and Confederates under General Braxton Bragg moved toward one another in Tennessee. When they met near Perryville on October 8, wind and atmospheric conditions created by the numerous hills in the vicinity created what are known as "acoustic shadows"; because of them, half of Buell's army did not even realize a battle was going on. Without these men as reinforcements, the Union soldiers fought the Confederates to a stalemate instead of crushing them; Bragg escaped with his remaining troops the next day.

Hills were not the only topographical features that changed the shape of battles. As Henry Spooner had noted after Antietam, "the mere presence of a hill here, a creek there & a gully yonder" influenced military strategy; waterways and swamps were significant obstacles to armies on the move. In Vicksburg, Mississippi, for example, the great southern citadel on the Mississippi River was an almost impregnable fortress due to its surrounding natural features. The city sat 200 feet above the water on bluffs. Annual flooding created wide and deep levees on Vicksburg's western side, and the city was flanked on its eastern side by the Big Black River's winding streams and mucky swamplands. These natural features shaped the Union campaign in 1862–1863 in two ways. First, Vicksburg's hydrological obstacles prompted Union General Ulysses S. Grant to cut loose from his supply line and swing around the city's eastern side, living off the country in a month-long march. This success convinced Grant that the destruction of the South's agricultural base would win the war, and he used this strategy in subsequent campaigns. Second, the streams and swamps defending Vicksburg's "backdoor" defeated all attempts of Union soldiers to assault them in 1862–1863; a disappointed Grant ultimately gave up on the strategy of invasion and instead bombarded the city from a distance, laying waste to its houses, businesses, and churches.

Like hills, swamps and ravines, rivers shaped all manner of battle strategies during the war. For both armies, they provided access to markets and to much-needed military supplies; but they were also a conduit for the enemy's foot soldiers and sailors. Therefore, each side sought to control rivers. In an effort to prevent Union warships and ironclads from entering southern waterways, Confederate soldiers, white civilians, and slaves cut trees and threw them into the water. In May 1862, for example, during the Confederate evacuation of Pensacola, Colonel Thomas Jones of the 27th Mississippi Infantry sent the steamboat *Turel* up the Escambia River in northwest Florida with orders to cut down trees and create obstructions. The wood-choked river would stymie Union gunboats and protect Confederate soldiers and sailors retreating into Alabama. This was an effective strategy, especially along the Gulf coast, where Union boats were trying to make inroads in the South's major river and stream systems. Sometimes rivers did not need any additional help from soldiers; during intense rainstorms and spring "freshets," some waterways raged high above their normal levels, wiping out bridges and stopping armies in their tracks.

By 1864, many landscapes across the South had been trampled down and deforested. Moving, feeding, sheltering, killing and burying hundreds of thousands of soldiers over three years took an immense toll on the South's roads, roadsides, agricultural fields, and woodlots. The war had created landscapes of ruin in many places—especially northern Virginia—and this desolated country came to represent the war's costs for many Americans.

Farmland took hits from all directions. Because large armies prefer to fight in open spaces, farmlands and pastures became battlefields across the South. As men and animals moved into position they churned up earth and when the battles began artillery barrages "plowed" the ground. And even as fields became sites of battle, they were also optimal spaces for establishing camps. According to northern journalist Joel Cook, who traveled with Union troops during the Peninsula Campaign in 1862, soldiers were often choosy when scouting for campsites. "Grass or grain fields were always preferred for camping-grounds," he reported, "and a ploughed field or one containing the long stalks and spongy soil left by the last year's corn-crop was never taken, except when nothing better could be had" (43–44).

The presence of encamped soldiers compressed still-standing crops and killed them, unless foraging soldiers harvested them first. Survival depended on agriculture and so both Union and Confederate soldiers foraged widely in the farmlands of the South, picking fields clean of their corn and wheat. They looted trees of their fruit and took chickens, pigs, and other domesticated animals from southern farms and plantations. Natural forces also took a toll on southern fields during the war; long months of drought hit the South in 1862 and again in 1864. Whether they were stripped by soldiers' hands or by the withering heat, empty agricultural fields forced soldiers to forage further afield. By the winter of 1865, Confederate General Robert E. Lee was sending his soldiers and their horses from camps in Virginia to take food and fodder from the swamps and fields of North Carolina.

Soldiers razed farmlands to feed themselves and their horses and mules but also as a way to fight the enemy. During the Union's "hard war" campaigns, which intensified in 1864, soldiers confiscated crops and set fire to fields in order to destroy the Confederacy's ability to feed both soldiers and civilians. In the summer of 1864, General Grant famously ordered Phil Sheridan and his cavalry units to end the Shenandoah Valley's reign as the "Breadbasket of the Confederacy" and to devastate its farms and plantations so completely that "crows flying over it for the balance of this season will have to carry their provender with them" (United States War Department 223). Attacking southern agriculture in this way, Union troops ruined the South materially and psychologically, exposing the fragile control that Southerners held over the landscape and destroying Confederate soldiers' and civilians' morale.

In the most intensively fought over areas of the South these devastated agricultural fields were then transformed into a landscape of trenches, tunnels, wreckage, and corpses. During the Civil War, the massive armies in the eastern theater tended to leave their camps, maneuver toward one another, pause to build fortifications, and then send out charges against one another's defenses. In 1863 outside of Vicksburg, Mississippi, and in 1864 around Petersburg, Virginia, and Atlanta, Georgia, Union troops also laid siege to southern cities for long periods, necessitating the construction of vast acreages of fortifications. These alterations of the environment often rendered it unrecognizable. Northerner Charles Carleton Coffin, wandering among the Union forts east of Petersburg in 1864, came upon the Dunn house, which sat two miles outside of the city. The house had previously been surrounded with lush fields and forests; by 1864, "in front of it is a fort; another south; a third north, and other works, with heavy embankments and deep ditches. The woods in front of the house of Mr. Dunn were cut down in 1862, when McClellan was on the Peninsula, and the trunks of the trees, blackened by fire, are lying there still" (357).

The exigencies of war turned much of the rural landscape of Virginia into desolate, windswept plains, stripped of crops, grass, and increasingly, trees. As Coffin noted, the woods around the Dunn residence had been cut down; "bomb-proof" shelters, stockades and magazines, battery platforms, and signal towers, all elements of the protective landscape of battle, were constructed of wood, and almost all of the wood came from nearby forests. Soldiers built earthworks using dirt and clay as their primary materials and anchored them with "gabions," cylindrical baskets made of twigs or tree branches that soldiers weaved together and filled with earth. In order to hold the baskets together soldiers bundled small poles (called fascines), placed them on top of the gabions, and staked them into the earthwork as well. To provide more of a buffer against the charging enemy, soldiers also created *abatis*—felled trees with their branches sharpened—or *chevaux de frise*, rows of pointed stakes projected at right angles. As well, soldiers cut down nearby trees if they obscured their view of the enemy.

This kind of clearing took a heavy toll on southern forests. As central constructive elements of earthworks, trees protected soldiers; they also shielded men from harm on the battlefield. Skirmishers and other soldiers under fire were likely to take up positions behind trees because even young saplings could provide protection against musket or rifle fire. Northern journalist James Julius Marks could not believe the damage that a "storm of bullets" did to Virginia's trees along the Williamsburg road in 1862: "A small sapling tree of about twenty-two feet in length and about the size of a man's arm, I singled out as the one on which to count the number of balls that struck it. I numbered twenty-five musket-balls as having pierced one side of the tree alone" (200). Rifle and artillery fire buried bullets and shells in tree trunks, knocked the leaves from trees and slivered smaller tree branches. When Joel Cook visited the Fair Oaks battlefield, he was amazed. "Timber originally covered three-fourths of the surface," he noted, "but military operations had converted the whole into a most forbidding wilderness. This destruction gives the most shocking appearance imaginable to a wood—that of an abandoned waste without any thing to redeem its barrenness" (226). The survival needs of soldiers—warmth, food, and shelter—and the destructive capabilities of military weapons, ruined southern forests and created a "forbidding wilderness" where only five years before, pines, oaks, and hemlock had grown in lush profusion.

By the fall of 1865, parts of Virginia, Mississippi, Georgia, and South Carolina had become—as Henry Spooner anticipated—scenes of desolation. Some wild animals and birds had disappeared, farmlands were little more than fields of mud, and thousands of acres of tree stumps covered hills and valleys. The networks of fortifications that soldiers constructed in the later years of the war remained, barren marks of war on the countryside. Soldiers had burned fields and used up trees to protect themselves. But sometimes these destructive acts resulted in the creation of new landscapes that also shaped the war and the experiences of soldiers waging it.

Part of this new landscape was the transportation network. Moving hundreds of thousands of men through southern landscapes was no easy feat. Union and Confederate armies were in almost constant motion nine months out of the year, packing up and transporting themselves, their kits, and their animals as little as half a mile or as many as 25 miles a day. As armies trod along, pioneer and engineering corps were often called up to repair or create components of the wartime roads and routes. Just as they threw trees into roads and rivers, Civil War soldiers burned bridges in order to obstruct the enemy's pursuit. And then, of course, they rebuilt them. Sometimes soldiers built bridges and roads from scratch, constructing some of the most impressive examples of transportation infrastructure in the nation at that time. Joel Cook looked with awe upon the Woodbury Bridge, a mile-long structure composed of a roadway and a 200-yard long and 15-foot wide bridge surface spanning the Chickahominy River in Virginia. The bridge, he wrote, "is firm and solid as a rock. Piles, beams, and braces, all of rough hewn timber, support a corduroy roadway which is capable of bearing the heaviest burdens" (274).

Even more common than bridge building was road building, which engineer and pioneer corps did in order to move men, horses, and wagons more efficiently through the muddy paths and tangled swamps of the South. To build these new "corduroy" roads, soldiers laid tree trunks and limbs side by side on the surface of the mud, anchoring them with wooden "piles" driven down through the soil until they came to rest on stable bedrock. After the pile drivers set the anchors, the men would cut down trees and then saw them into sections of equal length; two more groups of soldiers would then stand on each side of the road and pull the logs across them, place them tightly next to each other, build a cross-layer, and then cover the road with gravel to smooth it out. Soldiers also built and repaired railroad beds and bridges, another vital component of the war's transportation infrastructure. Both Northerners and Southerners felled trees to build bridges and roadways to enable themselves to move more quickly and efficiently through the South's various environments. And when they finally stopped marching and threw down their knapsacks, they continued this process of destructive creation, transforming the southern countryside into a string of military villages.

When their time in camp was believed to be of a long duration, both Union and Confederate soldiers built themselves log cabins. One northern soldier described the process of converting forests into camp towns in 1863: "The small pines were soon leveled to the ground and our dingy looking tents occupied their places. Let as many men as there are here go into a piece of woodland to camp, and in half a day where the giants of the forest stood in all their towering majesty, a large city of tents with their inhabitants will appear, putting one in mind of the Arabian tales" ("Convalescent Camp" n.p.). Virginian George Caperton also noted how quickly forests became camps in December 1861. "Sunday meets with no observance," he wrote in his diary. "Men busy chopping and building huts. It requires little time to build a village" (n.p.).

Despite the ephemeral nature of their wooden lodgings, most Civil War soldiers found great comfort in them, beyond their basic function as protection from the elements. Although New Hampshire soldier Sylvester Hadley was caught out in "a regular New England north Easter [sic]" in Virginia in January 1863, he was relieved to see the snow falling so thickly. "The Army will have to lay still as long as there is snow upon the ground," he wrote in his diary. "It is much better for us than rain as it will last longer." Hadley spent the next few days reading inside his hut, and then went on an excursion to procure "some poles and fixed up a good Bunk [sic], and some other little matters about the house so that it will be more comfortable" (n.p.). Soldiers constructed furniture and shelves for their cabins not only for practical purposes but also to recreate a sense of domesticity in the landscape of war. Union photographer Alexander Gardner was impressed with these domestic acts, finding the hut of one Chief Quartermaster to be delightfully "homelike." The house boasted "a fireplace worthy of a New England mansion house" and walls "partly papered with illustrated weeklies" and maps. In such a pleasing domestic environment, "round the blazing hearth, on many a sullen winter night, the ennui of camp were forgotten in pleasant re-unions of the General's staff" (Plate 52). Soldiers' cabins were utilitarian buildings, meant to provide shelter and warmth, but they also offered opportunities for camaraderie and a sense of comfort in wartime.

Civil War soldiers left their cozy cabins reluctantly, but when they did they emerged into a gridded, planned military landscape of regimental "streets" and open squares. Each army's camps, no matter where they were located, looked the same because U.S. military regulations (which both armies followed) dictated their layout. In the *Revised Regulations of 1861*, each company of infantry was directed to pitch its tents or build its huts in two rows, "facing on a street perpendicular to the color line" (the regimental front) and ten paces from it; the street "should not be less than 5 paces" wide (515–16). To the rear of the soldiers' tents were the kitchens, the lodgings of non-commissioned officers, the company officers, and the field and staff, each separated by streets 20 paces wide. This camp landscape reflected the hierarchy of military rank and also probably reminded soldiers of their hometowns, where the grid pattern held sway by the mid-nineteenth century.

To bolster these feelings of familiarity (each camp the same, each camp reminiscent of home) during a time of great upheaval, soldiers went to great lengths to "improve" the camp landscape. One way they did this was to go into the forests and bring nature back with them. During the winter of 1862, Delaware soldier Charles H. Ashton's father visited him at Camp Hamilton, his winter quarters in Virginia. In April Ashton wrote to his mother that the camp "has been greatly improved since pap was down here." His company had paved the streets with wooden planks and now "we have flower beds before our doors and paved walks" (n.p.). Responding to such scenes, photographer Alexander Gardner lauded the "ingenuity and taste of the American soldier," which resulted in well-built and refreshingly decorated quarters. "The forests are ransacked for the brightest foliage, branches of the pine, cedar, and holly are laboriously collected," he noted approvingly, "and the work of beautifying the quarters continued as long as material can be procured" (Plate 57). Soldiers also sought to reinsert nature into their lives by transplanting trees, which provided shade and visual relief in a camp environment that often looked like a moonscape. As they worked to create a picturesque camp, many soldiers gained a sense of place in what was often a disorienting wartime experience.

Of course, soldiers actively created bare and stump-filled acres by cutting trees and transplanting them; however, most of them did not see or appreciate this irony. When they constructed fortifications, bridges, roads, and camp villages across the South, Union and Confederate soldiers were engaging in almost simultaneous acts of environmental destruction and creation. The labor of these men (and the awed wonder with which they viewed the results) suggests that the relationship between soldiers and the environments through which they marched, camped, and fought—the relationship between war and nature—was not a simple matter of exploitation. Thus, a soldier like Massachusetts cavalry-man Howard Dwight could write to his mother from Rolla, Missouri, and tell her that their camp "was lately a forest with trees of all ages & sizes & a dense undergrowth. Now everything except the largest and handsomest trees has been cleared away & it now presents the appearance of a beautiful grove, the intervals between the trees being occupied by tents." Dwight thought this camp scene was "truly picturesque & will not soon be forgotten" (n.p.).

The southern landscape continued to transform after 1865. The forests that soldiers cleared grew over with new tree species within two generations. They were different woodlands—more pines—and their strong limbs and soft needles served to hide and then erase altogether many of the marks of war in the southern landscape. In the wake of war, nature endured. When northern poet and novelist John T. Trowbridge "followed in the track of the destroying armies" on his way to battlefields large (Gettysburg) and small (South Mountain) in 1866, he found "wayside trees" that were "riddled with bullets," giant oaks, chestnut, black-walnut and hickory trees "with their great, silent trunks, all so friendly, their clear vistas and sun-spotted space." He recognized Bull Run battlefield by its "boundaries" of scarred trees and was deeply affected by the contrast between the "disfigured" pines and the blooming hollyhocks and peach trees surrounding the ruined foundation of Judith Henry's house. Virginia's "old fields" were covered with "briers, weeds, and broom-sedge—often with a thick growth of infant pines coming up like grass." These overgrown areas were common in the South as early as 1866. "Much of the land devastated by the war lies in this condition," Trowbridge noted, and nature would reclaim it in the near future: "In two or three years, these young pines shoot up their green plumes five or six feet high. In ten years there is a young forest" (iii, 24, 85, 225). These two faces of nature—one disfigured, one blooming with new life—constitute the environmental history of the Civil War: a story of both destruction and creation.

## Further Reading

Ashton, Charles H. *Letters*. Virginia Historical Society, Richmond, VA.

Barr, James. *Let Us Meet in Heaven: The Civil War Letters of James Michael Barr, 5th South Carolina Cavalry*. Abilene: McWhiney Foundation Press, 2001.

Brady, Lisa. "The Wilderness of War: Nature and Strategy in the American Civil War." *Environmental History* 10.3 (2005): 429–31.

Caperton, George Henry. "Diary, 1862." Virginia Historical Society, Richmond, VA.

Coffin, Charles Carleton. *Four Years of Fighting: A Volume of Personal Observation with the Army and Navy.* Boston: Ticknor and Fields, 1866.

"The Convalescent Camp" (1863). Broadsides Collection. American Antiquarian Society, Worcester, MA.

Cook, Joel. *The Siege of Richmond: A Narrative of the Military Operations of Major-General George B. McClellan during the Months of May and June, 1862.* Philadelphia: George W. Childs, 1862.

Dwight, Howard. *Letters.* Dwight Family Papers. Massachusetts Historical Society, Boston, MA.

Hadley, Sylvester. "Diary, 1863." New Hampshire Historical Society, Concord, MA.

Faust, Drew Gilpin. "Equine Relics of the Civil War." *Southern Cultures* 6.1 (2000): 23–49.

Gardner, Alexander. *Gardner's Photographic Sketch Book of the War, Vol. 2.* Washington, D.C.: Philip & Solomons, 1865.

Hitchcock, Watson. *Letters.* Watson C. Hitchcock Papers. Connecticut Historical Society, Hartford, CT.

Marks, James Junius. *The Peninsular Campaign in Virginia, or Incidents and Scenes on the Battle-fields and in Richmond.* Philadelphia: J.B. Lippincott & Co., 1864.

McPherson, James and James Hogue. *Ordeal By Fire: The Civil War and Reconstruction*, 4th edition, New York: McGraw Hill Companies, 2010.

Meier, Kathryn S. "'No Place for the Sick': Nature's War on Civil War Soldier Mental and Physical Health in the 1862 Peninsula and Shenandoah Campaigns." *Journal of the Civil War Era* 1.2 (2011): 186-88.

Moore, Josiah. "Diary, 1861." Moore Family Papers. Virginia Historical Society, Richmond, VA.

Morse, Charles F. Papers. *Letters.* Massachusetts Historical Society, Boston, MA.

O'Connor, Arthur Emmet. *Letters.* Virginia Historical Society, Richmond, VA.

Spooner, Henry J. "Correspondence 1862-1864." Spooner Family Papers. Rhode Island Historical Society, Providence, RI.

*Revised Regulations for the Army of the United States, 1861.* Philadelphia: George W. Childs, 1862.

Trowbridge, John T. *The South: A Tour of Its Battle-Fields and Ruined Cities.* New York: Arno Press, 1969.

United States War Department. *The War of the Rebellion: A Compilation of the Official Records of the Union and Confederate Armies, Series I, Volume 40.* Washington, D.C.: Washington Printing Office, 1880–1901.

Woodruff, George Egleston. *Boyhood Sketches.* Columbia: South Caroliniana Library, 1914.

# PART III
# Religion and Reform

# 8

# RELIGION IN THE SOUTH

*Thomas Lawrence Long*

In his Second Inaugural Address, delivered in March 1865, Abraham Lincoln said of the North and South that during the Civil War: "Both read the same Bible and pray to the same God, and each invokes His aid against the other." Lincoln referred to the religious commonalities that characterized the conflict. Yet even the South itself was not monolithic in its spiritual culture. The antebellum and Civil War South was religiously diverse and, in some respects, southern regional identity shaped religious beliefs and practices more than religion shaped culture.

The South has been a stewpot of religious creeds and practices since its colonization predominantly by Spanish, French, and English settlers, who initially mingled with Native Americans (and eventually displaced them). The initial European attempts to convert southeastern Native Americans to Christianity were conducted by the Catholic Spanish and French. The Church of England's Society for the Propagation of the Gospel in Foreign Parts (founded in 1701) attempted to evangelize Native Americans as well as unchurched whites and African slaves in the rural South, though it was largely unsuccessful. Africans who were brought to the Americas came from a variety of religious cultures, including traditional animist religions, Islam, and, sometimes, at least nominal Christianity (with some slaves having been baptized before the Atlantic crossing). Syncretism between African religious traditions and Christianity was more evident in the Caribbean and Catholic Americas (including Louisiana) than in Protestant North America. African gods could be disguised as Catholic saints, and Africans could appropriate Catholic festivals. An exception to this pattern occurred in regions with greater continuous contact with Africa, like the coastal South, particularly Georgia and South Carolina.

After its initial mission to evangelize Native Americans and unchurched whites in the rural South met with mixed results, the Anglican Society for the Propagation of the Gospel in Foreign Parts eventually won the concession from slave owners to evangelize and baptize slaves. Slave-owning planters long resisted such missionary work for fear that their relationships and legal obligations with their "property" might be compromised if the chattel were fellow Christians and equal in the eyes of God. When slave owners were eventually convinced of the utility of Christian virtues of meekness and doctrines of a passive acceptance of slavery or an eternal reward in the hereafter for temporal subservience in the here and now, chaplaincy among African slaves flourished. Christianity among enslaved African Americans developed as a segregated institution; even domestic slaves, though permitted to attend the masters' Sunday worship, were contained in one part of a church building and not permitted to receive the sacraments, and black-only styles of worship developed, often as underground communities of faith away from the monitoring eyes of white overseers. The reformist evangelical communions like the Baptists and Methodists, rather than the socially elite Episcopal or Presbyterian churches, were particularly attractive to African Americans, and, by the time of the Civil War, their black members in the South constituted half a million.

African American slaves appropriated and adapted the liberation themes of the Hebrew scriptures and the Christian scriptures. By means of biblical typology, they imagined themselves to be the recapitulation of the Israelites enslaved in Egypt, awaiting a Moses who would lead them to a new promised land, or they borrowed the apocalyptic language of the Book of Revelation and saw themselves as the Church awaiting the return of King Jesus. These consoling messages, and, in some instances coded subversive messages, were employed in the classic spirituals, the origins of which are lost but which reached a wide audience in print with the 1867 publication of *Slave Songs of the United States* and Thomas Wentworth Higginson's article "Negro Spirituals" in the *Atlantic Monthly*. Among the best known today of the slave's spirituals or sorrow songs are "Lay Dis Body Down," "Deep River," "Roll, Jordan, Roll," "Michael Row the Boat Ashore," "Steal Away to Jesus," "Go Down, Moses," and "My Army Cross Over." The symbolic ambiguity of these songs have led some commentators to assume that the surface message of spiritual deliverance at the end of time also might have encoded a message encouraging a slave's escape from bondage or even providing encrypted directions for doing so. Later slave narratives, including Frederick Douglass's autobiography, were less coded in their criticism of the discrepancy between Christian pieties and slave-owning realities. In fact, Douglass's critique of southern Christians' hypocrisy was so extensive that he added an appendix to *Narrative of the Life of Frederick Douglass, an American Slave* (1845), in which he distinguished the false slaveholding religion from true Christianity.

As slave owners' Christianity attempted to manage slaves' behavior with exhortations to obedience and promises of eternal reward, and slaves' Christianity encouraged endurance and awaited deliverance, the biblical prophetic and apocalyptic traditions took on a more literal form of slave resistance. This occurred in the slave revolts of Gabriel Prosser, Denmark Vesey, and Nat Turner. The best known of these, the 1831 uprising of the Virginia slave Nat Turner, seems by all accounts to have been the product of his reading and literal interpretation of biblical texts. A transcription by attorney T.R. Gray of Turner's "confession" and a later article about Turner by the northern abolitionist Thomas Wentworth Higginson depict a literate and deeply religious man who came to imagine himself as a prophetic avenger doing God's work in his murders of white households during the brief rebellion. It also prefigures the imagery of later militant white abolitionists, including John Brown.

But although Christian churches (Catholic and Protestant) dominated the religious landscape of the South before the Civil War, Judaism established and maintained a small but influential presence from the early Colonial Era forward. The first Jewish settlers (mostly Portuguese Sephardic Jews) arrived in the late seventeenth century, and English-speaking Jewish communities were founded in Savannah, Georgia, in the 1730s and in Charleston, South Carolina, in the 1740s. The charter of the Carolina Colony ensured some measure of religious freedom and had been drafted by no less a political philosopher than John Locke (whose ideas would later inform the drafters of the Declaration of Independence and of the United States Constitution). Virginia's Statute for Religious Freedom (drafted by Thomas Jefferson in 1779 and adopted by the Virginia General Assembly in 1786) also provided some measure of legal tolerance. By 1800, more Jews lived in Charleston than in New York City (a distinction retained until the mid-1800s when a second stage of European Jewish immigrants, mostly German Ashkenazi Jews, emigrated into northern industrial cities).

Although the North tended to be far more explicitly and consistently anti-Semitic than the South, where Jewish assimilation was far more likely, southern Christian anti-Semitism was sometimes evident in the antebellum culture of the region. During the evangelical revival known as the Second Great Awakening (1790s-1830s), groups like the American Society for Meliorating the Condition of the Jews and the American Sunday School Union were formed, and, in some instances, prompted more than a passive endurance on the part of Jewish individuals. For example, Jewish women writers promoted a "domestic Judaism" that called for an unabashed revival of Jewish spiritual traditions. Rachel Mordecai engaged the popular Anglo-Irish author Maria Edgeworth in an exchange of letters for over two decades, prompted by Mordecai's revulsion at a stereotyped Jewish character in Edgeworth's *The Absentee* (1812). Confederate hospital matron Phoebe Yates Pember's short story "Miss Magdalena Peanuts," submitted to the *Atlantic Monthly* and published in September 1879, took a satirical tack when a dying Christian mother directs that a Jewish pharmacist become her daughter's guardian.

During the Civil War, Jewish Southerners, like their Christian neighbors, tended to give their allegiance to the Confederacy and served in the government and the military of the Confederate States of America. There were large Jewish communities in the major cities of the South, including New Orleans (with the seventh largest Jewish population in the United States), Charleston, Savannah, Richmond, Petersburg, Atlanta, Memphis, Nashville, Galveston, and Houston. Assimilated into Southern society and identified as white, Jewish Southerners frequently adopted proslavery opinion, for which Southern Christian apologists could find legitimation in passages of the Hebrew scriptures.

Southern Jews enlisted in the Confederate cause for many reasons. In a racial caste system they enjoyed benefits that they did not have elsewhere, either in Europe or in the North. Acculturated in southern values of valor and honor, Jewish men responded in kind. Aware of the stereotypes of Jews as clannish among each other and disloyal to Gentiles, they were determined to disprove those characterizations. Jewish immigrants in particular were eager to demonstrate their loyalty to their adopted homeland. And many Jewish families had deeper southern roots and a greater cultural and economic investment in the region than some of its Gentiles. General Robert E. Lee's correspondence with Jewish religious leaders seeking furloughs for soldiers during Jewish holy days indicates the exigencies of wartime and the respect that Lee had for Jewish soldiers, while letters from Jewish soldiers convey the difficulties in attempting to observe kosher dietary laws and Levitical observances, particularly problematic in the South where salt-cured and sugar-cured pork was a staple of civilian and military diets.

Perhaps the most significant Jewish figure in the Confederate government was Judah P. Benjamin (1811-1884). Born a British citizen in the West Indies, Benjamin emigrated with his parents to South Carolina where his father helped to found the Beth Elohim Reformed Synagogue in 1841. Benjamin moved to Louisiana, married into a prominent New Orleans Creole family, and became a lawyer, sugar plantation owner, and slave owner. Eventually he became a Louisiana legislator, and in 1850 sold his plantation and slaves. In 1852, Benjamin was appointed by the legislature as United States Senator for Louisiana, and in the next two years, he was twice nominated to (but declined) the U.S. Supreme Court. Upon Louisiana's declaration of secession, Benjamin gave his allegiance to the Confederacy, serving as its Attorney General, Secretary of War, and Secretary of State. Famous as an orator and debater, Benjamin's most famous exchange on the U.S. Senate floor erupted from the connection of his Judaism and the biblical precedent of the Israelites' deliverance from Egyptian slavery in the Exodus. The abolitionist and Radical Republican Benjamin Wade of Ohio characterized him as an "Israelite in Egyptian clothing." Judah Benjamin responded: "It is true that I am a Jew, and when my ancestors were receiving their Ten Commandments from the immediate Deity, amidst the thundering and lightnings of Mt. Sinai, the ancestors of my opponent were herding swine in the forests of Scandinavia" (Feldberg 53).

If the South has never been monolithically Christian, southern Christianity has likewise never been monolithically evangelical Protestant. The earliest Christians in the southeast of North America were Catholics, Spanish missionaries who by the late sixteenth century had traveled as far north as the Chesapeake Bay, establishing a short-lived mission there. However, aside from the Spanish settlements of the Mexican gulf region and the later French settlements of the lower Mississippi, Catholicism in the English-speaking South was constrained by British Protestant animosity, both religious and political, toward Roman Catholicism. It was not until after the American Revolution that the Vatican created the first Catholic diocese in the United States, Baltimore, and appointed its first bishop, John Carroll, in 1790. Baltimore became an archdiocese in 1808 with the creation of the next southern diocese, Bardstown, Kentucky. Charleston, South Carolina, and Richmond, Virginia, were created as separate dioceses in 1820. With the westward expansion of the United States early in the nineteenth century, the South began to absorb ethnic Catholicism, including French Cajuns and Spanish Creoles. Much like Jews before them, ethnic immigrant Catholics faced the challenge of finding a place in the South. They encountered prejudices about their languages and folkways, their allegiance to a foreign religious leader (the Pope, bishop of Rome and head of state of the Vatican), and their mysterious worship conducted in an ancient language by an unmarried clergy.

However, Catholics did rise to significant positions in the South, even in the Confederacy. For example, as secession loomed, the Catholic bishop of St. Augustine, Florida, Jean-Pierre Augustine Verot, preached on slavery and abolitionism, a sermon later published as a Confederate tract, giving Verot the name "Rebel Bishop." And during his presidency of the Confederate States of America, Jefferson Davis appealed to Pope Pius IX to intervene on behalf of the Confederacy by counteracting the Union's attempts to secure European allies, resulting in a sympathetic reply by the Pope. Davis had attended the St. Thomas Aquinas school run by the Catholic Dominican order in Washington County, Kentucky, and he counted Catholics among his circle of friends.

Southern Catholic priests and nuns also served during the Civil War. Catholic nuns, notably the Daughters of Charity founded in Emmitsburg, Maryland, by Elizabeth Ann Bayley Seton in 1809, served as nurses to both sides, without political allegiance. A Catholic chaplain to the First Georgia Volunteers, Father Peter Whelan, became a Union prisoner of war when the rest of his regiment was captured in 1862. He was sent to New York's Governor's Island, where he remained until those troops were repatriated (despite being previously paroled) in 1863. He returned to the South, sent by Bishop Verot to be a chaplain at the notorious Confederate Andersonville prisoner of war camp, where he worked to ameliorate the horrible conditions of Union prisoners. Even the South's poet laureate was a Catholic priest, Father Abram Joseph Ryan, a native of Norfolk, Virginia, who also served as a military chaplain. His most famous poem, "The Conquered Banner," published in 1866, became an anthem of the Lost Cause ideology.

Southern Protestant Christianity developed in many forms in the years leading up to and during the Civil War. Economic and social elites tended to belong to the Episcopalian and the Presbyterian churches, derived from the Anglican and Scots Calvinist communions respectively. Baptists and Methodist missionaries evangelized rural areas. Though representing a small minority in the South, the Society of Friends (the Quakers) first appeared in the region in the late 1600s when its founder, George Fox, visited the Carolinas in 1672, laying the groundwork for the North Carolina Yearly Meeting, which began in 1698. Derived from Scots-Irish Presbyterianism, the Disciples of Christ were founded in the early 1800s as a congregational communion (with independent congregations) committed to restoring the simplicity of the early Christian community found in the Acts of the Apostles.

As the nation became divided prior to the Civil War over the question of slavery, the national Presbyterian, Baptist, and Methodist communions likewise split. The Episcopal communion remained united until secession. The first Episcopal bishop of Virginia, James Madison (a cousin of the president), had been consecrated in 1790, and during his episcopacy the church struggled for members with competition from the actively evangelizing Baptist and Methodist churches. These were far more effective in Southern rural areas and, unlike the Episcopalians, they were not associated with the political and economic elite. The character of the Southern Episcopal church eventually became more evangelical than its counterpart in the North and after the secession of the southern states and the creation of the Confederate States of America, southern dioceses formed the Protestant Episcopal Church in the Confederate States in 1862. Led by Bishop Leonidas Polk, the missionary bishop for the states of the Deep South, and Bishop Stephen Elliott of Georgia, it dissolved at the end of the war.

The Methodist denomination can also claim an old Southern pedigree. Initially a reform movement within Anglicanism, Methodism eventually constituted a breakaway denomination. Its founders, John Wesley and Charles Wesley, first came to America in 1736 as chaplains to the Georgia colony created by James Oglethorpe as a penal refuge. There they met Moravian congregations that influenced their own spirituality and worship. Methodists were fiercely evangelical and energetically missionary, creating a system of "circuit riding" clergy who traveled from place to place in the rural South. As a result of Methodist missionary work in the late Colonial era, half of all Methodists in North America lived in the southern colonies, and by the time of the Early Republic, nearly 90 percent of Methodists in the United States lived below the Mason-Dixon line. Methodism's evangelicalism tended to be inclusive, more democratic, and more working class in its appeal, which included African Americans. However, this inclusiveness created the conditions for schism over the issues of slavery and abolitionism. In 1784, a Methodist conference prohibited slaveholding in states where emancipation was legal, but by 1808, southern

Methodists had succeeded in winning a compromise that allowed each state Methodist organization to rule on the issue of slavery. By 1836 New England Methodists began to call for a return to the earlier understanding. By 1844, northern and southern Methodists had separated. Southern Methodist chaplains and missionaries served Confederate soldiers during the Civil War, and its tract societies provided soldiers with devotional reading material.

Other denominations split over the issues of slavery and secession as well. The Presbyterian Church in the Confederate States of America formed in 1861, claiming a spiritual rather than political mission. After the Civil War, this denomination continued as the Presbyterian Church in the United States until reunification in 1987. The Baptist denomination in the South, which dominates the religious landscape of the region today, already had several versions by the time of the Civil War, including General Baptists, Free Will Baptists, and Primitive Baptists. By 1845, northern and southern Baptists had split over the issue of slavery.

Southern apologists for slavery frequently employed religious rhetoric to defend the institution. They could use proof texts (scriptural passages taken out of context) or make typological arguments (employing a past biblical precedent to make sense of a present circumstance). Neither the Jewish scriptures nor the Christian scriptures (what Christians call the Old Testament and the New Testament of the Bible) offered outright prohibitions against slavery, and both scriptural traditions admonished masters and slaves to behave ethically toward each other. For example, ancient Jewish society recognized three forms of slavery: the Israelite who was a servant to another Israelite (either voluntarily as financial security or by birth or purchase), the non-Israelite taken as war captive by an Israelite, and the Israelite who sold himself to a non-Israelite as debt collateral. Depending on which of these conditions pertained, slaves might be afforded seventh-year sabbaticals or fiftieth-year jubilee release (Exodus 21: 2–6; Leviticus 25: 10, 38–41, 47–55), or at the very least protection against oppression (Exodus 22: 21; 23: 9). In the Christian tradition, the gospels describe the presence of household slaves during the ministry of Jesus. In one case, Jesus heals the slave of a Roman centurion (Luke 7: 1–10), and, even upon his arrest in the Garden of Gethsemane when Simon Peter attempts to protect Jesus by cutting off the ear of the High Priest's slave, Jesus restores the ear to the injured slave (Matthew 26: 47–56). Slaves appear in Jesus' parables. For instance, Jesus compares his watchful and hopeful followers to attentive slaves who are ever vigilant for their master's return (Luke 12: 37–46; Matthew 24: 45–51). For St. Paul, slavery was the metaphor for Jesus' role as the preeminent servant of humankind (Philippians 2: 7), which the Christian is called to imitate (Philippians 2: 5); St. Paul also characterized himself as a slave of Christ (Romans 1: 1; Philippians 1: 1).

The chief typological arguments concerned the mark of Cain and the curse of Ham. Adam and Eve's son Cain murders his brother Abel, is cursed, outcast, and physically marked (Genesis 4: 11–16). This would be used as a rationale for the slavery of dark-skinned peoples. Ham the son of Noah, who sees his father naked, is cursed to perpetual slavery (Genesis 9: 20–27). Slavery proponents interpreted this story to mean that people of African descent, Ham's descendants, were marked for perpetual slavery. Proslavery writers also employed *ad hominem* attacks on abolitionist writers whom they characterized as atheists bent on undermining the authority of the Bible. Some also adopted a racist pseudoscience emerging in the nineteenth century, particularly theories of polygenesis, the notion that different human races were not descended from the same First Parents, Adam and Eve. Polygenesis allowed proslavery advocates to remove African Americans from the salvation narrative passed down from Adam and Eve through Abraham and Sarah (and their descendents) and from the human community entirely. Proslavery religious arguments were made in a variety of genres, including the sermon, of which James Henley Thornwell's "The Christian Doctrine of Slavery" (1850) is exemplary.

Perhaps one of the more carefully calibrated representations of the different religious positions in the slavery debate is found in the first published novel by an African American, *Clotel, or The President's Daughter* (1853), by William Wells Brown. An escaped slave who worked among abolitionists in England, Brown used the legend of the slave daughter of Thomas Jefferson to create his protagonist. Brown depicted a southern Presbyterian pro-slavery minister, a disreputable missionary among slaves, an agnostic rationalist, and a courageous southern heroine whose religious convictions bring her to abolitionism. Brown also noted wryly that the landing of the Pilgrims on Plymouth Rock coincided with the arrival of the first enslaved Africans in Jamestown, contrasting the religious convictions of the New England founders with those of the Virginia founders.

But although most religious institutions of the Old South accepted and often endorsed slavery, some religious whites in the South dissented from the mainstream view. The North Carolina Meeting of the Society of Friends, which had practically eliminated slavery among its members by 1814, provided leadership in Southern abolitionism, manumission societies (that raised funds to purchase and to free enslaved African Americans), African resettlement societies, and the Underground Railroad. Leadership of the Methodist Church, bishops Francis Asbury and Thomas Coke, Baptists ministers John Leland and David Barrow, and Presbyterian leaders David Rice and George Bourne, each argued that slavery was inconsistent with Christianity and that Christians could not compromise on this point. Evangelical revivalism, though frequently focused on personal salvation, did aspire to reforming society at large and spawned efforts to repatriate emancipated African American slaves to Liberia, Africa.

Perhaps the most eloquent religious dissent articulated by a Southerner is Angelina Grimké's "Appeal to the Christian Women of the South" (1836), a call for civil disobedience to unjust laws, written a decade before Henry David

Thoreau's more famous (and less pragmatic) essay, "Resistance to Civil Government" (1849). With her sister Sarah, Grimké moved from South Carolina to Philadelphia in 1819, so great was their antipathy to Southern slavery, where both became Quakers. In her appeal, Grimké critiqued the religious rationalizations for slavery and called upon women to pray, to read, and to act on behalf of its abolition. She used biblical precedents to defend her call for conscientious objection to slavery and suggested biblical female exemplars of such dissent. She also armed her readers with a combination of secular legal and religious propositions against slavery. Obeying a higher Divine law, Grimké argued, must take precedence over adhering to unjust human laws.

A region as religiously diverse as its northern counterpart, the South and its culture shaped its religious expression more than its theologies shaped the culture. The ideologies of land, honor, agrarian economy, and race provided social cohesion across lines of religious belief and practice. In the antebellum era and during the secession, Southerners frequently found religious ways of defending and explaining what soon would become the Lost Cause.

## Further Reading

Feldberg, Michael. "Judah Benjamin, the Jewish Confederate." *Blessings of Freedom: Chapters in American Jewish History.* New York: American Jewish Historical Society, 2002. 52–53.

Ferris, Marcie and Mark I. Greenberg, eds. *Jewish Roots in Southern Soil: A New History.* Hanover: University Press of New England, 2006.

Genovese, Eugene D. *Roll, Jordan, Roll: The World the Slaves Made.* New York: Random House, 1974.

Hill, Samuel S. *One Name but Several Faces: Variety in Popular Christian Denominations in Southern History.* Athens: University of Georgia Press, 1996.

Hill, Samuel S., ed. *Varieties of Southern Religious Experience.* Baton Rouge: University of Louisiana Press, 1988.

Miller, Randall M., Harry Stout, and Charles Reagan Wilson, eds. *Religion and the American Civil War.* New York: Oxford University Press, 1998.

Rablee, George C. *God's Almost Chosen Peoples: A Religious History of the American Civil War.* Chapel Hill: University of North Carolina Press, 2010.

Raboteau, Albert J. *Slave Religion: The "Invisible Institution" in the Antebellum South.* New York: Oxford University Press, 1978.

# 9

# RELIGION IN THE NORTH

*James R. Rohrer*

When South Carolina guns opened fire upon Fort Sumter in April 1861, commencing the most devastating war in American history, countless citizens looked to their churches for guidance in responding to the attack. Religious opinion throughout the North had been deeply divided during the months leading up to Fort Sumter, with many ministers and Christian reformers urging peaceful reconciliation or even acceptance of secession. Antislavery poet John Greenleaf Whittier, a Quaker and pacifist, expressed the views of many abolitionists when in the midst of the secession crisis he penned these lines (333):

> They break the links of Union: shall we light
> The fires of hell to weld anew the chain
> On that red anvil where each blow is pain?
> Draw we not now even a freer breath,
> As from our shoulders falls a load of death.

Many Protestants and Catholics who did not share Whittier's pacifism nonetheless doubted the right of the federal government to coerce southern states into union. The vast majority of northern clergy agreed with their southern counterparts that slave ownership was consistent with the Bible as well as the Constitution, and that abolitionism was both politically incendiary and theologically heretical. Without any united theological stand against the South's "peculiar institution," and wishing to avoid bloodshed, northern Christians moved through the secession winter confused about the appropriate path the republic should follow.

The firing upon Fort Sumter, which northerners regarded as a sign of southern aggression, ended all confusion and brought the vast majority of northern

Christians solidly behind military force to suppress the rebellion. Massachusetts Unitarian pastor Edmund B. Wilson observed that where "one week before all was uncertainty ... apathy, doubt, gloom," now "we are one people" (Chesebrough 84). The famous Presbyterian preacher, Henry Ward Beecher, who had advocated acceptance of secession before the attack upon Sumter, suddenly experienced a conversion to militancy. The day after federal troops surrendered the fort, Beecher mounted his pulpit in Brooklyn to declare:

> I love our country.... I hold that to be corrupted silently by giving up manhood, by degenerating ... is infinitely worse than war.... We want no craven cowards; we want men.... They have fired upon the American flag.... Let every man that lives and owns himself an American, take the side of true American principles;—liberty for one, and liberty for all; liberty now, and liberty forever.
>
> *(Chesebrough 84)*

Ministers in both the North and South played key roles in preparing the way for a civil war. During the 1830s and 1840s the largest Protestant communions—the Baptists, Methodists, and Presbyterians—had all split into sectional denominations that differed in theology and attitudes toward social reform. The drifting apart of southern and northern churches made it easier to divide the nation politically and when the secession crisis came, ministers in both regions were quick to shore up popular cultural positions with theological justifications. Christians could give themselves heart and soul to rival political causes with full assurance from their churches that God was on their side. In the words of historian Sydney Ahlstrom, "When the cannons roared in Charleston harbor, two divinely authorized crusades were set in motion, each of them absolutizing a given social and political order. The pulpits resounded with a vehemence and absence of restraint never equaled in American history" (119).

Clergy also played a crucial role in interpreting the struggle once it began, and offering Americans consolation and hope as the human cost of the war escalated. In 1860, no other center of culture even closely rivaled the influence of organized religion. Between 1800 and 1860 religious revivals had repeatedly swept across the United States, adding countless Americans to the ranks of evangelical churches. By 1860, over 10,000,000 Americans, roughly 40 percent of the total population, identified with evangelical Christianity, making it the largest single subculture in the United States. Countless citizens affiliated with various other Christian traditions, including Lutheran, Episcopalian, Quaker, and the rapidly growing Roman Catholic community. Approximately two-fifths of Americans were formal church members in 1860, while twice that number attended religious services regularly.

The Civil War, then, must be understood as a theological as well as constitutional and political crisis. The war tested common American assumptions about divine providence and the role of the United States in God's redemptive plan for the world. The failure of Church leaders to find common ground in the Bible on such fundamental issues as slavery and obedience to the government tested Protestant notions about the sufficiency of private interpretation of scripture. Americans of every stripe, as they surveyed the wreckage of their nation, were acutely aware of the irony that Abraham Lincoln voiced so poignantly in his Second Inaugural Address. Both sides, Lincoln observed, "read the same Bible, and pray to the same God; and each invokes His aid against the other."

As Protestant clergy in the North struggled to make sense of the Civil War, they drew upon deeply rooted traditions that stretched back to the Puritans. Certainly, the most important of these was the belief in America's unique covenant with God. First articulated as early as 1630 by John Winthrop, the idea that America was called to be a "City on a Hill," a beacon to all humanity, pervaded Protestant American rhetoric during the antebellum years. Even so unorthodox a writer as Herman Melville nonetheless took for granted that "We Americans are the peculiar, chosen people—the Israel of our time; we bear the ark of the liberties of the world" (149). Referencing the Old Testament, the comparison to Israel recalled that God's covenant bound the Israelites to faithful obedience, and that the Lord chastened His people with dreadful punishment whenever they forgot their covenant and wandered away from Him.

In sermons and editorials in religious periodicals, northern ministers assured their people that a sovereign God was using both sides in the conflict to purge the nation of sin. Methodist minister George Peck informed his flock that "as God often uses one wicked people for the punishment of another, he is permitting this slaveholders' rebellion to inflict upon us terrible chastisement" (Moorehead 48). On April 30, 1863, designated as a national day of fasting by President Lincoln, Reverend Byron Sunderland, a Presbyterian and chaplain to the Congress, assured his Washington, D.C., congregation that "We have sinned, while holding in trust the noblest heritage ever held by any people, while having charge in effect of the last and most precious hopes of human nature." Unless the nation repented and returned to righteousness, Sunderland declared, the country would "sink into an abyss of shame and infamy such as no people ever contracted, not even the doomed and wandering house of Israel" (Moorehead 47).

Although very few ministers had supported the abolitionist movement in the years preceding Fort Sumter, once the carnage of the war hit home, Protestant clergy increasingly came to see slavery as the root cause of the nation's intense suffering, a blight that had to be removed if all the sacrifice of life was to have ultimate meaning. The logic of their providential understanding of history pointed toward slavery as the great sin that God now purposed to wipe away. Increasing numbers of ministers throughout the North came to favor the emancipation of slaves as a national necessity, and in the months before Lincoln issued the Emancipation Proclamation on September 23, 1862, he was deluged with petitions from churches urging him to take action.

Lincoln himself seems to have grown increasingly immersed in religious reflection as he grappled with the national crisis and responded to religious leaders who sought to shape his policies. Although never a church member or formally aligned with any Christian body, his rhetoric became increasingly biblical during the course of his presidency. Like the Christian public that endlessly petitioned him, he came to regard the war in providential terms, and to see himself as a tool of the divine will. Lincoln later reflected that the Emancipation was a "covenant" he had made with "his Maker" that he could not break. By accepting the mythic role into which northern religious sentiment cast him, Lincoln contributed to the apotheosis that would occur in the wake of his assassination on Good Friday, 1865, linking him forever in the popular imagination with Christ as well as Moses.

Although most Americans in 1860 were Protestant, Roman Catholicism was the fastest growing religious community in the North. Catholic bishops drew upon Catholic teaching about submission to earthly powers to make sense of the war. Bishops generally followed their state governments into either the Confederacy or the Union; Catholics fought and died on both sides of the conflict. Northern Catholic leaders, disappointed that southern Catholics did not uphold the United States government, regarded Jefferson Davis and Robert E. Lee as no better than Italian revolutionaries seeking to overthrow the papacy. Despite a lack of enthusiasm for the emancipation of slaves, and a suspicion of their nativist Protestant neighbors, Catholics in the North generally rallied behind the Constitution, supporting the war as a noble cause.

The belief that the war, with all of the suffering it engendered, ultimately served some higher purpose was essential for both soldiers and their loved ones on the home front. The war's horror could be faced and endured only if it was invested with a transcendent meaning. Protestant and Catholic chaplains alike faced the task of helping soldiers to fight and die courageously as "Christian soldiers" in a sacred war. Preachers at home labored to sustain the flagging hopes of those who followed the conflict from afar, and to shore up public support for the government and the troops. The higher the death toll mounted and the longer the conflict dragged on, the more crucial it was to believe that the slaughter was purposeful and the sacrifice somehow necessary.

The immense popularity of Julia Ward Howe's famous "Battle Hymn of the Republic" clearly suggests the consoling power of this optimistic millenarian message. First penned in late 1861 and published in the *Atlantic Monthly,* by the close of the war it had become one of the most beloved songs in the nation. Modern Americans, products of a more secular era and not immersed in the devastation of war, cannot easily appreciate the desperate hunger for purpose that Howe's sentimental lyrics satisfied:

> In the beauty of the lilies Christ was born across the sea,
> With a glory in His bosom that transfigures you and me:

As he died to make men holy, let us die to make men free,
While God is marching on.

The Civil War, Gardiner Shattuck has observed, was regarded by Americans as a "channel of grace" for the nation. Those who died were considered Christian martyrs, whose sacrifices "brought redemption to both the soldier himself and the nation for which he fought" (15).

Military chaplains played a crucial role in ministering to the spiritual and physical needs of Civil War soldiers and preparing them to fight and die for the cause. Ever since the Mexican War, there had been persistent criticism of the use of public money to finance clergy; according to Warren Armstrong, the Civil War "rescued the chaplaincy from possible extinction as an American military tradition" (x). At the outbreak of hostilities there were only thirty post chaplains serving 17,000 regular army troops. Lincoln's call for volunteers to suppress the rebellion brought a dramatic increase in the number of both soldiers and chaplains. Volunteer regiments, organized locally, often included chaplains as a matter of course. These men were chosen by the field commanders, approved by state governors, and appointed by the War Department at a salary of roughly $1,400 per annum. Chaplains for regular army units, government hospitals, and military posts received their appointments directly from Lincoln at the same salary. Altogether, some 2,300 ministers, priests, and rabbis held the chaplaincy in Union armies, although not more than three hundred served at any one time during the war.

The quality of these "Holy Joe's" varied considerably. At the outset of the war, appointment of chaplains was rather haphazard, and sometimes fell to well-connected but inexperienced political appointees eager to earn the salary. Early soldier's diaries and letters frequently contain derogatory comments upon cowardly and inept chaplains who did more harm than good. After July 1862, an Act of Congress required chaplains to have the endorsement of some "authorized ecclesiastical body of not less than five accredited ministers belonging to the said religious denomination" (Wiley 289). Over time, the quality of chaplains dramatically improved as incompetents disappeared and more dedicated men filled the ranks. Many letters and journals penned by soldiers testify to the devotion of chaplains and the high esteem in which officers and enlisted men generally held them.

Chaplains played myriad roles, depending both upon circumstances and need but also on the whim of regimental commanders. They served as spiritual advisors and friends, confessors, evangelists, nurses, and essential contacts between soldiers and family at home. Often they acted as financial agents for soldiers. Frequently it was the chaplain who wrote letters of condolence to the loved ones of fallen heroes. Chaplains distributed regimental mail, went shopping for supplies, and, during the weeks and months between battles, sometimes taught school for Union troops and black freedmen. Perhaps the most beloved chaplains were those who fought as combatants alongside the enlisted men, demonstrating their own willingness to kill and be killed in the cause.

Although chaplains played a vital if at times intangible role in maintaining morale and combat efficiency, there were too few of them to meet the tremendous needs of the armies that waged the Civil War. Home missionaries and Christian relief organizations, the latter staffed heavily by lay volunteers, had perhaps an even greater impact upon Union troops. By 1860, American churches had experience organizing and operating a plethora of benevolent societies. Antebellum churchmen had erected a vast network of local, state, and national associations to distribute Bibles and tracts, establish Sunday Schools, plant churches in "destitute" towns, reform drinking habits, and distribute charity to the poor or infirm. This so-called Protestant benevolent empire reached into virtually every city and village in the Union and commanded the dedicated support of countless citizens. Upon the outbreak of war, reformers were quick to see the army itself as the largest and neediest mission field in the nation, and began to channel the energy and resources of the "empire" toward the welfare of the soldiers.

Initially, many local churches and benevolent groups acted on their own to provide Bibles and reading material, clothing, medical supplies, and comfort articles for troops. It was also common for ministers to make brief missionary trips to soldiers in camps, hospitals, or even occasionally on the front lines. But soon efforts were made to create a more systematic and coordinated mechanism to mobilize the resources of the Christian public. Two distinct and sometimes rival organizations emerged that became an omnipresent part of the war effort: The U.S. Sanitary Commission and the United States Christian Commission.

The Sanitary Commission was organized largely at the instigation of Unitarian minister Henry W. Bellows, a theological liberal whose Church of All Souls in New York City included some of the wealthiest and most renowned citizens. Sometimes nicknamed "The Church of the Holy Zebra" because of its Italianate architecture, All Souls was doctrinally alien to northern evangelicals. Bellows regarded both evangelism and moralistic reform with disdain. He had outraged many New York City Protestants in 1857 by publicly defending the theatre and criticizing those who attacked "the recreations rather than the sins of society" (Bremner 37–38). Having carefully studied the English sanitary reformers Edwin Chadwick and Thomas Southwood Smith, Bellows believed that most social ills could be prevented by the application of reason and scientific organizational techniques. While praising the spontaneous outpouring of Christian charity at the commencement of the war as noble, he believed that piecemeal efforts and moralizing were inappropriate. Soldiers did not need Bibles and occasional preaching so much as healthy food and a clean environment, intellectually stimulating literature, and the best physicians and nurses available. To provide these necessities required careful rational planning by experts.

Bellows helped organize in April 1861 the Women's Central Association of Relief to coordinate the efforts of the various aid societies in metropolitan New York. Then, in May, he enlisted several of the city's leading physicians to accompany him to Washington, D.C., where they lobbied the Lincoln administration to create a national commission of military officers, medical men and civilian philanthropists to "methodize" and reduce "to practical service the already active but undirected benevolence of the people toward the army" (Bremner 39). Secretary of War Simon Cameron and President Lincoln were both cautious about civilians meddling in army affairs, but, in June 1861, approved the formation of a Sanitary Commission with the understanding that it would confine its efforts to volunteer regiments. Reverend Bellows was named President of the Commission, while the well-known architect and city planner, Frederick Law Olmstead was tapped to direct field operations as general secretary.

By 1864, the Sanitary Commission employed a salaried staff of about 450 people, and directed the activities of many thousands of mostly female volunteers throughout the Union. Local auxiliaries raised funds and gathered needed supplies, forwarding the latter to strategic warehouses for distribution to needy troops. The commission established hospitals, libraries, and reading rooms, as well as recreational "lodges" and "refreshment saloons" for needy soldiers, recruits, and discharged veterans. The commission also operated allotment, pension and back-pay offices, and kept a directory of the names and locations of men confined to hospitals. Field agents visited and encouraged troops on the front lines, delivered boxes of food and care packages, and lectured on camp hygiene.

Although most volunteers certainly considered the Sanitary Commission to be an expression of Christian charity, the organization appealed primarily to theological liberals whose religion focused upon practical benevolence. Evangelism had no place in the Sanitary Commission agenda. For the vast pool of evangelical Protestants, this lack of concern with explicitly Christian outreach was a source of frustration. Many ministers and parents worried that their young people in uniform would be left bereft of spiritual support, and might pass into eternity without a strong relationship with the Savior. They feared the deleterious effects of army life upon the morals of the soldiers. They also recognized that constant exposure to sickness and death often opened men in uniform to spiritual reflection. Believing that practical relief needed to be linked to specifically evangelical ministry, a group of YMCA leaders from fifteen cities launched the United States Christian Commission in November 1861.

The Christian Commission tapped into the existing network of evangelical churches and local reformers. Soon it far outstripped the Sanitary Commission in both funds and volunteer support. Although delegates of the two organizations remained cordial and avoided open competition, behind the scenes rivalry could be fierce. The Sanitary Commission concentrated upon wealthy donors to sustain its operations, while the Christian Commission reaped the small contributions of countless ordinary citizens. But sometimes both groups targeted the same sources of funding. When the wealthy New York merchant William E. Dodge, a staunch evangelical, accepted appointment as Chair of the Christian Commission's New York branch, Henry Bellows begged him to reconsider. The nation could not support two rival organizations, Bellows warned, and he predicted that "the Christian Commission, without accomplishing its own object, will weaken and defeat ours" (Bremner 60).

Bellows was wrong; each organization thrived throughout the war. Field agents of both agencies roamed battlefields, visited prisons and hospitals, and tried to comfort soldiers in any way possible. Often volunteers of the rival commissions worked side by side as nurses, gravediggers, and distributors of relief. But as "ambassadors of Jesus" the Christian Commission added preaching and prayer meetings, passed out Bibles and hymnals, and attempted to bring soldiers to faith in Christ. Judging from comments in Civil War diaries and memoirs, many soldiers felt grateful to the work of both organizations.

The liberation of tens of thousands of black slaves by Union troops soon created a monumental humanitarian and logistical challenge that easily rivaled the problems posed by needy soldiers. As early as late 1861, countless escaped slaves made their way as "contraband" to Union lines. Military leaders pleaded with the northern public for food and clothing to provide to these destitute runaways. Herded into "contraband camps" scattered along the Atlantic coast from Washington, D.C., to South Carolina, and along the Mississippi River from New Orleans to Cairo, Illinois, the refugees included not only able-bodied men, women, and children, but also the elderly, sick, and disabled. The task of housing, clothing, and feeding former slaves, educating them, and treating their illnesses, did not generate the same enthusiasm among northern Churches as did relief efforts for soldiers. A later report by the New York National Freedmen's Relief Association summarized the problem:

> The masses of people had never been anti-slavery in sentiment. The number was small of those who had faith in the black man's capacity, or hope in his future, or interest in his fate. The Sanitary Commission was pressing for money to aid and comfort the sick and wounded soldiers. Few heard the freedmen's sigh; few that heard it heeded it.
>
> *(9)*

The first agency that heeded the "freedman's sigh" was the American Missionary Association, an antislavery organization established in 1846 to offer an alternative to Protestant missions that equivocated on slave holding. Refusing to take money from slaveholders, the AMA already had more than a decade of experience raising funds from such dedicated abolitionists as the wealthy New York merchant Lewis Tappan, funds which were used to support such causes as a mission among freedmen in Canada. The AMA took up the plight of the "contraband slaves" in September 1861, sending their first volunteer missionary to Fortress Monroe in Virginia. During the course of the war, hundreds of additional AMA volunteers, approximately one-third of them single women, went south to serve as nurses, teachers, and physicians in the refugee camps.

Soon the work of the AMA among freed slaves was augmented by volunteers from many other freedmen's aid societies. Mirroring the division between the Sanitary and Christian Commissions, freedmen's aid groups also split over theology, as well as race. Boston Unitarians, many of them already active in the Sanitary Commission, launched in early 1862 the Educational Commission of Boston to work among southern blacks. Later renamed the New England Freedmen's Aid Association, they eschewed evangelism. The new organization sought to cultivate in freedmen "habits of cheerful voluntary labor in place of the constrained toil of slavery, teaching them to read and write, and interesting them in lessons of honesty and frugality" (Bremner 103).

Late in 1862, black churches in New York City and Brooklyn launched the American Freedmen's Friend Society, seeking to meet the concrete physical needs of the freedmen but also to promote their patriotism and loyalty to the United States government. In the field, where volunteers from these various agencies often worked side by side, hostility sometimes sprouted between evangelical and Unitarian teachers. White volunteers of either persuasion often felt chagrined by the apparent preference of the freedmen for teachers and preachers of their own race.

The Civil War harnessed the energy and resources of countless northern Christians and channeled it into the cause of the Union. The unprecedented association of cross and flag, the sanctification of patriotism, became a hallmark of northern Christianity into the twentieth century. Many northern evangelicals during the Gilded Age would push to have the United States recognized officially as a "Christian Republic," an impulse unleashed by the rhetorical fusion of God and Country during the Civil War. As historian Gaines Foster has observed, the campaign to pass a "Christian amendment" to the United States Constitution rested upon the assumption that the American Union must ultimately depend upon a more stable footing than state sovereignty or majority will. The secession of the southern states had convinced many northerners that government needed to be grounded upon a formal covenant with God, who alone could forge a "more perfect union." Spearheaded by the National Association for the Amendment of the Constitution, petitions flooded into Congress asking that God, Christ, and the authority of the Bible be inserted into the preamble of the Constitution. Religious liberals and Jewish leaders roundly condemned these efforts to establish Christianity, and Congress paid no heed to the campaign. Nonetheless, the crusade for a Christian amendment reflected widespread Protestant ideals in the post-war years.

The Civil War clearly promoted closer ecumenical relations between different northern denominations, and, at least temporarily, helped to lessen animosity between Protestants and Catholics. Soldiers of all faiths fought and suffered together during the war. Protestant, Catholic, and Jewish chaplains served bravely in the same armies, offering spiritual support and consolation to soldiers without distinction to faith. Although anti-Catholic nativism would still be a factor in politics after the war, many Protestant veterans recalled with gratitude the patriotic sacrifices Catholic troops had made in the struggle. The shared Civil Religion of American patriotism was beginning to erode the ancient prejudices that divided the churches.

The close of the Civil War saw church attendance at unprecedented heights across the North. Unlike the American Revolution, which had a deleterious effect upon popular piety, the Civil War seems to have sparked a great revival of support for organized religion. The late nineteenth century witnessed the migration of masses of rural Christians into America's growing cities, which became centers of great evangelistic crusades and reform efforts. Many of the leading organizers were preachers like Washington Gladden and Dwight L. Moody, who had first honed their skills as delegates of the Christian Commission during the Civil War.

Beneath the surface of post-war piety, however, the war unleashed economic and social forces that were pushing America in a more secular direction. The war generated large-scale industrialization and a dramatic increase in bureaucratic efficiency. The federal government and American corporations grew in size and scope with breath-taking swiftness. Churches would never again be the unrivaled power centers of American public life. Some Christians responded to the expansion of federal power by lobbying for national laws to promote morality, but many other churches shifted their energies away from efforts to shape American politics, emphasizing instead the need for personal holiness and conversion. Although piety and faith remained a powerful source of comfort for countless Americans, increasingly this energy was directed inward and had less impact upon the formulation of public policy.

## Further Reading

Ahlstrom, Sydney E. *A Religious History of the American People, Vol. 2.* New York: Doubleday, 1975.

Armstrong, Warren B. *For Courageous Fighting and Confident Dying: Union Chaplains in the Civil War.* Lawrence: University of Kansas Press, 1998.

Bremner, Robert H. *The Public Good: Philanthropy & Welfare in the Civil War Era.* New York: Knopf, 1980.

Chesebrough, David B. *"God Ordained This War": Sermons on the Sectional Crisis, 1830–1865.* Columbia: University of South Carolina Press, 1991.

Fredrickson, George M. *The Inner Civil War: Northern Intellectuals and the Crisis of the Union.* New York: Harper & Row, 1965.

Goen, C. C. *Broken Churches, Broken Nation: Denominational Schisms and the Coming of the Civil War.* Macon, GA: Mercer University Press, 1985.

Foster, Gaines. *Moral Reconstruction: Christian Lobbyists and Federal Legislation of Morality, 1865–1920.* Chapel Hill: University of North Carolina Press, 2002.

Melville, Herman. *White Jacket; or, The World in a Man-of-War.* New York: Holt, Rinehart & Winston, 1967.

Moorehead, James H. *American Apocalypse: Yankee Protestants and the Civil War, 1860–1869.* New Haven: Yale University Press, 1878.

Noll, Mark. *The Civil War as a Theological Crisis.* Chapel Hill: University of North Carolina Press, 2006.

Shattuck, Gardiner H., Jr. *A Shield and a Hiding Place: The Religious Life of the Civil War Armies.* Macon: Mercer University Press, 1987.

Whittier, John Greenleaf. *The Complete Poetical Works of Whittier.* Boston: Houghton Mifflin, 1894.

Wiley, Bell Irving. "Holy Joes" of the Sixties: A Study of Civil War Chaplains." *The Huntington Library Quarterly* 16:3 (1953): 287–304.

Woodworth, Steven E. *While God is Marching On: The Religious World of Civil War Soldiers.* Lawrence: University of Kansas Press, 2001.

# 10

# REFORM AND WELFARE SOCIETIES

*Lauren Brandt*

"In the history of the world, the doctrine of Reform had never such scope as at the present hour." With these words, the philosopher Ralph Waldo Emerson summed up the dominant social climate of the mid-nineteenth century in the United States. Speaking before an eager audience of young men, members of the Mechanics' Apprentices' Library, in Boston on January 25, 1841, Emerson described the tenor of the times as one of "judgment" in which "Christianity, the laws, commerce, schools, the farm, the laboratory" were all succumbing to the "new spirit" and its effects. This new spirit, as Emerson described it, found expression in many forms, yet at its heart, consisted of one core impulse: "the conviction that there is an infinite worthiness in man which will appear at the call of worth, and that all particular reforms are the removing of some impediment" (218, 237).

Not surprisingly for such an astute social observer, Emerson's words to the young apprentices of Boston that night accurately captured the tremendous energy expended on projects of social reform in the United States during the nineteenth century. Through ways and means too numerous to count, Americans of all classes, races, and regions were drawn by a single impulse to the project of re-forming the existing society in the hopes of achieving a new and better nation. Again, Emerson proved prescient in his diagnosis: underlying the broad proposals was a kernel of belief that could not be shaken in the "worthiness in man," which demanded complete recognition and fulfillment. At its heart, the project of reforming American society was inextricably linked to questions of religious identity and belief. Indeed, one historian defines all reformers of this time period as sharing a single trait: "the tendency to apply religious imagination and passion to issues that most Americans considered worldly" (Abzug 3). The increase in religious revivals and the emerging emphasis on the relationship between the human individual and the divine (as expressed by the Unitarians, the Mormons, and the Transcendentalists, to name but a few) brought the existing state of American social and political relationships into sharp relief. Their philosophies focused attention on definitions of the individual self and posited new theories to regulate man's interactions with his own mind and with others. Yet this new emphasis on selfhood led back to the cosmos, as Abzug notes. The roots of human individualism lay in the attempt to parse out man's relationship to the divine, as embodied in the world surrounding him. Emerson's essay, *Nature*, published in 1836, promulgated this new understanding of man even as it raised questions about man's ability to transform the world.

Transforming the world was the goal of the numerous reform and welfare societies that emerged during the mid-nineteenth century. While the reformers were united in their desire to redefine American society, the transformations that they sought and the mechanisms which they used were not always the same. In fact, one could divide these societies into several categories along the axes of race, religion, and region. The "new spirit" expressed itself differently according to the dominant political, social and economic factors present in each town, state and region. Ultimately, however, reform movements could also be divided into two main categories—first, those concerned with transforming the individual and one's personal behavior, and second, those oriented towards transforming others by emphasizing their innate worth and value.

Nineteenth-century Americans actively sought to uncover the "worthiness" noted by Emerson in their own personalities. The concept of "individual worthiness" was intrinsically linked to the sense that each individual was linked to the divine, whether through Emerson's idea of the "oversoul" or the more traditional relationship between an omniscient God and the individual sinner. This pursuit led to such disparate outcomes as the growth of temperance societies which required their members to abstain from alcohol, to Sabbatarianism, which advocated for Sunday as a day of rest, to the growth of utopian agricultural communities in New England. In keeping with the emphasis on the individual, these movements sought to restore humanity to its proper relationship to the divine. They effectively treated the physical environment as a manifestation of divine power and significance (Abzug 6–7). Religion and morality became a matter of self-discipline, which was seen as evidence of the individual's commitment to a Christian identity and the goal of a more Christian community.

The temperance movement proved emblematic of these concerns. Initially focused on curbing the use of alcohol in the individual, it quickly gained followers who were focused on ridding their communities of the substance. The American Temperance Society, founded by Lyman Beecher and Justin Edwards in 1826, used pledges of abstinence and statistics to persuade its audiences of the benefits of tee-totaling. The Washingtonian Movement and the Knights of Father Mathew offered a similar structure (the first for any denomination, the second for American Catholics)—both linked temperance to ideals of personal and civic virtue. Sabbatarians took this one step further; they sought to implement legislation on the local level that would protect Sunday as a day of rest for the individual citizen. This would accomplish two goals: it would force recognition of the Sabbath and, ideally, curb any excessive materialistic cravings on the part of individual citizens

Both of these movements demonstrate how the personal goals of individuals became intertwined with the broader goal of improving the surrounding community. Sabbatarians and members of temperance groups viewed recruitment as essential to their efforts, not only to improve individual lives, but also to raise the tenor of the nation itself. Personal transformation fueled the improvement of American society. For many activists, the goal of individual transformation only accomplished so much—rather, it was to coming generations that they entrusted the fulfillment of their social goals. To this end, the need to properly instruct and train children became a pressing one. Bronson Alcott's Temple School in Boston and Catherine Beecher's Hartford Female Seminary in Connecticut are representative of their time and the widespread interest in education. In his classroom, Alcott encouraged Platonic dialogues as a means of teaching, rather than the rote memorization that was then popular in schools. His use of question-and-answer format, his use of parables, and his emphasis on students' self-expression placed him well ahead of his time. Beecher's focus on female education originated in her insistence on women's moral influence: only properly educated women could be trusted to employ this influence wisely and for the betterment of the nation. The Hartford Female Seminary was merely one of her many attempts to educate women for their future role as teachers and arbiters of the national moral culture.

The optimism embedded in this idea of the person as an improvable entity ultimately moved beyond the bounds of the individual self and expanded to include the others with whom the individual interacted. One historian affirmed that "rather than the privilege of the few," philanthropy was "the practice and the prerogative of the many" in the decades immediately preceding the Civil War (McCarthy 3). This outward impulse proved a natural corollary to the initial impulse: once one recognized his own innate worthiness, how could one fail to recognize it in other people?

Some of the main channels of this energy were the benevolent societies that emerged in the 1830s and 1840s. Whether they consisted of different ethnic and racial groups attempting to aid members of their own community, or groups who targeted a specific audience for their efforts, these organizations, often sustained by women's voluntary efforts, provided crucial economic buffers for the poor and destitute of the time. Christian benevolence found a natural object in the idea of the poor, and, during the 1840s, many religious denominations formed associations and organizations to provide aid for the impoverished of their community. These associations relied on a system of volunteers who would visit individual families to assess their needs. One of the earliest formal expressions of this occurred in New York City with the formation of the Association for the Improvement of the Conditions of the Poor in 1843. Concern for children was particularly acute; the Children's Aid Society of New York was formed only ten years later in 1853. In focusing on the poor and the young in urban environments, reformers found it easy to justify the need for social reform.

A significant subset of this concern linked outreach to others with the educational goals promulgated by many reforms. The linkage between Christian benevolence and education reached perhaps its fullest expression in the establishment of schools designed to prepare its pupils for foreign missionary work. Mt. Holyoke, one of the first female institutions of higher education, opened its doors to fulfill precisely this purpose. In time, it became one of the feeder institutions for a larger organization, the American Board of Commissioners for Foreign Missionaries (ABCFM), an agency that supervised the recruitment, organization, and support for evangelical Christian missionaries both domestically and abroad. Chartered in 1812, the ABCFM placed missionaries in India, China, Latin America, and even among Native Americans throughout the nineteenth and early twentieth centuries. In 1860, even amidst the national turmoil of the Civil War, Reverend Dr. Fisher assured his Boston audience that "God educates us to leave the paternal roof for distant homes" in order to join "a great army of missionaries of the Cross" (22). Women, in particular, found missionary work attractive as it gave opportunities for travel, education, and leadership roles that would have been difficult to experience in the United States. In time, women would form the majority of American foreign missionaries.

The zeal of the missionary impulse came a distant second to the work of the antislavery societies. Of all reform and welfare societies during the mid-nineteenth century, these were perhaps the most active and arguably the most influential in terms of national politics. While those who fought for the end of slavery often divided over the means of ending it, they shared a common horror of the system that effectively stripped individuals of their humanity. Prior to the Civil War, activists relied heavily on methods of persuasion. If they could appeal to the individual through reason, logic, and sentiment, they could then persuade others to support their cause. Borrowing from the self-education movement, they adopted lectures, newspapers, and publications as their ammunition. Lectures often proved to be the medium of choice, as individual speakers sought to convince their audiences to support their arguments. In the North, the lecture circuit quickly became the most popular method of promulgating one's individual message. In keeping with the emphasis on individual agency, reformers focused on eradicating the obstacles that kept individuals from expressing their full humanity. William Lloyd Garrison's American Anti-Slavery Association (AAS), founded in 1833, relied on lectures by abolitionists Garrison, Frederick Douglass, William Wells Brown and others both to expose the dangers of slavery and to garner support for their cause.

While many reformers shared an understanding of the necessity of ending slavery, they disagreed over the means to achieve that end. Abolitionists called for an immediate end to slavery, arguing that the system should be abolished immediately. Others, worried about the political, social, and economic consequences of disrupting such an established system of labor, sought to gradually end slavery through the means of legislative measures. This led to fierce disagreements and, eventually, the proliferation of various abolitionist groups. Garrison and his followers formed the AAS in 1833; a group of members split from the AAS in 1840 and created the American and Foreign Antislavery Society as a more politically-focused group. Still others adopted more violent means. John Brown's infamous raid on Harper's Ferry was merely the culmination of efforts by a contingent of reformers who actively sought the end of slavery. Thoreau's eloquent defense of Brown embodied the strong emotions provoked by this radical figure. Thoreau praised Brown as "brave and humane" and publicly shamed the broader American public as ineffective reformers, advocating "that philanthropy which neither shoots me nor liberates me" (Redpath 28, 37). Thoreau's pleas for direct action reflected his own impatience with the lectures, pamphlets and writings aimed at education rather than decisive action.

Black Americans found themselves faced with multiple options and similar frustrations. Not only did they form their own antislavery organizations, but they also promulgated the ideals of a truly non-racist American society. Figures like James Forten, Richard Allen, and Frederick Douglass all sought to establish themselves not just as black Americans, but as knowledgeable and virtuous citizens. For example, in 1855, black activists were instrumental in forming the Equal School Rights Committee in Boston, which led to the integration of Boston's public schools. In 1862, Douglass urged his audiences to support emancipation, crying, "But why, O why should we not abolish slavery now? All admit that it must be abolished at some time. What better time than now can be assigned for that great work?" (n.p.). Such statements revealed both Douglass's faith in the strength of the abolition movement, as well as demonstrating his efforts to constantly push its members to take a more forceful stand. Black women followed his example, building on the structure of religious organizations to push for reform and recognition of their identities as individuals, wives, mothers, and members of the American public sphere. Some turned to literary pursuits to attract an audience and then to persuade their readers; some employed a mixture of autobiography and fiction, such as Harriet Jacobs; others wrote poetry, such as Frances Watkins Harper. Both women employed popular literary techniques of their time, not only to establish themselves as female authors, but as free blacks as well.

White women attracted to the abolitionist movement found themselves applying its principles to their own situations. They drew similarities between the legal definition of slavery and the legal status of women, who lacked representation and once married, were subject to the legal principle of coverture, in which their legal identity was merged with that of their husbands. Elizabeth Cady Stanton, Lucy Stone, Lydia Marie Child, and the Grimké sisters served as prominent examples of this trajectory; their advocacy on behalf of abolitionism led directly to their efforts to address women's status in the United States. In 1848, this impulse was codified in the Declaration of Rights and Sentiments, a result of a convention held at Seneca Falls, New York. Drawing on language similar to that resounding in abolitionist circles, the women argued that gender should not bar women from full participation in the national government. Just as abolitionists argued for an end to slavery because of its effect on both slave and master, so too did these women target the evil effects of women's lack of status. Reflecting the philosophical roots of the movement, Stanton and her colleagues advocated for numerous changes in the legal treatment of women, for women's rights as wives, workers, and mothers, not just for the vote alone. Some historians have suggested that this trajectory of women's activism had a significant impact on American political culture; in her work, Julie Jeffrey argues that women's participation in abolitionist societies helped to create pub- lic culture of "new mass participatory politics" (162). Scholar Nancy Isenberg suggests that "antebellum activists had not only conceived of women's rights in broader terms, but they also developed a rich theoretical tradition that con- tributed in significant ways to a national discourse on constitutional practices in a democracy" (6).

This new attention to the role of women grew in part out of the transforma- tion of nineteenth-century gender norms. As the rise of industry transformed the household from an economic workplace to a private sanctuary, women's actions were redefined as part of the domestic sphere. This ideology, which melded religious belief, economic conditions, and gender stereotypes, associ- ated women's work with the creation and maintenance of the family. As wives and mothers, women were regarded as responsible for the moral tenor of the home. While the association between women and religious emotion could have been regarded as restrictive, women instead turned the rhetoric of the domestic sphere to their advantage. In the North, women used the language of Christian morality to justify their claims for social reform and their criticism of the cur- rent status quo.

Educator and reformer Catharine Beecher offered a striking example of this simultaneous pull-and-push of public activism. Beecher based her career on her identity as a Christian woman, even as she moved far beyond the domestic sphere to encourage the education of women and their training as public school teachers. According to Beecher, "woman is to win every thing by peace and love; by making herself so much respected, esteemed and loved, that to yield to her opinions and to gratify her wishes, will be the free-will offering of the heart" (101). To this end, Beecher denounced the calls for immediate emanci- pation, instead focusing on the influence of the "domestic and social circle" to achieve gradual change.

Beecher's defense of women's domestic focus would have found many allies in the southern part of the United States. In the South, reformers focused less on work itself and more on the nature of social interactions. Southern women turned to reform societies as a way of affirming and marking their class status. For example, in Virginia, reform and welfare societies became a vehicle for white women to exert public pressure. Historian Elizabeth Varon argues that "elite and middle-class women played an active, distinct and evolving role in the political life of the Old South" (1). They used petitions, voluntary associations, appeals and fiction to express their opinions on the salient political issues of the day, including slavery and secession. One primary example was the American Colonization Society, first established in 1816, but primarily active during the 1830s and 1840s. Virginian women promoted the ACS for multiple reasons. It served their own class interests to protect the status quo, but also corresponded to the cultural values of Christian benevolence. By advocating for colonization, these southern women effectively operated as mediators between the nation's cultural regions: drawing on a common gender identity, they sought ways to address slavery in a limited fashion.

The impulse towards reform noted so succinctly by Emerson contained within it an internal paradox. Even as reformers worked to liberate the individual from whatever bonds they characterized as oppressive, the means of doing so often led them to endorse collective solutions. The move from an emphasis on persuasion to legislative enforcement occurred within many charitable organizations during the Civil War itself, most notably the United States Sanitary Commission (USSC). As the war progressed, civilians began to recognize the inefficiency of volunteer organizations rooted in the local level. While the efforts of local leaders and volunteers were appreciated, they often miscarried. One common complaint concerned the waste of resources, such as food, clothing, bedding and medical supplies, which were meant for the soldiers, but languished in railroad depots. Inspired by the thought of the men deprived of the basic necessities, a group of northern elites led by Henry W. Bellows organized the USSC. At the height of its powers, it spread across the North and Midwest acting as a clearinghouse for soldiers and for medical supplies, becoming "the largest, most powerful, and most highly organized philanthropic activity that had ever been seen in America" (Fredrickson 98).

The USSC proved crucial to nurturing the skills of women reformers, many of whom became involved in its work as leaders on the local or city level. The organization allowed them to model the type of benevolent Christianity previously relegated to the domestic sphere on a national stage. Women literally followed the soldiers to the battlefield, acting as nurses, supervisors, letter-writers, and distributors of supplies in military hospitals and camps. The women often referred to their work as an attempt to keep a sense of "civilian" life alive in the soldiers; they saw their role as essential to maintaining the connection between the military men and the home front. They gained experience in institutional bureaucracies, while simultaneously raising their public profile. Their experience "combined grassroots women's activism with centralized access to political authority and created a new political culture for women" (Giesberg 8). After the war, many of them transferred their new expertise to other areas of reform.

The success of the USSC effectively signaled a shift in the nature of reform and welfare societies. By demonstrating the power of centralized authority, it served as a prototype for the numerous welfare organizations that began to emerge in the post-bellum era. In many ways, the Freedmen's Bureau was the culmination of these numerous strands of reform history. The Bureau, created in March 1865, combined the narrowly focused concern for the individual with the economic and political measures enforced by the federal government. The Bureau sought to encourage economic self-sufficiency among the newly freed blacks by establishing farms and plots of land to be cultivated. In addition, it established schools, began to register marriages, served as supervisors and inspectors for existing plantations, and worked to regulate the hours and wages of the freedmen.

In 1864, the report of the Freedmen's Bureau superintendent in Tennessee and Arkansas reported that over two thousand acres of cotton, corn, and vegetables were planted. The sale of the cotton left the population with an estimate of $500 to $2,500 per worker for the season. With the schools, which were often located in cities or farms, the report noted that "soldiers and laborers carry about them their speller or reader and are frequently overheard reciting to each other." The "lady teachers" were praised as "most devoted to their work" (Eaton 68, 69). Schools for the newly emancipated slaves relied on northern women and men who eagerly engaged in the process of collective racial uplift. Viewing education as the primary means of personal liberation, they sought to provide their pupils with the tools they viewed as necessary to truly emancipate them from the legacy of slavery. Historian Jacqueline Jones argues that "their activities and problems reveal not only the strength of the neo-abolitionist impulse as well as the limits of liberal reform, but they also incorporate the three Rs of mid-nineteenth century American history: race, reform, and Reconstruction" (3). According to Jones, black attendance at these schools was in essence political participation, symbolizing "defiance to white authority and an expression of community self interest" (3). Schools, hospitals, jobs and labor contracts, were all part of the Freedmen's Bureau's mission in the southern states. In this sense, the Bureau embodied the multi-faceted nature of Civil War-era reform societies. As an institution, it regulated matters both public and private, involving itself in practically every facet of an individual's life. This encompassing approach reflected the organization's roots in antebellum reform and the lessons learned during the war itself.

The new emphasis on formal organizations as a means of encouraging reform proved to be an enduring one. In the years to come, most notably among women, reform and welfare societies would emerge at a rapid rate. The skills that women such as Mary Livermore and Jane Hoge acquired during the Civil War proved integral to the efforts to achieve their goals in the post-bellum era. Livermore, for example, leveraged her work during the war into a successful post-war career as a journalist and suffragist. As one historian observes, "these women of the war generation created a model organizational structure for women's organizations in the postwar era" (Giesberg 7). The Women's Christian Temperance Union, the National Women's Suffrage Association and the settlement house movement all drew upon the experience and legacies of activists who emerged from the Civil War with a new understanding of how to meld individual transformation with the demands of collective action. Black Americans similarly benefited from this experience. But due to the political backlash of Reconstruction, their path followed a different route. Even as the male and female white reformers reached new levels of influence in the postwar era, black Americans increasingly focused on building within their own communities. While women such as Mary Church Terrell and Anna Julia Cooper built success as black clubwomen, they fought a battle to define themselves and their work on two fronts—both as women reformers and as activist members of the black community.

The Civil War transformed the size, scope, and pattern of American welfare and reform efforts. Brought about by the insistence on an individual's right to respect and dignity, the national struggle highlighted the tension at the heart of the movement—the fight between moral suasion and political action. Through reform societies, many of those who lacked a formal role in the national government found ways to accomplish political action. Women and black Americans found reform and welfare societies to be the most effective means of channeling their multiple voices into powerful instruments of public change. As historian Kathleen McCarthy notes, these groups "assumed the power to define by creating institutions ... that shaped the 'public interpretation of reality," and indeed, had a profound impact on the modern United States (193). McCarthy argues that the triumph of the North in the Civil War effectively signaled the end of an era, because "wartime philanthropy helped to forge a more comprehensive version of civil society—and citizenship" and "swept away many of the vestiges of patriarchal philanthropy, opening expanded opportunities for independent social action both by white women and African Americans" (200). Through their concern for others, those citizens who existed on the margins of American political power were able to generate power, influence, and authority for themselves and for the improvement of the nation.

Other historians have challenged this optimistic narrative about the legacy of these reform and welfare societies. Rather than opening the doors to political participation by these marginal groups, some have suggested that in fact, the war strengthened the barriers against full participation, with Reconstruction restructuring the obstacles that kept women, blacks, and the poor from full involvement in the public world. As these reformers moved away from their religious motivations and as Emerson's transcendental definition of the individual gave way to the pragmatism of William James and his contemporaries in the late nineteenth century, the spark that lit the reform movement grew dim as its focus was divided. James himself astutely noted that individuals needed to retain the vision of the ideal, criticizing the city of Chautauqua (the site of numerous reform-minded assemblies) as "this atrocious harmlessness of all things" and suggesting that "what our human emotions seem to require is the sight of the struggle going on" (288, 289). Turning the reform impulse on its head, he argued that reform was not necessary for the good of the broader community, nor should it hope to transform the world. Rather, the reform impulse, the striving for the ideal, was, to use his phrase, "what made life significant" (286). Reform benefited the individual more than it benefited the community by providing the citizen with "the solid meaning of life" (302). Although his predecessors might have quarreled with James' conclusions, this statement reflected the central role that reform had come to play in American culture and in the definition of an American citizen. In that sense, reformers would have felt that their various missions had succeeded.

## Further Reading

Abzug, Robert. *Cosmos Crumbling: American Reform and the Religious Imagination*. New York: Oxford University Press, 1994.

Beecher, Catharine. *An Essay on Slavery and Abolitionism with reference to the Duty of American Females*. Philadelphia: Henry Perkins, 134 Chestnut Street, Perkins & Marvin, Boston. 1837.

Bremner, Robert H. *The Public Good: Philanthropy and Welfare in the Civil War Era*. New York: Knopf, 1980.

Douglass, Frederick. "The Future of the Negro People of the Slave States." *Douglass' Monthly*, March 1862.

Eaton, John. *Report of the General Superintendent of Freedmen, Volume 1*. Memphis: no imprint, 1865.

Eggleston, G.K. "The Work of Relief Societies During the Civil War." *The Journal of Negro History* 14:3 (1929): 272–99.

Eiselein, Gregory. *Literature and Humanitarian Reform in the Civil War Era*. Bloomington: Indiana University Press, 1996.

Emerson, Ralph Waldo. *The Works of Ralph Waldo Emerson, Volume 4*. Boston: Jefferson Press, 1883.

Fisher, Samuel Ware. *God's Purpose in Planting the American Church*. Boston: T.R. Marvin, 1860.

Frederickson, George. *The Inner Civil War; Northern Intellectuals and the Crisis of the Union*. New York: Harper & Row, 1965.

Giesberg, Judith Ann. *Civil War Sisterhood: The U.S. Sanitary Commission and Women's Politics in Transition*. Boston: Northeastern University Press, 2000.

Isenberg, Nancy. *Sex and citizenship in antebellum America*. Chapel Hill: University of North Carolina Press, 1998.

James, William. *Pragmatism and Other Writings*. New York: Penguin, 2000

Jeffrey, Julie Roy. *The Great Silent Army of Abolitionism: Ordinary Women in the Antislavery Movement*. Chapel Hill: University of North Carolina Press, 1998.

Jones, Jacqueline. *Soldiers of Light and Love: Northern Teachers and Georgia Blacks, 1865–1873*. Chapel Hill: University of North Carolina Press, 1980.

McCarthy, Kathleen D. *American Creed: Philanthropy and the Rise of Civil Society, 1700–1865*. Chicago: University of Chicago Press, 2003.

Redpath, James. *Echoes of Harper's Ferry*. Boston: Thayer and Eldridge, 1860.

Varon, Elizabeth. *We Mean to Be Counted: White Women and Politics in Antebellum Virginia*. Chapel Hill: University of North Carolina Press, 1998.

# PART IV

# Health and Education

# 11

# HIGHER EDUCATION

*A.J. Angulo and Kimberly Cook*

Thomas Jefferson once described the differences between North and South in the starkest of terms. The North, he said, was "cool, sober, laborious, independent ... interested, chicaning" (McCardell 13). He gave all the rational, systematic, and, some might say, masculine and untrustworthy traits to Northerners. As for Southerners, they were "fiery, voluptuary, indolent, unsteady ... generous, candid" (13). The South, he argued, was a stormy cauldron of passions. Jefferson was no stranger to reading the character of a people or of a place. He wrote voluminously about his experiences in various parts of the United States and Europe. His final reading of America was that it was a country divided, with the North guided by reason and the South driven by emotions.

Jefferson's characterizations relate not only to tensions between the sections that led to the Civil War. They also relate to higher education during the war. How scholars and teachers on each side approached the war and how the war ultimately impacted their work offers insight into what Jefferson once read into the nature and character of American society.

If the South was "fiery," as Jefferson put it, then what about southern professors and students? Many became effective "fire-eaters," promoting the war effort and the cause of Confederacy on their campuses. Charleston, home to the opening battle of the Civil War at Fort Sumter, was also home to the College of Charleston and its war-promoting faculty. Officials met in 1861 to allow the senior class a "leave of absence for an indefinite period" given the "present circumstances." Professors awarded degrees to some of them, not because they had completed courses and examinations, but because of "meritorious engagement in the service of the state" (Easterby 146–47). Most Charleston faculty remained in their teaching posts even when the student body dropped to a total of seven, but one professor of mathematics, and later natural history, John

McCrady, joined a company of his brothers to fight for the South. Franklin College (later the University of Georgia) followed a similar path with its share of fire-eating faculty who stirred student passions about the war. Joseph Henry Lumpkin lectured on the U.S. Constitution and on the "Glorious South, cut loose from the North, with King Cotton and Free Trade" (Coulter 307). Faculty there also decided to grant degrees to any student called to military service, regardless of academic performance and completion of coursework and exams. At Davidson College in North Carolina, faculty initially responded tepidly to the idea of having students join the Confederate Army. As the war progressed, entire classes were called to battle as Professor William Bigham Lynch organized a company of student volunteers. In the same manner as Charleston and Franklin, Davidson faculty granted degrees to seniors who would have finished their studies were it not for the "crisis" (Shaw 104–05). The University of North Carolina faculty adopted the same practice of granting degrees to students who enlisted and even created courses on military tactics to prepare the new recruits, as did Trinity College (later Duke University) and Emory College in Atlanta.

Southern faculty did more than ease requirements for degrees and offer military-oriented tactics in support of the war. They also helped establish cadet corps units that formalized student preparation for combat. These corps grew out of student and faculty desire to do their part in defending the region, as well as reflecting the patterns of pride and honor characteristic of antebellum southern life. Acceptance into this campus culture meant adherence and conformity to the values undergirding southern nationalism. The formation of cadet corps and subsequent pressure to join these units under threat of dishonor intersected with these values. Few students who understood honor and dishonor in the context of "the greatest dread," that of "public humiliation," or as "total conditions" like "mastery and slavery," as some scholars have put it, would have selected dishonor or, worse, being branded an enemy of the state (Wyatt-Brown viii). For these reasons, many southern institutions of higher education chose to convert their campuses into military academies. The University of Virginia, according to one student, had become "little more than a military school" with three companies drilling "in front of the Rotunda ... every evening" (Pace 104). Trinity organized its own "Trinity Guard" and a military department to prepare students for war during the vacation period. The University of Mississippi called together a cadet corps within a month of Fort Sumter and trained by parading their bravery and honor around the Oxford community.

Southern students hardly needed much prodding from their professors. Student enthusiasm was high when it came to supporting the war and the Confederacy. Franklin College students, for instance, cheered when they heard about the caning of Charles Sumner on the floor of Congress. They organized a fund to purchase another cane for Preston Brooks. One Franklin student, Thomas

R.R. Cobb, talked of slavery as "worth the price of the dissolution of the Union," while another was "thrilled" about the war and "wished to get at the invader!" (Coulter 307). Still others in Athens felt so wrapped up in the fervor of war that they could hardly wait for their chance at combat: "I remember the first time I heard 'Dixie' [I] felt like I could take a cornstalk, get on Mason and Dixon's line and whip the whole Yankee nation" (Coulter 308).

Similar levels of eagerness to participate in the war appeared across the South. Students at Davidson went home to join companies from their home states. Some left by foot; others purchased horses and wagons to make their way back. With the hemorrhaging of college students, Davidson began to resemble a grammar school and to rely increasingly on an affiliated feeder school for survival. University of Mississippi students took pride in joining the 11th Mississippi Volunteer Infantry Regiment as the "University Greys." When an area farmer complained that he had heard one of his pigs squeal when it was shot by students during rifle practice, they responded proudly that "if a University Grey shoots a hog … it doesn't squeal" (Sansing 106–07). That sense of pride took many of them straight to the frontlines with dire consequences; Gettysburg became a cemetery for almost every University Grey who participated. Students at the University of North Carolina left almost *en masse* in their hurry to enlist. Over 1,000 students and alumni entered the army during the war. More than half of Trinity College's student population disappeared as a result of departures during the first year of the war. Their enrollments dropped from 212 to 82.

Not all southern university officials promoted the war effort. In the lead up to the first battles, some officials who had either come from northern states or who weren't swept up by southern honor and nationalism attempted to temper the drive for war. William T. Sherman, famed Union general during the war, served as "superintendent," or president, of Louisiana Seminary of Learning (later Louisiana State University) shortly before the conflict started. He found students there increasingly restless as sectional tensions increased. Sherman stayed on as long as he could, "solely for the pay," and remained optimistic to his students and colleagues that disunion would never occur (Hirshson 75). In private correspondence to family, he worried that his Ohio origins raised eyebrows on and off campus. Sherman resigned and left for his home state a few weeks after a cadet threatened him "with a loaded pistol" and after questions about his loyalty to Louisiana and the region began to emerge (Hirshson 76).

At Washington College in Lexington, Virginia, President George Junkin found himself increasingly at odds with the student body over a series of secessionist flags raised on campus. Junkin's multiple attempts at removing and destroying the student-raised flags created an uproar, winning him such dishonorable labels as "Pennsylvania Abolitionist" and "Lincoln Junkin" (Pace 99). His students submitted a petition demanding that the flag be raised and emphasizing that opposition to the "old Mother State" would be interpreted as "treason." Junkin found little support from the faculty, so he packed his bags and left for Pennsylvania. And at the University of Mississippi, Chancellor Frederick A.P. Barnard pleaded with town and gown not to hand their boys over to the Confederate Army. He wanted parents to keep their sons in school and petitioned the state's governor not to put students into units. Although his petitions fell on the deaf ears of the governor and the students, Confederacy President Jefferson Davis agreed. Sending these boys to war, suggested Davis, was like "grinding the seed corn of the republic" (Sansing 106). Not long after the fall of Sumter, Barnard went the way of Sherman and Junkin by packing his belongings, heading northward, and eventually assuming the presidency of Columbia University.

A year into the war, the Confederacy discarded any reservations it might have had over whether to use college students in combat. Southern congressional leaders instituted a military draft, the first conscription in U.S. history that required the service of all white men between the ages of eighteen and thirty-five. Doing so nearly doubled the size of the Confederate army, from approximately 250,000 to 450,000 soldiers. Union generals recognized the impact the draft had across all segments of the southern community, but, at times, took special interest in student combat units. Both George B. McClellan and William W. Averell responded to captured southern students by releasing these prisoners and telling them to "go back to your books and study your best" (Pace 108). In some cases, these southern students had been captured by northern students who were of the same fraternities and, as one prisoner described it, "made their stay very pleasant and comfortable" (Pace 107). In other cases, Union generals made a point to punish southern student units for their participation in the war. After a Virginia Military Institute (VMI) unit helped with the trouncing of Union forces in a major battle in New Market, Virginia, Union forces sought revenge. When northern soldiers reached VMI's campus in subsequent skirmishes, they got their chance for revenge and burned campus buildings to the ground.

As southern faculty, students and leaders pressed forward with war, many physical campuses like VMI faced fire, destruction, closure, and conversion into hospitals. This shut down centers of intellectual activity in the South. One of the first institutions to close its doors due to the war was the University of Mississippi. It remained closed from fall of 1861 to the end of the war. Emory couldn't continue past the summer of 1861, but reopened immediately after the war. South Carolina College (later the University of South Carolina) closed in 1862. It too reopened after the final battles were over. Franklin's campus was closed in 1864. Davidson dismissed faculty and students shortly before being visited by William T. Sherman's famous march. The College of Charleston moved their most valuable documents, artifacts, and other possessions to a remote location in Camden, South Carolina. It was a prescient move that preserved records that would have been destroyed in battles that tore into the campus. Efforts to rebuild the college continued for years after 1865.

During the war, some of these colleges became places of healing. The Confederate government seized control of the University of Mississippi and converted it into a hospital. From 1861 to 1862, patient numbers rose from a few hundred to approximately 2,000 who were tended to by 85 slaves serving as orderlies at the hospital. Franklin's facilities became an infirmary for soldiers with eye injuries. These cases suggest that the purpose of southern campuses dramatically changed during the war. Their close proximity to the battlefront made southern colleges and universities attractive sites to military leaders on both sides of the conflict.

Northern colleges and universities were far less affected by the heat of war. The fiery rhetoric as well as the fire and destruction visited on southern campuses did not have an equivalent in the North. Free from direct experience with bullets and bayonets, northern campuses could respond to the idea of war from what Jefferson would describe as the "cool" and "sober" perspective. Northern professors engaged in a rhetoric of suppression of rebellion and freedom for slaves, rather than an eagerness to defeat the South or to defend the glory of the North. Oberlin College's commencement exercises included a resolution that it was the "duty of the American people to demand of the Government immediately to abolish Slavery in the seceded States by the exercise of the war-power" (Fletcher 878). Faculty at Oberlin consented to student enlistments within this context and moved to repeal a prohibition at the institution against participation in military companies. Mount Holyoke prepared their students to see themselves as the "true army of occupation." Local pastor and trustee member Hiram Mead meant they should be "Yankee schoolteachers" who would do the real work of holding "the conquered territory" (Cole 148). At Williams College, faculty delivered instruction to undergraduates in the "military arts." They put students through drilling for at least an hour every day starting in November 1862. Dudley Field, an influential alumnus and benefactor, believed that "all peaceful pursuits must accommodate themselves to the demands of war" (Rudolph 205–06). He had much to do with the introduction of "military art" in the college's curriculum.

Unlike their southern counterparts, northern faculty members were far less inclined to give degrees without completing course work. At least two institutions—Columbia University and Rutgers—did make this an occasional practice, but few others followed. Yale faculty resisted giving any special status for those who left as a result of the war. "Those students who leave College to serve in the army," they stated, "can have a regular dismissal on the usual conditions, but cannot have a leave of absence" (Kelley 197). Earlham College, a Quaker institution, wanted to restrict any celebratory mention of the war. The Board of Trustees recommended that "the production and reading of essays eulogistic of wars and warriors, or which, in any way, tend to cultivate the spirit of war, be discouraged" (Hamm 55). Earlham's pacifist, Quaker tradition became explicitly institutionalized during the Civil War.

Some of the more hawkish faculty at northern and borderline institutions could be found at Rutgers, the University of Maryland, and Missouri's Columbia College. Rutgers President Theodore Frelinghuysen was a full supporter of the Union Army and the war effort. He promised the governor of New Jersey in a campus address that "when he wants more soldiers ... he can have one hundred able-bodied and able-throated men from Rutgers College on one day's notice" (Demarest 388). At Maryland, a very large presence of Southerners created a stormy campus climate. The professors there refused to fly the U.S. flag at commencement at more than one of these ceremonies during the war. Union Army officials raised the flag against their wishes. Furor over faculty "disloyalty" appeared in the local papers. One Maryland paper reported that they should be required to "take an oath of allegiance" (Callcott 154–55). In Missouri, Columbia experienced a similar "loyalty" concern. Raids from Confederate soldiers made this a pressing campus issue that led to a call for all faculty to support the Union. After Union troops occupied the campus, faculty were asked to support the U.S. Constitution and to refuse to give "aid and comfort to the enemies ... during the present civil war" (Batterson 41).

Students on northern campuses held a wide range of sentiments toward the war. Many felt disengaged, distracted, or uneasy about it. College of the Holy Cross may have been home to some of the most detached students. According to one observer, "it really is striking what little interest the boys take in the war. They seem to have no enthusiasm at all.... I can assure you if you may judge of the sentiments of the parents by the sons, there are not many here who would prosecute this war" (Kuzniewski 114). Yale students—with O.C. Marsh, William Graham Sumner, and J.W. Gibbs among them—approached the war with a similar degree of detachment. Out of four hundred, a mere thirteen Yale students enlisted in the war in 1861. By 1863, recognition of "Yalies" serving in the war effort virtually ceased. The campus literary magazine barely mentioned the war and ceremonies honoring enlisted students disappeared.

Oberlin College students were more distracted and uneasy than disengaged. A total of 48 forty-eight enlisted in the first company that was formed and 150 more followed. One of these, Lucien Warner, wrote: "I cannot study. I cannot sleep. I cannot work." His mind was consumed with all the campus talk and debate about "WAR! and volunteers are the only topics of conversation or thought." Studies themselves had turned into a "mere form" (Fletcher 845). After Oberlin's E.B. Stiles enlisted, the sense of distraction turned to unease with the call to military service and the duties required. "I begin to realize," he ruminated, "that a soldier is nothing but a machine and is supposed to know nothing, or care nothing" (848). The remaining students at the college followed political developments closely, debating Lincoln's early positions on slavery, celebrating what they believed was the late but critical Emancipation Proclamation, putting Jefferson Davis on mock trial and finding him "guilty of High Treason" (884).

To varying degrees, northern students tended to follow the Oberlin pattern of treating war topics as an intellectual exercise in the politics of secession, the requirements of military service, and the realities of war. Princeton students certainly did, with one important exception. They were similar to Oberlin students in closely tracking political developments, and yet different in that approximately half of the student body was from the South on the eve of the Civil War. In early 1861, Southerners quietly began leaving the campus and keeping secret the relationships with their northern friends. Respectful was the tone of the Princeton campus to its southern population as they left. After Fort Sumter, Princeton's president created a fund for southern students to facilitate their travel home. They were given a formal farewell and celebratory send off with live music. The only recorded instance in which passions flared at Princeton was over the words of a southern sympathizer once the war had begun. This student, observers recalled, gloated over a specific Confederate victory in the battlefield. Three other Princeton students subjected the sympathizer to a "ducking." The three were suspended for their behavior, but were celebrated by the town with a parade.

Higher levels of student engagement appeared in Ann Arbor and Cambridge. At the University of Michigan, the student response to the war was almost immediate: fifty-three graduating students left soon after graduation exercises, two-thirds of the medical students served as surgeons and assistants, while undergraduates were taken as stewards. By the fall of 1861, half of the student population had enlisted and established drill companies. Although some students considered Michigan weather too cold for outside drills, U.S. government funds supplied a tent-like structure along with uniforms and guns. The tent became the student company headquarters. Once the war began, three student companies formed and were called for duty. During the war, each graduating class lost approximately 50 percent of its students. At Harvard, student James Savage, Jr. and his colleagues began drilling with local companies within days of Fort Sumter. They became a few of the 1,311 Harvard students and alumni who enlisted and served in the Union Army. Ten percent of them never returned from battle. Savage's regiment made its way to Cedar Mountain, Virginia, and fought in the clash that decimated one-third of the troops in his cohort. Captured by Confederate soldiers, Savage was carted back to the University of Virginia, which had been turned into a hospital. He became, like many others, a northern student-turned-soldier who died of wounds on a southern campus.

Northern colleges and universities—their facilities, buildings, and purposes—were virtually untouched by the ravages of war when compared with their southern counterparts. At many institutions, it was business as usual with fewer students, although some smaller ones closed due to lack of funding or very low student numbers. St. Joseph's College, a fairly young Philadelphia institution, closed in 1863 and reopened after 1865. In Boston, the Massachusetts

Institute of Technology was attempting to get its start when the war intervened. William Barton Rogers, conceptual founder of the Institute, successfully petitioned and received a charter to establish the Institute just days before the outbreak of war. Essential funding for building the Institute dried up and forced the idea of MIT into hibernation until the first classes were held in 1864. But these instances of closure or delay were not the norm. Some northern institutions, like the University of Michigan, experienced growth during the war. Two buildings were constructed for the campus: one for law, the other for medicine. Vassar's president received authorization to make $2,500 worth of library purchases. Williams raised ten times that amount for an endowed professorship in astronomy and Rutgers concluded a campaign that raised $130,000 for an endowment—all of which occurred during the Civil War. Northern campuses, by and large, were free from worry about enemy soldiers appearing at their gates. This had obvious implications for creating very different conditions for faculty, students, and campuses in both sections of the country.

But the most telling difference between regions, and the most important Civil War era development for higher education, was the enactment of the Land-Grant Act of 1862. The federal bill was hardly a new idea when it was passed, but it was one that did not gain traction until after the southern states left the Union. Vermont Senator Justin Morrill had talked for years about the need to establish federal support for agriculture and mechanics education. When Morrill successfully pushed the bill through Congress and received Lincoln's signature in July 1862, the South was shut out of the first federal support for American higher education. The South's resistance to the Act before the war and its inability to access the funds until after the war meant that northern campuses would receive unprecedented support at the very time southern campuses were under greatest duress. As mandated by the bill, states were granted 30,000 acres of land in western territories for each of their congressional representatives. Consequently, the formula favored the more populous states, which received larger appropriations. Morrill's bill allowed for states to then sell, rent, or otherwise derive an income from the scrip to finance the establishment of a new institution or to support existing ones. The legislation, however, required that those institutions receiving the funds must promote the education of agriculturists and mechanics of the state.

The Land-Grant Act ultimately distributed over 17 million acres to various states of the Union. It provided a significant source of stability for northern institutions of higher education, although it was not always clear which new or established institutions would receive funds from the act. Established institutions became fiercely competitive with one another to assure their institutions would clinch the land-grant funds. Such was the case in both Pennsylvania and Massachusetts. Pennsylvania's Farmer's High School changed its name to the Agricultural College of Pennsylvania in May of 1862, just prior to the passing of Morrill's bill in hopes of edging out the neighboring private Polytechnic

College of the State of Pennsylvania in being able to have a legitimate claim to the funds. This tactic proved successful and the Agricultural College of Pennsylvania was awarded all funds from the grant. A similar situation arose in Massachusetts between the newly formed Massachusetts Institute of Technology and Harvard University, the oldest institution of higher education in the United States. Both institutions insisted they were deserving of the grant; both had proposed courses in agricultural or mechanical science. In the end, a state-level committee decided to use the appropriations to establish a separate and independent agricultural and mechanical school, with the remainder divided between MIT and Harvard. The new land-grant school became the University of Massachusetts.

Students, faculty, and leaders on both sides of the Mason Dixon line—from VMI to MIT—responded to the Civil War crisis with the characteristics Jefferson once attributed to each region. Although painting southern and northern traits with broad strokes, his views capture well the campus culture that could be found on both sides of the conflict. The South's fire-eating rhetoric in antebellum newspapers and political speeches spilled over into the classroom and student halls. With Sherman and others cutting large, fiery swaths through the South, these campuses saw more than rhetoric. They often fell victim to serious destruction. In the North, students and faculty focused less on glory, pride, revenge, and defense; rather, they questioned, debated, and took the cool, sober approach Jefferson had identified decades before. This might have been due to the nature and character of the region. It might also have been partly because these campuses stood at a greater physical distance from any battlefields.

The successful passage and implementation of Morrill's Land-Grant Act highlights these important sectional differences. Northern schools competed for unprecedented levels of federal support while southern campuses were closed, burned, or turned into military outposts. The North welcomed federal support for higher learning. Southern states, or at least their politicians and leaders, rejected the idea. As northern colleges and universities received a significant boost, the South lagged behind. Northern institutions put federal funds to work for the expansion of their campuses in their effort to promote mechanical and agricultural studies. Southern higher education, meanwhile, followed a fire-eating path, succumbed to the devastation and destruction visited upon their institutions by the war, and did not fully participate in this milestone of American higher education history until long after the Civil War had come and gone.

## Further Reading

Angulo, A. J. *William Barton Rogers and the Idea of MIT.* Baltimore: Johns Hopkins University Press, 2009.

Batterson, Paulina A. *Columbia College: 150 Years of Courage, Commitment, and Change.* Columbia: University of Missouri Press, 2001.

Callcott, George H. *A History of the University of Maryland*. Baltimore: Maryland Historical Society, 1966.

Cole, Arthur Charles. *A Hundred Years of Mount Holyoke College: The Evolution of an Educational Ideal*. New Haven: Yale University Press, 1940.

Coulter, E. Merton. *College Life in the Old South*. New York: Macmillan Co., 1928.

Demarest, William H. S. *A History of Rutgers College, 1766–1924*. New Brunswick: Rutgers College, 1924.

Easterby, J. H. *A History of the College of Charleston, Founded 1770*. Charleston: Trustees of College of Charleston, 1935.

Fletcher, Robert Samuel. *A History of Oberlin College from Its Foundation through the Civil War. Vol. 2*. Oberlin: Oberlin College, 1943.

Hamm, Thomas D. *Earlham College: A History, 1847–1997*. Bloomington: Indiana University Press, 1997.

Hirshson, Stanley P. *The White Tecumseh: A Biography of William T. Sherman*. New York: John Wiley & Sons, 1997.

Kelley, Brooks Mather. *Yale: A History*. New Haven: Yale University Press, 1974.

Kuzniewski, Anthony J. *Thy Honored Name: A History of the College of the Holy Cross, 1843–1994*. Washington, DC: Catholic University of America Press, 1999.

McCardell, John. *The Idea of a Southern Nation: Southern Nationalists and Southern Nationalism, 1830–1860*. New York: W.W. Norton, 1979.

Pace, Robert F. *Halls of Honor: College Men in the Old South*. Baton Rouge: Louisiana State University Press, 2004.

Rudolph, Frederick. *Mark Hopkins and the Log: Williams College, 1836–1872*. New Haven: Yale University Press, 1956.

Sansing, David G. *The University of Mississippi: A Sesquicentennial History*. Jackson: University Press of Mississippi, 1999.

Shaw, Cornelia Rebekah. *Davidson College: Intimate Facts*. New York: Fleming Revell Press, 1923.

Wyatt-Brown, Bertram. *Honor and Violence in the Old South*. New York: Oxford University Press, 1986.

# 12

# MILITARY SCHOOLS

*Bradford A. Wineman*

During the two decades preceding the Civil War, military education enjoyed a huge success in the United States, particularly in the southern states. After the establishment of the nation's first state-supported military school, the Virginia Military Institute, in 1839, an estimated ninety-six military colleges were founded throughout the slaveholding states between 1840 and 1860. The North, which was home to the nation's oldest private military college, the American Literary, Scientific and Military Academy (ALSMA) at Norwich, Vermont, did not embrace military education to the same extent as the South and only established twelve such schools during this time period. All of these institutions, however, were built upon the pedagogical foundation of the nation's first military school, the United States Military Academy, founded in 1802 to formally educate and train the officers of the United States Army. The structure, which consisted of a unique curriculum and disciplinary system, was created by one of its most celebrated superintendents, Colonel Sylvanus Thayer, and became the template for the increasing number of military schools that opened during the antebellum period, almost exclusively in the South.

There is no singular explanation why military schools experienced such a meteoric rise in popularity during the antebellum years. But much can be traced to the distinctiveness of the educational environment that these academies offered young men, as opposed to that of the more traditional civilian colleges. Many of civilian institutions had become infamous for the behavior of their adolescent students (drinking, gambling, and womanizing) in the absence of parental supervision. Academy cadets, on the other hand, lived in a regimented system centered on the concept of *in loco parentis* with the entirety of their daily activities arranged according to a strict military schedule. This rigid system of discipline reinforced the philosophy of instilling specific traits within each cadet: self-control, responsibility, contentiousness and patriotism. Proponents of military education lauded the system for shaping the "whole" man—not just in strength of mind but strength of character and imbuing him with the skills, as well as the values necessary to succeed in adult life.

Regardless of their martial character and structure, southern states created these institutions, ironically, for the purpose of the betterment of civilian society, not for military preparation. The military academies offered a more modern and practical curriculum focusing on engineering, mathematics and the hard sciences as opposed to conventional university classes that maintained curriculum concentrating on languages, classics and philosophy. This more functional education, coupled with the inculcation of the values of service, duty and self-sacrifice, gave military schools the unique function of educating a rising middle class: teachers, engineers, merchants, and other professional occupations for their respective states. Military schools also extended this opportunity, unlike their civilian counterparts, to a broader segment of the male population. The academies sought out young men of great intellectual potential but limited financial means to attend their schools with the state government paying their tuition. With the curriculum crafted toward developing practically skilled professionals and a disciplinary system that created a sense of service and industry, both politicians and taxpayers supported these institutions as means to improve their states and local communities both socially and economically. The recognition for the broader good of the population built the public support needed to procure the public funding to maintain the military schools in days when government-supported education was in its infancy.

Aside from their economic impact, military academies generated profound social phenomena. All cadets wore the same clothing, endured Spartan living conditions and handed over to their superintendents whatever personal money they brought with them (which they only had access to with his permission). This leveled the disparity in social classes, which was of particular necessity given the number of poorer cadets attending with state-funded tuition. With all students dressed alike, conforming to the same grooming standards and forced to follow a uniform set of behavioral rules, distinction between social classes was nearly non-existent—a unique egalitarianism contrasting much of the South's cultural identity, which rested on the construct of a stratified social class system. Each individual cadet sacrificed his own individual freedoms while embodying a democratic construct rarely duplicated in any other institution in the antebellum slaveholding culture.

Rising sectional tensions of the 1850s encouraged the establishment of even more military schools and civilian institutions began to teach courses in military studies and create drill companies among student bodies. The volatile political climate drove the academies to take on a noticeably more martial configuration, while other civilian colleges, such as the University of Alabama, converted completely to become military institutions. In 1859, the VMI Corps of Cadets served as the escort of Virginia Governor Henry Wise at the execution of abolitionist John Brown, with Superintendent Francis H. Smith giving the final command at the gallows. South Carolina Military Academy (SCMA, later renamed the Citadel) cadets also participated in the inauguration of the war by firing one of the first shots on Fort Sumter from a shore battery in Charleston, South Carolina, in April 1861.

The growing sectional crisis also had profound effects on America's national military academy at West Point. As each state from the Union was represented in the cadet ranks, the corps became a microcosm for broader nationwide political controversy. Many of the political issues of the day became common topics of discourse at West Point, either in formal debate or in private conversation between students from the North and South. After the first states left the Union during the winter of 1860-61, the corps endured numerous resignations, many became tearful farewells, as several popular cadets left their comrades in order to serve their now seceded states. By the time of Fort Sumter, nearly all the Southern cadets and professors had departed, drastically reducing the numbers at the academy. Superintendent Major Alexander Hamilton Bowman then struggled to keep the remaining students (and faculty) functioning in light of all of the resignations to accept commissions in the volunteer army being raised to subdue the rebellion.

Once the South seceded from the Union, several confederate state governors called upon their military schools to provide cadets to train the thousands of raw recruits of state military forces. The state governments had little difficulty in finding volunteers to fill their regimental rosters. The challenge instead lay in how to prepare them most expediently for combat. Few in the South had greater mastery of basic drill and military movements than the cadets at the military academies. Drill had become a cornerstone of their daily activity at their respective academies, not so much for the perfection of violence, but for its value in applying obedience, precision, teamwork, and leadership. Cadets traditionally drilled in basic marching and manual of arms daily and concluded the duty day with an evening dress parade.

As early as January 1861, the governor of South Carolina organized a battalion of SCMA cadets to augment and train the state's forces. He moved them to various camps throughout Charleston so the cadets could provide instruction in basic drill and ceremony to the inexperienced recruits. Cadets from the Georgia Military Institute (GMI) assembled in late April in Marietta to train a regiment that GMI Superintendent Francis W. Capers had organized in the town. The corps then moved on to Camp McDonald in Big Shanty where they drilled a larger group of "four regiments of infantry, two artillery batteries and a squadron of cavalry" (Livingston 52). Superintendent Landon C. Garland chose to divide his cadets into small cadres and distribute them to camps throughout Alabama, eventually having his students prepare nearly 12,000 new Confederate soldiers by the summer. When their native Virginia seceded, the

Virginia Military Institute sent 185 cadets to Camp Lee in the capital of Richmond where large crowds had gathered to watch the spectacle of the teenage military students training grown men twice their age with noticeable vigor. One Confederate soldier wrote home about his training experience with his VMI drillmaster:

> I was three and thirty years old, a born invalid, whose habit has been to rise late, bathe leisurely and eat breakfast after everybody else was done. To get up at dawn to the sound of fife and drum, to wash my face in a hurry in a tin basin, wipe on a wet towel and go forth with a suffocates skin, and a sense of uncleanliness to be drilled by a fat little cadet, young enough to be my son, of the VMI, that indeed, was a miser. How I hated that little cadet! He was always so wide-awake, so clean, so interested in the drill; his coattails were so short and sharp and his hands looked so big in white gloves. He made me sick.
>
> *(Couper 107)*

By the end of June, Francis H. Smith estimated that his corps had trained nearly 20,000 recruits in the Confederate capital.

But once the training was over, superintendents had to contend with a new challenge: keeping their schools open. As the armies prepared to leave camp to being their respective campaigns, each military school endured a flood of resignations and desertions. The allure of war's glory and adventure was too much to keep them attentive to their studies. Meanwhile at West Point, cadets from both northern and southern states made the "bitter choice" to resign their cadetships in order to offer their services to their respective "nations," with many of these departures resulting in tearful farewells for young men who had spent their formative years as classmates and friends but who now would be enemies (Morrison 127).

Attempting to educate adolescent males in the wake of an impending military conflict, often proved distracting for the faculties of the military academies. Many of the schools held informal graduations that summer for their senior cadets who remained long enough to receive their diplomas. They had an equally difficult time preventing their faculty members from joining the army, as nearly all were themselves graduates of military academies and in high demand for their skills and experiences. One by one, the South's military schools were forced to close due to lack of both students and faculty as the boards of trustees placed the needs of the Confederate army before the operation of their institutions. Some superintendents, like VMI's Smith, exemplified this prioritization by writing recommendations for their own graduating cadets and alumni for commands and commissions in the army.

Statistics do not exist accounting for all southern military school alumni and their service but those available for more famous institutions provide an example for their contributions overall. SCMA provided 193 men to the Confederate

the fiscal realities of war-torn state governments with even fewer resources to offer. Administrators attempted to beg, borrow, and steal from any sources they could find to provide the basic necessities for their cadets and staff, while others preached the practice of conservation to get the most out of what few amenities they could procure. State governments typically diverted their most basic resources, such as food, fuel, uniforms, weapons and ammunition, to the armies in the field rather than the military academies. The money to buy supplies from other sources was even scarcer, forcing schools to rely more on bartering and purchasing on credit. Shortages later in the war caused by the tightening blockade made the resourcing dilemma even worse, as it did in the rest of the South.

In spite of these challenges, military schools continued to press forward with their educational mission, even in the concurrence of the war. Each of the academies maintained same scientific curriculum based on the West Point model. Cadets conducted daily recitation on lessons for which they received a daily grade. At the end of the academic year, each student would be given an oral examination by a panel of faculty members on each of their subjects and occasionally attended by Board of Visitors members or state political figures who would observe the showcase of the corps' academic progress. Superintendents, however, had to often borrow textbooks, use outdated equipment for science and engineering classes and cover a full class schedule with and understaffed and under-qualified faculty but still meet pre-war standards for academic excellence. Although much had changed the structure and operations of these military schools because of the war, the academic curriculums, for the most part, remained unaltered. Occasionally, class time spent on languages or other such subjects, would be reduced in the name of increasing more hours for drill or gunnery practice but overall, the academic programs reflected those prior to the outbreak of hostilities. The academies endeavored to live up to their new label as "West Points of the Confederacy" and resisted the pressures to supersede the mission of learning with that of military preparedness.

The rigid structure of the curriculum and pedagogy purposely integrated with the broader philosophical mission of the schools overall which continued to center on discipline and order. Every student enrolled as a member of the Corps of Cadets, wore a uniform, learned military drill and ceremonies, and observed a daily schedule that reflected the arrangement of a military unit. Cadets also were expected to follow a demanding set of regulations to control and shape their behavior. These rules were framed within a structured daily schedule which included all of their daily activities from reveille (wake up) to taps (lights out) and specific times for class, dress parade, study, and inspections. Students were forbidden to swear, use tobacco, or leave the grounds without permission and had to keep a clean and orderly personal appearance. Each violation of which was enforced through a system of demerits, confinement, and potential dismissal. To monitor their development, both academic and behavioral, the administration calculated their classroom progress (recitation grades) with their number of demerits and compiled the collective scores into an "order of merit" ranking for each cadet. This performance–based assessment system, combined with the uniforms, fostered an atmosphere of equality within the corps. Military students were judged by their faculty and their peers through their merit and talents versus their family heritage or social standing. The assignment of military rank and billets within the corps gave the young men a unique opportunity to develop a sense of responsibility and accountability for themselves and their peers.

Even enduring the demands of the challenging curriculum, firm discipline, and deprivations of wartime, cadets found various ways to break monotony of their regimented environment. Throughout the war, military schools maintained many cadet organization such as debating clubs, musical groups, and intellectual societies. As adolescents, however, many coped with the stresses of the academies through more mischievous means. Some turned to vice such as card playing, smoking, or sneaking off grounds into town after hours (dubbed "running the blockade"). Cadets at all schools notoriously played practical jokes on their comrades as a way to find levity in the otherwise serious and humorless environment. These pranks on fellow students, particularly the newest members of the corps, occasionally came in the form of rites of initiation or some form of hazing. These cases of cadet abuse drew the ire of administrators and parents and even occasionally forced the intervention of state politicians to legislate preventative measures. Superintendents struggled to find balance of keeping their young charges energetic and spirited but not to let their youthful proclivities devolve into deviant acts. To counter this roguish conduct, several superintendents promoted evangelical religion among their cadets to reinforce the goals of proper behavior and self-control. Nearly all schools required mandatory religious services on Sundays and many were implicitly encouraged to commit to a Christian way of life. Several schools sponsored religious revivals and Bible studies while others had cadets initiate their own temperance pledges for their comrades to inhibit the vice of drinking.

As manpower shortages ravaged the southern ranks and Union forces pushed deeper into the southern heartland, several Confederate commanders reluctantly called upon the services of local military schools to augment their undermanned forces during operations of critical danger to the areas surrounding their respective academies. Most often, cadets functioned in the role of a "home guard" by either searching for deserters, escorting prisoners, or doing guard detail. The close proximity of Federal troops often inspired rumors of slave uprising, forcing various corps of cadets to mobilize in their local communities to deter such an insurrection. Cadets immediately reacted with excitement, but this enthusiasm eventually waned when they finally confronted the realities of life on the campaign: bad weather, fatigue duty, and endless footsore marches across the countryside. Superintendents valued the opportunity to contribute to the needs of the Confederate army and the protection of their communities but inwardly resented the often unjustified distraction from classwork and cadet daily schedules. The growing number of times where local commanders mobilized cadets, who were never used in combat after miles of marching, lost sleep, and time away from their academic lessons, frustrated the administration and faculty. In May 1863, the cadets of VMI would take on more somber duty of escorting the body of their former faculty member, General Stonewall Jackson, to his final resting place. He was buried at the local Lexington cemetery where he had fallen at the Battle of Chancellorsville.

By the later years of the war, the need for manpower within the Confederate forces became so great that military academy cadets were eventually compelled to fight in pitched battle. The most famous of the instances occurred on May 15, 1864, when 257 cadets from VMI helped turn back the Federal Army under General Franz Siegel at the Battle of New Market. Ten cadets were killed during the engagement. Cadets from SCMA and GMI also distinguished themselves in fighting at the Battles of Tulifinny and Resaca respectively, while the corps of cadets from the University of Alabama contributed in smaller skirmishes during the latter campaigns of the war.

In spite of their contributions on the battlefield, cadets could do little to protect their institutions from invading Union armies. Throughout 1864 and 1865, nearly every southern military school still in operation was destroyed or severely vandalized by Union troops. Displaced corps of cadets attached themselves to larger Confederate armies to fight out the rest of the war or disbanded altogether. After the surrender at Appomattox in April 1865, only the Virginia Military Institute would reopen immediately, albeit under destitute conditions, and maintain its exclusive military character. SCMA was forced to close and did not reopen again until 1882. Some schools, such as the University of Alabama and Louisiana State Seminary and Military Academy (renamed Louisiana State University) would become permanently civilian institutions. However, the majority of these nearly one hundred institutions would never reopen their doors.

The southern military school tradition, however, did not die. It experienced a revival after the war and the implementation of the Morrill Land Grant Act of 1862. This legislation, which established the state land grant universities (including several in the former Confederate states, such as Texas A&M University, Clemson University, Virginia Polytechnic and State University, and Auburn University) all created corps of cadets and took on an exclusively military structure. Each of these schools based their structure and curriculum on the model of the antebellum military academies, often drawing from the alumni of the original schools to staff its faculty and administration. These institutions enjoyed popularity and success comparable to their antebellum predecessors in the late nineteenth and early twentieth centuries.

## Further Reading

Allardice, Bruce. "West Points of the Confederacy: Southern Military Schools and the Confederate Army." *Civil War History* 43.4 (1997): 310–331.

Andrew Jr., Rod. *Long Gray Lines: The Southern Military School Tradition, 1839–1915.* Chapel Hill: University of North Carolina. Press, 2001.

Couper, William. *One Hundred Years at VMI, Volume II.* Richmond: Garrett and Massie, 1939.

Hsieh, Wayne Wei-siang. *West Pointers and the Civil War: The Old Army in War and Peace.* Chapel Hill: University of North Carolina Press, 2009.

Livingston, Gary. *Cradled in Glory: Georgia Military Institute, 1851–1865.* Cooperstown: Cassion Press, 1997.

Morrison, James L. *The Best School in the World: West Point, the Pre-Civil War Years, 1833–1866.* Kent: Kent State University Press, 1986.

Smith, Francis H. *History of the Virginia Military Institute.* Lynchburg: J. P. Bell and Company, 1912.

# 13

# MILITARY MEDICINES

*Guy R. Hasegawa*

Union private Albert Morton Hayward, writing home from his camp in Virginia, reported that an officer had "got the Dr to give me some medicine for my diseese 'what it is I dont no but I have got about well again.'" The typical Civil War soldier or sailor could hardly be expected to know the content of proffered pills or powders or understand the reasoning behind giving them. The prescribing decision, after all, was influenced by the physician's individual and specialized knowledge, experience, and style. In fact, the entire process of medication use in the military reflected a complex interplay of diverse and often conflicting practices, beliefs, and attitudes. It included a wide array of players from drug merchants in faraway lands to patients like Hayward, who could accept or reject treatments and usually had something to say about them either way.

The Civil War is known for its battlefield deaths and wounds. Yet, roughly twice as many soldiers in that conflict died from disease as from combat injuries. Crowded conditions, exposure to the elements, lax sanitary practices, polluted drinking water, and food that was nutritionally poor, incompetently prepared, or contaminated all contributed to a high prevalence of illness. Among personnel in the field or at sea, it was the rare soldier or sailor who never became sick or injured enough to require medical attention. Ailments that did not require surgery could be treated with nondrug interventions such as rest and changes in diet. Nonetheless, medicines were an exceedingly familiar part of military life.

Drugs of the era can generally be divided into those derived from plants (e.g., quinine from South American cinchona bark) and those of mineral or chemical origin (e.g., ether, mercurial compounds). Before the war, mainstream medicinal substances were largely imported into the United States, although some were derived from North American vegetable or mineral resources. American pharmacists often processed indigenous or imported raw materials into medicinal forms, such as tinctures or extracts, which could be incorporated into prescriptions.

The official military medical supply lists in use at the start of the war were developed by medical officers (surgeons) in the regular armed forces of the United States and reflected the military's needs as seen by practitioners of regular (orthodox or allopathic) medicine. The supply tables indicated the drugs to be procured and issued by medical supply officers (medical purveyors). In 1862, the Union Army liberalized its practices to address the needs of its many physicians—in fact, most surgeons serving at the time—who had only recently left civilian practice for the military. "The volunteer medical officers being many of them country doctors, accustomed to a village nostrum practice," reported Medical Director Charles S. Tripler of the U.S. Army of the Potomac, "could not readily change their habits and accommodate themselves to the rigid system of the army in regard to their supplies. To meet this difficulty I attempted within reasonable limits to disregard supply tables, and to give the surgeons articles of medicine and hospital stores to suit even their caprices, if in my judgment such articles could be of any avail in the treatment of disease" (*War of the Rebellion*, ser. 1, vol. 5, 79). The Union Army also expanded the supply table on the recommendation of a board consisting of two army surgeons and Edward R. Squibb, a drug manufacturer and former navy surgeon. The decision-makers in the Confederate Medical Department, also allopaths, sought not to reinvent the wheel and adopted the 1861 Union supply table almost without change. They were later forced to add drugs made from southern plants, as described below. Civilian relief agencies (particularly in the North), state governments, and local merchants also supplied drugs and other medical supplies, especially when official army channels seemed inadequate.

Allopaths had been known for their tendency to favor drastic or "heroic" therapy—for example, bloodletting, inducing vomiting and defecation, and vigorous administration of harsh mineral drugs. Among the more notorious allopathic mainstays were tartar emetic (antimony potassium tartrate) and the mercurial compound known as calomel, which was known for causing oral gangrene and other toxic effects. Although such practices had lost much of their popularity among allopaths by 1860, they had contributed to the rise of various medical sects that promoted milder treatments, most often with plant-based drugs. There was no love lost between sectarians—homeopaths and "eclectic" physicians were among the most organized and numerous—and allopaths, many of whom considered the sectarians to be quacks. The leaders in the Union and Confederate medical departments were allopaths and so were most physicians who were allowed into the military as surgeons. Allopaths and sectarians prescribed many of the same plant-based drugs, but for the relatively few sectarian physicians who managed to obtain an appointment as surgeon, the standard supply tables fell miserably short in terms of overall selection.

Standard drugs were absolutely unsatisfactory to homeopathic surgeons, who prescribed medicines in extraordinarily dilute formulations.

In 1863, Surgeon General William Hammond of the Union Army, a progressive allopath, removed tartar emetic and calomel from the supply table on the grounds that the drugs were being misused by surgeons to the detriment of patients. This move delighted the sectarians, for whom those two drugs had exemplified the harsh agents with which allopaths were supposedly killing and disabling patients. Many allopaths were enraged—some because they found the excluded drugs useful, and others because Hammond's action gave comfort to their sectarian foes. Hammond, who had clashed with Secretary of War Edwin Stanton, was subsequently ousted from his position after being convicted of flimsy charges by a court martial. Tartar emetic and calomel remained stricken from the supply table, but they could still be obtained upon request. Furthermore, other mercurial drugs remained on the table, including the familiar "blue mass" (mercurial pill mass), from which "blue pills" were formed.

During the Civil War era, drugs were largely treated as commodities, with their market prices reported in trade publications and speculators buying up goods whose value they thought would rise. Quinine, in particular, was carefully watched. "Beyond all other articles," said Squibb, "[quinine] has tempted outside persons to invest in it for speculation, and as such are generally easily frightened, they get 'weak kneed,' as it is called, and by selling out in a falling market, aid to depress it often to extremes upon which opposite extremes find surest basis" (182).

Raw drugs were commonly adulterated with less costly substances to increase profits for the sellers. Belladonna leaves, for example, might be mixed with cheaper digitalis leaves, and raw opium might contain stones or bullets to increase its weight. Regulations were in place for drugs entering U.S. ports to be inspected and, if of poor quality, turned away, but the appointment of inspectors was politically motivated and did little to protect the public. "The prostitution of this office [of inspector] for political purposes," lamented a pharmacist, "is the surest way to counteract the good intentions of the law" (Maisch 125). Even medicines prepared and sold in American drugstores often exhibited "a low character discreditable alike to the professions of medicine and pharmacy, and to human nature in general" (Squibb 192). The laissez-faire attitude of the times assumed that the public's demands and market pressures, rather than regulation, would eventually drive off businesses that offered poor goods or services. The public, however, was not in a position to discern high- from low-quality medicines, and there seemed to be no shortage of buyers for disreputable medicinal goods as long as the price was right.

Pharmacy, popularly considered more of a trade than a profession, was so loosely regulated that practically anyone could buy or sell medicines. Despite there being a core of highly educated and conscientious pharmacists, no pharmacy degree or license was needed to operate a drugstore, and customers who wanted to treat themselves could purchase any items, including opiates and poisons, that the store operator was willing to sell. Physicians wrote prescriptions but often dispensed medicines personally or through drugstores that they owned.

The North had several drug companies—such as Edward R. Squibb, M.D., Charles Pfizer & Co., John Wyeth and Brother, Schieffelin & Co., Powers & Weightman, and Rosengarten and Sons—with a large-scale capacity to manufacture chemicals and turn raw materials into finished medicines. During the war, importation of goods into the northern states continued, although Confederate commerce raiders sometimes hampered it. Early in the war, the Union Army bought drugs on the open market but tended to favor the large drug companies, whose goods were more predictable in price and quality than those obtained elsewhere. In the second half of the war, the Union Army—eager to ensure quality, standardize packaging, and control costs—established medical laboratories that inspected raw materials, manufactured medicines, and repackaged bulk purchases of drugs. These facilities—the primary ones were in Philadelphia, Pennsylvania, and Astoria, New York—were modeled after the U.S. Navy medical laboratory in Brooklyn, which had been established in 1845 and continued operation throughout the war. Union medical supplies were distributed through a series of depots to surgeons stationed at hospitals or other military bases, in the field, or at sea.

President Lincoln's imposition of a naval blockade of the Confederate states, although not particularly effective at first, became more efficient as the war progressed. Among the items classified as contraband were medical supplies, a circumstance condemned in the South as barbaric but regarded with mixed reactions by Northern citizens. At first, Confederate medical purveyors relied heavily on local druggists for supplies. In the spring of 1862, when the capture of Savannah, Georgia, seemed likely, the medical purveyor stationed there, William H. Prioleau, reported to Chief Purveyor Edward W. Johns that he was safeguarding his own cache of purchased goods while letting city druggists fill his requisitions. "Should the City be taken," he explained, his own goods "will be saved and the Stocks of the Druggists will have been reduced in the service of the Government" (*Letters Sent* 60).

Other important but unreliable means of procuring drugs in the Confederacy included capturing Union military goods and the open bartering of southern products, usually cotton, for northern merchandise. The latter practice, which occurred in the Union-occupied South, was tolerated by the U.S. government if it was deemed advantageous to Federal interests, but Union military men typically condemned such trade as enhancing the enemy's strength. The Confederate government generally prohibited this trade, although Confederate medical authorities thought it a useful means of obtaining high-quality drugs at reasonable prices. The Confederate War Department did, on occasion, authorize agents to enter the United States to purchase medical supplies, but it prohibited them from engaging in personal profiteering.

Medicines were also smuggled into the South from the North—often by speculators who sold the goods to druggists or medical purveyors—or snuck into southern ports by blockade runners. Cargoes were typically auctioned to druggists or speculators from whom medical purveyors were then forced to purchase. At times, medical purveyors were authorized to seize goods from speculators and pay them only the cost price. Such measures were unlikely to elicit objections from common citizens, who generally agreed with Richmond's *Daily Dispatch* that speculators were scoundrels who would "coin the generosity of a glorious people into gold for their own dirty pockets, and who, if they could ever get to Heaven, would rob the saints of every pearl in their crowns before they had been there five minutes" ("Be Economical" 2). Some drugs were imported for government use, but disputes over the price could lead to purveyors impressing the goods and the government determining a "fair valuation."

Drugs arriving in Southern ports were likely to be adulterated, perhaps more so than those shipped to the North. According to Squibb, medical supplies arriving by blockade runners were largely "shipped for a hazardous venture by the lowest class of traders in the foreign markets whence they came, and ... must naturally be the refuse of the markets" (193). Southern newspapers angrily reported that "poisoned" quinine sold by Northerners to southern smugglers was finding its way to Confederate medical purveyors. Any adulteration or mix-ups, of course, could have occurred before or after the quinine was in the hands of northern dealers.

The South had no preexisting large-scale drug industry, so the unreliability of existing sources of medical supply and the ever rising cost of goods forced the Confederacy to commence the collection of native resources, especially plants, from which medicines could be made. "It is the policy of all nations at all times, especially such as at present exists in our Confederacy," explained Surgeon General Samuel Preston Moore, "to make every effort to develop its internal resources, and to diminish its tribute to foreigners by supplying its necessities from the productions of its own soil" (*War of the Rebellion* ser. 4, vol. 1, 1041).

Some medicinal plants could be collected by troops in the field or by hospital personnel and used with little preparation. Many, though, had to be processed into medicines, so army medical laboratories—perhaps up to a dozen—were established throughout the South to accomplish this task. Laboratory directors published notices asking citizens to collect certain plants, for which they would be paid. Southern women were urged to grow poppies and deliver the raw opium to medical purveyors. Poppies, flax, castor beans, and other plants with medicinal uses were cultivated in large scale. Plants were not the only resources collected. Minerals such as lime and Epsom salts were mined, and citizens were asked to collect and dry potato flies as a substitute for Spanish fly, which was used as a blistering agent.

The army medical laboratories also manufactured standard drugs such as chloroform and ether; the lone Confederate Navy laboratory, in Richmond, evidently manufactured nothing but conventional drugs. Silver nitrate, used to cauterize wounds, was produced from silver cups and plates purchased from citizens and from coins provided by the government. Whiskey, considered a valuable medicinal agent, was obtained through contracts or manufactured in government-owned distilleries. "Being anxious that our sick soldiers should not be poisoned by the vile stuff sold as whiskey," said Medical Purveyor J. J. Chisolm to a distiller, "I have written to you to know whether you can furnish any quantity for Government purposes under a State license" (*Letterbook* 15). Among the opponents of distilling was the governor of Georgia, who was adamant that grain should be used to feed citizens and soldiers and not be made into liquor, even for medical purposes.

The Confederate medical laboratories were usually associated with purveying depots, which received, stored, and issued medical supplies. The facilities were targets for thieves, who set their sights on valuable and highly saleable items like quinine and morphine. Surgeon-in-Charge A. Snowden Piggot of the Lincolnton, North Carolina, laboratory had other fears. "With the absurd prejudice however which you know exists throughout the neighborhood against this Laboratory," he wrote, "I think you will agree with me that it is unsafe to leave the Government property exposed there with a less force to guard it than I have named. I know that numerous threats have been made against it & I do not consider them altogether idle." The basis of this hostility is unclear, although some speculation has centered on distrust of Piggot because of his Northern roots.

Medical purveyors sometimes had to turn to sectarian practitioners for assistance in collecting and processing native flora. "As I am not at all conversant with the appearance of these plants," wrote Medical Purveyor Prioleau to Chief Purveyor Johns, "I would like very much to have some one who understands them" (*Letters Sent* 295). Prioleau consequently worked with Willliam T. Park, who "belongs to the so styled reformed Medical School, who practices exclusively with Indigenous remedies." At about the time Park left his position, Prioleau began working with another botanical physician, Methvin Thomson, who was also mayor of Macon, Georgia, to build and operate a laboratory. Prioleau also paid these practitioners for plants that they sold out of their own stores or purchased as agents.

In spite of such cooperation, tensions between allopaths and sectarians remained. Surgeon General Moore had to urge his surgeons to keep an open mind about the usefulness of indigenous remedies. In explaining his break from Prioleau, Park contended that Prioleau "reported me to the Surgeon General as endeavoring to promote the Reform Profession, thereby arousing his antipathy to the Reform Profession and causing him to discontinue my agency" (2). The services of sectarians to Confederate medical authorities evidently did not include advice about the selection or therapeutic use of native plants.

Physicians during the Civil War era were generally unaware of the underlying causes of illness; in particular, they were ignorant of the role of microorganisms in infectious diseases. An important theory of the day, at least among allopaths, held that disease could be accounted for by derangements in the level of "excitability" in the tissues. An excess of excitability, associated with congestion of blood vessels, might manifest as fever or a fast or forceful pulse and could be countered with drugs such as sedatives. If "overexcitability" were localized to a certain region of the body, it might be reduced there by producing stimulation (and diverting excess fluids) elsewhere—by the administration of emetics or laxatives, for example, or application of blistering agents at a distant site. An insufficiency of excitability might be evident in prostration or a weak pulse and call for administration of tonics or stimulants. Tonics were known for their relatively gentle and prolonged action, whereas stimulants—alcohol was so classified—had short-lived excitatory effects that were followed by depression. Some drugs, such as the mercurial compounds, were thought to act by altering the nature of the body's solids or fluids rather than increasing or reducing their actions and were thus called "alteratives."

Physicians often tailored their treatments to manage the patient's symptoms and needs rather than selecting a specific remedy for the diagnosed ailment. A notable exception was quinine—sometimes mixed with whiskey—which was well recognized for its remarkable specificity and effectiveness in preventing and curing malaria (commonly called "intermittent fever" or "periodic fever"). Quinine, however, was often prescribed as an antipyretic or tonic in nonmalarial illnesses, often with little success. "The proverbial prescription of the average army surgeon was quinine," said one Union soldier, "whether for stomach or bowels, headache or toothache, for a cough or for lameness, rheumatism or fever and ague" (Billings 175–76). Other valuable drugs included chloroform and ether, which were used as anesthetics for surgery or other painful procedures, and opium and morphine, which helped relieve pain, suppress cough, and reduce the severity of diarrhea. By today's standards, most other drugs would not be considered valuable, although they did often produce effects, such as vomiting or purging, that were sought by surgeons. Southern remedies made from native plants were generally considered inferior to standard medications.

Soldiers seeking medical attention reported to the surgeon at a specified time of day for "sick call." In hospitals, surgeons went from patient to patient and prescribed therapy. As much as surgeons may have wanted to ponder each patient's needs and thoughtfully prescribe accordingly, circumstances often dictated that they take a simpler course. Surgeons in the field charged with stabilizing wounded soldiers might do little other than dress the injuries and give opium or whiskey before having the patients transported elsewhere for more definitive treatment. Only a small variety of drugs were available when troops were on the march. In hospitals, the supply of medicines and the number of patients—surgeons were sometimes responsible for more than a hundred—also influenced what was prescribed. During epidemics, treatments may have been quite uniform. How drugs were prescribed for a specific illness depended heavily on the individual practitioner, since there was little or no standardization of treatment throughout the armies.

Surgeons were commonly accompanied by noncommissioned officers called hospital stewards, who prepared and dispensed drugs and assisted with surgery and other procedures. Hospital stewards—some had been physicians in civilian life, while others had no little or no medical training at all—commonly made therapy decisions on their own and generally took on as much responsibility as their supervisory surgeons allowed. Medical cadets—medical students who had not yet graduated—assisted Union surgeons, especially in general hospitals. Permission to prescribe was generally not extended to other personnel, such as nurses or hospital matrons.

With the exception of chloroform and ether, which were inhaled when used as anesthetics, the vast majority of drugs were given orally or applied topically. Oral medicines were usually in the form of liquids, powders dispensed in folded papers, or pills. Pills, if not premade, were pinched off of a wad of dough-like material (a pill mass) on the spot. If time and facilities allowed, surgeons could prescribe drug mixtures to be prepared by hospital stewards. Otherwise, patients were likely to receive whatever was immediately available. Large batches of medicines, such as quinine in whiskey, were used for mass dosing of troops.

Physicians did not rank particularly high in social status, a circumstance that contributed to the relative lack of respect accorded surgeons by volunteer troops. As was the case for pharmacy, medical practice was largely unregulated in civilian life, such that practically anyone could claim expertise and treat patients. Obtaining a medical diploma required attending two usually identical courses of lectures, each of which lasted several months, writing a thesis, and passing an examination. Lax or totally absent standards accounted for a great many unqualified physicians entering the military as surgeons early in the war. Treatments at the time were not notable for their success, and many troops, especially those from rural areas where physicians were scarce, were accustomed to treating themselves. The constant and acrimonious bickering among allopaths and sectarians about which group provided superior treatment eroded any image that physicians may have had as trusted and knowledgeable caregivers. To be sure, many—perhaps most—surgeons were caring and capable men, especially later in the war. Judging from death rates among sick and injured patients, Union and Confederate surgeons compared favorably with European military surgeons, whose training was supposedly superior. Yet even the most skilled Civil War surgeons were often powerless to alleviate suffering, and problems with crowding and logistics hampered their ability to provide the quality of care that might have been possible had conditions been different.

The preexisting doubts that troops had about the abilities of surgeons were exploited by various factions, each with its own agenda to press. Sectarians wanted more of their members allowed into the military, so they disparaged the practices of allopaths. Authors of medical self-help books argued that physicians could not be relied upon and that citizens must look out for themselves. "The honest fears of some that the physician should alone prescribe, is a mistake," said John C. Gunn in his best-selling family medical book. "There is not that strangeness and marvelousness about medicine which many suppose; the administration is to be guided by good judgment and common sense, necessary qualities, which all physicians, and young practitioners generally, do not always possess" (5). Merchants of patent medicines claimed that their wares were superior to what troops could expect from surgeons. "Soldiers see to your own health, do not trust to the Army supplies," read an advertisement for a nostrum (Holloway's). "Cholera, Fever and Bowel complaint will follow your slightest indiscretion. Holloway's Pills and Ointment should be in every man's knapsack. The British and French troops use no other medicines. Only 25 cents per Box or Pot."

Physicians did not necessarily hold themselves to a lofty standard of behavior. They seemed as susceptible as common soldiers, for example, to the temptations of alcohol and had unusual access to it, since it was often kept nearby as a medicinal agent. Observing intoxicated surgeons was not likely to inspire confidence in them as caregivers.

Given their doubts about physicians and the propensity of soldiers to grumble rather than praise, it is not surprising that patients often thought of their surgeons as uncaring, ignorant, and more harmful than helpful. "It has ever been my opinion that a man is no better than a dead man when placed under the hands of almost any of our army surgeons," said an infantryman from Pennsylvania (Hill 229–30). "This is startling, but *it is true*. An ordinary army surgeon can, by a course of treatment, bring the stoutest man to the grave; and they seldom fail to do it."

Allopathic drug therapy by its nature often produced obvious and unpleasant effects, such as vomiting, without a commensurate improvement in the underlying illness. Not surprisingly, then, soldiers tended to shy away from the surgeon and his "poisons," especially if more benign treatments were available. Ailing soldiers, especially those who were self-reliant as civilians, were likely to treat themselves. "Once I caught a bad cold," remembered a Union private, "but I treated it myself with a backwoods remedy and never thought of going to the surgeon about it. I took some of the bark of a hickory tree that stood near our quarters, and made about a quart of strong hickory-bark tea. I drank it hot, and all at once, just before turning in for the night. It was green in color, and intensely bitter, but it cured the cold" (Stillwell 19). Other self-treatments could consist of patent medicines, remedies sent from home, or cures suggested around the campfire by comrades. Citizens did not hesitate to send newspapers their own recommendations for medicating soldiers.

Soldiers often commented that surgeons prescribed exactly the same thing for every patient regardless of the illness or gave different remedies for patients who had exactly the same symptoms. Quinine, calomel, and blue mass or blue pills were the usual medicines mentioned in such accounts. Multiple explanations might be offered for such behavior: incompetence or laziness on the part of the surgeons, certainly, but also having only a small variety of medicines from which to choose, or a legitimate belief that the same agent might help relieve a multitude of ailments. In any event, surgeons' seeming lack of thought was not likely to inspire confidence in their medical prowess. Troops sometimes made light of the situation by giving their surgeons nicknames like "Old Salts" or "Opium Pills" or attaching lyrics like "Come and get your quinine" to the notes blown by the bugler to announce sick call.

Although many soldiers avoided surgeons, others feigned or exaggerated illness to escape unpleasant assignments. When detected, the "shirkers" might be given a benign or unpleasant drug before being declared available for duty, but they might also fool a surgeon and receive truly harmful drugs. These fakers, said one soldier, "degraded their bodies by swallowing drugs, for the ailments for which they laid claim" (Billings 174). Indeed, receiving drugs was expected as a routine part of receiving medical attention. "I believe there are no class of men," wrote a Union surgeon, "so willing to take medicine as sick soldiers" (Josyph 60). Sick or not, soldiers did not hesitate to discard medicines they regarded as distasteful, harmful, or unnecessary.

The supply chain for Civil War military medicines might stretch from Peruvian cinchona forests or Turkish opium fields to battlefields or hospitals in Pennsylvania or Georgia. Factors other than logistical difficulties, however, affected how drugs were provided and used. Unprincipled drug suppliers, unfettered by effective regulation, offered adulterated or poor quality goods, and profiteers forced prices up for medical purveyors and other purchasers. Physicians' beliefs and practices were far from uniform, and the sheer numbers of patients requiring treatment often favored prescribing that was hurried and expedient rather than contemplative and individualized. Patients themselves often distrusted surgeons and feared or scoffed at the medicines they prescribed. Far from being governed primarily by purely scientific considerations, the use of military medicines was subject to a wide variety of practical, economic, social, and cultural influences, many of which were not directly related to the war.

## Further Reading

Adams, George Worthington. *Doctors in Blue: The Medical History of the Union Army in the Civil War.* Baton Rouge: Louisiana State University Press, 1952.
"Be Economica." *Daily Dispatch (Richmond).* October 31 1861: 2.

Billings, John D. *Hardtack and Coffee or the Unwritten Story of Army Life*. Boston: George M. Smith & Co., 1887.

Bollet, Alfred Jay. *Civil War Medicine: Challenges and Triumphs*. Tucson: Galen Press, 2002.

Cunningham, H. H. *Doctors in Gray: The Confederate Medical Service*. Baton Rouge: Louisiana State University Press, 1958.

Gunn, John C. *Gunn's New Domestic Physician: Or Home Book of Health*. Cincinnati: Moore, Wilstach, Keys & Co., 1863.

Hasegawa Guy R. "Pharmacy in the American Civil War." *American Journal of Health-System Pharmacy* 57 (2000): 475–489.

Hasegawa Guy R. "'Absurd Prejudice': A. Snowden Piggot and the Confederate Medical Laboratory at Lincolnton." *North Carolina Historical Review* 81 (2004): 313–334.

Hasegawa Guy R. "Quinine Substitutes in the Confederate Army." *Military Medicine* 172 (2007): 650–655.

Hasegawa Guy R., and F. Terry Hambrecht. "The Confederate Medical Laboratories." *Southern Medical Journal* 96 (2003): 1221–1230.

Hayward, Albert Morton. "Letter, January 27, 1863." Albert Morton Hayward Papers. Pearce Civil War Collection, Navarro College, Corsicana, Texas.

Hill, A. F. *Our Boys. The Personal Experiences of a Soldier in the Army of the Potomac*. Philadelphia: John E. Potter, 1864.

Holloway's Pills and Ointments, advertisement. *Vanity Fair*. September 14, 1861: 122.

Josyph, Peter, ed. *The Wounded River: The Civil War Letters of John Vance Lauderdale, M.D.* East Lansing: Michigan State University Press, 1993.

*Letterbook of J. J. Chisolm, Columbia, South Carolina, May 24 to November 14, 1862*. Wessels Library, Newberry College, Newberry, South Carolina.

*Letters Sent, Medical Purveyor's Office, Savannah, Georgia, Depot 1862,* War Department Collection of Confederate Records (Record Group 109), ch. 6, vol. 572. National Archives and Records Administration, Washington, D.C.

Maisch, J. M. "On Commercial Belladonna Leaves." *American Journal of Pharmacy* 34 (1862): 123–129.

Park, W. T. "Communicated," *Savannah (Georgia) Republican*, 3 October 1862: 2.

Piggot, Aaron Snowden, to unknown, n.d. Maj. A. Snowden Piggot Papers. War Department Collection of Confederate Records (Record Group 109). National Archives and Records Administration, Washington, D.C.

Smith, George Winston. *Medicines for the Union Army*. Madison: American Institute of the History of Pharmacy, 1952.

Squibb, E. R. "Report on the Drug Market." *Proceedings of the American Pharmaceutical Association at its Eleventh Annual Meeting, Held in Baltimore, Md., September, 1863*. Philadelphia: Merrihew & Thompson, 1863: 175–195.

Stillwell, Leander. *The Story of a Common Soldier of Army Life in the Civil War*. 2d ed. Kansas City: Franklin Hudson Publishing Co., 1920.

*The War of the Rebellion: A Compilation of the Official Records of the Union and Confederate Armies*. Washington, D.C.: Government Printing Office, 1880–1901.

# 14

# CIVILIAN HEALTHCARE

*James M. Schmidt*

Civilian healthcare differed greatly from military healthcare during the Civil War era. For all its faults, the military paradigm had its advantages: sophisticated general and specialized hospitals, the emergence of the professional nurse, an improved ambulance service, and surgeons trained and experienced in trauma and emergency surgery. For those Americans at home or the farm during the era, the state of medicine was less progressive. It also had divisions and inequities that mirrored the state of the Union: whites vs. African Americans, North vs. South, rich vs. poor, city vs. farm, professionals vs. quacks, empiricism vs. rational invention, among many others. In brief, there was no *one* home-front medical experience in the mid-nineteenth century. Even within these divisions there were distinctions with a decided difference. For example, medicine and healthcare looked different among the era's African American population, with distinctions between free and enslaved, male and female, children and adults, plantations and industrial centers.

No less a personality than Mark Twain—whose life spanned the better part of the nineteenth century—discussed the state of civilian medicine in the Civil War era. He wrote often on medicine and doctors in his essays, satire, and fiction. In his autobiography, Twain declared: "Doctors were not called in cases of ordinary illness; the family's grandmother attended to those. Every old woman was a doctor, gathered her own medicines in the woods, and knew how to compound doses that would stir the vitals of a cast-iron dog" (10–11). In these few sentences of his autobiography, Twain managed to touch on several important elements of civilian medicine before the war: the treatment of illness in the home rather in the hospital or office, the herbal and mineral compositions of purported cures, the primary role of women as caregivers, and the complementary (rather than antagonistic) relationship between professional physicians and domestic caregivers. In other passages, he wrote of the medical traditions of Native Americans and ancient remedies that influenced the medical practices of enslaved African Americans. While his musings aptly describe the state of medicine up to and including the Civil War, what's missing is some of the effects that the war had on civilian medicine for the balance of the century. Though admittedly slow in fruition, they included the continued professionalization of the medical and pharmaceutical ranks and the increasing influence of politics and the law on medicine, especially when applied to the medical care of the war's veterans. In this way, the Civil War influenced civilian medicine well beyond the years 1861–65.

Before the war, it was the rare letter in which the writer did not include news of the health of the household, express concern over the sickness of the recipient, voice fears of a real or rumored epidemic, or post an accounting of deaths in the family. It is fitting that such news came in letters from home, because it was in the home where the vast majority of ministrations occurred. A physician might be called in the most desperate circumstances but, generally, families relied on newspapers, almanacs, business or farm ledgers, and magazines for diagnosing illness and finding treatments, all written in "common sense terms." Especially popular were household books such as William Buchan's *Every Man His Own Doctor* (1816). One historian even suggests that the two most widely read books in some households, especially in the South, were the Bible and John C. Gunn's *Domestic Medicine* (1830) (Cavender 33).

All but a few medicines did no good (and sometimes great harm), but mid-nineteenth century Americans at least had choices. If purported cures were not gleaned from books, they might be borrowed from neighbors, secured at the druggist, dispensed by the doctor, or passed down through generations by oral tradition or even penned in last wills and testaments. One mother's letter reveals the panoply of medicines employed by a typical antebellum city-dwelling family in the East:

> How you must be wondering at my long silence but we are all dependent upon circumstances even in this land of independence. Your letter … did not reach me until Monday afternoon and then I had just returned from the city unwell and much fatigued … I took the cholera remedy but without removing my distress … [Your father's] leg troubles him much but he will take no one's advice. One day he flies to one remedy, next day to another. Last Sunday he took the advice of a physician here and after taking the medicine for one day and bandaging his leg as directed he went to the city on Monday … [Tuesday] went to a druggist, got some other nostrum. Our old neighbor Mr. Platt recommended me to take some vinegar salt which I have done and think it has done me some service, though I feel excessively weak.

> *(Collection of James M. Schmidt)*

Mothers, wives, and daughters were expected to provide medical care to their families. Of the role of females, historian Emily K. Abel recently declared that "Caregiving dominated women's lives throughout the nineteenth century," beginning "as early as girlhood and extending into middle and old age" (37). Furthermore, women did not limit their care to their own families, but also extended it to neighbors and even strangers. Indeed, care for neighbors could be quite hazardous, as "women moved from house to house ... exposing themselves and their own families to disease" (Abel 39).

Several social, economic, and even technological factors forced caregiving into the hands of women. The period domestic "code," popular culture, and a personal sense of duty explain the obligation and the self-motivation to care. Many families could not afford a doctor and only the very well off could afford an in-home nurse, and—curiously—most chose not to. Limited communication and transportation meant that a doctor would be hard to reach, and if he was contacted, it would be a long wait to finally see him. Of course, these same factors limited the practical sphere of a doctor's practice and in turn his potential income. To be sure, there was prejudice against the medical profession, but there is some debate among historians on the relationship between professional (and orthodox) doctors and domestic caregivers. Paul Starr points to the period assessment that physicians should be on guard against "jealous midwives, ignorant doctor-women, and busy neighbors" as a sign of a "weak profession" with "no confidence in its own authority" (88–89). However, others suggest that the real hostility was not between the orthodoxy and domestic caregivers, but rather "physicians [who] were more concerned with eliminating sectarian competitors than with halting self-care" (Wilkie 686).

The female duty and motivation to extend care had a mixed record on the plantation, at least as far as the "mistress" was concerned. To be sure, the wives and daughters of slave owners did provide medical care; their reputation spans the range of "chief medical officer" (Scott 36) to those who complained of their responsibilities—and the sickness of their slaves—in letters and diaries. In fact, as Todd Savitt pointed out in *Medicine and Slavery* (1978), male owners and overseers took significant responsibility for the medical care of the slaves, being in an "unenviable position" as "taskmaster, judge, and physician, simultaneously" (156). Period manuals, such as *Planters' Guide and Family Book of Medicine* (1849) or *Plantation and Farm Instruction* (1852) outlined the overseer's medical obligations.

Slaves were not completely dependent on their owners and overseers for their medical care, nor were they passive recipients. They too had a dubious notion of the effectiveness, if not adequacy, of white care, but also their retention of beliefs and practices born of their African roots and a natural inclination to trust in their own practitioners and remedies. Their freedom—such as it was (and it was indeed only reluctantly assented to by their owners)—to treat the members of their own community also provided some little control over their own lives. The *materia medica* of enslaved African Americans was composed of proven plants, herbs, and minerals, and—just as it had for centuries for whites—the influence of their interactions with Native Americans. Interestingly, white orthodox physicians reported on the more successful slave remedies in period medical journals.

Post-war slave narratives, especially those gathered in the Federal Writers' Project of 1936-38, often include descriptions of favorite remedies and opinions on practitioners. As an example, ninety-year old ex-slave Victoria Adams recalled: "Us had medicine made from herbs, leaves and roots; some of them was cat-nip, garlic root, tansy, and roots of burdock. De roots of burdock soaked in whiskey was mighty good medicine. We dipped asafetida in turpentine and hung it round our necks to keep off diseases" (*Born in Slavery* 14:12). Likewise, eighty-year old ex-slave Josephine Baccus declared: "Oh, de people never didn' put much faith to de doctors in dem days. Mostly, dey would use de herbs in de fields for dey medicine. Dere two herbs, I hear talk of. Dey was black snake root and Sampson snake root. Say, if a person never had a good appetite, dey would boil some of dat stuff en mix it wid a little bit of whiskey en rock candy en dat would sho give dem a sharp appetite" (*Born in Slavery* 14:20). A number of other primary sources further reveal the health and medicines of slaves, including Patricia Lambert's analysis of skeletal remains removed from plantation cemeteries, which, as she explains, complements the historical record by "providing a more direct accounting of the biological impacts of slavery" and a "means to test [hypotheses] about health and disease experience" on the plantation (107).

But it is impossible to *completely* separate military and civilian medical experiences during the Civil War. War, especially civil war, necessarily disrupts local populations through battles, disease, loss of income, the wounding and death of family and friends, and other impacts. During the Civil War, people on the homefront—especially women—participated in charitable "war work" which supplemented the activities of the government and the military medical establishment. Sustaining medical care at home, especially in rural areas, sometimes required the kindness of aid societies and the continued reliance on domestic medicine.

Several wartime situations could result in a medical impact on the civilian population. Historian James McPherson has suggested that a "fair estimate of war-related civilian deaths might total 50,000" from the effects of malnutrition, exposure, and disease during the war (619). Certainly, those parts of the country—especially in the Confederate states—that were subject to invasion were more likely to suffer the direct costs of war. Interactions of soldiers with local populations did result in civilian disease; indeed, few places during the war were more perilous to the health of civilians than proximity to standing camps or prisoner of war (POW) facilities and conflicts between military and civil authorities ensued on that account. For example, in his recent study of Union POW camps, James Gillispie notes that the construction of a smallpox quarantine hospital—best located outside the confines of the POW camp—was delayed because the local population of Alton, Illinois, protested that there would no barrier between themselves and infected prisoners (231).

Where there was disease and poor diet, especially in the South and more particularly in rural areas, access to professional medical care was limited as increasing number of physicians gave their attention to the armies in the field. Even where doctors were available, some families—bereft of the support and income of husbands and fathers—had to rely on charitable organizations, especially to subsidize the cost of medical care. A number of local and state relief societies were organized to provide the funding. Still, relief was not assured: recipients often had to provide proof of marriage and their husbands' service records, and that the locality received "credit" for the enlistment. Other societies required that beneficiaries swear that they had no alternative means of support. And as historian Judith Giesberg points out, another important string attached to relief was conforming to standards of respectability. Some women were denied aid for "not acting as a virtuous wife should" (31).

Women also participated in "war work" that had a medical component. In keeping with Kate Cumming's declaration that "the war is certainly ours as well as that of the men" (28), women participated as nurses and aid society members. Historian Drew Gilpin Faust found a distinction between women in the South who primarily entered hospital work as volunteers or visitors, and women in the North who used their wartime experiences to build a new sense of purpose and calling. While female graduates of medical schools were uniformly rejected as military surgeons in an official capacity, the war did provide an opportunity for women to advance in professional medicine.

As the war opened up these avenues for progress, it also opened avenues for marketing and brought to a head the competition between traditional and alternative medical practices. Quackery in all its forms was in its golden age in the mid-nineteenth century: patent medicines, health reform movements, and pseudo-science. These practices can be traced to a number of social and economic factors, including the rapidly growing population (a good part of which had limited access to physicians), the limited efficacy of and negative attitudes towards traditional medicine, technological improvements in printing and advertising, and the influential philosophy of self-improvement. By the Civil War, patent medicines were popular, including among soldiers, and the nostrum makers took advantage of the moment and made clever uses of patriotic and wartime symbolism in their marketing. Likewise, makers of items such as patriotic envelopes employed medical motifs in their products: bullets were referred to as "Lincoln Pills," cannonballs as "Union Pills," and terms such as "remedy" and "cure" were employed to humorous, yet effective rhetorical effect. The gimmickry even began before the war. Taking advantage of Abraham Lincoln's popularity prior to his inauguration, the maker of "Bellingham's Onguent' declared (falsely) in an advertisement in the *New York Times* that the president-elect had raised his whiskers in six weeks using their popular hair restorative.

While peddlers of patent and proprietary medicines peddled their nostrums, a change in policy in 1860 at the United States Patent Office generated applications for compounds, oils, ointments, salves, and other remedies. Indeed, while fewer than thirty patents were issued for medicines from 1837-1860, nearly eighty patents for medicines were issued during the war years alone. To be sure, some of the patented medicines were explicitly born of wartime needs, such as John Weaver's "Improved Medical Compound for the Cure of Diarrhea" (a "speedy and effectual remedy for the disease ... from the attacks of which soldiers in camp are great and frequent sufferers"). Jeremiah Hascall's "Improved Medical Compound for Miasmatic Diseases" also was particular to wartime needs. But most patents were designed for the home or farm, including a variety of "hair restoratives," improvements in treatment for hog cholera, and treatments for common diseases.

Like many remedies of the era, most of the patented medicines had a vegetable or mineral origin, sometimes of an exotic nature. For example, Anson Dart's "Improved Compound Oil" for the treatment of venereal diseases was purportedly composed of "an oil of the dwarf olive" and an oil from the seeds of a musk-melon "not known to grow anywhere except in Hindostan." Dr. Caleb Sanborn's "Improved Medicine for Croup" contained *Lobelia inflate* ("Indian tobacco"), the herb *Scutellaria lateriflora* ("blue skull-cap"), alcohol (high proof), best West India molasses, and pure water. Still, the sanction of the Patent Office did not lend the "therapies" any more scientific merit than the secret remedies marketed by quacks. Dart claimed his treatment was "as sure a prevention to taking the venereal diseases as that water will quench fire." Even more outlandish was Henry F. Wiesecke's patent for "Improved Sugar Tablet for Taking Medicines." The inventor claimed he had endowed sugar crystals "with a healing power"; the tablets were distinguished "by four hundred and twelve different numbers ... designed to cure four hundred and twelve various phases of sickness" (a full description is given in his work, "Fountain of Health"). *Scientific American*—the leading technical journal of the day—was justifiably dubious of the medicines and remarked on them with bemusement. On the other hand, the magazine reported enthusiastically and presciently on the promise of the future age of synthetic chemistry, writing that although the "fruits of chemical inquiry" had been valuable, "still more may be expected from the further prosecution of this study," and the "connexion [sic] between medicine and chemistry ... will be productive of benefits, the importance of which we can scarcely venture to estimate in the present state of our knowledge" ("Chemistry and Medicine," 99).

While the modern age of "rational" drug discovery predicted by *Scientific American* would have to wait fifty years for the discovery of the "magic bullet" of salvarsan in Paul Erlich's laboratory in 1908, the American pharmaceutical industry certainly came of age in the Civil War era. The drug houses of Edward R. Squibb, M.D., Charles Pfizer & Co., and John Wyeth and Brother, were already recognized and reliable suppliers of medicines before the war, and their future success in the civilian market was ensured by their wartime experience in large-scale manufacturing. Other well-known names in the industry would emerge shortly after, such as Union veteran Eli Lilly's enterprise.

Just as important as this development of large-scale manufacturing was the dawn of the industry's increasing reliance on patent protection. Professional ethics had prevented doctors and orthodox pharmacists from securing patents for medicines and devices. Indeed, the American Medical Association proclaimed that it was "derogatory to professional character ... for a physician to hold a patent for any surgical instrument or medicine," and forbade its members to secure patents (Baker 328). However, soon after the Civil War, the growing pharmaceutical industry tried to "redefine patents as an ethical means of encouraging scientific and commercial innovation" (Gabriel 135).

The wartime civilian medical experience did not end with the surrender at Appomattox in 1865. Veterans continued to live with wounds and diseases contracted during the war. And increasingly they encountered a newly professionalized politico-medico-legal movement (and industry). The pension policy instituted by the federal government in 1862 first sought to compensate disabled veterans injured during the war. Revisions to the law in 1864 and 1866 increased the compensation for certain disabilities. Under pressure from a powerful veterans' political lobby, Congress expanded the benefits in 1873 and 1875 to compensate veterans for conditions contracted during the service that resulted in a later disability, and they extended back payments for disabilities not already applied for. Another major reform in 1890 allowed veterans to apply for a pension due to disabilities not necessarily related to their military service. The system was modified again 1907, transforming the pension system into an insurance scheme under the premise that old age was itself a disability.

From its origins in 1862, the Civil War pension system had an important civilian medical component in that local physicians examined applicants to confirm their medical conditions and rate the severity of their disabilities. The Pension Office then scrutinized the reports and passed final judgment on the claims. There was little controversy in the early years of the pension system, but the subsequent policy expansions forced (and allowed) physicians to make conclusions on disease states and disability without the benefit of modern diagnostics, and "led to charges that corrupt doctors validated veterans' false and exaggerated claims of disability" (Blanck and Chong 147).

Hand-in-hand with the inspecting physicians was a growing cottage industry of pension attorneys who prosecuted pension claims on behalf of the veterans. Indeed, if the post-war era was a new time for medicine, it was also a new time for the law, and pension attorney firms were among the largest professional organizations of their time. Their ubiquitous advertisements in period newspapers and circulars were a forerunner to modern medico-legal advertising and lobbying efforts. This flurry of changes in the law must have been dizzying for veterans; even more so, for widows, parents, and orphans who could also claim benefits. The Pension Bureau, rightly or wrongly, served as a gatekeeper to minimize fraud and abuse in the system, and there was fraud and abuse. People were hard-pressed to produce the documents that were required to secure pensions, especially in proving wartime diseases. Veterans and their families sometimes went to great lengths to secure affidavits from comrades, years after the guns fell silent. Pension attorneys were also known to drop cases due to frustration at their clients' inability to produce the required information for claims.

Civil War veterans in the North and South also encountered quackery in the continued influence of patent medicines. While the impact of patent medicines in the Civil War veteran community may not have been as important or long-lasting as the politico-medico-legal implications of pension policy, it was important nonetheless. Just as they had during the war itself, patent medicine firms marketed their wares specifically to Civil War veterans in the post-war years, and—as during the war—counted on testimonials from the erstwhile soldiers to prop up their "snake oil" to the American public. The stakes were high: patent medicine sales grew to nearly $80 million by the turn of the century. Accordingly, the solicitation of testimonials from veterans was vital. Patent medicines were especially popular in the South, which did not have the same maturing base of pharmaceutical industry that the North enjoyed. Especially popular was the Chattanooga Medicine Company's "Black Draught" (ironically marketed by some Union veterans); it became a southern staple and was heartily endorsed by old soldiers in *Confederate Veteran* magazine. Likewise, the company that sold "Pink Pills for Pale People" sent a brochure to Union veterans inviting them to fill out and return a list of questions about their health, so that they could be advised on a cure by return mail, free of charge.

The century closed with a curious—and humorous—intersection of pension policy and patent medicines. In 1897, an issue of the *Boston Medical and Surgical Journal* reported on the (perhaps apocryphal) case of a Massachusetts veteran who had given a testimonial to a patent-medicine manufacturer, stating that he had been entirely cured by his nostrum: "It seems that he was receiving a pension for the ills of which the medicine cured him, and that when the authorities learned of his recovery, his pension was cut off." The *Journal* wondered: "Is he likely to suffer relapse? And if he does will he get back his pension?" ("An Expensive Testimonial" 7). The *British Medical Journal*, seeing reports of the veteran's plight in American newspapers, had the answer: the authorities "would, we imagine, be more likely to recommend him a further course of the patent remedy which had proved so efficacious before" ("A Warning to Givers of Testimonials" 353).

## Further Reading

Abel, Emily K. *Hearts of Wisdom: American Women Caring for Kin, 1850–1940.* Cambridge: Harvard University Press, 2002.

"An Expensive Testimonial." *Boston Medical and Surgical Journal* 136 (1897): 7.

"A Warning to Givers of Testimonials." *British Medical Journal* 1 (1897): 353.

Baker, Robert B. (ed.). *The American Medical Ethics Revolution: How the AMA's Code of Ethics Has Transformed Physicians' Relationships to Patients, Professionals, and Society.* Baltimore: John Hopkins University Press, 1999.

Blanck, Peter and Cheng Chong. "Civil War Pension Attorneys and Disability Politics." *University of Michigan Journal of Law Reform* 35.1/2 (2002): 137–217.

*Born in Slavery: Slave Narratives from the Federal Writers' Project, 1936–1938.* Library of Congress Manuscript Division, Washington, D.C.

Cavender, Anthony P. *Folk Medicine in Southern Appalachia.* Chapel Hill: University of North Carolina Press, 2003.

"Chemistry and Medicine." *Scientific American*, August 17, 1861: 99.

Cumming, Kate. *A Journal of Hospital Life in the Confederate Army of Tennessee.* Louisville: John P. Morton, 1866.

Faust, Drew Gilpin. "The Civil War Homefront." In *Rally on the High Ground: The National Park Service Symposium on the Civil War.* Ed. Robert K. Sutton. Washington, DC: Eastern National, 2001.

Gabriel, Joseph M. "A Thing Patented is a Thing Divulged: Francis E. Stewart, George S. Davis, and the Legitimization of Intellectual Property Rights in Pharmaceutical Manufacturing, 1879–1911." *Journal of the History of Medicine and Allied Sciences* 64.2 (2009): 135–172.

Giesberg, Judith A. *Army at Home: Women and the Civil War on the Northern Home Front.* Chapel Hill: University of North Carolina Press, 2009.

Gillispie, James M. *Andersonvilles of the North: The Myths and Realities of Northern Treatment of Civil War Confederate Prisoners.* Denton: University of North Texas Press, 2008.

Lambert, Patricia M. "Infectious Disease Among Enslaved African Americans at Eaton's Estate, Warren County, North Carolina, ca. 1830–1850." *Memórias do Instituto Oswaldo Cruz* 101, Suppl II (2006): 107–117.

McPherson, James M. *Battle Cry of Freedom: The Civil War Era.* New York: Oxford University Press, 1988.

Savitt, Todd L. *Medicine and Slavery: The Diseases and Health Care of Blacks in Antebellum Virginia.* Urbana: University of Illinois Press, 1978. Reprint 2002.

Schmidt, James M., and Guy R. Hasegawa, eds. *Years of Change and Suffering: Modern Perspectives on Civil War Medicine.* Roseville: Edinborough Press, 2009.

Scott, Anne F. *The Southern Lady, From Pedestal to Politics, 1830–1930.* Chicago: University of Chicago Press, 1970.

Starr, Paul. *The Social Transformation of American Medicine.* New York: Basic Books, 1982.

Twain, Mark. *The Autobiography of Mark Twain.* Ed. Charles Neider. New York: Harper & Brothers, 1959.

Wilkie, Jennifer S. "Enter the Physician: The Transformation of Domestic Medicine, 1760–1860, by Lamar Riley Murphy." *Journal of Social History* 26.1 (1993): 686.

# PART V

# Ethnic American Lives

# 15

## SLAVE EMANCIPATION

*Sharon A. Roger Hepburn*

One of the most significant changes wrought by the Civil War was the abolition of slavery. Yet the Civil War was not fought specifically or solely to abolish the institution. The official rhetoric at the onset of war in 1861 was that the North was fighting to restore the Union—as a slaveholding union. In his inaugural address and then again in a July Fourth message to Congress, President Lincoln pledged that he had "no purpose, directly or indirectly, to interfere with slavery in the States where it exists" (170). At the end of July, Congress overwhelmingly approved the Crittenden-Johnson resolution affirming that the war was not being fought with the intention or purpose of "overthrowing or interfering with the rights or established institutions" of the states but rather to "defend and maintain the supremacy of the Constitution and to preserve the Union" (*Congressional Globe* 1861, 222–23).

Despite the official pronouncements and public stance, there were those, abolitionist William Lloyd Garrison among them, who saw slavery as the root cause of the war and prophesied that the institution would not survive the conflict. In his newspaper, *The Liberator,* Garrison espoused his opinion that slavery was the underlying cause of the conflict between North and South: "out of the slave system comes this terrible civil war, with whatever ghastly horrors may follow in its train." Garrison warned that if the war did not remove the institution then, "in due time, a still more fearful volcanic explosion" would erupt (n.p.). In May 1861, black abolitionist Frederick Douglass wrote that "the American people and the Government at Washington may refuse to recognize it for a time; but the 'inexorable logic of events' will force it upon them in the end; that the war now being waged in this land is a war for and against slavery" (n.p.).

Slaves, too, had a different understanding of the war than that proclaimed by Lincoln. They saw themselves at the heart of the conflict and knew that their future depended on the war's outcome. Recognizing in the war the potential to end slavery, they took actions to ensure that abolition became an integral part of the wartime agenda. Slaves began to liberate themselves as soon as the fighting began, pouring into Union lines, seeking refuge, protection, and freedom. In a letter of May 1861, Union General William S. Harney, made note of the actions of slaves within the first month of the shots at Fort Sumter: "Already since the commencement of these unhappy disturbances, slaves have escaped from their owners, and have sought refuge in the camps of United States troops" (Berlin et al. 1992, 7). Slaves then took advantage of the intense disruption of war in the area between Washington and Richmond in the summer of 1861. By August, more than nine hundred fugitives had sought and gained protection with the Union forces. Slaves who found de facto freedom behind Union lines often took the next step in securing the liberty of their families as they returned south and brought out their wives, children, and other family members. These actions were dangerous. Fugitives might be recaptured by owners who were deemed "loyal" by Union officers, as was the case when two runaways who sought refuge with the 10th Indiana were dragged away by slave hunters after receiving permission by the regimental commander to search through the encampment. When one owner captured his fugitive slaves in the District of Columbia, he had them severely whipped and confined for the duration of the war.

The development of Union political and military policy often lagged behind slaves' actions. Military authorities initially followed no set policy and sent out mixed messages, including Henry Halleck's order returning escaped slaves to their owners in the Ohio Valley and Benjamin Butler's declaration of fugitive slaves as contraband in Virginia. Meanwhile, Lincoln, fearful of retribution from the border states whose loyalty he deemed essential to the Union's war effort, treaded lightly and pushed his agenda for voluntary, gradual, compensated emancipation with support for colonization. But as the war progressed, there was a perceptible shift in its apparent objectives. In response to Major General Butler's classification of slaves who were used in the Confederate military effort as contraband, Congress passed the First Confiscation Act in July 1861 that provided for the confiscation, and de facto freedom, of such slaves. When Congress assembled in December 1861 John J. Crittenden reintroduced his resolution that declared the war was being waged solely to save the union, a resolution that had passed almost unanimously just a few months earlier. Now, with Republicans voting overwhelmingly against it, the House resolution was soundly defeated. Sentiment within Lincoln's party was hardening against slavery. Congress then proceeded to pass a series of laws designed to chip away at the institution. In April 1862, slavery was abolished in the District of Columbia. A new article of war was enacted on May 13, 1862, that prohibited army officers from returning fugitive slaves to their owners. The next month, defying the Supreme Court's ruling in the 1857 Dred Scott case, Congress prohibited slavery in the territories. In August, it passed a Second Confiscation Act that not only authorized the seizure of the property of persons in rebellion but also specified that all slaves who came within Union lines were captives of war and free.

Meanwhile, Lincoln believed that emancipation should occur under state auspices and continued to work toward that end. He was convinced that if the border states adopted emancipation, their action would shorten the war. Throughout the first year of the war, Lincoln repeatedly urged the border states to adopt a program of gradual, compensated emancipation—they demurred. In the fall of 1861, Lincoln proposed the "Delaware Plan" to apply to border states with less than 2,000 slaves. His proposal called for a gradual abolition program that would immediately free slaves over the age of thirty-five as well as those born after passage of the plan, and then gradually free others as they reached the age of thirty-five. The proposal further provided for compensation to owners for the loss of their property. His proposal was rejected.

Putting preservation of the Union first, Lincoln remained concerned with the legal, political, and social constraints on emancipation. As late as August 22, 1862, only a month before the preliminary emancipation proclamation was announced, Lincoln responded to a plea from Horace Greely, editor of the antislavery *New York Tribune*, by underscoring his guiding principle of the war—preservation of the Union. Even as he marched towards the issuance of the proclamation, Lincoln advocated a program of gradual, compensated emancipation. In his December 1862 annual message to Congress, he urged Congress to pass three constitutional amendments to provide federal bonds to any state that abolished slavery before 1900; to secure the freedom of all slaves freed by "the chances of war" with compensation to loyal owners; and to authorize federal funding for colonizing free blacks.

The Emancipation Proclamation consists of two executive orders. The first was announced on September 22, 1862, shortly after the bloody battle of Antietam. This Preliminary Proclamation declared that slaves in any state of the Confederacy that did not return to the Union by January 1, 1863, would be free. Then the Emancipation Proclamation, signed by Lincoln on January 1, 1863, enumerated the specific states, and parts of states, still in rebellion and thus subject to emancipation. Slaves in the remaining parts of the country, including the border states of Delaware, Maryland, Missouri, and Kentucky, that had not seceded from the Union, were unaffected by the Proclamation. Although it was widely criticized for freeing only those slaves over which Lincoln had no real power, the document committed the Union to ending slavery. It made emancipation an irrevocable war aim, profoundly changing the character of the Civil War.

Enslaved and free African Americans awaited Lincoln's official proclamation with great anticipation and excitement. As they waited, celebrations took place throughout the nation. On New Year's Eve 1862, black communities held prayer and worship services. These "watch night meetings" welcomed the new year with thanksgiving and prayer. In Washington, D.C., hundreds congregated in a chapel in a contraband camp located on 12th and Q streets. Other members of Washington's black community gathered at a celebration at the Israel Bethel Church where Henry McNeil Turner read the Emancipation Proclamation. Reports in the *Washington Evening Star* the next day spoke of unrestrained celebration, with men shouting and women fainting.

In New York City, black abolitionist and clergyman Henry Highland Garnet presided over an emancipation Jubilee. The crowd of both white and black congregants filled the Shiloh Presbyterian Church to capacity. They listened to numerous speeches focused on the trials and tribulations faced by slaves, and the contributions of blacks in the fight to save the Union. Other speeches focused on the struggle of abolitionists to bring about the day of freedom, and the hand of God in the history and destiny of slaves. In Boston, three thousand people, including Frederick Douglass, assembled at Tremont Temple on New Year's Eve. And on New Year's Day in Boston, the Philharmonic conducted a jubilee concert. Similar celebrations occurred throughout the North—in Philadelphia, Rochester, Chicago, Albany, Pittsburgh, and Buffalo.

Emancipation celebrations took place in the South as well, even in places where slaves were not freed by the proclamation. At Norfolk, Virginia, a city already in Union hands and thus exempt from its provisions, four thousand freedmen paraded through the streets. At Port Royal, South Carolina, also under Union occupation, there was an elaborate celebration at Camp Saxton on January 1. Slaves from the surrounding area came to Camp Saxton by the hundreds to participate. The *New York Herald* reported that around four thousand blacks came from surrounding plantations. Some walked, while others came in by steamers. The *Boston* brought several hundred blacks from Hilton Head, and the steamer *Flora* arrived from Beaufort around midday with upwards of a thousand passengers. The three-hour-long service then consisted of music, prayers, hymns, speeches, and a reading of the Emancipation Proclamation by Dr. William Brisbane—a planter turned abolitionist who had freed his own slaves years before. A flag donated by a church in New York bearing the embroidered inscription "The Year of Jubilee has Come" was presented to the 1st South Carolina regiment members who were also in attendance. Their commander, Thomas Wentworth Higginson, gave one of the several addresses that day, before the crowd adjourned to the parade ground and partook of a barbecue.

Some slaves did reject all notions of Lincoln as their deliverer. Thomas Hall, born a slave in North Carolina, held nothing back. "Lincoln got the praise for freeing us, but did he do it? He give us freedom without giving us any chance to live to ourselves and we still had to depend on the southern man for work, food and clothing, and he held us through our necessity and want in a state of servitude but little better than slavery. Lincoln done but little for the negro race and from living standpoint nothing" (Rawick 14:47). Hall and other members of the black community clearly connected physical freedom with economic and social opportunity and criticized Lincoln for his failure to provide the latter.

But despite the limitations of the Emancipation Proclamation, many slaves revered Lincoln as a Moses figure. To Elijah Marrs, a runaway slave who enlisted in the Union Army, Lincoln was "our Moses." Another black soldier recalled: "Lincoln was indeed our Moses. He gave us our freedom" (Blackett 294). Many other black men and women simply associated Lincoln with freedom. "I know that I am free, for I have seen father Abraham and felt him" exclaimed one former slave (Blackett 294). Some slaves described their deliverance as coming from God through Lincoln. Hannah Crasson, a former slave from Mississippi, recalled: "I thank de will of God for setting us free. He got into Abraham Lincoln and the Yankees. We are thankful to the Great Marster dat got into Lincoln and the Yankees" (*Born in Slavery* 11:193). Another former slave, Sarah Waggoner, exclaimed: "Abe Lincoln was jes' next to Jesus Christ. Yes, Oh Lord! Yes! Dat he was! Jes' next to Jesus Christ! I remember when I was freed!" (*Born in Slavery* 10:358).

Even those who were unclear who Lincoln really was linked him with emancipation: "Lincoln was the man that set us free. He was a big general in the war," wrote Charlie Moses, a former slave from Mississippi (Rawick 7:135–42). Another slave said: "I thought Abraham Lincoln wuz the Medicine man, with grip in his han', cause he said every borned man must be free" (*Born in Slavery* 9:116). Others, like Susan Snow, "didn' know nothin' 'bout Abe Lincoln," but heard "he was a-tryin' to free de [slaves] an' my mammy say she want to be free" (*Born in Slavery* 7:135–42). Henry Cheatam, from Alabama, remarked that he did not "know nothin' 'bout Abe Lincoln 'ceptin' dey say he sot us free, an' I don't know nothin' 'bout dat neither" (*Born in Slavery* 1:71). Gabe Emanuel, from Claiborne County, Mississippi, recalled merely that "Lincoln was de man dat sot us free. I don't recollec' much 'about 'im 'ceptin' what I hear'd in de Big House 'bout Lincoln doin' dis an' Lincoln doin' dat" (*Born in Slavery* 9:47).

Lincoln's death elevated him into a state of martyrdom. Many set aside the limitations of emancipation and Lincoln's penchant for colonization and inequality. Freedmen on St. Helena Island, South Carolina, prayed for him. Laura Towne reported from the Sea Islands, where she had gone to help teach newly emancipated slaves, that upon hearing the news of Lincoln's death, the freedmen prayed for him in church and said that "he was their Savior—that Christ saved them from sin and he [Lincoln] from Secesh" (Rose 346). Towne recalled that another freedman said: "Lincoln died for we, Christ died for we, and me believe him de same mans" (Towne 159–60). Christ saved them from sin while Lincoln rescued them from slavery. In speaking of Lincoln's death, Mattie Lee, an ex-slave from Missouri, remarked that she "often thought how hard it was to give up his life for de United States. But Christ died for to save de world an Lincoln died to save de United States. And Lincoln died more Christ-like dan any other man dat ever lived" (*Born in Slavery* 10:226).

The manner in which slaves learned of the Emancipation Proclamation varied. Some slaves read the proclamation themselves and then told others of its contents and meaning. Some heard whites talking about the document while others heard of emancipation through the slave "grapevine." Still other slaves were told by their masters or were informed of their freedom by Union soldiers. Black soldiers of the 1st South Carolina Regiment, for instance, carried stacks of printed copies of the Emancipation Proclamation with them when they engaged in a raid in Florida in the early months of 1863. Willis Anderson, a former slave from Texas, recalled how Union soldiers came through Centerville "telling the slave owners to free their slaves" (*Born in Slavery* 16:22).

Just as varied was the behavior of slaves in response to news of emancipation. A southern white landowner in Port Gibson, Mississippi, complained to the state's governor that blacks were acting as they pleased. Widespread disloyalty and general "strikes" followed the Emancipation Proclamation. Beginning on Christmas Day, the slaves on Magnolia Plantation in Mississippi simply refused to work anymore. Elsewhere slaves danced and sang. William Adams recalled that "dere was a lot of excitement 'mong de niggers. Dey was rejoicin' and singin'. Some of 'em looked puzzle, sorter skeered like. But dey danced and had a big jamboree" (Rawick 4:8-11). And when Caddy, a slave who had been sold numerous times for her defiant attitude, learned of her freedom, she found her mistress, flipped up her dress and told the white woman to "kiss my ass" (Litwack 187). Still other slaves reacted not with gestures of joy and abandon, but with tears. William Adams recalled that when he and fellow slaves on their plantation in Texas were told of emancipation, "They's lots of cryin' and weepin'.... Lots of them didn't want to be free, 'cause they knowed nothin', and had nowhere to go" (*Born in Slavery* 16:3).

The slave community often viewed military service as a key step in the process of emancipation. Emery Turner remembered how the adult males on her plantation left to join the Union Army as soon as they learned of Lincoln's proclamation. Others recalled that when their communities heard about emancipation, the "grown-up negroes on the place left to join the Union Army" (*Born in Slavery* 5:8). Thomas Long, former slave and Union soldier, acknowledged that if slaves "hadn't become sojers, all might have gone back as it was before, our freedom might have slipped through de two houses of Congress and President Linkum's four years might have passed by and notin' been done for us" (Litwack 102). In fact, a majority of the roughly 180,000 African American troops who fought in the Civil War had been slaves. Their enlistment and service assured them of their freedom, and helped liberate others.

But freedom came about by degrees and the death of slavery proved to be agonizingly slow for many. The precise moment when slaves could safely think of themselves as free men and women was not always clear. Some only found out about their freedom after the war, and without mention of the Emancipation Proclamation itself. Barney Alvord recalled how he found out he was free: "ole Marse cum home to stay an' he looked mi'ty sad. One day he rung de big bell an' had all de darkies to cum to de house an' told dem dey wus freed" (Rawick 6:23–49). Isaac Williams remembered: "One day he [master] went into Arcadia and come home and told us the war was over and we was free" (Rawick 7:1–5). Even in instances where slaves realized they were free, some waited to hear their masters confirm it rather than assert their free status independently themselves.

Particularly for slaves in Texas, freedom came late. News of emancipation finally reached the people of Texas, on June 19, 1865. Stories still circulate about why it took two and a half years for news to travel: some say a messenger was murdered on his way to Texas, others that Union troops waited for the end of the cotton harvest to enforce the proclamation, still others that the news was deliberately withheld by slave-holders. Texas slaves were emancipated by General Gordon Granger, who on June 19 announced in Galveston that all slaves were free. And even beyond Texas, freedom was not instantaneous. Mary Shaw, a slave born in Bolivar County, Mississippi, recalled that she did not know anything about the war or freedom at the time, and that her mother "said it was a long time after freedom 'fore she knowed anything about it. She said there was just lots of the folks said, to their knowin', they had been free three years 'fore they knowed anything about it" (*Born in Slavery* 2:141).

Some masters refused to give up their slaves until forced to do so by slaves themselves or a federal officer. John Bates remembered that his owner "never call us up like everybody else the slaves, us has to go up and ask him 'bout it" (*Born in Slavery* 16:52). Frank Bell testified that when the war was over, his master refused to set him free. "Master helt me long years after the war. If anybody git after him, he told them I stay 'cause I wants to stay, but told me if I left he'd kill [me]" (*Born in Slavery* 16:60). One master did not tell his slaves they were free until he saw a group of soldiers coming down the road, at which point he called the slaves "in quick, and told them they were free" just before the soldiers arrived (*Born in Slavery* 16:98). Issabella Boyd and her fellow slaves on a plantation near Beaumont, Texas, continued to work as slaves for months after they first heard about freedom in part because their master waited "de long time lettin' us know. Dey wants to git through with de corn and de cotton Befo' dey let's de hands loose" (*Born in Slavery* 16:115). Even when told by people from nearby plantations that they were free, the slaves on Boyd's plantation refused to believe it and kept working, thinking that "de gov'ment tell us when we's free" (*Born in Slavery* 16:115). Only after Boyd's master went to town to "see what de gov'ment goin' do" and returned home to say "yo'r jus' as free as I is" did his slaves fully realize their freedom (*Born in Slavery* 16:115).

Freedom was often heavily dependent on the proximity of the army. Many slaves, even before the Emancipation Proclamation, assumed they were free when the Yankees arrived. Samuel Elliot, born in Liberty County, Georgia, stated that he became free "when the army came into the County" (n.p.). Nancy Johnson similarly testified that she "became free when the army came" to her part of Georgia (n.p.). Of course, the southern white attitude was that the Union army passing through, proclaiming freedom to the slaves, was not sufficient to make freedom a reality. One southern white woman noted that as soon as the Union soldiers moved on from their area, local confederates assembled the slaves and instructed them to return to their duties as if the federal troops had never been there. North Carolinian Ambrose Douglass remembered that "every time a bunch of No'thern sojers would come through they would tell us we was free and we'd begin celebrating," but then "somebody else would tell us to go back to work, and we would go" (Guelzo 240).

With good reason, slaves were often cautious about exercising their freedom and realistically perceived that the degree of their freedom often rested with the proximity of federal authorities. When the Union Army moved on, those blacks remaining were often confused and frightened, fearing retribution for action they had taken while the soldiers were protecting them. Such retribution, enacted by masters upon their slaves, did occur. On one plantation near Columbia, South Carolina, a master vented his anger on a young slave girl who had helped the Yankees find the master's hidden valuables. After the Yankees departed, the master hung her. Further west, another master let his slaves know that if the Yankees reached them in Oklahoma, the slaves were not going to be freed because "when dey git here dey going to find you already free, 'cause I gwine line you up on de bank of [the creek] and free you wid my shotgun" (Rawick 7:275–84). Such acts and promises of violence made slaves wary of acting on their freedom.

This wariness, however, did not reflect a lack of understanding about what freedom *was*. Despite this common misconception among whites, in both the North and the South, many slaves did indeed know what freedom entailed. Of course, not all slaves fully understood the meaning of freedom: "I heare some slaves shoutin' glad cose they was free. I didn't know what 'free' meant," remembered one former slave (Rawick 8:3082–86). But many others knew that freedom meant that they now belonged to themselves; that they were their own masters. When asked who they belonged to, former slaves responded: "Ise don't b'longs to nobody ... Ise owns self" (Litwack 226). Barney Alford recalled that fellow slaves on his plantation "wanted to be sot free. Dey jes' didn't want to work under a whup; dey all wanted to be free to cum an' go when dey wanted" (Rawick 6:23–49). Whatever remained vague about their new status, freedman realized that they were no longer merchandise, subject to sale at the whim, bankruptcy or death of their owners. They recognized that freedom secured their families from involuntary disruption.

The Emancipation Proclamation itself did not provide much in the way of guidelines for freedom. It only instructed blacks to "labor faithfully for reasonable wage," and "to abstain from all violence, unless in necessary self-defense." So freedmen had to carve out their new lives as best they could, within the constraints of their varied circumstances. Some, albeit a small number, were provided with what some might call "freedom dues." Sarah Ashley, freed from a cotton plantation in Texas, recalled: "when de boss man told us freedom was come he didn't like it, but he give all us de bale of cotton and some corn" (*Born in Slavery* 16:9). More often slaves entered freedom with little more than their own capacity for physical labor to establish their independence. Barney Alford of Mississippi remembered that "when de slaves wus sot free, dey had nuffin an' ole Marse didnt give 'em anything" (Rawick 6:23–49). Throughout the South, freed people confronted the vast changes that were sweeping through their world amid the disruption and dislocation of war.

Of the many decisions facing newly freed slaves, the dilemma of whether to remain with their former masters or leave for the unknown was perhaps the most pressing. Former owners often tried to hold onto their laborers, with varying success. Alford recalled that his master, after telling his slaves that they were free, "tole dem if dey wud stay wid him dat year he wud contract wuf dem; sum uf 'em left right den, an' sum uf 'em stayed on" (Rawick 6:23–49). Alford and his mother remained on the Mississippi plantation for almost five years, leaving only when the landowner could no longer pay for their labor. Several factors may explain why they did not immediately leave the site of their former bondage. Alford makes no mention of the presence of his father and so perhaps he and his mother had no other family members with whom to travel. Alford left when his former owner could no longer pay him wages, so perhaps economic motivations played a role in the decision.

Some slaves chose not to leave for years. In Texas, Will Adams stayed with his former master and his family "mos' twenty years after the war" before striking out on his own to farm and do odd jobs around town (*Born in Slavery* 16:3). On a plantation in Texas, slaves apparently responded with fear or loyalty and "cheer[ed] and say day want to stay" when the master explained that they could stay and work for pay (*Born in Slavery* 16:82). And in Louisiana, when Isaac Adams's master informed his slaves that they were free, they "didn't know what to make of it" and about half chose to remain on the plantation and work for shares. Adams was among those who left, explaining that he was "jest a boy and he [master] didn't need me at the house anyway." Adams left with his father to try to "do better somewhere else" (Rawick 7:1–5). Many former slaves who stayed on the site of their former enslavement did so not out of loyalty to their former owners but a desire to live among kin in familiar surroundings. And although they did not leave, some declared their independence in a different way—by asserting family names for themselves. By taking their own surnames, they declared their freedom and claimed their own identities.

For decades afterwards, the black community commemorated freedom annually with Emancipation Day celebrations. Although not a legal holiday recognized by the government, this day was commemorated as early as 1864. More than a day of remembrance, it was a day to celebrate liberation and mark the progress of African Americans since the Emancipation Proclamation. One of the first such celebrations was held in Charleston on January 1, 1866, when over 10,000 African Americans crowded the racetrack there to celebrate the end of slavery. But due to the different pace of liberation across the states, various other days served as "emancipation day" as well. While in some locations it was January 1, the date of the Emancipation Proclamation, other communities celebrated on September 22, the date of the Preliminary Emancipation Proclamation, and still others celebrated on July 4 (American Independence Day) or August 1 (West Indian Emancipation Day). Most Emancipation Day celebrations were sponsored by black churches. Festivities accompanied such celebrations, including a reading of the Emancipation Proclamation, sermons and speeches, music, barbeques, and parades.

Another common day of celebration was Juneteenth, June 19, marking the date of the announcement of slavery's abolition in Texas in 1865. Elvira Boles remembered that "Freedom was given on January 1, 1865, but de slaves didn' know it 'till June 19" (*Born in Slavery* 16:108). Near San Augustine, Texas, Harrison Beckett was told by his mother that when the war was over, their master called the slaves together and told them "you's free as I is…. Dat near June 19th" (*Born in Slavery* 16:57). Gus Johnson, of Beaumont, Texas, remembered that after freedom they would have a big celebration on Juneteenth every year (*Born in Slavery* 16:210). Josh Miles recalls similar Juneteenth celebrations in Texas in which "de white folks give us beeves and hawgs to barbecue" (*Born in Slavery* 16:81). Today, forty-one states recognize Juneteenth as an official holiday.

## Further Reading

Berlin, Ira, et al., eds. *Free at Last: A Documentary History of Slavery, Freedom, and the Civil War.* New York: New Press, 1992.

Berlin, Ira, Marc Favreau, and Steven F. Miller, eds. *Remembering Slavery: African Americans Talk About their Personal Experiences of Slavery and Emancipation.* New York: New Press, 1998.

*Born in Slavery: Slave Narratives from the Federal Writers' Project, 1936–1938.* Library of Congress, Manuscript Division.

Blackett, R.J.M., ed. *Thomas Morris Chester: Black Civil War Correspondent.* Baton Rouge: Louisiana State University Press, 1989.

*Congressional Globe: Debates and Proceedings 1833–1873.* 37th Congress 1 Session, 1861. Washington, DC: Globe Office, 1833–1873.

Douglass, Frederick. "Nemesis." *Douglass' Monthly.* May 1861.

Elliott, Samuel. "Testimony, July 17, 1873." Liberty County, Georgia case files, Approved Claims, ser. 732, Southern Claims Commission, 3rd Auditor, RG 217.

Garrison, William Lloyd. "The War—Its Cause and Cure." *The Liberator.* May 3, 1861.

Guelzo, Allen. *Lincoln's Emancipation Proclamation: The End of Slavery in America.* New York: Simon & Schuster, 2004.

Johnson, Nancy, "Testimony, March 22, 1873." Georgia case files, Approved Claims, ser. 732, Southern Claims Commission, 3rd Auditor, RG 217.

Lincoln, Abraham. "First Inaugural Address, March 4, 1861." *Complete Works of Abraham Lincoln, Volume 6.* Harrogate: Lincoln Memorial University, 1894.

Litwack, Leon F. *Been in the Storm So Long: The Aftermath of Slavery.* New York: Vintage, 1980.

Rawick, George P. *The American Slave: A Composite Autobiography.* Westport: Greenwood Press, 1973–1976.

Rose, Willie Lee. *Rehearsal for Reconstruction: The Port Royal Experiment.* Oxford: Oxford University Press, 1964.

Towne, Laura M. *Letters and Diary: Written from the Sea Islands of South Carolina, 1862–1884.* New York: Negro Universities Press, 1969.

# 16

# BLACK TROOPS

*Maggi M. Morehouse*

In a rousing 1863 recruiting speech, Frederick Douglass said: "Once let the black man get upon his person the brass letters, U.S, let him get an eagle on his button, and a musket on his shoulder and bullets in his pockets, and there is no power on the earth or under the earth which can deny that he has earned the right to citizenship in the United States" (Blassingame 592). In this speech "Negroes and the National War Effort," delivered at a mass meeting in Philadelphia, Douglass informed the mostly black audience of the opportunity to enlist in the Union Army. He also linked the ideas of black citizenship and military service. He exhorted the large crowd: "Young men of Philadelphia, you are without excuse. The hour has arrived and your place is in the Union army" (598).

If the audience was skeptical, because many black men had been denied the right to participate in any capacity in the armed forces, Douglass cleared up their uncertainties: "We are American citizens. We can import goods, own and sail ships, and travel in foreign countries with American passports in our pockets" (592). Douglass noted how some states had refused enlistment and service of black soldiers, but he said that this policy of discrimination would not continue and reassured his listeners that the federal government's policy of open enlistment would take precedence over any state policies. Then, he announced a significant change in the government's view on black enlistment and participation in the "War of the Rebellion": "The President at Washington, the Cabinet and the Congress, the generals commanding, and the whole army of the nation unite in giving us one thunderous welcome to share with them in the honor and glory of suppressing treason and upholding the star-spangled banner" (592). The transcription says his speech was met with "immense cheering" (598). Judging from the number of recruits who flooded the enlistment stations, including two of his sons, the open-door policy was a turning point for African American participation in the war effort.

Two years into the Civil War by this point, President Lincoln had finally allowed for the enlistment of black soldiers. He hoped black participation in the armed forces would bring an end to the war more quickly. Lincoln knew the Confederate Army was already using black individuals as laborers. Confederate generals were also discussing whether to arm black men in defense of their goals. Shortly after Lincoln's change of policy, black men were officially allowed to serve in the Union Army, and the Confederate Army began to employ more soldiers of African descent. While no social survey results exist, black men likely viewed participation in the armed services of the Civil War as a road to citizenship and more liberties. Douglass told them to remember, "the musket—the United States musket with its bayonet of steel—is better than all mere parchment guarantees of liberty. In your hands that musket means liberty; and should your constitutional rights at the close of this war be denied, which, in the nature of things, it cannot be, your brethren are safe while you have a Constitution which proclaims your right to keep and bear arms" (Blassingame 598).

African Americans have always understood the relationship between military service and civil rights. Enslaved and free black men participated in every military engagement since the colonial battles; at times offered freedom in exchange for their military service, at other times extended civil rights. The connection between liberty, citizenship, and military service was especially relevant during the Civil War when more than four million people of African descent awaited freedom from bondage. Participation in the war was one avenue toward freedom and citizenship within the nation and after the first battle of the Civil War in secessionist South Carolina, African Americans attempted to enlist in the armed forces.

At the onset of the Civil War, both the Union and the Confederate Armies were reluctant to arm African Americans. Both governing military hierarchies were operating under the Militia Law of 1792 that specifically banned black enlistment. Should the nation require a fighting force, each state was authorized under the law to provide a uniformed militia of "able-bodied white male citizens" eighteen years or older. African Americans were regularly used in service and support of military operations—they were employed to cook and feed the troops or do laundry, build the military quarters and storage facilities, and do other manual work. Over the years, there were exceptions, including the black men and children who were brought into the service as musicians. In addition, when white troops were worn out during wars and battles, military commanders would make exceptions and muster in black units. But black soldiers were not seen as assets in combat, and thus were underutilized. Military commanders were never sure if armed black men would shoot at them or the enemy, or simply vanish. They crafted policies to keep African Americans in service and support rather than combat operations because they believed in black inferiority.

By 1861, the North remained reluctant to recruit and arm black soldiers, fearing that even non-slaveholding states would lean toward the Confederacy if black soldiers were used in the service of the Union. The Confederates also refrained from enlisting slaves or free black men for fear of an armed rebellion. And so, although both sides contemplated arming black soldiers, writing memos and policy proposals throughout the war, the most frequent use of African Americans came in the form of labor for the military. Early in the war, Confederates impressed black men and women to build fortifications and prepare food for the troops, while the Union put white officers in command of the black infantry volunteers and assigned them to be used for scouting purposes.

But both governing military powers changed their policies during the four years of the war. These policies evolved alongside the aims of the war. In 1861, President Lincoln stated that the war aims were crafted to maintain the Union. Writing to Horace Greeley, the editor of the *New York Tribune*, Lincoln stated: "My paramount object in this struggle is to save the Union, and is not either to save or to destroy slavery. If I could save the Union without freeing any slave I would do it, and if I could save it by freeing all the slaves I would do it; and if I could save it by freeing some and leaving others alone I would also do that" (388). Lincoln was also pursuing a policy of black repatriation or colonization as a way to rid the Union of slavery. Congress approved an act authorizing the president "to make provision for the transportation, colonization, and settlement, in some tropical country beyond the limits of the United States, of such persons of the African race, made free by the provisions of this act, as may be willing to emigrate" (U.S., *Statutes at Large, Treaties, and Proclamations of the United States of America* 592). When this repatriation became too costly, the president and Congress looked for other ways to get rid of the problem of slavery.

During this early period of the Civil War, most northern military officers did not want open enlistment for African Americans who might misconstrue the war aims as a strike against slavery. For example, as Brigadier General Thomas W. Sherman entered South Carolina to secure the coast for Union forces, he sent words of greetings to calm the people. He said: "I have passed some of the pleasantest days of my life" here and "we come among you with no feelings of personal animosity; no desire to harm your citizens, destroy your property, or interfere with any of your lawful laws, rights, or your social and local institutions" (Nalty and MacGregor 22). As the Union Army advanced along the coastline, hundreds of enslaved individuals took shelter in the Union camps and offered their services to the northern forces. These "contraband of war" were not to be utilized as fighting forces but could provide labor services to the Union defenses. Both northern and southern military officials recognized the value of slavery to the Confederate war effort, and Union forces accepted the labor of the "contraband" in order to strip the Confederates of the wage-free work force upon which they had become dependent. Union officers who employed "contrabands as servants" were instructed to pay "at least eight dollars per month for males, and four dollars per month for females" (Nalty and MacGregor 22).

The same year, the First Confiscation Act passed by Congress established a policy that had been in practice at Union strongholds in the South. The act denied masters the labor of slaves who had been permitted to labor for the Confederacy. This punitive policy helped to turn war efforts toward the idea of emancipation, and the loss of Confederate labor and the addition of a labor pool for the Union strengthened the northern army. Then, the following year, in 1862, Lincoln asked the slaveholding states that had not seceded from the Union to consider a plan of compensation for the emancipation of slaves. Although they refused his ideas, Congress pushed ahead with a Second Con-fiscation Act in concert with an amended Militia Act that emancipated slaves who were able to labor for the Union forces, and allowed for people of Afri-can descent to be mobilized into any branch of the military where they were deemed competent. Congress declared that "the President of the United States is authorized to employ as many persons of African descent as he may deem necessary and proper for the suppression of this rebellion, and for this purpose he may organize and use them in such manner as he may judge best for the public welfare" (U.S., *Statutes at Large, Treaties, and Proclamations of the United States of America* 592).

This policy shift served a severe blow to the Confederacy and signaled a change in thinking about the use of black soldiers in warfare. At the beginning of the war, Lincoln had established the northern fighting forces through a pro-gram of volunteers, militiamen, and regular army men. Each state in the Union recruited and trained the volunteers in their own state militias. The governor of Massachusetts and a senator from Kentucky, plus some Union field generals, asked for black troops to be recruited. Lincoln stalled until white troop recruit-ment and reenlistment was so low and the manpower shortage so extreme that he had to craft a policy to conscript or enlist black men—contraband, free and enslaved.

Both before and after these policy shifts, however, black men and women involved themselves in the struggle in a variety of ways. After the war, former slaves remembered how they entered the military and what happened next. "Soldier" Williams recalled: "I run away to Louisville to j'ine the Yankees one day. I was scared to death all the time. They put us in front to shield themselves. They said they was fighting for us—for our freedom. Piles of them was killed; I got a flesh wound. I'm scarred up some. We got plenty to eat. I was in two or three battles. I wanted to quit but they would catch them and shoot them if they left. I didn't know how to get out and get away" (*Born in Slavery* 2:191). Other slaves had an even more dramatic entry into the war. In 1862, a Union navy commander off the coast of Charleston, South Carolina, reported on a steamer he saw flying a white flag: "I immediately boarded her, hauled down the flag of truce, and hoisted an American ensign, and found that it was the steamer *Planter*, of Charleston, and had successfully run past the forts and escaped. She was wholly manned by Negroes, representing themselves to be slaves" (Nalty and MacGregor 34). Since the Navy had no policy to address these exploits of Robert Smalls, the black captain who steered the *Planter* into Union hands, the commander was writing for authorization to commandeer the steamer and its passengers.

Regiments of black soldiers also began to organize, with white officers in command. Volunteer corps included the Louisiana Native Guards, the 1st South Carolina Volunteers, and the 1st Kansas Colored Volunteers, who fought Confederates at Island Mound, Missouri, in late 1862. Their commanding officer described the battle between his 225 soldiers and the counter force of 500 rebels: "After a severe engagement the rebels were defeated with severe loss. Our loss was 8 killed and 10 wounded" (Nalty and MacGregor 26). He was pleased to report this "first engagement in the late war in which colored troops were engaged."

The shift to a federal authorization of black troops came that year, in 1862. The Emancipation Proclamation, sent to Union troops as a General Order in September 1862 following the Union victory at Antietam, signaled Lincoln's acknowledgement of the value of utilizing free African Americans in the war. This order was followed by a congressional mandate requiring all men between the ages of twenty and forty-five to sign up for military service, with selection provided by conscription through a lottery. A conscript could pay $300 for a replacement individual (called a commutation fee), and this, along with the open recruitment of black men, led to anger and disenchantment among many white recruits. Further inequality existed within the troop hierarchy. In all cases of black recruitment into military service, the men served in segregated units with the officer corps filled by white men. Still, African Americans flooded the recruiting stations, sometimes traveling to other states so that they could enlist. Douglass interpreted the proclamation and military service as a positive advancement and he exhorted men to enlist immediately, even supporting his two sons when they joined the 54th Massachusetts Infantry.

Another change wrought by the Emancipation Proclamation was that black men laboring in the South could serve in the armed forces, thereby changing their status from "contraband" to soldiers. In addition, the family members of the men serving could obtain their freedom if they came over to the Union. This led to floods of African Americans trying to get to the areas of the Confederate South occupied by Union forces. Men and women would hear about the Emancipation Proclamation through announcements by occupying northern soldiers and try to join the Union encampments, prompting plantation owners to complain about their laborers being "kidnapped" or impressed into service. In Florida, Captain Sears enlisted black workers to build Fort Clinch, but he complained that his men were being kidnapped. He wrote that his "work should be protected from the interference of men, who are enlisting and drafting soldiers for the African Regiments" (Berlin 55–56). Then, he detailed how five of his men "were seized night before last and were forbidden permission to see me before leaving—an officer with them declaring that he 'didn't care a damn for Capt. Sears; if they didn't go he would give them the bayonet'." One of these "kidnapped" men was told that the "orders came from high authorities" that they should be made to be soldiers. He testified that he did not go of his own free will and he wished to go home (Berlin 57–58). Even as numerous slaves would free themselves and join the Union Army, still others were pressed into service.

Along with the confusion about what to do with contraband men and women, military officials pondered the appropriate use of free black men who had enlisted in the federal regiments from the North, now designated as the United States Colored Troops (USCT). In May 1863, the government established the Bureau of Colored Troops to deal with the issues of enlistment, pay, and officer selection. One of the most glaring problems was the pay disparity between white and black enlistees. White enlistees were paid $13 per month with a $3 deduction for uniforms, while black enlistees were paid $7 per month after the $3 uniform deduction. Some black soldiers mutinied until the military finally equaled their pay.

Another major problem centered around the policy to commission only white officers for the black regiments, and to relegate black men to noncommissioned officer status. Black chaplains and some medical personnel could be promoted to higher ranks but only if they were never in command of any white personnel. This policy seriously hampered the advancement of black men who might have climbed the ranks during wartime service. In 1864, Congress revised the inequities and commutation fees from its earlier Conscription and Enrollment Act, yet it continued with press gangs to bring men into the service against their will. And in regions like Georgia, Alabama, and Texas, where heavy concentrations of black people resided, Union forces were not numerous enough to provide safety, shelter, and freedom to the individuals who wanted to serve.

Once enlisted, the warfare began and black troops soon discovered the horrors of battle and occupation. Black soldiers and their commanders were suspicious that they were always assigned the dirty work, or the lowest and meanest tasks. Many felt they received unequal treatment and they complained in letters and conversations. In one letter to his wife, Colonel Robert Gould Shaw, who commanded the 54th Massachusetts Infantry, described his feelings of disgust when his black troops were ordered to destroy the town of Darien:

> The reasons he [Colonel Montgomery] gave me for destroying Darien were, that the Southerners must be made to feel that this was a real war, and that they were to be swept away by the hand of God, like the Jews of

old. In theory it may seem all right to some, but when it comes to being made the instrument of the Lord's vengeance, I myself don't like it. Then he says, "We are outlawed, and therefore not bound by the rules of regular warfare" but that makes it none the less revolting to wreak our vengeance on the innocent and defenceless. By the time we had finished this dirty piece of business, it was too dark to go far down the narrow river" *(Duncan 343).*

In the South, too, the Confederate government and military officials studied whether to enlist and arm black men. But they only agreed to arm them when the war was in its last weeks. Initially, so many black men and women left the plantations to serve in the Union that some Confederates offered money and freedom to slaves who continued to labor. Others threatened black men who slipped away to Union lines that their family members would be sold. Then, the Confederacy announced that any captured black soldier would be executed, rather than imprisoned, and any white officer of black troops would be dealt with similarly. In early 1864, Lincoln issued an order to treat Confederates in kind if they would not offer black soldiers the rights due of any captured soldier. But infamously, in April 1864, General Nathan Bedford Forrest's troops slaughtered black soldiers who had surrendered at Fort Pillow, Tennessee.

Yet, in spite of this Confederate mistreatment and the widespread African American distrust of the Confederacy, not all African Americans in the military served the Union forces. As the military hierarchy in the South argued out a decision about arming black men and offering freedom—Confederate Emancipation—some African Americans entered the service of the Confederacy. Estimates of the total number vary widely from 5,000 to 50,000. Many African Americans were utilized to build fortifications and support Confederate encampments. Some masters took their male slaves into the military to serve as attendants and valets. Richard, an enslaved man traveling with a Confederate unit, wrote to his "Mistress" about the death of her husband, the "Master," while Martin Jackson, another black man in the service of the Confederacy, recalled attending to a fatally wounded Colonel whom he served: "He was too far gone. I just held him comfortable, and that was the position he was in when he stopped breathing. That was the worst hurt I got from when anybody died. He was a friend of mine" *(Born in Slavery* 2:191).

Black women experienced an equally complicated set of choices during the Civil War. Women could not serve in the armed forces, although they could provide services and support for the troops. Sojourner Truth assisted in the recruitment of black men into the military, and raised money and supplies for the men. Black women also provided intelligence information to Union forces and many African American women became laborers to the military operations—laundering uniforms, preparing and serving meals, and providing nursing services. Some women were offered asylum if they had been enslaved in the South and could enter Union lines. Always, the women were met with suspicion whenever they offered their services. Mrs. Susie King Taylor, the wife of a noncommissioned officer in the 1st South Carolina Volunteers, was a laundress in the regiment, as well as a nurse and teacher. Suspicious of her skills, her first commander asked her to prove herself. She recalled:

> Captain Whitmore, commanding the boat, asked me where I was from. I told him Savannah, Ga. He asked if I could read; I said, "Yes!" "Can you write?" he next asked. "Yes, I can do that also," I replied, and as if he had some doubts of my answers he handed me a book and a pencil and told me to write my name and where I was from. I did this; when he wanted to know if I could sew. On hearing I could, he asked me to hem some napkins for him. He was surprised at my accomplishments (for they were such in those days), for he said he did not know there were any negroes in the South able to read or write. He said, "You seem to be so different from the other colored people who came from the same place you did." "No!" I replied, "the only difference is, they were reared in the country and I in the city.
>
> *(9)*

By the end of the war, nearly 10 percent of the men serving in the military were black. Overall, approximately 180,000 black men served in the armed forces as laborers or combat soldiers. The death toll of black men is estimated at around 38,000 people, from disease or injury in battle. Some of the decisive battles that engaged black servicemen were in Louisiana, Milliken's Bend and Port Hudson, also at the Battle of the Crater in Petersburg, Virginia, and most memorably, at Fort Wagner, South Carolina, where half of the black troops of the 54th Massachusetts died. In his *Farewell Address* to the black troops of the 33D USCT, Lt. Colonel Trowbridge spoke to the troops in the vicinity of Fort Wagner. He lauded the soldiers:

> The hour is at hand when we must separate forever, and nothing can ever take from us the pride we feel ... It seems fitting to me that the last hours of our existence as a regiment should be passed amidst the unmarked graves of your comrades, at Fort Wagner. Near you rest the bones of Colonel Shaw, buried by an enemy's hand in the same grave with his black soldiers who fell at his side; where in future your children's children will come on pilgrimages to do homage to the ashes of those who fell in this glorious struggle.
>
> *(Taylor 46, 48)*

Still, by the end of the war, the question of whether black men could be good soldiers went unanswered. Military officials were still apprehensive about arming black men, no matter the glowing reports. Congress instituted a new federal policy that established permanent black military units as part of the regular army, but they choose to keep the units segregated, with white officers in command. The four "Negro Units," the 9th & 10th Cavalry, and the 24th & 25th Infantry Regiments, were out-posted to segregated military bases in the West, and continued to serve the nation as free men, albeit with curtailed citizenship rights.

Freedom was not universally achieved at war's end, nor as an automatic outcome of military service. In Texas, 250,000 black men and women were still enslaved two months after the end of the war, and two and a half years after the Emancipation Proclamation. Shortly after Union troops arrived to occupy Galveston, General Gordon Granger, the commanding general of the Union forces, read military orders declaring freedom to all enslaved people and warned the newly freed slaves not to loiter around the military post and become idlers and ne'er-do-wells. But former slave Felix Haywood remembered those first days of jubilee when the news of emancipation reached him in the summer of 1865 in San Antonio, Texas, in particular the sense that African Americans had achieved this liberation for themselves:

> Soldiers all of a sudden was everywhere—coming in bunches, crossing and walking and riding. Everyone was a-singing. We was all walking on golden clouds. 'Hallelujah! Union forever, Hurrah, boys, hurrah! Although I may be poor, I'll never be a slave—Shouting the battle cry of freedom.' Everybody went wild. We all felt like heroes, and nobody had made us that way but ourselves. We was free. Just like that, we was free.
>
> *(Born in Slavery 2:133)*

Most black soldiers left the military after the end of the war, but some stayed and joined the occupying forces of Reconstruction, and others continued on in all-black militias. In the South, white Democrats bridled at the civil rights that black people, now voting Republicans, exercised. In South Carolina, for example, 61 percent of the newly reconstructed state legislature was of African descent. And in Aiken, a small, upcountry town, three newly elected black politicians carved out a county from the most powerful territory in the state. Those three men illustrate the legacy of the Civil War for even the smallest town: one man had served in the Union Army, one man had served in the Confederate Army, and one man was a "carpetbagger," a free black who moved South after the war's end.

## Further Reading

Ash, Stephen. *Fireband of Liberty: The Story of Two Black Regiments that Changed the Course of the Civil War.* New York: Norton, 2008.

Berlin, Ira, ed. *The Black Military Experience.* New York: Cambridge University Press, 1982.

Berry, Mary Frances. *Military Necessity and Civil Rights Policy: Black Citizenship and the Constitution, 1861–1868.* Port Washington: Kennikat Press, 1977.

Billingsley, Andrew. *Yearning to Breathe Free: Robert Smalls of South Carolina and his Families*. Columbia: University of South Carolina Press, 2007.

Blassingame, John W., ed. *The Frederick Douglass Papers, Series One: Speeches, Debates, and Interviews, Volume 3: 1855–63*. New Haven: Yale University Press, 1985.

Blatt, Martin H., Thomas J. Brown, and Donald Yacovone, eds. *Hope & Glory: Essays on the Legacy of the Fifty-Fourth Massachusetts Regiment*. Amherst: University of Massachusetts Press, 2001.

*Born in Slavery: Slave Narratives from the Federal Writers' Project, 1936–1938*. Library of Congress Manuscript Division, Washington, D.C.

Duncan, Russell, ed. *Blue-eyed Child of Fortune: the Civil War Letters of Colonel Robert Gould Shaw*. Athens: University of Georgia Press, 1992.

Glatthaar, Joseph T. *Forged in Battle: the Civil War Alliance of Black Soldiers and White Officers*. Baton Rouge: Louisiana State University Press, 2000.

Levine, Bruce C. *Confederate Emancipation: Southern Plans to Free and Arm Slaves during the Civil War*. New York: Oxford University Press, 2006.

Lincoln, Abraham. *The Collected Works of Abraham Lincoln, Volume 5*. Springfield: Abraham Lincoln Association, 1953.

Looby, Christopher, ed. *The Complete Civil War Journal and Selected Letters of Thomas Wentworth Higginson*. Chicago: University of Chicago Press, 2000.

McPherson, James M. *The Negro's Civil War: How American Blacks Felt and Acted during the War for the Union*. New York: Ballantine Books, 1991.

Nalty, Bernard C., and Morris J. MacGregor, eds. *Blacks in the Military: Essential Documents*. Wilmington: Scholarly Resources, 1981.

Quarles, Benjamin. *The Negro in the Civil War*. New York: Da Capo Press, 1989.

Redkey, Edwin S., ed. *A Grand Army of Black Men: Letters from African-American Soldiers in the Union Army, 1861–1865*. Cambridge: Cambridge University Press, 1992.

Rollins, Richard, ed. *Black Southerners in Gray: Essays on Afro-Americans in Confederate Armies*. Murfreesboro: Southern Heritage Press, 1994.

Smith, John David, ed. *Black Soldiers in Blue: African American Troops in the Civil War Era*. Chapel Hill: University of North Carolina Press, 2002.

Taylor, Susie King. *Reminiscences of My Life in Camp with the 33d United States Colored Troops Late 1st S. C. Volunteers*. Boston: Published by the Author, 1902.

U.S., *Statutes at Large, Treaties, and Proclamations of the United States of America, vol. 12*. Boston: Little, Brown & Co. 1863. 589–592.

Westwood, Howard C. *Black Troops, White Commanders, and Freedmen during the Civil War*. Carbondale: Southern Illinois University Press, 1992.

Wilson, Keith P. *Campfires of Freedom: The Camp Life of Black Soldiers during the Civil War*. Kent: Kent State University Press, 2002.

# 17

# IMMIGRANTS

*Jennifer A. Stollman*

Thousands of immigrants participated in the Civil War as soldiers and supporters. In many ways, they experienced the war in the same way as native-born
soldiers and civilians. Immigrants debated the issues of slavery and state sovereignty. They fought and died on military and home fronts. But they also felt the
war's impact differently. Nativism and outright hostility to ethnic and religious
differences impacted how both Northerners and Southerners treated immigrants, who faced discrimination, segregation, and violence. Cognizant of their
differences, immigrants endeavored to demonstrate their patriotism throughout the war while preserving their own ethnic identities and communities.

European migrations began and continued throughout the first half of the
nineteenth century. Immigrants steadily poured into the country during the
early republic period, with about 13,000 people arriving each year. Beginning
in 1830, the immigrant population exploded. Access to cheap land, higher
wages, expanded labor opportunities, failed revolutions and famines drove
individuals from Germany, Ireland, Britain, Scandinavia, and Eastern Europe.
In the decades after 1845, over three million immigrants made the trip.

The infusion of large numbers of immigrants exacerbated already growing tensions within the United States. Working-class Americans viewed these
immigrants with suspicion and fear. Convinced that immigrants competed for
jobs, undercut wages, held dangerous religious customs, and corrupted American religious traditions, native working-class people resorted to protests and
violence. During the 1840s and 1850s, several riots broke out in northeastern
cities. Age-old fears regarding papal control resurged and anti-Catholic rioters
vandalized and burned the homes and businesses of Catholic immigrants. Individuals were shot or hung. Facing similar xenophobia and threats of violence,

German immigrants sought to migrate in groups. They settled in rural towns, to enable the preservation of traditional customs and values.

Concerned by the new immigrants' faith and leisure traditions, early nineteenth-century temperance advocates directed their efforts at immigrant populations. Reformers worked diligently to prohibit public drinking and the distribution of alcohol, and directed their activities at German and Irish ethnic and religious customs. To support their legislative attempts at restricting the consumption of liquor, temperance advocates pointed towards the disproportionate violence and arrest rates within these immigrant communities. What began as a national campaign aimed to improve labor and social productivity quickly devolved into verbal and physical attacks on immigrants.

Reform movements, the groundswell of violence, continued immigration, and rising regional tensions all enabled xenophobia to rise in the country and encouraged a formal anti-immigrant political organization, the Know Nothing party, to gain strength during the 1840s and 1850s. Born out of covert fraternal societies that restricted membership to native immigrants, the party accused immigrants of conducting subversive religious and political activities and undercutting labor opportunities. Influenced by increased labor and wage competition, young white middle- and modest-class individuals joined such groups decrying the negative effects of immigrants on American political and economic systems. Fearful that incoming migrants would sway political elections against their own interests, these individuals called for measures that proscribed immigrant access to political and economic power. Native-born citizens viewed the ethnic ghettoization of immigrants in newly created urban tenements as havens for crime. Crime rates and public relief rolls increased dramatically. When the Plenary Council of American Bishops responded to nativist sentiments, challenged that public education supported Protestant philosophies and decided to push for public support of Catholic schools, nativists' worst fears seemed confirmed. While ultimately slavery replaced nativism as the central national issue, xenophobia still remained. Yet despite these challenges, immigrant communities managed to develop counter-mechanisms that enabled them to thrive and foster pride in their ethnic traditions. Often residentially segregated, they managed to retain their old country lifestyles, languages and cultural values.

In this context, Chinese immigrants entered the United States. Responding to the labor opportunities that accompanied the gold rush, they arrived from 1848 onward. Initially, the Chinese were considered industrious immigrants. According to Dennis Wepman: "At first these newly arrived immigrants, many whom were serious, sober and hard working, were welcomed in America. They patiently accepted strenuous and disagreeable tasks few natives wanted to undertake and they often worked harder than whites" (138). Many Chinese gained employment as domestics, launderers, and cooks, and helped to construct the transcontinental railroad. But economic instability and the growth of nativism meant increased anti-Asian sentiment. In 1855 California legislators imposed a $55 head tax on every Chinese immigrant and in 1860 they passed a law that prohibited Chinese children from attending public schools. In 1862, however, the U.S. Congress took action *against* American abuse of Chinese natives and passed legislation against the excesses of the coolie trade. As indentured servants, the coolies were shipped from China to the Americas as part on an international traffic in human beings. Numerous uprisings resembled slave rebellions aboard ships. And as the Civil War raged, Congress finally turned its attention to this other form of slavery.

The Civil War also brought a temporary halt to European immigration. In 1861, only about 90,000 immigrants traveled to the United States—the lowest level in more than twenty years. Yet war opportunities did still encourage European immigration. The Irish continued to arrive. Between 1861 and 1880, around 870,000 Irish immigrants settled in America. They accounted for 17 percent of total immigration to the United States. Like other immigrant populations, they settled in urban areas, and a large Irish presence in cities enabled a strong political voice in urban politics. Irish communities facilitated immigrant settlement by creating benevolent societies that helped new arrivals find jobs and acculturate.

Germans also continued to emigrate. Between 1861 and 1870, over 90,000 German immigrants arrived in the United States. They settled in Pittsburgh, Pennsylvania, throughout the Midwest and Texas, in cities like Milwaukee, St. Louis, and Cincinnati and created strong ethnic enclaves. Preserving ethnic customs and traditions, they worked in the mills and factories and as skilled craftsmen, bakers, cabinet-makers, machinists, brewers and distillers. They also settled in southern rural and urban areas including South Carolina and Louisiana.

But by 1862, more immigrants were desperately needed to provide economic and military labor. Shipping companies actively embarked on recruitment campaigns. Throughout Europe, broadsides hung in public spaces and ports hailing the benefits of immigration to America and offering jobs, land, high wages and bonuses. To provide an even greater incentive, Congress passed the 1862 Homestead Act that offered 160-acre plots to any immigrants whose end goal was citizenship. Thousands of immigrants responded and climbed aboard ships to the United States. As historian Dennis Wepman concludes, "to land hungry Europeans, the opportunity to find lucrative employment and to establish holdings of such size was irresistible" (131).

Immediately upon arrival, immigrants went to work in mines and on farms and railroads. Civilian immigrants also supported the war effort. Different populations collected funds and created benevolent societies. They worked to combat anti-immigrant legislation, stereotypes, and violence. In editorials and articles, they championed immigrant soldiers' efforts in the major battles such as Chancellorsville and Gettysburg. Scores of immigrant groups marked 4th of

July celebrations by commemorating their countrymen's service in the Civil War. For example, British immigrants feted their efforts with parades and patriotic recitations of the Declaration of Independence.

Still others came to serve in the Union and Confederate Armies. Bounties and substitution fees provided attractive immigrant opportunities. Many had not even gained citizenship when they began military service. The federal government offered bonuses of several hundred dollars to immigrants who would enlist and promised some Union soldiers immediate citizenship upon completion of their military service. Port cities often housed recruitment stations and army officers fluent in several languages encouraged newly arrived immigrants to sign up. The recruitment campaigns were so successful that many new immigrants wore Union uniforms within days of their arrival. Many British soldiers even enlisted *before* arrival. Then, as the Civil War progressed, demand for immigrant labor in the military and in the broader workforce increased still further until, on Independence Day in 1864, President Lincoln signed into law the Act to Encourage Immigration, which ensured the continued flow of immigrants. Reminiscent of an indenture system, the act allowed employers to fund immigrants' passage to the United States in exchange for a term of labor. The act was repealed in 1868, when the demand for labor waned after the end of the Civil War.

Although these individuals brought with them to the United States their own ideas about slavery and the war, many hoped to protect their own social, economic, and political positions and so avoided engaging the debates. In editorials for immigrant newspapers, writers argued that newly arrived immigrants should not involve themselves in the war, rather leave it to the native born. But the war's protracted nature eventually forced immigrant populations to choose sides. In print and through public demonstrations, immigrants pledged allegiance to the North or the South.

Several immigrant populations frowned upon the institution of slavery. For example, historian William Van Vugt suggested that most British immigrants viewed the institution as not "peculiar" but "evil" (139). Previously exposed to transatlantic abolitionist efforts and literature, British immigrants were among the earliest and most enthusiastic Union volunteers. Other immigrant populations embedded their positions within religious rhetoric. German Pietists accepted the Civil War as God's judgment for slavery, and Northern Swedes understood the war as a manifestation of God's will to destroy the system of slavery in the South. Convinced that it was their religious duty to fight slavery, Swedish Lutherans formed regiments and wrote home in an attempt to recruit others. On the other side, some British and German Lutherans were pro-slavery advocates and used the Bible to justify slavery. And tensions rose within German and Irish communities as Protestants and Catholics split over the issues of secession and slavery.

Some populations feared the potential repercussions of taking "the wrong side." Antislavery Germans living in the South knew their safety and livelihoods depended on openly supporting the Confederacy. Those who opposed slavery were forced to leave, remain silent, or risk bodily and business harm, so self-preservation often dictated their public displays. Many Germans publicly proclaimed their loyalty to the Confederacy, and German immigrants proved invaluable to the Confederacy. The Confederate government solicited the expertise of high-profile German immigrants as political writers and cartographers. In Charleston, Germans supported slavery, were publicly quite loyal, and demonstrated this by forming several all-German militias and working as blockade runners. In New Orleans, which housed the South's largest German population, immigrants labored as workers and craftsmen. German ladies created benevolent associations to send soldiers packages and erect makeshift hospitals.

The strategy of public loyalty worked well for Germans in Texas, for example, until secession, when the Confederate Congress demanded that foreigners declare their loyalty or risk being "treated as alienable enemies" (Bailey 12). Eventually, public proclamation of loyalty did not immunize Germans against military raids that sought foreign soldiers who avoided conscription. Confederate military personnel sharpened their attacks against Germans based on stereotypes and xenophobia. Rampant violence reached the rural German communities in Texas and in turn caused immigrant disenchantment with the Confederate cause, which prompted more violence.

Violence even sparked tension among Germans from different migration waves. Each charged the other that either their lack of assimilation or their loss of German traditions fostered Confederate white rage. Anti-slavery Germans living in Gainesville, Florida, who opposed secession, also found themselves the target of violence. They formed the anti-Confederate Peace Party to oppose conscription acts and in 1862, pro-secessionists had several party members arrested. A mob killed two German immigrants as they tried to escape and vigilante courts sentenced several more to death.

The war politicized soldiers in particular. While some soldiers were integrated into non-immigrant fighting units, others belonged to all Irish or German brigades, because of rampant nativist sentiment. Entire regiments were made up of immigrant populations. Because there were so many German immigrants in the North, the Union Army boasted several German regiments. These all-German regiments exposed several generations of German immigrants to different ethnic customs and language, and also served to reinforce and reconstruct a unique German identity. This identity merged German and American military traditions, masculinities, and ideologies. Irish, Scandinavians, and Jews all organized their own military regiments as well. At times, officials rejected foreign units, refused to issues arms to immigrant soldiers, and failed to recognize immigrant officers. Ultimately and out of necessity, Union and Confederate officials accepted immigrant soldiers but according to historian Craig Kautz, "thoughts of arming Irish Romanists horrified them" (61).

Many immigrant soldiers fought for land, to prove loyalty, to counter stereotypes of laziness or shirking military responsibilities, to prepare for a future war against the British (the Irish), and to right the wrong of failed revolutions (the Germans). Northern German soldiers worked to combat negative stereotypes, and German newspapers routinely ran stories that focused on immigrant soldiers' bravery and valor. But immigrant soldiers—including the Irish and the Germans—still remained scapegoats in both armies. Suffering from nativist ideas, marginalization, discrimination, and violence, some German units mutinied just a few months into the war. Other immigrant populations resented fighting in the Union Army for a cause that directly threatened their economic interests, and some Irish immigrants strongly opposed emancipation because of the labor competition posed by ex-slaves.

Then, as casualties increased during the war, both Irish and German communities expressed anger at mandatory military service. The 1863 Conscription Act allowed individuals to purchase their way out of the war for $300, but few Irish or German immigrants could afford the fee. For example, in the state of New York, as many as three-fourths of the able-bodied men exempted from military service were American born, while three-fourths of those drafted were foreign-born. Immigrant editorialists proclaimed that conscription unfairly targeted poor men and immigrant soldiers expressed resentment that they experienced anti-immigrant hostility while incurring a disproportionate number of casualties. German and Irish immigrants protested the presence of recruiting stations in their neighborhoods. In New York City, publicly displaying their displeasure at the draft, the Irish rioted and directed their anger at free African Americans.

Immigrant soldiers also resented the vandalism of their homes and land by native-born Americans. Sometimes this violence escalated to murder. For example on May 11, 1864, the St. Louis German Home Guard marched alongside captured secessionist troops from Camp Jackson. Native citizens erupted and, in addition to torching houses and property, they shot two German immigrants. Bigotry was rampant in the Union and Confederate armies, and white soldiers and war commentators routinely assigned bad soldier behavior as pathologically ethnic.

In particular, the war produced a resurgence of anti-Semitism. Southern Jews were strong supporters of the Confederacy and slavery, even though many of them did not own slaves. Jews supported the South because they perceived northern abolitionists as anti-Semitic. Jews fought as Southerners in support of southern honor and duty, to support Jewish tradition, to prove their loyalty and capability, and as one historian observes, "to make a place in Southern society for Jews who would come after them" (Ural 163-64). There were Jewish soldiers holding all ranks in the Confederate Army.

Yet, the fact that up to 12,000 Jews served in the Confederacy and 15,000 Jews served in the Union Army did not shield them from discrimination. To combat anti-Semitism and demonstrate their loyalty, Jews in the South raised two Jewish companies: the first in West Point, Georgia, during the first month of the war and the second in Macon, Georgia, in 1862. Northern Jews formed several companies including the 82nd Regiment of the Illinois volunteers. This troop was made up of recent émigrés from Lithuania, Russia, and Poland.

Despite these efforts, charges of profiteering plagued both northern and southern Jews. Unionists and Confederates alike charged Jews with disloyalty and greed. Grant's "Order No. 11" in 1862 exemplified this type of anti-Semitism. In a carefully worded statement that accused Jewish merchants of stealing, corruption, and unreasonably benefiting from the war, Grant expelled all Jews from his military jurisdiction in Tennessee. The order was carried out but due to much local and national protest, Lincoln revoked it three weeks later. Throughout the duration of the war, Jews continued to fight similar charges.

British immigrants, on the other hand, experienced the war differently. American soldiers did not see British immigrant soldiers as "foreign" and were not uncomfortable with their traditions. For their part, British military recruits worked harder than most immigrants to demonstrate their loyalty because of historical tensions caused by the Revolution, the War of 1812, and existing western border disputes. Nonetheless, when Britain considered recognizing the Confederate States of America (later announcing its neutral position), the federal government required that British-born recruits take special loyalty oaths renouncing forever all allegiance to Queen Victoria. In this sense, the war provided British recruits with the perfect opportunity to allay any fears of disloyalty. Soldiers recalled that their reasons for fighting for the Union included: "to show loyalty to [their] adopted country, to defend the honor of [their] adopted country" (Van Vugt 145-46).

Throughout the war and even afterwards, immigrant soldiers and veterans were targets of discrimination and scapegoating. In the South, according to historian James McPherson, the presence of immigrant soldiers in the Union army confirmed the myth that it was comprised of "foreign hirelings" (606). Claiming unfair advantage after the war, Southerners routinely complained that they would have won had it not been for the overwhelming immigrant presence in the Union army—although in reality, immigrants constituted 25 percent of the servicemen and only 30 percent of males of military age in the Union States were foreign born.

Politicized by the draft, by ongoing nativism and by the debate over emancipation, immigrant populations developed a stronger ethnic consciousness. Before 1861, immigrants may have attempted to assimilate into American life but the war stymied such efforts. All-immigrant regiments exposed individuals to ethnic customs and languages, thereby reinforcing their immigrant identities. And in response to discrimination and scape-goating, immigrants defended and fostered a distinct cultural identity. Even after the fighting was over, nativists continued to target immigrant communities with temperance laws, reform efforts, and xenophobic violence. But much like they did during the war, immigrants publicly responded by preserving their native languages and traditions, proclaiming their unique contributions to American society, and combating negative stereotypes. Proud of their regional accomplishments at home and in battle, immigrant veterans celebrated their own war efforts.

## Further Reading

Bailey, Anne J. *Invisible Southerners: Ethnicity in the Civil War.* Athens and London: The University of Georgia Press, 2006.

Burton, William L. *Melting Pot Soldiers: The Union Ethnic Regiments.* New York: Fordham University Press, 1998.

Creighton, Margaret S. *The Colors of Courage: Gettysburg's Forgotten History Immigrants, Women and African Americans in the Civil War's Defining Battle.* New York: Basic Books, 2005.

Keller, Christian. *Germans in Civil War-Era Pennsylvania: Ethnic identity and the Problem of Americanization.* New York: Fordham University Press, 2007.

Kautz, Craig Lee. "Fodder for Cannon: Immigrant Perceptions of the Civil War—The Old Northwest." Ann Arbor, University Microfilms, 1976.

McPherson, James. *Battle Cry of Freedom: The Civil War Era.* New York, Oxford University Press, 1988.

Mahin, Dean. *The Blessed Place of Freedom: Europeans in Civil War America.* Washington, D.C.: Potomac Books, 2003.

Ofele, Martin W. *True Sons of the Republic: European Immigrants in the Union Army.* Westport: Prager, 2008.

Rosen, Robert N. *The Jewish Confederates.* Columbia: University of South Carolina Press, 2000.

Samito, Christian. *Becoming American Under Fire: Irish Americans, African Americans, and the Politics of Citizenship During the Civil War Era.* Ithaca: Cornell University Press, 2009.

Ural, Susannah J., ed. *Civil War Citizens: Race, Ethnicity, and Identity in America's Bloodiest Conflict.* New York: New York University Press, 2010.

Van Vugt, William E. *Britain to America: Mid-Nineteenth Century Immigrants to the United States.* Urbana: University of Illinois Press, 1999.

Wepman, Dennis. *Immigration: From the Founding of Virginia to the Closing of Ellis Island.* New York: Facts on File, 2002.

# 18

# NATIVE AMERICANS

*W. Craig Gaines*

Since European immigrants arrived in North America, a series of cultural conflicts and wars began over the immigrants seizing Native American (Indian) lands. New diseases, especially cholera and measles, carried by the European immigrants, destroyed whole tribes and weakened Native American resistance to invasion. Before the Civil War, Native Americans east of the Mississippi River had been decimated; resettled onto lands in present Arkansas, Oklahoma, Kansas, and Texas; or absorbed into the new Anglo American culture.

Tribes in the northeastern United States had been conquered in a series of colonial wars, the French and Indian wars, the American Revolution, and other Indian wars. The powerful Iroquois Confederacy, consisting of the Mohawk, Oneida, Onondaga, Cayuga, Seneca, and the Tuscarora, became divided with tribes settling in reservations in Ohio and New York as well as Canada. Some Cayugas, Shawnees, and Senecas also immigrated to the Indian nations in present-day Oklahoma and Kansas.

In the southeastern United States, the Five Civilized Tribes, consisting of the Cherokees, Creeks (Muscogees), Choctaws, Chickasaws, and Seminoles (several groups), were originally found in present-day Alabama, Florida, Georgia, Kentucky, Mississippi, North Carolina, South Carolina, and Tennessee. Often, members of these tribes had divided loyalties with members of each tribe serving in wars with and against the United Sates. By 1850, about 84,000 Native Americans had been removed or voluntarily emigrated from the eastern United States to the Indian nations, in Arkansas, Kansas, and Texas. In the Indian nations, the tribes set up their own governments. Missionaries converted many Native Americans to Christianity, and several young men attended universities in the northeast such as Harvard and Yale.

The United States–Cherokee Treaty of Echota and the United States–Creek Treaty of Dancing Rabbit Creek caused great divisions in these two tribes. The Five Civilized Tribes were forced by these and other treaties to abandon their ancestral lands and emigrate in the Trail of Tears to Indian Territory (the Indian nations) and Arkansas. In Indian Territory, Native Americans were put on reservations. Old animosities between tribal members, usually dictated by tribal political and removal issues, caused some revenge murders among several tribes.

The California, New Mexico, Arizona, Texas, and Florida Indians had been part of the Spanish mission system before the United States took over these lands. The California Indians had been decimated by venereal disease, cholera, and smallpox. The discovery of gold in 1849 brought hordes of Anglo Americans, Mexicans, Chinese, and others who destroyed traditional California Native American food sources and forage.

Some Native Americans resisted the settler and miner intrusions into their traditional fishing, farming, and hunting grounds. The Apaches, Navajo, and other tribes in Arizona and New Mexico had resisted Spanish and Mexican settlements for two centuries and continued to resist the new Americans. In the western United States, many tribes followed traditional ways and were policed by the United States Army from a number of forts.

When the Confederate States of America was established, the United States was plunged into a civil war, with an immediate effect on Native Americans. With the withdrawal of United States Army troops and Indian agents from the western United States, they experienced more freedom. Native Americans raided settlements, ranches, and roads to reclaim their lands and drive out the Americans. The Navajos and the Apaches attacked frontier settlers and travelers in their lands.

Native Americans in the eastern United States had either been integrated into the local culture or lived peacefully on reservations with limited rights. The need for soldiers during the Civil War caused social separation in the East to become less pronounced. The Union 98th New York Volunteer Infantry Regiment enrolled 25 St. Regis Indians in October 1861. After the battles of 1862, it was apparent that more Union soldiers would be needed and volunteers would be lacking. The draft began in August 1862 to enroll male citizens between 18 and 45 years old. Drafted men could hire replacements. Many Indians in the North joined the Union Army due to bounties of $300 for a 3-year enlistment, which helped support their families. The most famous Union Indian was Ely Samuel Parker, a lawyer, civil engineer, and a sachem of the New York Seneca tribe. Although initially rejected for an officer's commission due to being an Indian, he was a friend of General Ulysses S. Grant and became a Union officer, engineer, and Grant's military secretary.

The Iroquois had at least 628 volunteers in the Union Army. The Tuscarora Company of the 132nd New York Infantry Regiment had 25 Iroquois, including Lieutenant Cornelius Cusick, a "peace chief" or sachem. The 53rd

New York Regiment of Zouves had many members with some Indian blood. Forty-nine Oneidas, mostly farmers, joined the 14th Wisconsin Infantry Regiment, which was in Sherman's Atlanta campaign. In Wisconsin, 125 Menominees joined the Union Army. The 37th Wisconsin Regiment contained soldiers from the Oneida, Menominee, Chippewa, and Stockbridge tribes. The Wisconsin Oneidas numbered about 1,100 reservation Indians, with 111 to 142 enlisting in the Union Army and 46 to 65 of them dying during the war. The 9th Minnesota fought at Brice's Crossroads on June 10, 1864, and Native Americans helped repulse Confederate attacks during their retreat. The regiment saw seven enlisted men killed, 272 enlisted men missing, and 8 officers missing out of the original 30 officers and 635 enlisted men in the campaign. Company K of the 1st Michigan Sharpshooters Regiment had Ottawa and Chippewa Indians, who chased Morgan's Confederate raiders in Indiana and Ohio and fought in Virginia.

Native Americans served in many colored regiments, as some states chose not to put them alongside white soldiers. Pequots served in the 30th Connecticut Colored Infantry Regiment, which later became the 31st U.S. Colored Troops. But at the Battle of the Crater, Petersburg, Virginia, Native Americans fought on both sides. At Petersburg, the 31st contained Pequots and the 1st Michigan Sharpshooters Regiment with Ottawas and Chippewas fought on the Union side, while the 17th South Carolina Infantry Regiment with Catawbas fought on the Confederate side. All 19 Catawba adult males joined the Confederate Army in the 5th, 12th, and 17th South Carolina Infantry regiments, which fought in the Peninsula Campaigns, Second Bull Run, Antietam, and Petersburg.

Native Americans from the Five Civilized Tribes, the Cherokees, Creeks, Choctaws, Chickasaws, and Seminoles, fought on both sides. During the war about 1,000 Cherokee soldiers changed sides, serving in both the Confederate and Union forces. Of 19,000 Cherokees in the Cherokee Nation and North Carolina, about 4,500 Cherokees served in the military during the war. When the Civil War broke out, about 2,000 Cherokees known as the Eastern Band of Cherokees lived in the Smoky Mountains of North Carolina and Tennessee. The Eastern Cherokees' protector was politician William Holland Thomas, a U.S. Indian agent, merchant, and adopted son of Cherokee Chief Drowning Bear. Confederate President Jefferson Davis was also related by marriage to Thomas. North Carolina refused to recognize Indian land ownership, so all Eastern Cherokee land titles were held in William Holland Thomas' name. Thomas organized a Confederate Cherokee company on April 9, 1862, at Quallatown (now Cherokee), North Carolina, and later raised three more companies of mostly Cherokees, led by white officers. On September 15, 1862, at Baptist Gap, Tennessee, Thomas' Cherokee Company A fought against Union Indiana troops and scalped several dead Union soldiers after the death of Cherokee Lieutenant Asttogatogeh during the attack. Confederate officers apologized for the scalping and returned the scalps so they could be buried with the dead Union soldiers.

The 400 Cherokees who served in Thomas' Legion were almost all of the adult Eastern Cherokees males. When the Cherokees were detached from Thomas' Legion, they remained near their homes in the Smoky Mountains to defend the area against Union sympathizers, raiders, and bushwhackers. They fought in a number of skirmishes. In 1863, a Confederate Eastern Cherokee party was captured during a skirmish near Bryson City, North Carolina. The captured Cherokees were so dissatisfied with the Confederacy that they joined the Union Army. About 30 Eastern Cherokees joined the Union 3rd North Carolina Mounted Infantry Regiment.

Many Eastern Cherokee families suffered from starvation, some reportedly existed on nothing but weeds and bark. Colonel Thomas requested that the Confederate government and state of South Carolina send food and cloth for destitute Cherokee women and children. Thomas wrote that nearly all the Cherokee men between the ages of 18 and 45 had volunteered for the Confederate Army, that the Cherokees had few slaves to do the farming for them, and that there had also been early frosts, which had destroyed their fall crops. South Carolina purchased 100 bushels of corn for the Cherokee families and the needy.

In the Indian nations, the war had a different impact. It involved tribes divided by politics, internal conflicts, and moral issues over slavery. In July 1861, Stand Watie raised a Confederate Cherokee company when the Cherokee Nation was officially neutral under Principal Chief John Ross, who was first elected chief in 1828. Ross was seven-eighths white and prosperous. Stand Watie was a one-quarter white attorney and merchant who led the Watie Party (or Treaty Party), the opposition party to the Ross Party.

A man of influence with Native Americans was Arkansas attorney Albert Pike, who had dealings with most tribes in Indian Territory before the Civil War. Pike was born in Boston, Massachusetts, had attended Harvard College, and had served with Robert E. Lee in the Mexican War. Attorney Pike represented many Indian nations in lawsuits against the United States government. Pike became a Confederate Commissioner of the Bureau of Indian Affairs in March 1861, and a Confederate brigadier general on August 15, 1861. He was trusted by most Native Americans and was the major influence in signing members of the Five Civilized Tribes in Indian Territory and many of the plains tribes into treaties with the Confederate States of America in 1861. Pike was a friend to both Watie and Chief Ross.

In an attempt to prevent a Cherokee civil war, Chief Ross led the Cherokee Nation into the Confederacy at an August 21, 1861, council attended by almost 4,000 Cherokee men at Tahlequah, Cherokee Nation (Oklahoma). Indian leaders from the Cherokees, Creeks, Senecas, Osages, and Quapaws signed treaties with the Confederacy on October 4, 1861, at Tahlequah. To counter Watie's forces, Chief Ross raised John Drew's Regiment of Cherokee Mounted Rifles, under 65-year-old John Drew. Chief Ross selected his heir-apparent and nephew, William Potter Ross, as its lieutenant colonel. Drew's Regiment's officers were generally mixed-blood Cherokees related to, or close friends of Chief Ross. Drew's Regiment had members with divided loyalty to both Chief Ross and the Keetoowah Society. The Keetoowah Society was a secret pro-Union full-blood Cherokee organization against slavery. The Keetoowahs were known as "pins" due to the insignia of crossed pins they wore on their clothes.

Watie's Regiment was raised initially as an Arkansas regiment in December 1861, and included Watie's nephew, Major Elias C. Boudinot, and Watie's brother-in-law, Captain James M. Bell. Watie's Regiment and Drew's Regiment were each referred to in documents and correspondence as the 1st Regiment of Cherokee Mounted Rifles, 1st Regiment of Arkansas Cherokee Mounted Rifles, 1st Arkansas Cherokee Rifles, and 2nd Arkansas Cherokee Mounted Rifles.

Other Native American units were raised by the Confederacy in various Indian nations, North Carolina, Mississippi, Missouri, and Arkansas. Like the Cherokees, the Creeks were split into several political parties. The McIntosh brothers, Daniel "Dode" M. and Chilly, formed the Confederate 1st Creek Regiment. Former United States Indian agent Douglas H. Cooper formed the 1st Choctaw and Chickasaw Mounted Rifles Regiment, the first Confederate Indian regiment.

In the fall of 1862, several hundred Choctaws who had avoided removal to the Indian nations served in the Confederate 1st Mississippi Choctaw Battalion. These Choctaws tracked down Confederate deserters in the Mississippi swamps. In May 1863, Union cavalry in Louisiana dispersed the 1st Mississippi Choctaw Battalion. Fourteen captured Choctaws were sent to Fort Columbus in New York harbor.

Confederate Brigadier General Douglas H. Cooper's force of Texans, Cherokees, Choctaws, Chickasaws, and Creeks attacked old Creek Chief Opothleyahola's pro-Union Indians in the Indian nations. Chief Opothleyahola and pro-Union Creeks, Choctaws, Chickasaws, Seminoles, Quapaws, Kickapoos, and members of other tribes requested aid from Union Indian agents in Kansas. Free blacks and escaped slaves also joined Chief Opothleyahola's pro-Union band. The Confederates feared that the pro-Union Indians would combine with Kansas Union forces and conquer the Confederate Indian nations.

On the night of December 7, 1861, about 440 Keetoowah Cherokees deserted from Drew's Regiment and joined Opothleyahola's pro-Union army. Colonel Drew and 28 Cherokees joined Cooper's Confederate force, which defeated Opothleyahola's pro-Union Indians on December 8, 1861, at the Battle of Caving Banks (or Chusto-Talash) near present-day Tulsa, Oklahoma. On December 26, 1861, Confederate Texas and Arkansas troops defeated Opothleyahola's pro-Union army at the Battle of Patriot's Hills (or Chustenahlah) in present Osage County, Oklahoma. Confederate Indian and white troops killed or captured many pro-Union Indians retreating toward Kansas. During the winter of

1861–1862, survivors of Opothleyahola's pro-Union army huddled in miserable refugee camps in southern Kansas, where many died of diseases or hunger.

The Confederate-Cherokee Treaty had a provision that the Confederate Indian soldiers did not have to serve outside the Indian nations, unless they agreed to do so. Many Native Americans feared that if they left the Indian nations, whites would confiscate their lands. When a Union army invaded Arkansas, Brigadier General Albert Pike's Indian Brigade joined Major General Earl Van Dorn's Confederate Army much to the anger of many Indians. On March 7, 1862, at the Battle of Pea Ridge, Arkansas, Confederate Cherokees and Texas troops captured a Union battery, where several Union soldiers were scalped. With much controversy, the northern press reported the scalpings.

In mid-1862 men from the Union Indian Kansas refugee camps enlisted in the 1st Kansas Indian Home Guard Regiment (Creeks, Chickasaws, Choctaws, Senecas, and Seminoles) and 2nd Kansas Indian Home Guard Regiment (mostly Cherokees, some Osages and Quapaws). Union forces with the Kansas Indian Home Guard regiments invaded the Seneca Nation and Cherokee Nation in June and July 1862. Watie's Confederate Cherokees were defeated and Clarkson's Missouri Battalion, Cavalry Independent Rangers with white and Indian soldiers, was mostly captured. Clarkson's Battalion was reorganized with Indian recruits and transfers, becoming Buster's Indian Battalion.

Chief John Ross and a large part of Drew's Regiment, including Lieutenant Colonel William Potter Ross and Major Thomas Pegg, were "arrested" on July 15, 1862, at Park Hill, Cherokee Nation by sympathetic Union forces, which included Union Cherokees. Most of Chief Ross' soldiers left the Confederacy and joined the Union 2nd and 3rd Kansas Indian regiments, but some remained loyal to the Confederacy. On July 27 to 28, 1862, a Cherokee and Choctaw Confederate raiding party en route to attack Chief Ross and his followers at Park Hill were ambushed and defeated by the Union 2nd and 3rd Kansas Indian Home Guard regiments. Confederate losses were at least 125, while only one Union private was wounded. This was the first major test of the Union Cherokee regiments against their Confederate tribal members.

Union and Confederate Indian units in the West had several differences in organization and supplies. Kansas Indian Home Guard regiment officers were primarily white Kansas citizens politically appointed, with some Native American officers. The Union Indian regiment's commanding officers were white. Many Native American soldiers did not speak English, so conflicts arose with the white officers who did not speak their language. Chief John Ross tried to get the Kansas Indian Home Guard regiments converted into Cherokee Nation units with Cherokee officers, but was unsuccessful. Confederate Native American unit officers appear to have been elected by their men, except for the most senior officers, who were appointed and normally Native American.

The 2nd Kansas Indian Home Guard Regiment was armed with Union supplied Prussian and Mississippi rifles. Confederate Indian units were armed with a wide variety of guns, mostly privately owned hunting rifles of various ages and usefulness. Confederate military supplies destined for the Confederate Indian units, were often intercepted by Confederate commanders who thought white soldiers could make better use of them. Kansas Indian Home Guard regiments were paid as infantry, but owned horses, which were cared for by the Union Army. By the end of the war, most of the Union Indians were afoot. Confederate Indian horses appear to have been owned by and cared for by the Confederate government. And finally, military drill and discipline was practiced in the Union Indian regiments. In contrast, the Confederate Indian units rarely drilled and had very loose discipline. Desertions and being absent without leave was rampant in all Indian units.

After their victories in the Indian nations, a junior Union officer, Colonel Frederick Salomon, arrested his commander Colonel William Weer on July 18, 1862, as his staff considered Colonel Weer to have endangered his command by putting them at risk of being destroyed by Confederate forces and lack of food supplies. Colonel Salomon and the Union troops retreated to Kansas. Colonel William A. Phillips' Union Indian Brigade, containing the 1st, 2nd, and 3rd Kansas Indian Home Guard regiments, retreated to Kansas in August 1862 and then fought in skirmishes and battles in Missouri and Arkansas. Chief Ross and his family left the Cherokee Nation and spent most of the war in Washington, D.C., and in Philadelphia, Pennsylvania.

Colonel Stand Watie became Principal Chief of the Confederate Cherokee Nation and a council was set up to govern the Confederate Cherokees. Major Elias Boudinot resigned from Watie's Regiment and traveled to Richmond, Virginia, as the Cherokee delegate to the Confederate Congress. A force of Shawnees, Delawares, and Kickapoos influenced by Union agents rode from Kansas and attacked about 200 Confederate Tonkawas at the Wichita Agency in the Indian nations on October 23, 1862. More than 100 pro-Confederate Indian scalps were taken.

As the war progressed, Indian uprisings began to take place. A brutal Dakota uprising in Minnesota in August 1862 killed 737 whites, and 40,000 American settlers fled to Wisconsin. Other Indian unrest occurred throughout the West, which often cut transcontinental communication by land between California and the East. Arizona Apaches caused much terror, and California Union troops eventually reached Arizona and New Mexico territories to quell the outbreak. Colonel Kit Carson led New Mexico Union militia to defeat the uprising Navajos in Canyon de Chelly, Arizona Territory. About 8,000 Navajos were forced into a reservation near Fort Sumner, New Mexico Territory.

On April 18, 1863, the Union Indian Brigade occupied Fort Gibson, Cherokee Nation, and then also operated out of Fort Smith, Arkansas, with a system of guard posts at river fords, hay camps, salt works, and mills to support Union troops and Indian refugees in the Indian nations. On April 30, 1863, General Douglas H. Cooper's Confederate Indian Brigade contained some Texas units and Colonel Stand Watie's 1st Cherokee Regiment, Colonel William Penn Adair's 2nd Cherokee Regiment, Colonel Tandy Walker's 1st Choctaw and Chickasaw Regiment, Colonel "Dode" N. McIntosh's 1st Creek Regiment, Colonel Chilly McIntosh's 2nd Creek Regiment, Lt. Colonel L. M. Reynolds' 1st Choctaw Battalion, Major Broken Arm's Osage Battalion, and Colonel John Jumper's Seminole Battalion.

But the largest battle in the Indian nations was the Battle of Honey Springs or Elk Creek on July 17, 1863. Confederate units in the battle under Brigadier General Douglas H. Cooper included the 1st and 2nd Cherokee regiments, the 1st and 2nd Creek regiments, and the 1st Chickasaw and Choctaw Regiment. The Union forces under Major General James G. Blunt included the 1st, 2nd, and 3rd Kansas Indian Home Guard regiments. The Confederate forces were driven into southern Indian nations with losses reported by Cooper of 134 killed and wounded and 47 captured, while Blunt reported the Confederate losses as 150 killed, 400 wounded, and 77 captured. Blunt losses were 13 to 17 killed and 60 to 62 wounded.

Union Native American soldiers included elected officials of their tribes and delegates to represent Indian interests. Cherokee Lieutenant Colonel Lewis Downing, Sergeant George W. Scraper, and Captain Smith Christie served in an 1864 delegation in Washington, D.C., that appealed to President Abraham Lincoln, Secretary of War Edwin Stanton, and Congress for restoration of Colonel Phillips to command of the Union Indian Brigade, for aid to the Cherokee refugees, and other items. Colonel Phillips was to be court-martialed because he interfered with private contractors cheating Union Indians. These contractors were partners and friends of Union General James G. Blunt and Kansas politicians.

When Major General Frederick Steele's Union army made an expedition to Camden, Arkansas, Native Americans in Confederate Colonel Tandy Walker's Second Indian Brigade left the Indian nations and helped capture 200 wagons and four cannons at the Battle of Poison Springs on April 18, 1864. From camps south of the Arkansas River, Colonel Watie and his Confederate Indians made many efforts to recapture the Cherokee Nation. Watie was promoted to brigadier general on May 10, 1864, and commanded the Confederate First Indian Brigade. Watie's Brigade captured and burned the steamboat *J. R. Williams* on June 15, 1864, which was en route to Fort Gibson, Cherokee Nation from Fort Smith, Arkansas, with supplies for Union troops and refugees. On July 11, 1864, Chief Stand Watie asked the Confederate Cherokee Council to conscript all Cherokee males between the ages of 18 and 45. Confederate Indian regiments were so depleted that even white conscripts from Texas became members.

Watie's Indian Brigade and Gano's Texas Brigade destroyed a Union hay camp at Flat Rock Creek, Cherokee Nation, wiping out a company of the 79th U. S. Colored Infantry Regiment on September 16, 1864. Two days later, at the

Second Battle of Cabin Creek, the Confederates captured a supply train from Union Indians and white troops with more than 200 wagons full of supplies worth $1.5 million. The supplies were brought back to the Confederate military and refugee camps in 120 captured wagons. The war in the Indian nations reached a stalemate for the rest of the Civil War as supplies and troops were directed to eastern operations.

Several Union expeditions invaded the Dakota lands to end their uprising and put them on reservations. In a series of battles in 1863 and 1864, Union forces defeated the Dakotas and forced them to flee to British Canada or to surrender. Among the captured Dakotas, 38 of their leaders were tried and hung for the Minnesota uprising.

Widespread Indian raids in western Kansas, Nebraska, and eastern Colorado made travel dangerous. Undisciplined and often poorly led Union militia had replaced the regular United States Army troops in the area. One such group on November 29, 1864, massacred a peaceful group of up to 600 Cheyenne and Arapaho men, women and children camped on Sand Creek, Colorado Territory.

General Ulysses Grant's military secretary, Seneca Colonel Ely S. Parker, wrote up the articles of Confederate General Robert E. Lee's surrender at Appomattox Court House, Virginia on April 9, 1865. Parker was promoted to brigadier general shortly afterward. Thomas' North Carolina Indian Battalion skirmished with Union forces on May 6, 1865, in North Carolina's last Civil War engagement. That night Confederate Cherokees in the hills above Waynesville danced and screamed around many campfires to unnerve the Union troops. On May 7, 1865, General James G. Martin, Colonel James R. Love, Colonel William H. Thomas, and Thomas' Cherokee guard came down from the hills into Waynesville to meet with Union Lieutenant Colonel Bartlett. Colonel Thomas and his Cherokee guard were stripped to the waist, painted for war, and wore feathers. Thomas threatened to attack Bartlett's 2nd North Carolina Mounted Infantry Regiment and scalp them all. Bartlett pointed out that the Confederacy was gone: General Robert E. Lee and General Joseph E. Johnson had already surrendered. General Martin agreed to surrender the Department of North Carolina, including Thomas' Indian Battalion. Not included in the surrender were the 20 Cherokees in Colonel Thomas' personal bodyguard and about 100 other armed Cherokee men in the Smoky Mountains not enlisted in Confederate service.

By early 1865, the Confederate Indians in the Indian nations were decimated by war, without military supplies, and living in camps scattered in the Chickasaw and Choctaw nations. The Union Indian Brigade controlled the Cherokee and Creek nations and other areas in Indian Territory. On May 26, 1865, General Kirby Smith surrendered the Confederacy west of the Mississippi River in the Trans-Mississippi area. Due to Confederate treaties with tribes, each tribe had to surrender separately or make peace with the United States. On June 23,

1865, near Doaksville, Choctaw Nation, Brigadier General Stand Watie became the last Confederate general to surrender. Watie also surrendered the Confederate Cherokee government and the Confederate Indian Division. Native Americans in the Indian nations lost most of their possessions during the war.

The Union Indian Brigade's Kansas Indian Home Guard regiments were mustered out of service on May 31, 1865, after fighting in at least 43 battles, skirmishes, and campaigns. The Confederate western Cherokees fought in at least 35 battles, skirmishes, and campaigns. At the end of the Civil War, the Indian nations were in ruins and would not recover for more than a generation. Military losses among Native Americans were very high due to illness, crowded conditions, and constant battle. The Union Indian Brigade had 3,530 men who served from the Indian nations, including Cherokees, Creeks, Seminoles, Osages, Iroquois, and other tribes. The Union Indian Brigade lost 1,018 dead or 28.8 percent, a higher percentage than any state force. Of the Union Indian Brigade dead, 107 died from combat, 775 died from disease, 7 were murdered, 1 was executed, and the rest died of accidents or unspecified causes. Confederate Native American losses were similar in the Indian nations.

The Indian nations were further weakened in the face of non-Indian settlement after the war. Eastern Cherokees faced difficult times trying to establish a Cherokee reservation in North Carolina. Thomas' health and financial problems threatened Cherokee lands that Thomas held in his name. It took many years of lawsuits and government legislation to clear land titles and form what became the Cherokee Qualla Reservation. The United States government confiscated many lands in the Indian nations in retribution for tribes signing treaties with the Confederacy and taking up arms against the Union. In addition, conflict persisted between many members of the Indian tribes as the tribal members had often fought on both sides during the war and sometimes killed one another.

## Further Reading

Abel, Annie Heloise. *The American Indian as Participant in the Civil War.* Cleveland: Arthur H. Clark Co., 1919.

Armstrong, William H. *Warrior in Two Camps; Ely S. Parker, Union General and Seneca Chief.* Syracuse: Syracuse University Press, 1978.

Durada, Patricia K. *The Menominee Indians.* Norman: University of Oklahoma Press, 1979.

Gaines, W. Craig. *The Confederate Cherokees: John Drew's Regiment of Cherokee Mounted Rifles.* Baton Rouge: Louisiana State University Press, 1989.

Godbold Jr., E. Stanly and Mattie U. Russell. *Confederate Colonel and Indian Chief: The Life of William Holland Thomas.* Knoxville: The University of Tennessee Press, 1990.

Hauptman, Laurence M. *The Iroquois in the Civil War.* Syracuse: Syracuse University Press, 1993.

Hauptman, Laurence M. *Between Two Fires: American Indians in the Civil War.* New York: Free Press, 1995.

Josephy Jr., Alvin M. *The Civil War in the American West.* New York: Vintage Books, 1993.

Wardell, Morris L. *A Political History of the Cherokee Nation: 1838–1907.* Norman: University of Oklahoma Press, 1977.

# PART VI

# Literature and Visual Culture

# 19

# NEWSPAPERS

*Brayton Harris*

Much of our knowledge and understanding of the Civil War comes from three primary sources: the *Official Records* of the governments and armies, correspondence and memoirs of participants, and the record left by journalists. The first two focus on battles, strategies, and personalities. The third—journalism—presents a time capsule, preserving the look and feel of life in America: not only descriptions of battles fought and political victories obtained, but also the price of gold in New York, of slaves in Charleston, and of cotton, ladies' shoes, and whiskey ($40 a gallon) in Richmond; archaic language, like "letters" for reporters' news dispatches, "the chivalry" for Southerners (so-called by Northern writers), and "Bohemian Brigade" for the war correspondents' self-assigned nickname.

Newspapers also included verbatim transcriptions of public speeches, thanks to Isaac Pittman's method of rapid, or "short-hand," writing—recently introduced, much to the delight of reporters and to the exasperation of politicians, who preferred to leave written, corrected, improved copies of speeches, which may or may not actually have been delivered, with favored newspapers. And they reported lurid tales of Native Americans in Confederate service scalping Union soldiers, of Rebel prisoners of war exposed to smallpox by "the Yankees," and of "flagrant outrages committed ... on the persons of females, the particulars of which are of too beastly a character to be recorded" ("The War News," n.p.).

By 1860, however, the American newspaper had just come through nothing short of a journalistic revolution. Through the first third of the nineteenth century, American newspapers did not contain much actual "news." They were journals of opinion, political cheerleaders, or vehicles for cultured discourse and cultural pretension. Much of what they published about the world came in through the mail: letters from subscribers and copies of other newspapers provided an informal system of exchange—encouraged by free postage—from which interesting items could be freely appropriated, if given credit to the source.

There were few professional reporters, and "war correspondents" were men who sent letters home from the army. At the smaller weeklies, printing was done on presses little changed from Ben Franklin's day, which might produce 250 impressions an hour as long as the pressman and his assistants could endure the pace. From the 1820s, larger papers enjoyed the luxury of improved machinery that raised the output to around 1,000 impressions an hour. However, as a practical matter, the size of a newspaper was limited to four pages (two sides of a single folded sheet) and the high-cost of production limited distribution to the upper classes.

Then, within 25 years, thanks to advancing technology and journalistic enterprise, the newspaper came of age. The enterprise came first. In 1835, Scottish immigrant James Gordon Bennett sensed a market for a more interesting and affordable sort of newspaper and founded the *New York Herald*. He reported on crime and scandal, initiated the Wall Street report, forced the Congress to admit non-Washington-based journalists into the press galleries, and invented the personal interview (the first, with the proprietor of a house of ill repute in which one of the residents had been murdered). In truth, Bennett invented the modern newspaper—and sold it for a penny a copy. His immediate success launched a gaggle of imitators and the day of the "professional" journalist soon arrived.

The technology was not far behind. The railroad, born about the same time as the *Herald*, allowed an expanded movement of people, goods and services across the nation. From the 1850s, steam-powered printing presses could produce as many as 20,000 impressions an hour and permit the wealthier newspapers to issue eight- and even twelve-page editions. The telegraph—invented in 1844 and with a 50,000-mile network by 1860—allowed reports of an afternoon event in Chicago to be off the press in New York by midnight and, be on the president's desk in the morning thanks to the convenience of rail service. (Three New York papers offered same-day home delivery in Washington, D.C.)

However, the high cost of telegraphy—the Washington-to-New York tariff for a typical 2,000-word newspaper column was about $100; from New Orleans to New York perhaps $450—had, early on, induced six otherwise competitive New York newspapers to form a cost-sharing cooperative, the Associated Press. This became a major business all by itself, with some 50 staffers stationed around the nation to cull local newspapers for interesting material. Other papers could use AP material, for a fee. As the war intruded, a Southern Associated Press stepped in to fill the gap, but midway through the war, when editors complained of high prices and poor service, a rival Press Association of the Confederate States of America was established, with headquarters in Atlanta and about twenty correspondents in the field.

One technical limitation continued: daily newspapers could not print illustrations any more complex than simple maps. Print makers such as Currier & Ives were able to turn out full-color lithographs, but at a rate of not more than 300 a day, and while photography—just then coming into wide-spread use—provided reference images for artists, no method had yet been devised for directly converting a photograph into a printing plate. The interim solution was the wood engraving, which was quite basic, yet easily transferable to newspapers. A drawing—at times, made by combat illustrators Winslow Homer or Thomas Nast—was transferred to the surface of four by five-inch blocks of hard-grained wood, and transformed into a relief printing surface by the hands of skilled craftsmen. Perhaps a dozen blocks might be used for a large illustration, the image coordinated by a master engraver who would lay out the plan, and then pass the blocks along to the printers to illustrate with their tools. When finished, the blocks were mounted in the printing frame along with the type or—as technology continued to advance—the whole image would be converted into an electrotype shell to be used on a high-speed rotary press.

The preparation was slow, expensive, and not feasible for the average deadline-driven daily newspaper, but well-suited to a special breed, the "illustrated weekly." The first such in America was launched in 1854, and bankrolled in part by the showman P. T. Barnum. It was a failure, barely making expenses, and soon abandoned. However, Barnum's head engraver went off on his own in 1855 with the eponymous *Frank Leslie's Illustrated Newspaper.* Leslie found the right balance of artistic style and newsworthy content, and, by 1860, was selling an average 100,000 copies per issue. In 1857, the Harper Brothers, who ran a book publishing house, began a competing weekly which they grandly named *Harper's Weekly Journal of Civilization.* The Confederates had less success in the illustrated realm. In an inaugural issue, September 1862, the editors of the *Southern Illustrated News* promised *truthful* engravings of battles, not scenes made up by the artists, and accurate battlefield maps. The paper struggled along for twenty-five months; it printed not a single battlefield scene, and only one map.

In the year Bennett founded the *Herald*, there were perhaps 900 newspapers in the nation; by 1860, there were more than 2500, of which at least 373 were published daily (80 of those, in the less-populous South). New York alone supported 17 daily newspapers; Washington, 3, and Richmond 4. By 1861, the larger papers in New York, Chicago, and Boston were publishing Sunday editions. Some began publishing both morning and evening editions.

But despite the technological and philosophical advances, newspapers continued to be unabashedly partisan; the 1860 U. S. Census categorized 80 percent of them as "political in nature" (*Preliminary Report* 103). Supported by local government printing contracts, many smaller weeklies favorably covered local office-holders. Newspapers in the North can be parceled—roughly—into one of four political categories:

1. Radical Republicans, for whom the only cause that justified going to war was the abolition of slavery. Chief among them were the *Tribunes* of New York and Chicago, and the Philadelphia *Inquirer.*
2. Moderate Republicans, who supported abolition but saw the war as a struggle to preserve the Union. These included the *New York Times*, the Cincinnati *Commercial*, and the Boston *Journal.*
3. Independents, who were against (or neutral on) abolition but for the most part supported the government. These are best represented by the *New York Herald* (although, to most Republican editors, the *Herald* was far from "Independent" and more likely "Democrat").
4. Democrats, who knew that their party could not regain political power in a heavily-Republican North unless reunited with the more populous southern Democrats. Many Democrats, from both the North and South, saw the war as a "Black Republican" plot to overthrow civil liberties and the rule of law and force full racial equality on the nation. The Democrat war aim was settlement, not conquest; ending slavery was not a goal, but an impediment; the path to peace was seen as enlightened discourse, not battlefield victory. These views are best represented by the Cincinnati *Enquirer* and the New York *World.* A subset called the "Peace Democrats" were militant, openly pro-southern, and tagged by the Radicals with the pejorative label "Copperhead," for the venomous snake of the same name. The Chicago *Times* best represents these views.

The allegiance of some papers was clearly indicated by the name on the masthead, although, the Missouri *Democrat* was a Republican paper and the Missouri *Republican*, an organ of the Democrats.

The quintessential radical paper was the *New York Tribune,* founded in 1841 by Horace Greeley, with the announced intention "to advance the interests of the people, and to promote their Moral, Political and Social well-being." Greeley promised that "the immoral and degrading Police Reports, Advertisements, and other matter which have been allowed to disgrace the columns of our leading Penny Papers [referring to the *New York Herald*] will be carefully excluded from this, and no exertion will be spared to render it worthy of the virtuous and refined, and a welcome visitant at the family fireside" (Hale 66-67). Early on, the *Tribune* supported the abolitionist cause, earning the undying enmity of the southern part of the nation.

The leading moderate was the *New York Times,* occupying the ground between the *Herald* and *Tribune.* It opened for business (as the *Daily Times*) on September 18, 1851. In his first edition, publisher Henry J. Raymond (whose was also speaker of the New York State Legislature) offered his own capsule philosophy: "We shall be *Conservative*, in all cases where we think Conservatism essential to the public good;—and we shall be *Radical* in everything which may seem to us to require radical treatment and radical reform. We do not believe that *everything* in Society is either exactly right or exactly wrong;—what is good we desire to preserve and improve;—what is evil, to exterminate, or reform" (Raymond 2).

Most southern papers were Democrat, although a few were Whig—the philosophical predecessor of the Republican Party that had largely ceased to exist in the North and was barely noticed in the South. Southern papers, of whatever persuasion, quickly fell in line; or went out of business. (A fair number of papers—from both the North and South—were forcibly *put* out of business, either by government edict or mob action.) Arguably, the most important of southern papers was the Richmond *Dispatch,* with a circulation that exceeded that of all other Richmond papers combined. This four-page, tabloid-size paper was founded in 1850, to bring New York-style journalism to the South. One of the editors was employed as a part-time clerk for the Confederate War Department, which gave the *Dispatch* an insider's edge. Unlike chief rivals in Richmond—the *Enquirer* (which was strongly pro-administration) and *Examiner* (which consistently criticized everybody)—the *Dispatch* supported the war, but stayed above politics in keeping with a long-stated editorial policy: "Devoted to the interest of the city and free and independent in its political views" (Andrews 1970, 32).

Few of the 2,500 papers, North and South, could afford to have reporters in the wartime field, although, from time to time, an editor might venture forth and interview a general or two. Editors could be overtaken by events when armies passed through town (or, came to stay). Nor could many papers afford the AP charges and almost all relied on official dispatches, letters from home-town men serving in the field, and the exchange system. But as war approached, the more affluent expanded their rosters with "special correspondents" (usually called, simply, "specials"), sent forth to cover the action.

Technically, they were not the first to serve as civilian war correspondents: five American newspapers had pooled their interests in the Mexican War of 1848 and sent a small team to the front. However, those efforts, while seminal, are largely invisible in any histories of that war, or in any histories of journalism. A few years later, two British newspapers and the *New York Evening Post* assigned a total of four reporters to cover the war in the Crimea (1854-56) with shocking results: the work of London *Times* reporter William Howard Russell exposed corruption, poor leadership, and woefully inadequate treatment of the wounded. Russell established a universal truth system in reporting. He said an unfettered journalist is a burden to the military, and anathema to the government, but vital to a democratic society. Russell set the tone for military-media relations that have transpired ever since the Crimean War.

As the nation dissolved and editors drifted into bombast, reporters rushed to prove their skills by uncovering details of military preparations for battle. On April 27, 1861, the Richmond *Enquirer* reported: "The rebel army stationed at Richmond numbers three thousand and seventy-two men." The May 5th edition of the Charleston *Mercury* reported: "Raleigh, North Carolina, is alive with soldiers.... Sixteen companies, comprising twelve hundred men, rank and file, are encamped at the Fair Grounds." The May 23 edition of the New York *Tribune* did its part to warn the Confederates: "A regiment left New York for Fortress Monroe; 350 men left New York to join the 69th Regiment at Washington; two regiments of Ohio volunteers, numbering altogether eighteen hundred men, reach Washington." The *New York Times* reported on May 25 the movement of 13,000 men into Virginia, "each man having sixty rounds of ball cartridge."

Governments from both the North and South, which likely had never heard of William Howard Russell, began to understand that, Constitutional issues aside, wartime freedom of the press could be a distinct liability. The Confederates passed a "Censorship" law which got the attention of the journalists, most of whom supported the cause and usually were careful to do no harm. The Union—where journalistic support was mixed to begin with and intense competition among the newspapers often trumped common sense—established a series of ineffective controls. Maj. Gen. Benjamin F. Butler told the Cincinnati *Commercial* (June 20, 1861) "the Government would not accomplish much until it had hanged ... half a dozen spies, and at least one newspaper reporter." At first, General-in-Chief Winfield Scott decreed that all dispatches must be approved by "the commanding general" (Russell 150-151). When he realized that he couldn't control a war and the news at the same time, he appointed the Washington agent for the AP as official censor.

The censorship was applied only to *telegraphic* reports being sent from Washington. Material sent in the mail, carried away in person, or published in the local Washington papers, was not subject to review. A clever reporter for a New York paper could arrange to have a touchy item planted in a Washington paper, which would then be borrowed with impunity. This ploy may have avoided the censor's scissors, but did little to bolster relationships with the War Department; ultimately, that loophole was plugged.

Both governments held meetings with journalists and editors to work out cooperative agreements, but soon learned that the most effective censorship was simply to keep journalists away from the troops. When he was appointed general-in-chief of the Union army, July 23, 1862, Gen. Henry Wager Halleck—who earlier had blocked reporters from his command in the field, just after the Battle of Shiloh/Pittsburg Landing—ordered Federal commanders to remove *all* newspaper reporters. Rebel commanders adopted a similar stratagem.

Over time, as commanders banned reporters; some journalists made "arrangements" to serve as a "volunteer aide" for a sympathetic senior officer, which gave them access, not only to information, but to food and shelter (in exchange for which, they may have been expected to write something appropriately flattering about their sponsor). Some journalists merely bought or borrowed uniforms and a horse and pretended to belong to nearby units. Notable was the *New York*

*Tribune's* George W. Smalley, who, during the battle of Antietam (September 17, 1862), was pressed into service by Maj. Gen Joseph Hooker to carry orders to various officers in the field. Smalley admitted to being a special correspondent for the *Tribune,* but Hooker didn't care, he needed help.

Notable also was an invitation to the editor of the Mobile *Register,* John Forsyth, to serve as special assistant with the rank of colonel to Confederate Gen. Braxton Bragg (who had banned all other journalists from his army). Bragg had political ambitions, but his plans were foiled. As the Columbus (Georgia) *Sun* noted, "All the silly efforts upon the part of a certain class of newspaper correspondents and 'small editors' to manufacture a great man out of General Bragg have failed" (Andrews 1970, 253).

Over time, most attempts to remove newsmen from the army fell aside, although commanders reserved the right to inspect and approve copy while in the field, a task usually assigned to a subordinate. Various infractions—publishing articles that revealed battle planning or insulted senior officers—got a handful of reporters banned from the field, North and South, some by order of court martial.

President Lincoln was universally hospitable and courteous to journalists. With General Grant, the policy was along Constitutional lines: no prior restraint was practiced. Grant trusted the gentlemen of the press, and unless someone demonstrated otherwise, he carried on without prior restraint. But the men at the top of the Confederate government were not so comfortable with newsmen—Jefferson Davis surrounded himself with a palace guard and rarely spoke with newsmen, or in public. It made little difference, because the newsmen of the South, almost without exception, willingly supported the cause even while some of them regularly ridiculed the government. For example, the Richmond *Examiner* observed on February 4, 1862: "In the midst of revolution, no greater calamity can befall a people, than for their affairs to pass into the control of men who could not understand it in the beginning, and are incapable of appreciating the demands of the crisis as they arise."

Overall, throughout the war, there were perhaps 500 "Special" correspondents in the field, although they did not work at the same time. A total of 350 special correspondents worked for the North, and 150 for the South. Of 78 northern specials for whom personal data survives, about half had attended college. Four out of five had been in newspaper work before the war began. The rest were lawyers, teachers, and adventurers. There were a few women, and at least one African American (Thomas Morris Chester of the Philadelphia *Press*). The average age was late 20s, although half-a-dozen were 19 or younger when the war started, and one was 16.

Most of this new breed of journalistic adventurers had to break fresh trail and arrange for their own support in the field. Of course, it helped to work for a wealthy employer. In the fall of 1862, while the *Tribune* had five men (who shared one horse, one messenger, and barely anything else) covering the

Army of the Potomac, the *Herald* fielded sixteen men with wagons, tents, boats, horses, money, and whatever supplies might be needed. By the end of the war, the *Herald* had sixty-three men in the field, each of whom was given firm guidance: "In no instance, and under no circumstances, must you be beaten.... Remember that your correspondence is seen by half a million persons daily and that the readers of the *Herald* <u>must</u> have the earliest news" (Starr 233).

A few of the specials were full-time military officers with newspaper experience; others in military service may have sought additional glory as "war correspondents" by responding to invitations such as that issued by the Charleston *Mercury*, April 22, 1861: "Officers of the army and navy of the Confederate States... will greatly oblige the proprietors... by furnishing sketches and incidents of the expected conflict between our gallant soldiers and their enemies.... When supplied exclusively, a liberal compensation will be allowed" (Moore 39). Both *Harper's* and *Leslie's* advertised for sketch artists with the army, offering free subscriptions to anyone who would at least send in a trial drawing; by war's end, each had arrangements with about 50 army artists, but their contributions were minimal.

For the most part, newspaper men in the field shared common challenges: to deal with an unfriendly military bureaucracy, to write their copy under the most primitive conditions (often by candlelight with a tree stump for a desk), and then to find some way to get it to the home office. For some material, mail service was sufficient. For more timely stories, the telegraph would be the logical choice, but terminals in the field were run by the army and usually busy with official traffic, and commercial terminals in nearby cities were subject to journalistic gamesmanship. Some specials had "arrangements" with friendly operators, to ensure that their copy would be moved to the head of the line; one *Herald* reporter, whose newspaper could afford the cost, was known at least once to have blocked waiting competitors—while he polished his own copy—by handing his pocket Bible to the operator with a simple instruction, "Start sending at Genesis" (Andrews 1955, 429). At times, the only practical solution was for the correspondent to entrust his copy to a messenger—or carry it himself—for a journey on foot, horseback, and train directly to his editor.

These reporters knew that "action" was the lifeblood of wartime journalism. A writer for the *New York Herald* challenged his readers, "Those who suppose that the labor of a news gatherer upon the battle field is facile and rapid, should stroll, as I have, over the ground where the dead yet lie unburied, and the survivors expect momentarily to resume the conflict" (News from the Peninsula," n.p.). In order to report battles properly, one *Tribune* special advised, a reporter must be "so closely observant of them as to be in danger of being killed" (Starr 148).

However, only a handful of reporters actually became victims of the combat that they observed. A few were killed by accident—drowning, or trapped under a fallen horse. About 50 news reporters became prisoners of war. Most of those were released after a very short time, with two glaring exceptions: Albert

Deane Richardson and Junius Henry Browne of the *New York Tribune*. They were held captive by the Confederate government under the most abysmal of conditions—and all attempts to negotiate their release failed—from May 1862 until they managed to escape in December 1864. They were held for the sole reason that they were correspondents of the hated *Tribune*.

Danger aside, the pay for a Civil War reporter was satisfactory. A typical reporter in the field, North or South, earned as much as a captain in the Union Army, roughly $27 a week. Some superstars rated $100 a week plus expenses, which in some areas—for example, Washington, D.C.—could run more than $35 a week for room and board. Many reporters pumped up their income, especially in the South, by contributing to multiple newspapers. The more prolific earned as much as $10,000 a year, at a time when the annual salary of Lincoln's Secretary of War was $8,000.

By general policy, few reporters were allowed to write under their full names. Some were permitted the use of initials, but most articles were published unsigned or under fanciful nicknames: Whitlaw Reid of the Cincinnati *Gazette* was "Agate" and Frank Wilkie of the *New York Times* was "Galway." One Southern reporter, George W. Bagby, sent copy to newspapers in four states as, variously, Hermes, Gamma, Malou, and Pan. The reasoning behind these pseudonyms was to enable freer speech. The editor of the Charleston *Mercury* advised his Washington correspondent, shortly before hostilities erupted: "The wisdom and consequent usefulness of your letters will depend entirely on [your anonymity].... If you are known, it is impossible to criticize and use names as you otherwise can do, to the great benefit of the southern cause" (Andrews 1970, 50). An executive of the *New York Tribune* wrote: "The anonymous greatly favors freedom and boldness in newspaper correspondence. I will not allow *any* letter writer to attach his initials to his communications, unless he was a widely known & influential man like Greeley.... Besides the responsibility it fastens on a correspondent, the signature inevitably detracts from the powerful impersonality of a journal" (Andrews 1955, 359). But in General Order 48 (April 30, 1863), Union General Joseph Hooker—frustrated over security leaks and personal attacks "by the publications of injudicious correspondents of an anonymous character"—declared that all copy must, thenceforth, be signed by the authors. This launched the "by-line." Some complied with this directive, and others did not.

As the war progressed, and Union forces moved inexorably South, many newspapers of the Confederacy became "loyal Union" sheets or else they shut down their operations. By the end of the war, there were only some 20 daily newspapers still being published in the South, fewer than in Virginia alone before the war. They were barely hanging on: most news came from Yankee papers smuggled through the lines. Shoe blacking substituted for ink—when there was enough paper on which to print even a greatly-attenuated edition—and the price of a subscription had jumped from $5 a year to more than $100.

Before the war, only five percent of American paper production was in the South and the cost of paper was about $5 a ream. The war cut off supply from the North and near the end of the war, the price for paper was $60 a ream. At various times during the war, newspapers resorted to printing on almost anything that would hold the ink, famously including, during the siege of Vicksburg, the blank reverse side of wallpaper. By contrast, the newspapers of the North were flourishing. James Gordon Bennett—who had started the *Herald* with $500 borrowed money—turned down a purchase offer of $2 million.

As newspapers had an impact on the war, for good or ill, the war impacted newspapers for the greater good. Where most news coverage before the war had been limited and local, after the war, reporting and news coverage became broad and national. A population of largely isolated groups, each knowing little of the rest of the nation, was brought together in the shared experience of the war—a war brought to them in the newspapers. As an observer noted in 1866, "It is plain that journalism will henceforth and forever be an important and crowded profession in the United States" and that emphasis had shifted from editorials (which "do not much influence the public mind, nor change many votes") to something much broader: "The word *news*paper is the exact and complete description of the thing which the journalist aims to produce" (Parton 376).

## Further Reading

Andrews, J. Cutler. *The North Reports the Civil War.* Pittsburgh: University of Pittsburgh Press, 1955.

Andrews, J. Cutler. *The South Reports the Civil War.* Princeton: Princeton University Press, 1970.

Hale, William Harlan. *Horace Greeley: Voice of the People.* New York: Harper & Brothers, 1950.

Moore, Frank, ed. *The Rebellion Record: A Diary of American Events.* New York: Putnam, 1861–63.

"News from the Peninsula." *The New York Herald.* June 7, 1862.

Parton, James. "The New York *Herald*." *North American Review* 102, April 1866: 373–419.

*Preliminary Report on the Eighth Census.* Washington, D.C., 1862.

Raymond, Henry. "A Word About Ourselves." *New York Daily Times.* September 18, 1851: 2.

Richardson, Albert D. *The Secret Service, the Field, the Dungeon, and the Escape.* Hartford: American Publishing Company, 1866.

Russell, William Howard. *My Diary North and South, Volume II.* London: Bradbury and Evans, 1863.

Starr, Louis M. *Bohemian Brigade: Civil War Newsmen in Action.* Madison: University of Wisconsin Press, 1987.

*The Richmond Examiner During the War or The Writings of John M. Daniel, with a Memoir of his life by his brother, Frederick S. Daniel.* New York: Printed for the author, 1868.

"The War News." *Richmond Dispatch.* June 18, 1864.

# 20

# LITERATURE

*Vanessa Steinroetter*

When the Civil War began, Americans soon realized that it would not only transform the political landscape forever, but also the ways in which they produced and consumed literature. From the very start of the hostilities, writers in the North and South commented on how the war was disrupting, fostering, or otherwise changing literature, reading habits, and book production. In Cambridge, Massachusetts, for instance, Henry Wadsworth Longfellow wrote in his journal in May 1861: "Nothing alive but the military. Bookselling dead." Having recently visited the Old Corner bookstore of Ticknor and Fields in Boston and seen the lack of business there firsthand, he concluded: "So much for war and books" (Fahs 20). Other writers found not only that popular demand for any literature besides war-related news was down, but that they themselves were so engaged in the events of the war that they were unable to continue writing as before. Southern author William Gilmore Simms complained in a letter to a friend that "nobody reads nowadays, and no one prints. My desks are already filled with MS.S. Why add to the number—the mass—when I so frequently feel like giving these to the flames?" (393–94). Simms, who nevertheless composed numerous poems on war-related themes and published them in southern periodicals throughout the war, worried that he would not be able to write anything more substantial, and that there would not be any possibility of publishing a book even if he did.

For some writers, the war meant disruption, distraction, and dwindling demand for books. Many others, however, including Walt Whitman, Emily Dickinson, and Herman Melville, found in it literary inspiration and material for some of their most powerful writing. As Herman Melville claimed in his foreword to *Battle-Pieces and Aspects of the War* (1866), the poems in this collection "originated in an impulse imparted by the fall of Richmond" (v). Hinting perhaps at the influence of current events and also representations of the war in the media during the volume's composition, Melville describes himself as someone who "but placed a harp in a window, and noted the contrasted airs which wayward winds have played upon the strings" (v).

Emily Dickinson wrote more than half of her known poems during the war years, and literary scholars have recently begun to recognize her importance as a poet of the Civil War, even though many thematic connections to the war remain indirect or hidden. Poems such as "It Feels a Shame to Be Alive" and "When I Was Young a Woman Died," which are now frequently read as poetic responses to the war in general, as well as to individual events and personal losses, reveal how much the work of this famously reclusive poet was actually immersed in the discursive contexts of her time—in spite of her comment in a letter to Thomas Wentworth Higginson in February1863 that "war feels to me an oblique place," three months after Higginson traveled to South Carolina to take command of a black regiment (Johnson and Ward 280).

Inspired by his contact with soldiers during his hospital visits in Civil War Washington, Whitman composed a sequence of fifty-three poems, which he published as *Drum-Taps* in 1865, and in which he expressed his thoughts on the fate of the country and his emotional responses to the war. Poems such as "Beat! Beat! Drums!" and "Come up from the Fields, Father" demonstrate the wide-ranging scope of Whitman's interest in the war's effect on the soldiers in camp and field as well as the civilians waiting for news at home. One of the most important poems in the book, "The Wound-Dresser," can be read not only as a poetic reflection on Whitman's work in the military hospitals during the Civil War, but also as an expression of his hopeful vision for reconciliation and the healing of the nation's wounds after the war.

While many books that had been popular before the war appeared to languish on booksellers' shelves, other print media saw a dramatic increase in popularity. Because there was suddenly a large market for literary responses and commentary on the war, newspapers and periodicals assumed a key role, as they provided publication venues for literary treatments of current events. Newspapers became vital sources for information on battles, casualties and political decisions, as well as for poems, essays, and fiction written in response to the war. As Oliver Wendell Holmes suggested in September 1861, newspapers had become as important as one's daily bread, thanks to the sudden hold that war-related reading material had taken in the minds of American readers. "The newspaper," he observed, "is as imperious as a Russian Ukase; it will be had, and it will be read. To this all else must give place. If we must go out at unusual hours to get it, we shall go, in spite of after-dinner nap or evening somnolence" (348).

The periodical press assumed a special importance in the Confederacy, as writers could no longer work through northern publishing houses to get their works published. Furthermore, due to paper shortages and other disruptions throughout the war, the few existing southern publishers such as West and

Johnston of Richmond often found themselves limited in what they could print. As a result, newspapers and magazines provided an important alternative for authors. As Alice Fahs has shown, at the beginning of the war, the South did not have a highly developed publishing industry: "Most Southern poetry was published in periodicals, and most newspapers and magazines in the South simply went out of business for lack of Northern markets, paying customers, advertising revenue, and materials" (5). As more and more southern poets, essayists, and fiction writers contributed to the few surviving periodicals, their moving and often highly patriotic contributions constituted the beginnings of a new national literature.

Some contemporaries, who felt keenly the importance of preserving this historical moment for future generations, took it upon themselves to collect and publish the poetry in anthologies. William G. Shepperson, for example, edited an anthology that he called *War Songs of the South* (1862), featuring poems about the war by famous Southerners such as Henry Timrod, William Gilmore Simms, and Paul Hamilton Hayne, and many celebrated women writers, including Caroline Howard Glover from Charleston, who contributed several poems to the distinguished magazines and newspapers of the South (for example, the *Charleston Mercury* and the *Southern Literary Messenger*), Constance Cary Harrison from Richmond (pen name "Refugitta"), and Julia Shelton ("Laura Lorrimer") of Bellefonte, Alabama. In the preface to his anthology, Shepperson explained the rationale behind his project: "Surely, these newspaper waifs have played no unimportant part in the actual drama which surrounds us. Convinced that their wealth of patriotic sentiment is too precious to be lost, I have gleaned through the fields of newspaper literature, and have bound up this volume as one binds up a sheaf of golden" (5).

Like newspapers, literary magazines quickly adapted to the change in their reading public's taste, offering an additional venue for writers to publish literature on topical issues without the longer wait associated with book publishing. Authors such as Louisa May Alcott and Thomas Wentworth Higginson published accounts of their wartime experiences, some fictional, some autobiographical, in the *Atlantic Monthly*. Other literary magazines such as *Harper's Monthly*, *Peterson's Ladies Magazine*, the *Magnolia Weekly* and the *Southern Literary Messenger* featured hundreds of contributions by professional writers and amateurs about the war.

The popularity of poetry, in particular, enjoyed during the war cannot be overestimated. Poets who are now less known, such as George Boker or Ethel Lynn Beers, and anonymous contributors to periodicals played an important role in shaping public perception of the war's contested meanings. Indeed, poetry formed one of the primary ways of writing and reading about contemporary events, and it was a regular feature in the majority of the newspapers, even in the regimental papers published by soldiers. Ordinary citizens responded to the outbreak of hostilities through an outpouring of patriotic poetry that, once published, was read by civilians and soldiers alike. Women in the North and South took advantage of these new opportunities and wrote much of the popular poetry produced during the Civil War.

The practice of reprinting and recirculating poems and fiction without the author's knowledge, let alone permission, was widespread in nineteenth-century America and helped to popularize some texts even across sectional borders. Northerner Ethel Lynn Beers (Ethelinda Eliot) wrote a poem titled "The Picket Guard," which took as its opening line a headline she had read in a newspaper: "All quiet along the Potomac." The poem was widely reprinted in northern newspapers, magazines, and anthologies, and set to music by a southern composer, John Hill Hewitt. Titled "All Quiet along the Potomac Tonight," the song based on her poem became one of the most popular of the war. As Ellen Gruber Garvey has shown, recirculation could make poems take on a life of their own, since it "had the capacity to increase greatly the circulation of a news item, poem, or story and give readers the impression that it originated in their own region" (161). For example, the two anonymous poems "A Rainy Day in Camp" and "Mortally Wounded" that Garvey traces across many different publication venues during the Civil War were attributed alternately to civilians and soldiers from the North and South, depending on the allegiances of the editors who reprinted it. Similarly, another poem about a dying soldier, "Somebody's Darling," appeared as both a northern and southern poem, sharing the fate of countless other works that were reprinted without acknowledgments or with a faulty attribution of authorship.

The themes and issues covered by these poems and other works of literature during the Civil War were as diverse as the authors themselves. Many works took as their inspiration and setting major events and battles of the war. Melville wrote many of the poems in *Battle-Pieces* about individual battles and titled them according to the location of the respective battles, such as "Donelson." This poem recounts the events of the battle at the famous Fort, but adds a twist by focusing on the home front and commenting on the production and reception of news during the Civil War. A speaker describes several scenes in which civilians follow events as they unfold through the medium of anonymously authored, mass-distributed texts such as newspaper reports or lists on bulletin boards. In addition to battles, Melville also turned his attention to major political disturbances, such as the New York draft riots ("The House-Top"), and to major figures in the war, including John Brown ("The Portent"), whom he calls "the meteor of the war," and General Thomas J. Jackson ("Stonewall Jackson").

The pages of books, newspapers, and magazines abounded with eulogies of great men and poetic and fictional retellings of major battles. The popular southern novelist John Esten Cooke turned many of the notes he had taken during the war into a volume of personal portraits of famous Confederate generals, which he published in 1867. Cooke's work, titled *The Wearing of the Gray,* features unapologetically exuberant praise for such major military figures as J.E.B. Stuart and P.G.T. Beauregard, and as such presents one writer's personal commemoration of the South's military successes even as the wider political discourse concerned the future of the South after its defeat.

Influential political figures, as well as generals and other military leaders, loomed large in the American literary imagination, starting before the war with John Brown and continuing up to the war's end with Abraham Lincoln, Jefferson Davis, and Robert E. Lee. In addition to Whitman's famous elegiac poems about Lincoln, "O Captain! My Captain!" and "When Lilacs Last in the Dooryard Bloom'd," other poets took the tragic assassination of the president as inspiration. William Cullen Bryant's moving poem "The Death of Lincoln" was read aloud by the Reverend Samuel Osgood to a crowd of mourners gathered in New York City's Union Square as the casket bearing the President's body traveled through the city on its way from the White House to his final resting place in Illinois.

But great men and battles did not constitute the only topics of Civil War literature. Women's experiences of the war, both on the home front and in military hospitals, figured prominently as well. Some popular fiction even focused on such notorious figures as Belle Boyd, the Confederate spy, and those highly publicized cases where women had joined the army and participated in battle while disguised as men. Wesley Bradshaw wrote sensationalist works of fiction that bore titles such as *Pauline of the Potomac, or General McClellan's Spy* (1862) and *General Sherman's Indian Spy* (1865) and challenged existing gender norms with scenes of cross-dressing female soldiers.

Even the poems, stories, and autobiographies that explored the more conventional roles of women in wartime could still challenge existing gender norms. In *Hospital Sketches* (1863), for instance, which was inspired by her experiences as a nurse in Civil War Washington, Louisa May Alcott presents female nurses as independent, strong, and unafraid of living and working among hundreds of male patients. Here Alcott inverts the traditional mid-nineteenth-century power dynamic between men and women, with the female nurse helping the male patient to recover his health and reintegrate into civilian society. In addition to hospital work, Alcott portrayed the domestic lives of women during the war, and in 1869 she published what would become her most popular novel, *Little Women*, set in part during the Civil War years and describing the lives of the four March sisters while their father is away at war.

Other writers addressed larger political issues and historical events through themes that suggested the invasion of the domestic sanctuary by war news, for instance in the form of condolence letters or casualty lists in newspapers. This became a literary trope: the reader wounded vicariously by receiving written news about the wounding or death of a loved one. Winslow Homer's illustration "News from the War," which appeared in *Harper's Weekly* on June 14, 1862, provides a good visual representation of the trope. The figure of a lonely woman bows her head in sadness after reading the letter that is still in her hand. As the caption beneath Homer's image suggests, the woman herself is "wounded" by reading a letter that relays news of a soldier's injury. Poems and stories used this trope to explore the effects of war on the individual and the nation. In July 1862, *Harper's Weekly* published a short story titled "Wounded," which begins with the narrator and his wife sitting together in their home, the husband reading a newspaper and commenting on the latest list of wounded and dead soldiers. His wife is deeply affected by the list's very existence, and the story attempts to teach the moral lesson that men should change their view of the casualty lists that populate the newspapers and realize that the mothers, wives, and sisters of soldiers bear scars: "the larger number never entirely recover. They may linger for years, but do not lose the marks of suffering," since "[f]lesh wounds close readily, but spirit wounds are difficult to heal" ("Wounded," 443).

In addition to the theme of the wounded reader, another theme in both northern and southern poetry was the dying soldier. In these poems, the speaker is generally a soldier, mortally wounded, who addresses his mother and other relatives in his imagination one last time, or asks a friend to relay his last words to his family. Unsure if his body will be buried, returned to his home, or even found, the soldier can only hope that he will be remembered by those he left behind. Often, such literary meditations on death and mourning are intimately connected to the characters' quest for spiritual solace in Christian faith, and they often conclude with a turn from expressions of sorrow to affirmations of faith and acceptance.

Elizabeth Stuart Phelps's bestseller *The Gates Ajar* (1868) illustrates this turn and offers a model of mourning that fosters this turn. Phelps also had dealt with the topic of grief in her short story "A Sacrifice Consumed," published in January 1864, which tells the story of a young seamstress, Ruth, and a young clerk, John. After a brief but happy courtship, Ruth's bliss is interrupted by the war and John's decision to join the army. She learns that John has fallen at Antietam and gradually accepts her fate as a war widow. The story ends: "So she lived very patiently at the foot of the altar where the ashes of her sacrifice lay, and knew that God had accepted it for the blessing of her country, herself, and John" (240).

A related theme in poems, short stories, articles, and essays during the war was letter writing—not only the role of letters in bringing bad news of death or wounds, but also letter writing as a means of maintaining emotional ties and uniting individuals. The power of letters to connect and reunite individuals separated by the war was celebrated in numerous poems and short stories that appeared in periodicals during the Civil War. *Harper's Weekly*, for instance, published the poems "A Soldier's Letter, and a Woman's Answer" (April 1862), "The Mother's Letter" (March 1863) and "Home-News in Battle-Time" (April 1864), while *Peterson's Magazine* featured the short story "The Soldier's Letter" by popular contributor T.S. Arthur (March 1863), and the New York *Ledger* published the poem "Mail Time in Camp" (March 1863) by Ethel Lynn—the author famous for another wartime poem, "All Quiet Along the Potomac"—and the short story "Wounded at Donelson" by Mary C. Vaughan (where letters reunite lovers separated by the war).

But although many writers chose to focus on the disruptions to the everyday lives of civilians during the war, others composed works designed to advance the cause of the North or South. In 1864, West & Johnston published Augusta Jane Evans's novel *Macaria, or, Altars of Sacrifice*, which celebrates the cause of the Confederacy and models the ways in which Southerners can serve it. By end of the novel, the female protagonist, Irene, having survived the war-related deaths of her father and fiancé, vows to become a war nurse and devote her life to the care of wounded Confederate soldiers and "to the hallowed work of promoting the happiness and gladdening the paths of all who journeyed with her down the chequered aisles of Time" (414). Evans referred to herself as "one who, although debarred from the dangers and deathless glory of the 'tented field,' would fain offer a woman's inadequate tribute to the noble patriotism and sublime self-abnegation of her dear and devoted countrymen" (3) and dedicated her novel to the "Army of the Southern Confederacy, who have delivered the South from despotism, and who have won for generations yet unborn the precious guerdon of constitutional republican liberty" (3).

The partisan rhetoric in *Macaria* and the author's unabashed support of the Confederate cause frequently earned it criticism and condemnation from the North, as in the alleged case of an officer in the Army of the Cumberland who is said to have ordered the confiscation and burning of all copies owned by the soldiers under his command. Nonetheless, *Macaria* was one of the bestselling books of the Civil War, selling over 20,000 copies. Other best-sellers of the war were translations of Victor Hugo's novel *Les Misérables*, including northern and southern translations with significant differences, designed to cater to widely divergent views on the slavery question.

Evans and the Hugo translators were not alone in enlisting their talents in the service of a political cause. Many writers on both sides of the conflict composed patriotic verses designed to rouse men into enlisting and persuade women to accept sacrifice. From James Ryder Randall's "Maryland, My Maryland" (1861) and Julia Ward Howe's "Battle Hymn of the Republic," first published as a poem in the *Atlantic Monthly* in February 1862 and later set to music, to poems by Southerner Henry Timrod such as "Ethnogenesis," "Carolina," and "A Cry to Arms," the Civil War produced a flood of politically motivated literature. For example, after the Union Army began recruiting the first African American regiments, the topic increasingly appeared in poems, essay, and fiction. In the *Atlantic Monthly*, Louisa May Alcott celebrated the courage of African American soldiers in the attack on Fort Wagner in her short story "The Brothers" (later renamed "My Contraband"). Thomas Wentworth Higginson's

"Leaves from an Officer's Journal," also published in the *Atlantic*, joined her in praise. Higginson later combined these "Leaves" with other notes and personal observations from the war and republished them as a book titled *Army Life in a Black Regiment* (1869), probably the most famous literary treatment of the topic of black soldiers in the Civil War. In 1864, *Harper's Weekly* published two short stories featuring escaped or freed slaves who joined the Union army, "Tippoo Saib," set against the attack on Fort Wagner, and "Buried Alive," focusing on the massacre at Fort Pillow. Often, the picture drawn of the black soldier in these texts was one of a physically strong man who performed well under the guidance of white officers and was willing to fight for the Union to his death.

White writers were not alone in addressing the topic of black soldiers in the war. In 1867, William Wells Brown published a book-length history titled *The Negro In the American Rebellion: His Heroism and His Fidelity* (1867), which describes the military accomplishments and intellectual backgrounds of particular black officers. That same year, Brown also published his novel *Clotelle, The Colored Heroine, A Tale of the Southern States* (1867) in the United States. Brown's novel appeared in four different versions between 1853 and 1867, and it is the last of these revised versions that directly incorporates the theme of African American participation in the military effort through the experiences of the two black protagonists, Jerome and Clotelle. Residing in Europe, which is described as lacking the overt racial discrimination of America, Jerome and Clotelle hasten back to the United States at the outbreak of the Civil War to aid in the cause of emancipation. Once home, Jerome and Clotelle use their "ample means" to assist "those whom the rebellion had placed in a state of starvation and sickness," regardless of color or sectional identity (105). As a result of her ministrations, Clotelle becomes known as the "Angel of Mercy," while Jerome soon follows the newly-issued "General Order No. 63 … recognizing, and calling into the service of the Federal Government, the battalions of colored men known as the 'Native Guard,'" one of the first black regiments to fight in the war (105).

In addition to Brown, numerous other African Americans wrote about the Civil War and black soldiers, and much of this intellectual and literary exchange took place in the African American press. Black newspapers such as the *Christian Recorder*, based in Philadelphia, had a large subscription base and readership during the war, and many of the featured news items, essays, and letters printed in the *Recorder* directly addressed the African American war experience. The *Recorder* printed contributions by soldiers in the United States Colored Troops (USCT), who in turn acknowledged receiving and reading the newspaper in camp.

With the end of the Civil War, literature gradually turned away from stories of battles and death, but loss and mourning still featured prominently in the literature of the early years of Reconstruction. In many cases these feelings expressed a sense of national grief. In the South, Father Abram Joseph

Ryan's poem "The Conquered Banner" (1865) became one of the most popular postwar poems, as did Henry Timrod's "Ode at Magnolia Cemetery" (1867), which is both a song of personal mourning and an elegy for the Confederacy. Sometimes simply called "The Charleston Ode," this poem commemorates the fallen Confederate soldiers buried at Magnolia Cemetery, South Carolina, calling them martyrs and the burial ground a holy site. It is an early testament to the ideology of the "lost cause" that so many Southerners espoused after the end of the war.

Northerners also mourned the loss of lives and the destruction of war. Sarah Morgan Bryan Piatt wrote a mournful poem with the same setting as Timrod's. Published in *Harper's Weekly* on August 25, 1866, "Arlington Heights" is set in Arlington National Cemetery, and the poem's speaker asks a spectral figure that seems to be the ghost of Robert E. Lee to answer for the many lives that have been lost.

Other writers focused on exploring reconciliation in the immediate aftermath of the war. These romances of Reconstruction, which include John William De Forest's novel *Miss Ravenel's Conversion from Secession to Loyalty* (1867), often explored sectional reconciliation through a marriage plot. And still other writers drew attention to troubling developments that seemed to threaten the long-term stability of reconciliation. Frances Watkins Harper described the persistent racism in the postwar South in her novel *Minnie's Sacrifice* (1869), which portrays the experiences of free educated African Americans from the North who head south to teach former slaves and end up facing threats, violence, and lynch mobs. As the title of Rebecca Harding Davis's 1867 novel *Waiting for the Verdict* implied, it seemed doubtful whether America was prepared for the societal and cultural changes set in motion by the Emancipation Proclamation. The fighting was over, but the struggle over the meaning of the war would continue in the pages of books, magazines, newspapers, letters, and journals.

## Further Reading

Aaron, Daniel. *The Unwritten War: American Writers and the Civil War.* New York: Knopf, 1973.
Alcott, Louisa May. *Little Women.* 1869, Boston: Roberts Brothers, 1890.
Alcott, Louisa May. *Civil War Hospital Sketches.* 1863. Mineola: Dover Publications, 2006.
Brown, William Wells. *Clotelle; or, the Colored Heroine. A Tale of the Southern States.* Boston: Lee & Shepard, 1867.
Brown, William Wells. *The Negro In the American Rebellion: His Heroism and His Fidelity.* Boston: Lee & Shepard, 1867.
Cohen, Michael C. "Contraband Singing: Poems and Songs in Circulation during the Civil War." *American Literature* 82.2 (2010): 271–304.
Cooke, John Esten. *Wearing of the Gray: Being Personal Portraits, Scenes and Adventures of the War.* New York: E.B. Treat & Co., 1867.
Dingledine, Don. "'The Whole Drama of the War': The African American Soldier in Civil War Literature." *PMLA* 115 (2000): 1113–117.

Evans, Augusta Jane. *Macaria, or, Altars of Sacrifice*. 1864, Baton Rouge: Louisiana State University Press, 1992.

Fahs, Alice. *The Imagined Civil War: Popular Literature of the North and South, 1861–1865*. Chapel Hill: University of North Carolina Press, 2001.

Fuller, Randall. *From Battlefields Rising: How the Civil War Transformed American Literature*. Oxford: Oxford University Press, 2010.

Gardner, Eric. "Remembered (Black) Readers: Subscribers to the *Christian Recorder*, 1864–1865." *American Literary History* 23.3 (2011): 229–259.

Gardner, Sarah E. *Blood and Irony: Southern White Women's Narratives of the Civil War, 1861–1937*. Chapel Hill: University of North Carolina Press, 2003.

Garvey, Ellen Gruber. "Anonymity, Authorship, and Recirculation: A Civil War Episode." *Book History* 9 (2006): 159–178.

Holmes, Oliver Wendell. "Bread and the Newspaper." *Atlantic Monthly*. September 1861: 346–52.

Homer, Winslow. "News from the War." *Harper's Weekly*. 14 June 1862: 276–277.

James, Jennifer C. *A Freedom Bought with Blood: African American War Literature from the Civil War to World War II*. Chapel Hill: University of North Carolina Press, 2007.

Johnson, Thomas H. and Theodora Ward, eds. *The Letters of Emily Dickinson*. Cambridge: Harvard University Press, 1958.

Kaser, David. *Books and Libraries in Camp and Battle: The Civil War Experience*. Westport: Greenwood Press, 1984.

Melville, Herman. *Battle-Pieces and Aspects of the War*. New York: Harper & Brothers, 1866.

Phelps, Elizabeth Stuart. "A Sacrifice Consumed." *Harper's Magazine*. January 1864: 235–240.

Richards, Eliza. "U.S. Civil War Print Culture and Popular Imagination." *American Literary History* 17.2 (2005): 349–359.

Richards, Eliza. "Correspondent Lines: Poetry, Journalism, and the U.S. Civil War." *ESQ* 54.1–4 (2008): 140–170.

Shepperson, William G. *War Songs of the South*. Richmond: West & Johnston, 1862.

Simms, William Gilmore. *The Letters of William Gilmore Simms, Vol. IV*. Columbia: University of South Carolina Press, 1956.

Sizer, Lyde. *The Political Work of Northern Women Writers and the Civil War, 1850–1872*. Chapel Hill: University of North Carolina Press, 2000.

Wilson, Edmund. *Patriotic Gore: Studies in the Literature of the American Civil War*. New York: Oxford University Press, 1962.

"Wounded." *Harper's Weekly*. July 12, 1862: 442–443.

Young, Elizabeth. *Disarming the Nation: Women's Writing and the American Civil War*. Chicago: University of Chicago Press, 1999.

# 21

# PHOTOGRAPHY

*Mandy A. Reid*

During the Civil War, more than two decades after daguerreotypes were intro-duced in the United States in 1839, photography still captivated Americans and was at the height of its popularity. Its inventor, Louis Jacques Mande Daguerre, had proudly boasted of his accomplishment in terms of harnessing nature to perform at his will: "I have found a way of fixing the images of the camera! I have seized the fleeting light and imprisoned it! I have forced the sun to paint pictures for me!" (Hirsch vii). In the mid-nineteenth-century United States, these 'sun-pictures' performed important cultural work. As Richard Rudisill explains, the daguerreotype influenced American life in three key ways:

> Initially the new medium directly encouraged cultural nationalism. Its pictures were clear affective images reflecting and reiterating many impulses toward the definition of an 'American' character. At another level of consciousness, the invention of photography helped Americans adjust themselves intuitively to the transition from an agrarian to a tech-nological society in that these images were produced with a reliable mechanical tool. Important as are both of these functions, however, it is at the level of the spirit that we must seek for the most essential operation of the daguerreotype in American life. It both reflected and activated national faith in spiritual insight and truth obtained from perceiving the works of God in nature.
>
> *(5)*

The idea that photography captured truth was a major selling point. Along with the fact that it literally offered Americans a new way of seeing themselves and relating to the world around them, this perceived truthfulness explains why it was used so extensively to document the events of the Civil War.

Although the Civil War broke out a mere 22 years after the introduction of photography in the United States, it was not the first conflict to be covered by photographers. The Mexican War of 1846-1848 was the first and the Crimean War of 1854-1856 was the second. But Civil War photographs mark the nascent beginnings of using visual testimony to report newsworthy events, and the Civil War was the most extensively photographed conflict of the nineteenth century. Photojournalism flourished on America's bloody battlegrounds, and successive improvements in technology increased in both depth and breadth what photographers were able to capture with their lenses. Civil War photography transformed the face of news in America. In the 1840s and 1850s, engravers hand-carved images into wooden blocks which then were used in the printing press for all illustrations published in newspapers and magazines. *Frank Leslie's Illustrated Newspaper* was unique in sending scores of correspondents into the field on both the Confederate and Union sides. The correspondents interviewed soldiers and gathered any and all information on the battleground, often flanking (or for the less courageous, following) soldiers in combat. They sent their missives, including hand-sketches, to the newspaper offices. Frank Leslie then employed hundreds of engravers to bring the images to the newspaper's readers. Even with the advent of Civil War photography, editors and publishers continued to use engravers; the primary change was that instead of working from a sketch, the engravers worked from—and even modified—photographs.

The most popular form of photography in the mid-century United States was the daguerreotype, which was typically used for portraits. In 1850, New York City alone was home to 71 daguerreian rooms, which were operated by 127 photographers and their 57 assistants. The final product was a highly glossy copper plate upon which an image was directly exposed; hence, the lack of negatives ensured that each image was unique. Daguerreotypes were easily portable thanks to small, often ornate, pocket-sized cases which housed the images. Some photographers branched out into scientific photography, using telescopes and microscopes to capture otherwise inaccessible subjects, including the moon, stars, lightning, and a fly's foot. Other unusual images that foreshadowed some of the subjects of Civil War photography included surgeries and the aftermath of disasters (such as fires and train crashes).

Americans were fascinated by the new technology and savvy daguerreotypists used the cult of celebrity to promote their products and services. Many, including Mathew Brady, perhaps the most well-known Civil War photographer, offered a free daguerreotype to celebrities in order for the right to display their likenesses. Presidents, politicians, authors, tradesmen, and countless others sat for their photographs, and many of those images were in turn sold to Americans who wanted to capture a piece of the sitter. The daguerreotype was popular with reformers, as well. The development of photography coincided with as the accelerating tensions over slavery, and so abolitionists, in particular, often sat for portraits. Many felt that photographs captured humanity at its best, and so presented a striking contrast to the slave system—humanity at its worst. Leading abolitionists knew that portraits offered excellent publicity, increasing both face recognition and name recognition. Frederick Douglass, for example, never missed an opportunity to sit for a photograph.

Most human subjects depicted in daguerreotypes are somber, however, perhaps because of fatigue. Initially development took a good 15 minutes. By the 1840s, the exposure times had been cut drastically—to about 30 seconds. The January 1, 1863 edition of the *American Journal of Photography* offers an insightful and humorous account of this experience of sitting for a photograph:

> You have a vague impression that to look smiling is ridiculous, and to look solemn is still more so…. You desire to look intelligent, but you are hampered by a fear of looking sly. You wish to look as if you were not sitting for your picture; but the effort to do so fills your mind more completely with the melancholy consciousness that you are. [The iron head brace] gives you exactly the appearance as if somebody was holding onto your hair behind.
>
> *("Having Your Photograph Taken" 292)*

Then, by placing two or more (typically 5 but up to 11) daguerreotype plates side by side, photographers were able to create a new product: the panorama. George Barnard, a photographer for the Union army, printed early panoramas which were highly valued by military generals, particularly those of contested terrain and enemy fortifications. While few nineteenth-century panoramas are still extant today, they served an important purpose during the Civil War. Unlike the personal photographs that soldiers and their families treasured, panoramas allowed an otherwise inaccessible form of military intelligence. In a nation divided by war, the work of photographers such as Barnard and George S. Cook made photography not only an art form and a form of communication, but a potential tool for spies.

Daguerreotypes began to be displaced in the mid-1850s due to market demands for faster and cheaper products. William Henry Fox Talbot's new positive/negative system—a repeatable system—shifted the focus of photography from unique images produced out of a scripted encounter between sitter and photographer to a potentially mass-produced product and a process in which almost anyone could participate. Visually fuzzy, two-dimensional images produced by the calotype highlighted the general over the particular, somewhat akin to Impressionist paintings. The artistic feel and flexibility of calotypes were far outweighed by a tricky developing process and uncertain results, as fading was a prominent concern. While calotypes never achieved the status of daguerreotypes in America, the negative/positive printmaking system offered photographers a more advanced means of producing visual images in mass.

By early 1855, two new forms of photography had been introduced— the ambrotype and the tintype. The ambrotype was remarkably like the daguerreotype: both were roughly the same size, offered a one-of-a-kind image, and were housed in special cases. The primary differences between the two were the ambrotype's lack of a glossy, reflective surface and its cheaper cost. It was the less popular cousin of the tintype and did not take off as quickly because one man, James A. Cutting, attempted to patent the ambrotype process. Other photographers, irritated at being sued for patent infringement, banded together and contended that Cutting was creating a monopoly on the scientific process. These photographers turned to tintypes and effectively rendered Cutting's actions moot.

Tintypes quickly became the most popular form of cased photographs. Despite their name, tintypes were actually made on thin sheets of iron. Their popularity was due in large part to the Civil War, as hundreds of thousands of soldiers—Union and Confederate—sat for their photographs in tent studios. Tintypes were often made by itinerant photographers who traveled on foot or by wagon, and the low level of professional skills required to make them, along with the low cost (as little as 25 cents), added to their appeal. Because they were so inexpensive, relatively durable and easily portable, tintypes were the most frequently used medium for soldiers who wanted to carry a piece of home into the battlefield, and family members who wanted to possess the image of a soldier. The process of making a tintype was roughly a minute, and the images were uniformly tonal and lacked the contrast and the reflective surface of daguerreotypes. But with the advent of the tintype, having one's photograph taken became less formal and more fun. No longer were smiles or mugging for the camera seen as disrespectful of a complex process.

Even the tintype, however, did not mark the peak of the public craze for photography. *Cartes-de-visite*, also called *cartes*, first appeared in the United States in 1859, and by the 1860s "cartomania" had taken hold. The *carte* was a widely popular form of photography and served multiple purposes in the United States. Americans exchanged *cartes*, sold them to support various causes or organizations, and compiled them in albums. Soldiers and family members sent the inexpensive images to one another in small envelopes, and Americans collected *cartes* of Abraham Lincoln, Ulysses S. Grant, and other Civil War celebrities. Printed on albumen paper and pasted onto a 2 × 4 inch card, *cartes* revolutionized the phenomenon of keeping and sharing images in photograph albums. "Everybody keeps a photographic album," a journalist observed in 1864. "It is a source of pride and emulation among some people to see how many *cartes de visite* they can accumulate from their friends and acquaintances" (Neely and Holzer 24).

However, what really differentiated *cartes* from previous forms of photography was the ease of duplication that the production of a negative allowed. Individuals only had to sit for a photograph once and could produce copies at a later date. Several million *cartes* were sold each year at the height of cartomania in the 1860s. In 1863, Oliver Wendell Holmes referred to them as "social currency, the 'green-backs' of civilization" (8), and in 1866 a journalist observed that "everyone is surfeited [with *cartes*] … everybody has exchanged with everybody"

(Gilbert 96). This frenzy continued into the early 1870s, when the *carte-de-visite* was replaced by the cabinet card—a similar, but larger albumen print.

At the same time that *cartes* were popular, stereoviews of the 1860s offered a new way of displaying images. Stereoviews were two identical 3 × 3 inch images pasted side-to-side on a thick 3 ¼ × 6 ¾ inch card to give a three-dimensional effect with viewed through a stereoscopic viewer. More significant than the physical layout, was the change in photographic experience:

> The stereoscopic view served a different purpose than the *carte de visite*. The card portrait was a photographic keepsake; the stereoview was a photographic viewing experience.... It was almost like being there and seeing the scene with one's own eyes. In that sense, it was the closest thing Civil War-era Americans had to movies or television, and it would remain so throughout the rest of the nineteenth century until the advent, in 1896, of actual motion pictures.
>
> *(Zeller 23)*

Stereoviews of Civil War photographs were quickly mass marketed and eagerly purchased.

Yet in spite of the popularity of their *cartes* and stereoviews, many Civil War photographers remain anonymous. Countless images from the Civil War did not display the photographer's name on the mount or reverse; others had misattributed credit. The photographers who *did* receive credit were Mathew Brady, George S. Cook, Jay D. Edwards, Alexander Gardner, J.W. Petty, A.J. Russell, R.B. Bontecou, and Timothy O'Sullivan. Of these, the three most famous were Cook, Brady, and Gardner.

George S. Cook was a southern photographer who had worked with Brady in New York and Washington, D.C., before moving to South Carolina. He served as a major supplier of photographic materials to other southern photographers, despite federal blockades of southern ports, and he kept open the doors of his very successful studio, even as his competitors closed up shop during the bombardments in Charleston, South Carolina. Cook served 3,566 customers in 1861 and 1862, prompting the *American Journal of Photography* to note in January 1863:

> There has been little photography in Jeffdom for the past two years. It is only in Charleston and perhaps Richmond that any photographs at all are made. By favor of our British cousins who run the blockade with powder and guns, our friend Cook of Charleston still has a precarious stock of photographic materials and still makes a business in the shadows of the people.
>
> *(Zeller 121)*

Aside from benefitting from blockade running and having a successful studio business, Cook made other photographic contributions during the Civil War. In 1861 he managed to enter the occupied Fort Sumter and photograph Major Robert Anderson and his men. By doing so, Cook "became history's first combat photographer—the first photographer to capture an image of enemy operations while himself under fire" (Zeller 2). In 1863 he captured combat photographs of Union ironclads, and he was also the first photographer to capture images of prisoners of war. Union prisoners captured at the Battle of Bull Run were held in a fort-turned-prison, Castle Pinckney, and Cook took several photographs of the Yankee prisoners and their guards.

In the North, Brady and Gardner joined forces at the beginning of the war, but dissolved their partnership sometime between November 1862 and May 1863. Historians have speculated that the split may have been due to Brady's practice of claiming credit for all photographs taken by those who worked for him (either intentionally or by not correcting the assumptions of observers and commentators), whereas Gardner meticulously credited each member of his team, even going so far as to divide the images equally in cases when exact authorship was unclear. For example, perhaps frustrating Gardner, no distinction was made between the graphic images taken by Brady and Gardner in the aftermath of Gettysburg, and the prevailing assumption was that the Gettysburg images were Brady's alone. Attributions were confused in spite of the fact that each man had a distinctive approach to the framing and taking of photographs. Brady's images were carefully and creatively constructed, and in more than a couple of images, the viewer can see Brady himself. Gardner focused less on the landscape and more on the dead. As one scholar observes: "The difference between Alexander Gardner's Gettysburg photographs and those of M.B. Brady is the difference between live bodies and dead ones. The enterprising Gardner was first on the battlefield, and he focused on the still-unburied dead. Brady arrived too late to photograph bodies, but not too late to imbue his inimitable style on the images" (Zeller 105).

Like George Cook, Gardner came under fire and was even called "Captain Gardner" after he joined General George B. McClellan's army forces in the early 1860s. He also worked with the nascent U.S. Secret Service by copying important maps and military documents and by taking photographs for the U.S. Topographical Engineers. But his best-known Civil War images came in 1862, when he arrived quickly on the scene at the Battle of Antietam and captured the aftermath of the fighting. His photographs—not merely engravings based on photographs—were featured in *Harper's Weekly* in October 1862 for the entire nation to see.

Brady photographed the aftermath at Antietam too, and displayed them in his New York gallery as an exhibition he called "The Dead of Antietam." Viewers were shocked by the images. Oliver Wendell Holmes acknowledged that "it was so nearly like visiting the battlefields to look over these views … and we buried them in the recesses of our cabinet as we would have buried the mutilated remains of the dead they too vividly represented" (12). A journalist for the *New York Times* commented that Brady had brought "home to us the terrible reality and earnestness of war," adding that if he "has not brought bodies and laid them in our dooryards and along the streets, he has done something very like it." This journalist felt a "terrible fascination" drawing him to look at the photographs, and empathized with the "hushed, reverend groups standing around these weird copies of carnage, bending down to look in the pale faces of the dead" ("Brady's Photographs" 5). Another *New York Times* article expressed shock at Brady's war photographs, explaining: "Photography came to us smilingly and trippingly, fragrant with meadows and beautiful with landscapes, seemingly the handmaid of Peace. She had a bucolic air.... Consequently one may be pardoned for starting with surprise when she suddenly flashes from the clouds, helmeted, plumed and be-belted, at once the Minerva and the Clio of the war!" ("Photographic Phases" 5).

The following year, both Gardner and Brady traveled—separately—to photograph Pennsylvania in the wake of the Battle of Gettysburg. Gardner and his team captured numerous images of the unburied dead, while Brady and his men, who arrived after most of the fallen were buried, took pictures of the damaged land. This time, however, it was Brady's images that were published in *Harper's Weekly*. Even though the images were most likely taken by Brady's assistants, given his own very poor eyesight, the photographs—and countless more from the war—all bore the same caption: "Photographs by Brady."

This time in Pennsylvania gave rise to a myth about Civil War photographers—that they frequently rearranged corpses to suit their own artistic purposes. While taking photographs at Gettysburg, Gardner and his team used the corpse of a Confederate soldier in two different images, and one image was staged after Gardner's team moved the corpse to a different site. Findings in the 1960s pinpointed the original camera locations of these "Sharpshooter" images, taken on July 7, 1863, and revealed that the same body was used in two different shots. But this rearrangement of corpses was not a typical practice. Most photographers left the dead alone and achieved the "look" they wanted with the addition of props (like shells and muskets).

Wounded and dead bodies were also photographed for medical purposes. Dr. R.B. Bontecou was the Surgeon-in-Charge at Harewood U.S. Army General Hospital in Washington, D.C. He was a pioneer in taking close-up photographs of medical procedures, including surgery, anesthesia, amputated limbs and appendages, and he documented soldiers' injuries with his camera as he treated them. In some cases, Dr. Bontecou took photographs of soldiers when he first treated them and, for those who survived, when they recovered. Initially, these images served as training manuals in field hospitals, and duplicates were appended to soldiers' military papers to document the nature of their injuries before they could receive their military pensions. Soldiers who could not prove that their injuries were sustained during battle were denied their pensions; more than 500,000 military pension claims were filed before 1885, and one-third were rejected. Photographs, rather than physical bodies scarred by war, provided evidence and subsequently compensation for many soldiers. These gruesome photographs detailed medical practices and also the physical cost of war. Image after image of dismembered bodies, soldiers leaning on crutches, gaps where limbs used to be, scars, wheelchairs, stumps, bullet holes and other wounds told their own story.

War photographs, whether filed with pension claims, displayed in galleries or published in newspapers and magazines, offered Civil War-era Americans as close a look at the war as they could tolerate. Then, after the war, they were able to relive it through photographs published in books. In 1866, George Barnard's *Photographic Views of Sherman's Campaign* and Gardner's *The Photographic Sketchbook of the Civil War* were both published. Amid calls for artists to help heal the nation's wounds, these albums of images helped Americans make sense of the war, and used sequenced images and captions to piece together a narrative of progress and reconciliation. As for Brady, he sold his collection of Civil War photographs to Congress for $25,000 in 1875. Additionally, what remained in the wake of the war was a technological legacy. In order to document the war's events as they happened or in the immediate aftermath, photographers needed faster methods. This resulted in shorter sitting times, easily transportable supply wagons, lighter and more effective equipment, and durable, easily reproducible and cheap images that soldiers could purchase and carry. Showing the impact of the Civil War on photography, all of these developments paved the way for modern technologies.

## Further Reading

"Brady's Photographs: Pictures of the Dead at Antietam." *New York Times.* October 20, 1862: 5.

Burns, Stanley B. *Shooting Soldiers: Civil War Medical Photography by R. B. Bontecue.* New York: Burns Archive Press, 2011.

Davis, William C. *Touched By Fire: A National Historical Society Photographic Portrait of the Civil War.* New York: Black Dog and Leventhal Publishers, 1997.

"Having Your Photograph Taken." *American Journal of Photography.* January 1, 1863: 292.

Gilbert, George. *Photography: The Early Years.* New York: Harper and Row, 1980.

Hirsch, Robert. *Seizing the Light: A History of Photography.* Boston: McGraw-Hill, 2000.

Holmes, Oliver Wendell. "Doings of the Sunbeam." *Atlantic Monthly,* July 1863: 1–15.

Huntzicker, William E. "Picturing the News: Frank Leslie and the Origins of American Pictorial Journalism." In David B. Sachsman, S. Kittrell Rushing, and Debra Reddin van Tuyll, eds. *The Civil War and the Press.* New Brunswick: Transaction Publishers, 1995. 309–324.

Neely, Jr., Mark E. and Harold Holzer. *The Lincoln Family Album: Photographs from the Personal Collection of a Historic American Family.* New York: Doubleday, 1990.

Newman, Kathy. "Wounds and Wounding in the American Civil War: A (Visual) History." *The Yale Journal of Criticism* 6.2 (1993): 63–86.

"Photographic Phases." *New York Times.* July 21, 1862: 5.

Rudisill, Richard. *Mirror Image: The Influence of the Daguerreotype on American Society.* Albuquerque: University of New Mexico Press, 1971.

Savas, Theodore P. *Brady's Civil War Journal: Photographing the War, 1861–1865.* New York: Skyhorse Publishing, 2008.

Trachtenberg, Alan. *Reading American Photographs.* New York: Hill and Wang, 1989.

Zeller, Bob. The *Blue and Gray in Black and White: A History of Civil War Photography.* Westport: Praeger, 2005.

# 22

# PAINTING AND ILLUSTRATION

*Jennifer Raab*

The Civil War presented both an opportunity and a dilemma for artists: here was a new subject—a war that definitively consumed the country's attention—but how to represent this violent struggle, and the more abstract issues it raised, was far from clear. War was traditionally the subject matter most suited for history painting, a genre of fine art characterized by large canvases, grand scenes, and heroic figures. American artists, inspired by European models, created such pictures following the Revolutionary War, including popular paintings of the signing of the Declaration of Independence, the Battle of Bunker Hill, and George Washington crossing the Delaware River. History paintings were often commissioned for large public spaces to commemorate important events and to shape collective memory. In scale and subject, they were designed to convey a moral message and to instill a sense of national pride.

But the Civil War did not produce any such canvases. No famous history paintings emerged during the war, nor in the years following the surrender at Appomattox. The artistic legacy of the Civil War is not a series of monumental paintings with clear narratives of victory and defeat and a cast of identifiable heroes, but rather a shift to a more direct and realistic form of representation. Instead of generals triumphing in battle, well-known artists produced paintings of camp life, nameless soldiers, and freed, or fleeing, slaves. Perhaps even more importantly, artists began working in greater numbers for newspapers and periodicals, creating images for print media that quickly and consistently reached a wider public eager to see and learn about all aspects of the war. The graphic arts provided a patriotic opportunity for artists and a means to reach a broader audience. While visual production during this period cannot be reduced to a single style, the most striking painted and printed images rely on observational realism to communicate the modernity and mass destruction of the Civil War.

The war was fought on the frontlines of battle and on the front pages of newspapers. "This is a war of opinion as well as of arms," one Alabama editor proclaimed (Coopersmith xviii). Each side had distinct advantages and disadvantages. The South was fighting to defend its way of life and its territory. There was a clear and compelling motivation for the Confederates: to protect their families, their land, and their livelihood from northern invasion. Meanwhile, the North had to both defend its own land and conquer the southern states. The Union's motivation, especially in the early years of the war, was also more abstract: to preserve the union. As historians have noted, this was a more difficult sell: "While that may have inspired patriotic songs and politicians' speeches, it was hardly the stuff that would make the citizen-soldier son of a Pennsylvania farmer look forward to yet another night sleeping in the mud" (Lewin and Huff 75). But the North certainly had significant advantages, namely, more manpower and more resources. These strengths had a direct impact on artistic production.

The Union controlled the centers of art and publishing on the eastern seaboard—New York, Boston, Hartford, Philadelphia, and Baltimore. The North could draw from a deeper pool of talented artists (and pay them more) to cover the war for the illustrated newspapers and journals that emerged at mid-century and became enormously popular as the conflict continued. These "sketch artists" worked for publications like *Frank Leslie's Illustrated Newspaper* (est. 1855) and *Harper's Weekly* (est. 1857). The Confederacy added their own version several years later with the *Southern Illustrated News*, launched in the fall of 1862 with this motto on its masthead: "Not a luxury, but a necessity." Southerners, cut off from northern publications and hungry for battlefront reports and pictures, subscribed in large numbers. But the paper was not able to send artists to the frontlines, as its northern competitors routinely did. There was, in fact, a shortage of illustrations in the *Southern Illustrated News*, and those that did appear in its pages were mostly portraits copied from outdated photographs, or even images reproduced from northern periodicals. There was also a lack of basic supplies—the wood that engravers required to cut their illustrations, the paper that the publication was printed on, and the ink that created the text and images. In the war of publishing and propaganda, the South could not begin to match the North.

To shape public opinion, one tactic that the Confederacy took was to connect southern secession with the American Revolution through both words and images. Titled *The First Flag of Independence Raised in the South by the Citizens of Savannah, Ga.*, a lithograph depiction of a rally in Savannah just over one month before South Carolina became the first state to secede, includes, as its focal point, a version of Benjamin Franklin's famous image of a rattlesnake. Franklin's cartoon, published on May 9, 1754 in the *Pennsylvania Gazette*, incited the American colonies to come together during the French and Indian War—to "Join, or Die." This was the first political cartoon published in an

American newspaper. The image gained even more power and historical import when it was used during the Revolutionary War against the British, with the slogan changing to: "Unite or Die." The image in the Savannah lithograph also includes another icon from the revolutionary period—the coiled rattlesnake with the motto "Don't Tread on Me," which had originally appeared on military flags. Even before secession and Fort Sumter, the South understood the importance of connecting its cause to previous struggles for freedom. The banner attached to the obelisk in the lithograph declares, "YOUR MOTTO ... Don't Tread on Me," and a sea of cheering people surround it in support of the Confederate cause. In an image reproduced on envelopes in the South—a common mode of disseminating patriotic propaganda and declaring individual allegiances—a snake divided into the southern states appears below the phrase "UNITE OR DIE" and above a quotation from the Confederacy's president, Jefferson Davis. "SLAVE STATES, once more let me repeat, that the only way of preserving our slave property, or what we prize more than life, our LIBERTY, is by a UNION WITH EACH OTHER." The reader is assured of linking the southern quest for "liberty" with that of the Founding Fathers; the image, and the secessionist strategy, are described as "The device of our Fathers in their first struggle for liberty,—1776."

The North, of course, viewed southern secession quite differently. This was not a "struggle for liberty," but a bloody act of rebellion. Jefferson Davis became, in a *Harper's Weekly* cartoon of October 26, 1861, a personification of death itself. Here was *Jeff Davis Reaping the Harvest*—a harvest not of wheat, but of men's skulls. A vulture is perched above a dangling hangman's noose, both clear symbols of death. More skulls remain to be "harvested," and thus the dark image foreshadows "the growing Northern acceptance that the war would not be pleasant nor would it pass quickly" (Lewin and Huff 67). But such acceptance is also accompanied by defiance. Almost camouflaged in the grass, curled up in the immediate foreground, is a small rattlesnake, tongue flickering up toward Davis. The snake takes a stand against Davis's grim reaper, as if providing a warning: taking another step could mean death for Davis, and his cause. This is a northern version of "Don't tread on me."

The toll of human life during the Civil War was unprecedented. The new medium of photography was capable of representing such losses, but only as a quiet aftermath. Because of the long exposure time necessary, photographic technology could not yet capture movement, much less frontline action. The battlefield was the purview of sketch artists. Their quick drawings, often with notations, would be express-mailed back to the publisher's office where engravers would translate the sketches into plates for printing. These images were then reproduced in the pages of illustrated periodicals like *Harper's* and seen by thousands of readers each week.

Artists like Thomas Nast brought the war back to the home front for the subscribers of *Harper's Weekly*. Images such as *After the Battle—The Rebels in*

*Possession of the Field,* published in *Harper's* on October 25, 1862, serve as chilling reminders of the horrors and chaos of war. In this picture of the carnage following the second battle of Bull Run, Confederates bury Union soldiers in mass graves, throwing body atop body into ditches so that all that is visible is a heap of contorted limbs. Soldiers on horseback supervise the operation from above and assess the charred landscape that stretches into the distance. In the foreground, other soldiers strip the dead bodies of clothes, shoes, weapons, and any valuable possessions before dragging them toward the graves. One soldier appears to be pulling out a filling from a dead man's mouth and a woman in the front center of the composition joins the men in their search to find desirable items among the corpses. At the margins, Nast includes the more tender casualties of war—a dead drummer boy, head still touching his drum, and a woman on the right edge of the picture, hands lifted in agony, her dead husband, we might imagine, lying across her lap.

Nash's image aims to shock, and it achieves this goal by skillfully combining a sense of documentary realism—limp and swollen bodies, mass carnage, scorched fields—with a clear political agenda. The Confederates in the image show no signs of mercy; Nast turns a Union defeat into a commentary on the ruthlessness of rebel soldiers and, by implication, the fundamental rottenness of their cause. Even a woman is not above picking through the pockets of a corpse. But, above all, the image conveys the fatigue and the casualties that both North and South suffered. There is nothing grand or majestic about this side of warfare.

The most important artist to emerge from the illustrated news business was Winslow Homer, who would become one of the most celebrated painters of the nineteenth century. Homer got his start at *Harper's Weekly* as an artist and engraver in 1861, and his images manage to convey a visceral sense of the randomness and inhumanity of war, the endless waiting and exhaustion, the discomfort and brutality. In essence, Homer depicts modern warfare.

Homer's detached, journalistic style is exemplified by his print, *The Army of the Potomac—A Sharp-Shooter on Picket Duty*, published in *Harper's Weekly* on November 15, 1862. Executed at the same time as his first oil painting, titled *Sharpshooter,* both images emerged from his observations and experiences while at the frontlines with the 61st New York Volunteer Infantry during the siege of Yorktown, Virginia. A Union soldier sits perched high in a pine tree, concealed by branches, his telescopic rifle resembling just another tree limb. But this "limb" is trained on the enemy, and this sharpshooter will pick off men when they least expect it. Rather than long lines of soldiers, led by their generals and their flags, converging upon each other in battle, the sharpshooter represents modern warfare, where enemies might never even see one another's face. The telescopic rifle provided the technological ability to shoot a man from a vast, concealed distance. Killing became efficient and ruthlessly cold-blooded; there was no opportunity for chivalric acts. Union sharpshooters were notorious and much-feared. They were also controversial with the northern public, which was skeptical of such mechanical warfare and its lack of clear moral codes. As if to demonstrate this, Homer obscures the soldier's face in both the print and the painting. The victim is kept entirely out of sight, but we understand with chilling clarity that the sharpshooter has found his mark.

A painting completed by Homer a couple of years later imagines what might be in the sharpshooter's scope. In *Inviting a Shot Before Petersburg, Virginia* (1864), a Confederate private challenges the Union troops—or perhaps a Union sharpshooter—to take a shot. And the North responds: a puff of smoke can be seen at the right and a flash of orange at the left, both indicating gunfire aimed at the defiant soldier. Homer gives us an instant in time, right before the potentially deadly outcome is made clear. His comrades look up at him, and a black laborer, banjo in hand, wears a startled, awe-inspired expression. The soldier breaks the horizon line and is dramatically silhouetted against the sky. His fist is clenched, his mouth open to shout, and his body tensed, as if to evoke the resolve, and desperation, of the Confederate forces toward the end of the war. At this late point, the Union army was relying on a strategy of deprivation as much as military confrontation to force the South into retreat and, eventually, capitulation. As Marc Simpson notes about Homer's painting, "the majority of the men in the trench, like the cut trees of the battlefield, were simply fuel to be used in the new war of attrition" (185).

The disposability and anonymity of men is made even clearer in an engraving titled *Army of the Potomac—Sleeping on their Arms* that Homer produced for the May 28, 1864 issue of *Harper's Weekly*. This image of the Battle of the Wilderness depicts scores of beleaguered Union soldiers scattered across a stretch of rough and barren land, most of them, as the title indicates, "sleeping on their arms." These men lack even the basic comforts of tents and encampments, sprawled out instead on the cold earth. A single soldier appears in the center foreground, presumably on picket duty. This sentry stands tall but looks worn and wane, his shoulders slumped, his cheeks sunken, his right hand clinging to his rifle as if to keep his balance. Around him, bodies appear in various states of sleep, lying huddled together against the chilly night or still seated, heads bowed over in exhaustion. Trenches stretch along the horizon and the few remaining trees echo the lean, scraggly quality of the soldiers, with their long muskets and sharp bayonets.

The Battle of the Wilderness, part of General Ulysses S. Grant's 1864 Overland Campaign against General Robert E. Lee's Confederate Army of Northern Virginia, was intense and inconclusive. Although Lee's army was greatly outnumbered, the dense, wooded, and uneven terrain in central Virginia favored his smaller force by rendering Grant's far-superior artillery less effective. The battle resulted in heavy casualties on both sides. In Homer's painting *Skirmish in the Wilderness* (1864), the artist conveys the confusing nature of such warfare by picturing a group of soldiers, amassed behind a large tree, facing and firing in all directions into the dark and tangled woods. One soldier appears to have been killed, while another crawls forward, possibly injured, to escape the fire. There is no sky above, nor any breaks of blue through the trees. Smoke from the gunfire appears in the middle of the composition, further obscuring vision. Where are the enemy soldiers or, rather, *who* is the enemy here? The wilderness becomes an equally formidable foe. The forest—normally a place of lush green and contemplative quiet—is transformed into the setting for a battle marked by uncertainty, fear, and blindness. Generally, Homer avoided painting battle scenes; the most notable exception is *Skirmish in the Wilderness*. "No less clear, directed, or unheroic action painting ever purported to present a scene of battle," the art historian Sally Mills writes (175). With its evocation of deadly confusion, Homer's painting presents the viewer with the feeling that veterans described experiencing during the Battle of the Wilderness. It was, according to one, "the strangest and most indescribable battle in history. A battle which no man saw, and in which artillery was useless and hardly used at all. A battle fought in dense woods and tangled brake, where maneuvering was impossible, where the lines of battle were invisible to their commanders, and whose position could only be determined by the rattle and roll and flash of musketry, and where the enemy was also invisible" (Mills 175).

A similarly menacing landscape is also the stage for Thomas Moran's *Slave Hunt, Dismal Swamp, Virginia* (1862). Moran was a successful landscape painter, known particularly for his sublime scenes of Yellowstone and the Grand Canyon. But in *Slave Hunt*, the artist imagines an environment that is, like Homer's *Skirmish in the Wilderness*, a place of darkness and claustrophobia. In the foreground, two slaves, a man and a woman, look back to see their pursuers: a pair of dogs poised to jump into the swampy waters, and a group of men emerging from a break in the trees, quickly closing the gap between pursuers and pursued. The painting has an eerie coloring, the reddish leaves and green vines appearing to sparkle in the filtered sunlight. But such fantastical light illuminates a distinctly tense and disturbing scene. Unlike Homer—whose painting evokes the confusion and indeterminacy of warfare—Moran conveys a clear sense of morality. Hunting black people as if they were animals is simply barbaric; slavery is immoral. As one historian notes, "the fugitive slaves appear like a horrific vision of Adam and Eve, chased through a swampy Southern landscape by savage bloodhounds" (Vendryes 97). The reference to Adam and Eve, the figures of human creation, is used to comment on the destructive inhumanity of slavery. As the name "Dismal Swamp" itself seems to suggest, rottenness and entropy are at the heart of the South's "peculiar institution."

But, with these notable exceptions, the Civil War proved to be a difficult subject for landscape painting. Frederic Edwin Church, the most famous painter in America at mid-century, directly addressed the Civil War in only one of his canvases, *Our Banner in the Sky* (1861), which was completed months after the outbreak of the Civil War. The landscape itself is transformed into the Stars and

Stripes, the most recognizable symbol of the Union. The small painting quickly became the basis of a chromolithograph, a new method of color printing that allowed for mass reproduction quickly and cheaply. With its populist brand of patriotism, Church's "chromo" turned a healthy profit, all of which the artist donated to the Union's cause.

The attenuated trunk of a dead tree provides the picture's single, stark vertical and doubles as a flagpole. The stars of the twilight sky appear in the upper left of Church's celestial flag, and the colors of sunset form the flag's tattered stripes. Little wisps of reddish clouds lend a sense of motion and danger to the bellicose tableau, as if flames might ignite and destroy the North's beloved symbol. But as fragile and faded as the "banner" might appear, such a sign writ large in the heavens was ultimately a declaration of faith in the Union cause and even of divine providence. *Our Banner in the Sky* is the pictorial equivalent of a sound-bite: visually accessible at a single glance and imparting a clear and uncomplicated message, especially in its chromolithographic form. The image exhorts its wartime audience to rally around the flag. Unlike Church's larger and more complex paintings, *Our Banner in the Sky* is a simple, but effective, piece of propaganda.

Although Church's landscape paintings rarely addressed contemporary events, the artist aided the Union cause in other ways. He donated the revenue from exhibition ticket sales to the newly created Union Patriotic Fund, a charity established to support soldiers' families. He, like many artists, loaned works to the 1864 Metropolitan Fair in New York, one of many fairs held to raise money for the Sanitary Commission, which aided wounded Union troops. Eastman Johnson's painting *The Field Hospital* (1867) portrays a wounded soldier dictating a letter to a female Sanitary Commission volunteer in a calm and pastoral setting, sun-dappled light spread across the soldier's bedsheets.

Women were cast in the rather limited roles of caregiver and comforter in Johnson's image, but the Civil War actually expanded economic opportunities for women. As men left to fight, and many never returned, women increasingly joined the wage-labor force to provide for their families and to help fill the gaps that men had left behind. The issue of appropriate gender roles is a recurring theme in images from the Civil War. For example, a cartoon titled *Scene, Fifth Avenue* published in *Harper's Weekly* on August 30, 1863, addresses the topic of class and the military draft by depicting a conflict between a man and woman. During the war, northern men from the upper classes paid "substitutes" to fight for them, but the cartoon suggests that the true man—the man that a woman would desire to marry—would fight in the war himself, or else his sweetheart might find herself a "substitute" as well.

Heroes and villains of the Civil War were also portrayed in terms of their masculinity. While Robert E. Lee became recognized by both Northerners and Southerners as a man of dignity and honor, a commander who fought and surrendered with stoicism, Confederate president Jefferson Davis was ridiculed by the northern press as he raced south to evade the Union cavalry after Lee's surrender at Appomattox. Just shy of the Florida border, the cavalry captured Davis and his party, but not before Davis reportedly tried to elude them by wearing his wife's raincoat and her shawl over his head and shoulders. Caricatures promptly appeared that capitalized on his disguise in order to emasculate the southern leader. Adding petticoats and bonnets made the president appear almost grotesquely, and certainly foolishly, feminine. On June 3, 1865, *Frank Leslie's Illustrated Newspaper* featured a woodcut illustration of the capture on its cover, titled *Capture of Jefferson Davis at Irwinsville, Ga,* and the image became the source for many succeeding pictures of the event. A lithograph published by John L. Magee of Philadelphia titled *Jeff Davis Caught at Last. Hoop Skirts & Southern Chivalry* (1865) depicts an old lady in a hoopskirt, brandishing a dagger as Union soldiers lift her shawl and peer under her skirt. Such images suggest that the South, personified by Davis, brought this humiliation upon itself. Its proud leader experienced the ultimate disgrace, appearing as a bearded old woman.

The war had ended, but the costs had been catastrophic and deep uncertainties remained. How could the nation heal its wounds and become the *United States* again? How would the thousands of men returning home from battle reintegrate into society? What would the reality of emancipation be for former slaves, and for African Americans across the nation? Images offered by such publications as *Harper's Weekly*, which supported racial equality, gave hopeful accounts. In *A Man Knows a Man*, from the April 22, 1865 issue, a white and a black veteran shake hands, putting aside racial differences to recognize their common sacrifice "for the good cause." Men are defined and made equal by their deeds. While Jefferson Davis was feminized and humiliated at the end of the war in the pages of northern journals, black men were praised for their manly bravery and sacrifice, at least in *Harper's Weekly.*

Thomas Nast, also working for *Harper's*, illustrated the hypocrisy in the argument against the enfranchisement of black men after the war in his wood engraving, *Pardon/Franchise*, published in *Harper's* on August 5, 1865. Columbia—the female figure who symbolizes the nation—contemplates whether she should reintegrate the southern secessionists while denying rights to African Americans, including disabled black veterans, as much of the public wanted. Should she "trust these men" who had betrayed her, "and not this man" who had sacrificed a limb for the Union cause? In a rare reversal of typical racial characterization, it is the white men, including General Lee at the center, who supplicate themselves before Columbia, while the lone black man stands tall and proud. Just four years earlier, a cartoon by Frank Bellew titled *Dark Artillery; Or, How to Make the Contrabands Useful*, published on October 26, 1861 in *Frank Leslie's Illustrated Newspaper,* a northern publication, had suggested that slaves fleeing across northern lines (dubbed "contrabands" since they were southern "property") could be used by the Union as "dark artillery." The cartoon cruelly represents black men jovially carrying Union canons strapped to their backs.

Northern attitudes toward blacks in the military did change as the war progressed. Black men were allowed to fight for the Union beginning in July 1862, and 180,000 black men eventually enlisted to fight for the northern cause. The most celebrated regiment was the 54th Massachusetts Colored Infantry which was immortalized by one of the great works of nineteenth-century American sculpture—and one of the most famous monuments dedicated to the Civil War—Augustus Saint Gaudens' *Shaw Memorial* (1897), installed on the edge of Boston Common, facing the State House. The monument portrays twenty-three black soldiers, distinct and individuated, along with their commander, in bronze relief and set in a marble and granite terrace.

Perhaps the most profound image to emerge from the Civil War period was Winslow Homer's *The Veteran in a New Field* (1865), painted right after the war's end. It is a minimal composition—a single figure in a sea of wheat, his hat slightly breaking the wide horizon line. Here is a soldier who has just returned home, his army jacket and canteen visible in the lower right. He has made the transition from the field of battle to a field of wheat, exchanging the sword for the plow—a biblical reference to the Book of Isaiah that viewers at the time would have understood: "And they shall beat their swords into plowshares, and their spears into pruninghooks: nation shall not lift up sword against nation, neither shall they learn war any more" (Isaiah 2:4). But death still lurks in Homer's new field. The veteran's scythe recalls the grim reaper, harvesting bodies as if they were stalks of wheat, like Jefferson Davis in the 1861 *Harper's Weekly* cartoon. Two of the bloodiest battles of the Civil War—Gettysburg and Antietam—were, in fact, fought in wheat fields. Homer's image also bears comparison to Timothy O'Sullivan's famous photograph, *A Harvest of Death, Gettysburg, July, 1863*, published in Alexander Gardner's *Photographic Sketch Book of the War* (1866), which captures the bloated corpses of Union and Confederate soldiers in the eerie aftermath of battle. But Homer's painting imagines the conversion of the destructive actions of violence into the productive promise of peace. This veteran who had done his brutal duty during the war is able to thrive in his new pastoral setting. Here is the hero of the war, Homer suggests—not generals parading on horseback, but an anonymous man, hard at work under a blue sky, a field of golden wheat stretching out before him, his uniform cast off behind him, at home at last.

For the visual arts, as scholars have argued, the Civil War "caused a crisis of representation" and resulted in "a failure of old narrative conventions" (Conn and Walker 63). How was it possible to depict a war of such mass casualties and modern tactics—characterized by telescopic rifles and heavy artillery—in which countrymen killed each other? Artists faced such new and difficult questions by moving away from the conventions of history painting—with its celebratory subject matter, allegorical vocabulary, and message of moral certainty—and by searching instead for new means to represent the violence and destruction. A clear style or theme did not result, but for the most innovative artists, like Winslow Homer, the Civil War provided an opportunity to communicate more directly with the audience. Homer's spare and evocatively journalistic approach seems most appropriate to the conflict—the brutal simplicity of the sharpshooter eyeing his unseen target, the startlingly defiant figure inviting a shot, the scores of crumpled bodies resting before the next battle, the confusion of a firefight in the wilderness, the nameless veteran in his Elysian fields. Death and life intersect, as if to remind the viewer that there were no real victors in this war.

## Further Reading

Bassham, Ben L. *Conrad Wise Chapman: Artist & Soldier of the Confederacy.* Kent: Kent State University Press, 1998.

Conn, Steven, and Andrew Walker. "The History in the Art: Painting the Civil War." *Art Institute of Chicago Museum Studies* 27.1 (2001): 60–81.

Coopersmith, Andrew S. *Fighting Words: An Illustrated History of Newspaper Accounts of the Civil War.* New York: The New Press, 2004.

Giese, Lucretia Hoover. "'Harvesting' the Civil War: Art in Wartime New York." In *Redefining American History Painting.* Eds. Patricia M. Burnham and Lucretia Hoover Giese. Cambridge: Cambridge University Press, 1995. 64–82.

Holzer, Harold, and Mark E. Neely. *Mine Eyes Have Seen the Glory: The Civil War in Art.* New York: Orion, 1993.

Lewin, J.G., and P.J. Huff. *Lines of Contention: Political Cartoons of the Civil War.* New York: HarperCollins, 2007.

Miller, Angela. *The Empire of the Eye: Landscape Representations and American Cultural Politics, 1825–1875.* Ithaca: Cornell University Press, 1993.

Mills, Sally. "Catalogue: *Skirmish in the Wilderness.*" In *Winslow Homer: Paintings of the Civil War.* Ed. Marc Simpson. San Francisco: The Fine Arts Museums of San Francisco and Bedford Arts Publishers, 1988. 174–177.

Neely, Mark E., Jr., and Harold Holzer. *The Union Image: Popular Prints of the Civil War North.* Chapel Hill: University of North Carolina Press, 1999.

Neely, Mark E., Jr., Harold Holzer, and Gabor S. Boritt. *The Confederate Image: Prints of the Lost Cause.* Chapel Hill: University of North Carolina Press, 1987.

Samuels, Shirley. *Facing America: Iconography and the Civil War.* Oxford: Oxford University Press, 2004.

Simpson, Marc. *Winslow Homer: Paintings of the Civil War.* San Francisco: The Fine Arts Museums of San Francisco and Bedford Arts Publishers, 1988.

Vendryes, Margaret Rose. "Race Identity/Identifying Race: Robert S. Duncanson and Nineteenth-Century American Painting." *Art Institute of Chicago Museum Studies* 27.1 (2001): 82–99.

# PART VII

# Leisure and Performance

# 23

# MUSIC

*Jack Hamilton*

Throughout the Civil War, at a time when there was arguably no "nation" of which to speak, there was no national music but rather national musics, no singular American musical community but rather numerous ones—from the parlor to army camps, from the sheet music press to the freedmens' schools and plantations, from star performers and hit songs to amateurs and flops, along with debates over perceived propriety and perceived profanity. Music served a diverse array of uses and often multiple uses simultaneously. It was a crucial forum for Americans to express their commitments and their ambivalence, to celebrate victories and mourn losses. While the basic fact of musical practices transcended region, race, gender, and class, the various meanings that music accrued often shifted widely between these divisions. The crisis of the Civil War also directly and indirectly altered the course of American music. Military bands became popular during the war and continued to influence music in the latter half of the century, while new songs and compilations such as *Slave Songs of the United States* (1867) cemented the spirituals as a foundation for modern black music.

Everyday musical practice and consumption was a crucial facet of life during the war, from parlors to churches, battlefields to plantations, camping grounds to concert halls. Thanks to the rise of the upright piano and a booming sheet music industry, songwriters such as George F. Root and Henry Clay Work became hit-makers. These Civil War-era musicians and composers continued the genre of nineteenth-century America's greatest songwriter, Stephen Collins Foster, who had exploded the possibilities of American music in the 1840s and 1850s, but died in 1864 in obscurity, at the end writing sentimental battle-field laments and campaign melodies for George McClellan and finding little success with either.

Three of the important modes of musical life during the Civil War were the lucrative "parlor song" industry of sentimental ballads, the vast proliferation of songs written for and about the war itself, and the emergence of the African American spiritual into the national consciousness. Although these three genres represent quite different manifestations of musical culture, they overlap, and many Americans would have been increasingly aware of all three as the 1860s progressed.

The origins of the American "parlor song" industry predate the Civil War and are tied to three key innovations: the rise of the "singing school" movement and its primary proselytizer Lowell Mason; the increasing affordability and availability of upright pianos; and the growing dominance of the sheet music industry, particularly in the North. Mason was a prolific and immensely influential musical figure in the first part of the nineteenth century, developing a philosophy of "edification" that regarded music as a central tool in intellectual and spiritual development. Generally considered America's first great musical educator, his ideas gained traction amidst a burgeoning middle-class ideology of moral respectability and self-improvement.

The rise of the upright piano parallels the rise of Mason and was tied to the manufacturing breakthroughs of the industrial revolution. By the 1840s, "home" pianos and other keyboard instruments had become increasingly common and affordable, and 1853 saw the birth of America's most famous piano company, Steinway and Sons. The new availability of pianos created an explosion in demand for musical products more generally, and countless composers and publishers of sheet music were happy to meet the demand. When Mason's ideas of musical edification became coupled with the technological and commercial innovations of the manufacturing and print industries, there emerged a sort of coalescence of an entire nineteenth-century musical worldview centered around the home. In much the same way that Americans of the era voraciously read literature of "sentiment" for its moral clarity and perceived spiritual benefits, in the minds of budding musical practitioners the piano and parlor offered new possibilities for intellectual and spiritual enrichment.

By the early 1850s, the American sheet music industry was publishing about 5,000 new pieces per year. Most of the country's most powerful publishing houses were in the North, and companies such as Root & Cady of Chicago, Firth, Pond & Co. of New York, and Oliver Ditson & Co. of Boston were extraordinarily successful before, during, and after the Civil War. However, the country's oldest music publisher—Siegling Music Company—was based in Charleston, South Carolina, and the South also boasted such well-known publishing houses as Blackmar (New Orleans and Augusta) and C.D. Benson (Nashville). The Civil War itself was initially a boost to the southern sheet music industry, as secession was believed to nullify northern copyright claims, thus rapidly expanding the landscape of musical material available to southern publishers.

Parlor music could be instrumental in nature or have vocal parts for solo or group performance. Indeed, for Americans of the mid-nineteenth century the pastime of singing around the piano was a favorite one. Perhaps most popular among these songs were traditional romantic ballads, sentimental, and fantastical songs that told stories of love, loss, and lament. For instance, the cover for "When the Swallows Homeward Fly" (published by Blackmar) advertises other titles from the same publisher: "I See Her Still In My Dreams," "Darling Little Blue Eyed Nell" and "Cottage By The Sea" are among the more maudlin selections. The loss recounted in a song such as "When The Swallows Homeward Fly" goes unspecified; while the language of death and mourning is consistently invoked, the vague generalities suggest the song's utility in another time-worn tradition—the break-up song. Its stilted language and affected bucolic imagery are by no means unusual, and in fact constitute an entire sub-genre of parlor song. Stephen Foster's first published composition, "Open Thy Lattice, Love" (1844) partakes in this tradition; while that song was a failure, two of Foster's later efforts, "Jeanie with the Light Brown Hair" (1854) and "Beautiful Dreamer" (1864, published posthumously) drew from the same well and became two of the nineteenth century's most famous songs.

Not all parlor songs were serious and lachrymose—among the more raucous and ribald songs played at home by Americans were several selections drawn from the minstrel stage. These were songs where white men donned blackface to enact various fantasies of African American life, performed before decidedly un-genteel audiences. While the coarse (and frequently dangerous) atmosphere of urban minstrel shows was ostensibly anathema to the average middle-class sheet music consumer striving for respectability, the baldly racist caricatures peddled by the genre were apparently welcomed with open arms. From instrumental pieces like "Plantation Dance" (1867) to the "comic song" stylings of "N.O.B." (a.k.a. "Nigger On the Brain," 1864) to the insidious pro-slavery longings of "Come Back, Massa, Come Back!" (1863), ideas of African Americans as child-like, lazy, and hyper-sexualized were practically a lingua franca of American music in the nineteenth century. Even amidst a war being fought for emancipation, such "satirical" lyric sheets as the one entitled "I Am Fighting for the Nigger," published in New York by H. de Marsan, were not uncommon:

> I calculate of niggers we soon shall have our fill
> With Abe's proclamation and the nigger army bill.
> Who would not be a soldier for the Union to fight?
> For, Abe's made the nigger the equal of the white.

Despite its reactionary sentiment, "I am Fighting for the Nigger" clearly illustrates that Americans were no strangers to voicing their political views through music, no matter how hateful those views may have been.

Certainly not all of the political stances vocalized in American song during the period were so anti–progressive, and much of this music found its way into parlors as well. Perhaps the most famous political songs of the period were sung by the Hutchinson Family Singers, a fiercely religious group who used four-part harmony to convey messages of abolition, temperance, and women's rights. It was not uncommon for a group's name or likeness to be prominently used in the advertisement of sheet music, and the Hutchinson name sold a great deal of music in the 1850s and 1860s. The Hutchinsons toured constantly through the northern United States and made numerous successful trips to Europe. Songs such as "King Alcohol" preached temperance and prohibition, while songs such as "Slavery is a Hard Foe To Battle" provided an effective counterweight to the increasingly pro-slavery minstrel oeuvre. The group's most famous song—"Get off The Track!"—used an extended train metaphor to drive home its abolitionist message.

The Hutchinsons were a sensation, inspiring rapturous devotion from their admirers and fierce antipathy from their detractors. In 1862, the family gave a concert at Lincoln's White House, where their sung performance of John G. Whitter's poem "We Wait Beneath the Furnace Blast"—which explicitly stated slavery as the cause of the war—almost led to a riot. According to historian Steven Cornelius, "General [William] Franklin, apparently acting on orders from General McClellan himself, subsequently revoked the Hutchinsons' singing permit … Such was the concert's notoriety that 'Furnace Blast' became an abolitionist rallying song" (172).

For mid-nineteenth-century Americans, performers such as the Hutchinson Family Singers, Christy's Minstrels, and Swedish soprano Jenny Lind (imported with stunning success by P.T. Barnum in 1850) were household names. While many flocked to see these performers in concert on any of their countless tours, many more knew them from the images and names that adorned the sheets of music that sat on their pianos and in their parlors. The songs that Americans played and sang in their homes during the Civil War era often served as a respite from the harsh realities of sectional strife, but amateur musical practitioners did not exclusively choose to escape the crises that surrounded them. As the success of songs like "Get Off the Track!" demonstrate, music could be as much a tool of confrontation as it was of evasion. As the war itself progressed, composers and consumers found new ways to draw musical meaning from the unthinkable destruction that surrounded them.

Historian Kenneth Bernard describes the Civil War as an unprecedented "musical war," and argues that "by the end of the war more music had been created, played, and sung than during all our other wars combined" (xviii). While a great deal of this activity can be chalked up to the boom in the music industry more generally that closely preceded the war, the sheer magnitude of the conflict inspired Americans to find new ways—including in music—of coping with and understanding tragedy. Thousands of war-related compositions emerged during the period, some of which remain famous, like "When

Johnny Comes Marching Home," "The Battle Cry of Freedom," and "The Battle Hymn of the Republic," and many more of which have long since been forgotten. There were songs of triumph and songs of tragedy, songs that celebrated the war effort and others that excoriated it. North and South each had their own songs, or sometimes simply their own lyrics to be sung to identical melodies: for instance, "Maryland, My Maryland"—the song from which Edmund Wilson's famous phrase "Patriotic Gore" derives—was sung with different lyrics depending on one's pro-slavery or anti-slavery allegiance.

Songs about the war appeared nearly simultaneously to the conflict itself. The first popular song of the war was fittingly composed by George F. Root, who would quickly become the war's most successful and memorable songwriter: "The First Gun is Fired! 'May God Protect The Right!'" was a decidedly pro-Union take on the happenings at Fort Sumter, and was published on April 18, 1861, just six days after the attack. Indeed, after years of crisis and compromise that served as an agonizingly protracted prelude to the war itself, when armed conflict finally broke out, songwriters such as Root were clearly well-prepared. Shortly after Root's wartime debut, a southern composition called "Sumter, A Ballad of 1861" appeared, later followed by "Dixie Doodle," in which songwriter Margaret Weir (prematurely) celebrated that "Dixie whipped old Yankee Doodle early in the morning."

The February 1862 edition of the *Atlantic Monthly* opened with a poem bearing the title, "Battle Hymn of the Republic," composed by abolitionist Julia Ward Howe. Sung to the well-known tune of "John Brown's Body," its text rang out with righteous triumphalism and a visceral religiosity. The poem's closing lines contained its most succinct and direct appeal to an abolitionist's sense of sacrifice: "As He died to make men holy, let us die to make men free, / While God is marching on." "The Battle Hymn of the Republic" ultimately overtook even the tremendous popularity of "John Brown's Body," and it is still well-known to many Americans.

Howe's poem was published two months before the Battle of Shiloh, six months before the Second Battle of Bull Run and seven months before Antietam, the bloodiest single-day battle in American military history. As the level of carnage reached increasingly unthinkable proportions, new and far more tragic genres of war songs emerged. According to Willard and Porter Heaps, the song "When This Cruel War Is Over" was "so mournful that generals were forced to forbid their troops to sing it," while a song such as "God Grant Our Soldier's Safe Return" gave voice to the anxiety of countless families grown increasingly convinced that return was a harsh impossibility (224).

Tragic war songs often trafficked in tropes and imagery borrowed from parlor ballads and the cultural key of sentimentality. "Mother" became a central figure, as songs such as "Break It Gently To My Mother" and "Is That Mother Bending O'er Me?" combined lachrymose fantasies of death with obsessive maternal longing. Children, those other stalwarts of sentimental culture, made frequent appearances as well, often in the form of the dying drummer boy. While the service (and not infrequent death) of young men remains one of the more brutal facts of Civil War history, in song the tragic drummer boy became a recurrent figure whose presence was often linked to that of the mother. For instance, "If I Sleep, Will Mother Come?" told the story of an eleven-year-old Minnesotan child fatally wounded on the battlefield. On the opposing side, the South had "The Little Drummer Boy of Shiloh," who "clasped his hands and raised his eyes / And prayed before he died." Even Stephen Foster, penniless and drinking himself to death in New York City, tried his hand at this market: one of his final compositions, "Give This To Mother," was about a dying drummer boy, although the song proved a commercial flop.

Chicagoan George F. Root was the rare composer who was able to mine both the triumphant and the tragic with equally stunning success. Not only did Root write the first popular song of the war, he wrote its first truly monumental piece of original music, "The Battle Cry of Freedom." "Battle Cry" weds an exuberant and instantly unforgettable melody to a stirring lyrical text, eschewing the religious pomp of "Battle Hymn of the Republic" for a straightforward, rollicking populism. Its structure and content are simple enough to learn, and remain exciting after countless repetitions. The song in fact proved so instantly popular that the South developed its own lyrics. Root, staunchly pro-Union, would have surely been incensed by this development, as by the fact that Herman L. Schreiner and William H. Barnes, the Confederate version's "composers," had altered the melody just slightly enough to claim credit for it as an original composition.

Root also wrote one of the war's most popular tragic ballads. His 1863 composition "Just Before the Battle, Mother," while forgoing the boundless enthusiasm of "Battle Cry," nonetheless employs a similarly deft directness to render itself both accessible and memorable. The song is essentially an imagined epistle from a soldier to his mother as he prepares for battle, and features the following chorus:

> Farewell Mother, you may never
> Press me to your heart again;
> But O, you'll not forget me Mother
> If I'm number'd with the slain.

Again, the simplicity of the song's theme is effective, as it gives voice to not merely a fear of death, but a fear of death unnoticed. In the context of a war in which tens of thousands were perishing in single battles, the song acknowledges that these soldiers were ultimately no more than "numbers," and that only a young man's mother is in a position to know otherwise. While Root would live and write music until he died in 1895, the songs he wrote during the Civil War were unquestionably the high point of his career, making him a wealthy man and his own publishing company, Root & Cady, a success. Root remained passionately committed to the Union cause throughout the war, and in 1865 wrote a piece called "Starved In Prison" that was a clear comment on the atrocities recently revealed at Andersonville prison.

Although Root was the most popular songwriter of the 1860s, his musical contributions would not prove to be the decade's most monumental: that distinction would go to a musical community well removed from both the gentilities of the parlor and entrepreneurial bustle of the sheet music industry. Indeed, the 1860s saw a historic rise in the attention that white musical devotees afforded to the music of African Americans, not simply as it had long been counterfeited and lampooned on minstrel stages, but as it was actually created, performed and disseminated. This growing interest and awareness was crucially linked to the realities of the Civil War itself, and reached its apotheosis in 1867 with the publication of *Slave Songs of the United States*, a small book compiled by three northern abolitionists that stands among the most significant musical publications in American history.

In June 1867, the *Atlantic Monthly* published an article by abolitionist Thomas Wentworth Higginson titled simply "The Negro Spirituals." During the Civil War, Higginson had served as colonel of the South Carolina Volunteers, the first federally-authorized army regiment to be comprised of former slaves. Higginson's article reads in many ways like an early attempt at ethnomusicology, as he attempts to describe, through both prose and exhaustive lyrical transcriptions, the music he heard in his camps. Higginson's transcriptions, rendered in dialect, reveal nearly as much about the author's expectations and biases as they do about the actual music he heard, evoking the lexicon of minstrelsy far more than that of scripture. When Higginson published a more complete collection of his diaries three years later, entitled *Army Life in a Black Regiment,* such tensions still held. Describing his soldiers as a "simple and lovable people, whose graces seem to come by nature, and whose vices by training" (18), Higginson's rapturous praises of his men and their music are tinged by condescension: "Give these people their tongues, their feet, and their leisure, and they are happy. At every twilight the air is full of singing, talking, and clapping of hands in unison … I wonder where they obtained a chant of such beauty" (21, 22).

The same year as Higginson published his *Atlantic* article also saw the publication of *Slave Songs of the United States,* a compilation assembled by William Francis Allen, Charles Pickard Ware, and Lucy McKim Garrison, three northern reformers, educators, and former abolitionists. A landmark text in both American music and folkloric study more broadly, the book originally sprang from the work of Lucy Garrison, who in 1862, while working with freedpeople in Port Royal, South Carolina (as Lucy McKim), began the first systematic attempt to transcribe African American spirituals. She was soon joined in her endeavor by fellow transplanted northerners Ware and Allen, and in 1867, they published the fruits of their labor in a single, thin volume. *Slave Songs of the United States* opened with the following statement:

The musical capacity of the negro race has been recognized for so many years that it is hard to explain why no systematic effort has hitherto been made to collect and preserve their melodies. More than thirty years ago those plantation songs made their appearance which were so extraordinarily popular for a while; and if "Coal-black Rose," "Zip Coon" and "Ole Virginny nebber tire" have been succeeded by spurious imitations, manufactured to suit the somewhat sentimental taste of our community, the fact that these were called "negro melodies" was itself a tribute to the musical genius of the race.

(i)

While this passage partakes in some of the prejudices and condescension on display in Higginson's writings, in another sense, it is both new and extraordinary. For instance, the emphasis on "systematic" collection places this text in a different class than the impressionistic descriptions of Higginson: these authors actually presented conventional musical transcriptions of their findings, and although they too employed the use of dialect, its presence was not nearly as oppressive and all-encompassing as in Higginson's writings. What is more, in the above passage the authors softly but explicitly critique the time-honored practice of white performers counterfeiting or burlesquing black music. The paragraph's second sentence stands as both an authenticity claim and a rebuke to those who had disingenuously claimed the veracity of various "Ethiopian delineations." For a large portion of the American public whose primary—indeed, perhaps exclusive—encounters with "black performance" were mediated by the minstrel mask, this statement is nothing short of revolutionary.

Many of the spirituals collected in *Slave Songs* are still famous today: "Roll, Jordan, Roll" opens the collection, for instance, and "Michael Row the Boat Ashore," "Nobody Knows the Trouble I've Had," and "Rock O' My Soul" have become classics of American music. There are also "secular" songs, such as "Charleston Gals," "I'm Gwine to Alabamy," and "Run, Nigger, Run!," the last of which deals explicitly with the omnipresent terror of slave patrols for escaped slaves. The significance of the spirituals in American and African American culture is nearly impossible to overstate; a few short years after the publication of *Slave Songs*, the "concert spirituals" of the Fisk Jubilee Singers, a group from Fisk University comprised of former slaves, became an international sensation. W.E.B. Du Bois called the "Sorrow Songs" "the most beautiful expression of human experience born this side of the seas ... the singular spiritual heritage of the nation and the greatest gift of the Negro people" (156), and in 1925, James Weldon Johnson put together his own *Book of American Negro Spirituals*. That same year, in his landmark Harlem Renaissance anthology *The New Negro*, Alain Locke declared the spirituals to be "the most characteristic product of the race genius as yet in America" (199).

In spite of the tremendous influence of the spirituals and the impact of both Higginson's memoirs and the publication of *Slave Songs*, there were occasionally troublesome ideological forces at work in their initial transcription, celebration, and dissemination. Both Higginson and the Garrison-Ware-Allen triumvirate celebrated the spirituals and their performers far more for their exoticism than for their artistry or intellect. Indeed, even *Slave Songs of The United States* contains well-worn stereotypes of black performance as wild and sensational, and advanced the stereotype of black music as the ideal of authenticity, "naturalness," and emotional purity. A whole host of ideological claims on black music can be traced to the collection of the spirituals.

Regardless of the numerous triumphs and missteps that accrued around the initial collection of the spirituals, the significance of their publication for American musical culture is immense. The emergence of the spirituals into the larger American consciousness was a direct result of the Civil War, and this music of African Americans would go on to become one of the nineteenth-century's great cultural legacies; the spirituals are nothing short of a foundational document.

## Further Reading

Allen, William Francis, Charles Pickard Ware, and Lucy McKim Garrison. *Slave Songs of the United States*. New York: A. Simpson & Co., 1867.

Bernard, Kenneth A. *Lincoln and the Music of the Civil War*. Caldwell: Caxton Printers, 1966.

Cornelius, Steven H. *Music of the Civil War Era*. Westport: Greenwood Press, 2004.

Crawford, Richard. *America's Musical Life: A History*. New York: Norton, 2001.

Du Bois, W.E.B. *The Souls of Black Folk*. New York: Dover, 1994.

Heaps, Willard A. and Porter W. *The Singing Sixties: The Spirit of Civil War Days Drawn from the Music of the Times*. Norman: University of Oklahoma Press, 1960.

Higginson, Thomas Wentworth. *Army Life in a Black Regiment*. Boston: Fields, Osgood & Co., 1869.

Kramer, Lawrence, ed. *Walt Whitman and Modern Music: War, Desire, and the Trials of Nationhood*. New York: Garland, 2000.

Locke, Alain Leroy. *The New Negro: An Interpretation*. New York: A. and C. Boni, 1925.

Lord, Francis Alfred. *Bands and Drummer Boys of the Civil War*. New York: T. Yoseloff, 1966.

Olson, Kenneth E. *Music and the Musket: Bands and Bandsmen of the American Civil War*. Westport: Greenwood Press, 1981.

# 24

# THEATER

*Laura M. Ansley and Renée M. Sentilles*

In January 1861, a New York newspaper editor asserted that the "Union and secession biases of the various sections are demonstrated in the theatres." Maggie Mitchell, a popular Bowery actress, had been caught "catering to the depraved tastes of Southern ruffians with 'secession songs.'" Secession and war put entertainers into an unenviable position. The editor proclaimed Mitchell outlawed "in all loyal communities for some time to come, and we advise her to remain among the rebels with whom she sympathizes" ("Amusements" n.p.). Mitchell did not heed his advice and a scant year later returned to the New York stage with her signature "shadow dance." Flush with cash created by wartime industry and hungry for distraction, New Yorkers made her a star. No paper mentioned her earlier transgression.

The Civil War period fundamentally changed American theater just as it did the world that theater reflected and parodied. Before the war, theater was shaped by arguments implicitly determined by a desire for clear class distinctions and segregated gender practices. But in the postbellum period, the race, gender, and class distinctions brought into conflict during the war itself, manifested into a topsy-turvy reflection of the world as played out on stage. New York City was America's theater capital and best illustrates wartime changes in touring patterns, production, material, the acting profession and even the physical theater structures. Maggie Mitchell became a celebrity in a theater world that was breaking a new middle road between high (Broadway) and low (Bowery) theater.

But the history and profile of New York is also regionally bound. Looking to the West suggests that theatrical influences moved back and forth across the continent, despite difficulties in travel and communication. San Francisco, for example, emerged with a sophisticated theater culture in place—much of it borrowed from New York. The unprecedented fluidity of capital in mid-century San Francisco—thanks to the mining of gold, then silver, copper, and ore—lured entertainers to camps before the tents became buildings. By the end of the war, far western sensibilities began to influence entertainment styles back East. Perhaps no theater region experienced so much change as the Confederate South. Performers like Maggie Mitchell, caught on one side or the other of the Mason-Dixon line found themselves pledging allegiance in order to earn their living (and sometimes to stay alive). Political fare overtook the repertoire and the traveling theaters and circuses that had long toured the largely agricultural region fell apart as money (and therefore audiences) became scarce. American theater changed over the course of the war in these three regions and their three main theater cities: New York City, San Francisco, and the Confederate capital of Richmond, Virginia.

Theater stars occupied a unique position in the struggle, as they traveled incessantly, even during the war. Although it became impossible to play on both sides of the Mason-Dixon line once the war was in full throttle, Maggie Mitchell's experience at the beginning of the war was symptomatic of the acting profession. Even in the war-torn 1860s, entertainers like Edwin Booth, Adah Isaacs Menken, and Laura Keene were household names throughout the former United States. But no family had more transregional recognition than the Booth family, and no theater family became more intimately tied with the war historically. Patriarch Junius Booth began shaping modern American theater in the 1820s. In the 1850s his oldest son, "June," saw gold rush California as a ripe theater market and knew that no one was better equipped than he to pick its fruit. He convinced his father and Edwin, the middle and most theatrically talented son, to give the opening performances at the first major theater in the city, the Jenny Lind, in 1852. After Junius returned to home in the East, Edwin remained and developed his own skills playing in the rough mining towns of California and Nevada. When he returned to the Northeast in 1856, Edwin brought with him fare learned on the western frontier, and immediately emerged as the reigning star of American theater. Meanwhile the youngest son, John Wilkes, also decided to make his future in the footlights. He went to Richmond to establish his own identity beyond the shadow of his great family. The Booth brothers linked together the various theater arenas of the Civil War period, and the war tore them apart.

In New York, at the outset of the war many Americans were sympathetic to the secessionist cause. Given the city's extension of commercial credit into the South, the *Evening Post* went so far as to announce that the "City of New York belongs almost as much to the South as to the North" (McKay 18). Mayor Fernando Wood even officially proposed the secession of the city if the union broke apart. But Wood's plan failed and prophesies of commercial doom proved wrong. New York City experienced an unprecedented financial boom starting in 1863, thanks to gold speculation and wartime industry that led to an expanded middle class and a marked demand for novelty. New Yorkers also felt the pain of the war through forced conscriptions that culminated in the Draft Riots of 1863. It was in such an atmosphere, far from the fighting yet shaken by reverberations of war, that New York's famed theater district developed.

The Civil War years brought dramatic shifts to New York's theaters in terms of structures, fare, performance, and cultural function. Some of the changes began before but were accelerated by the war, such as the move to attract the growing middle-class female market by making theaters family-friendly rather than bastions of male culture. Likewise, changes in theater fare continued to shift and specialize by venue, so that variety and minstrel shows became common even in theaters targeting middle-class audiences. "Leg shows" and burlesque, two forms of entertainment formerly confined to low-class establishments, became acceptable even for children's matinees. Shakespearean performers, such as James Macready, found themselves sharing the spotlight with variety entertainers and comedians. Lastly, the function of the theater itself shifted, returning to its roots as a site of subversive commentary and entertainment but now performed for a diverse white audience that included all classes, genders and ages.

In the antebellum period, two thriving and distinct theater districts served the city: the respectable Broadway and the bawdy Bowery. Their audiences differed in class but were made up of the same sex: male. Antebellum theaters were part of a male sporting world that included saloons, streets, firehouses, clubs, and brothels. "The notorious third tier" of most theaters was a site of prostitution, with respectable women welcomed to the theater as escorted guests (Butsch 381). But things began to change in the decade before the war, as industry prospered and theater owners noted the untapped market of respectable women with disposable income and leisure time. In an effort to create appropriate entertainment for women and children, savvy entrepreneurs created overtly "respectable" theaters by removing the rowdy pit and replacing it with immobile seating, and introducing the afternoon matinee. Over the war years, responding to a major influx of women into the cities, this process only increased, transforming theaters from primarily masculine spaces into sites that offered something for everyone.

As the spaces and audiences changed in the late antebellum period, so did the material performed. Moral melodramas became popular as more women attended the theater. Morality plays like *The Drunkard* and *Uncle Tom's Cabin* lured in spectators who previously would never have attended a theater for the sake of mere entertainment. Minstrelsy, already popular by 1850, expanded its reach into stable, middle-class theaters. "Blacking up" allowed white performers to parody African Americans for audiences who, for the most part, had rarely met a black person. These blackface figures gave their white performers a subversive voice for critiquing the larger culture and for elevating white male identity, and it is telling that by the end of the war white female performers would in many ways enact the same dynamic by cross-dressing as white men.

One of the century's most successful theater managers, Laura Keene, promoted cross-dressed burlesque spectacles. In 1856, Keene had opened her theater specifically to promote "Varieties," a style of melodrama referred to variously as the "immoral drama," the "sensation" drama, the "hydraulic emotional school," or "problem plays." The plots of such plays harkened directly from popular cautionary tales, such as Susanna Rowson's *Charlotte Temple* (1791) that centered on tragic heroines who allowed themselves to become lured into sexual transgressions while remaining sympathetic characters. Keene also favored burlesques, sensationalized sketches ringing with subversive commentary on contemporary culture and politics. Yet despite such titillating fare, Keene's theater boasted a respectable, middle-class audience because of the structure of the seating, ticket prices, matinees, and a lack of bawdy women on stage and off.

The internal structure of the city's theater stock also began changing during the war years, largely thanks to the efforts of James W. Wallack who opened the thoroughly respectable Wallack's Lyceum in 1852 on the site formerly known as Brougham's Lyceum. Unlike virtually every other theater manager, Wallack rejected the system of contracting stars who would come and go, and instead required that stars work as a part of the company. The strategy of creating a full in-house cast allowed Wallack to institute the now ubiquitous practice of fully rehearsing a play before its opening.

Dramatic theater fare most pleased the critics. Edwin Booth became internationally known not for his versatility but for his fresh portrayals of Shakespeare. For one hundred nights, as the war drew to a close, he headlined as Hamlet, from November 1864 to March 1865 at the Winter Garden, and became known as "the prince of players," the greatest actor on the boards (Smith 105). Shakespeare remained popular because it spoke to contemporary concerns. Cross-dressing, so prominent in Shakespeare comedies, became increasingly popular both offstage and on, in large part because the war itself put gender norms into question. The popularity of "breeches" performances grew during the Civil War as more women were compelled to run farms and businesses. Stories of cross-dressing women appeared in wartime novels, autobiographies, and even newspaper articles. Cross-dressing itself was not new; young men had done so on stage for centuries and earlier actresses of the period, such as Charlotte Cushman, achieved artistic adulation playing male roles. And cross-dressing of a more provocative sort had long appeared in low entertainment venues. But the Civil War heightened the popularity of breeches performances on the respectable stage.

Adah Issacs Menken, a sensationalist actress who published confessional poetry and fraternized with the highest literati, pushed the envelope still further by combining breeches roles with faux nudity and dangerous stunts. Menken's performance of an old equestrian drama, *Mazeppa; or the Wild Horse of*

*Tartary,* in 1861 included a treacherous ride up a paper mountain that took her into the rafters. Menken, supposedly playing a naked man tied helplessly to the back of a horse, was clearly a woman (clothed in flesh colored tights), suggestively jostling up and down with the rhythm of the horse. During the war years, Menken played Mazeppa throughout the United States, from New York to Baltimore to San Francisco to Milwaukee, and in the capitals of France, England, and Austria. Perhaps as important, Menken spawned an army of imitators who took the imagery of breeches roles into towns and cities across the country at a time when many women were crossing gender divisions of labor.

Menken's cross-dressed performances coincided with the rise of burlesque. Before the war, "burlesque" referred to parodies of popular plays. Laura Keene expanded burlesque to include spectacle when she pulled together a "motley combination of stage effects, platoons of amazon marchers, music, and burlesque comedy" (Allen 106) that comprised her play *The Seven Sisters.* She deliberately developed a flexible plot she could change to address contemporary circumstances, and the original run in New York lasted for 250 performances in 1861. Her creation proved a turning-point for American theater, heralding the potent combination of partial (or merely suggested) nudity and sexually charged performances as acceptable fare for respectable audiences.

Burlesque spectacle proved to be more appealing than appalling, and led to the post-war "leg show" that merged variety into vaudeville at the end of the century. Lydia Thompson led the way with British Blondes, a troupe of women dressed in men's clothing while sporting masses of bleached tresses, whose sly commentary on gender norms made their production *Ixion; Or Man at the Wheel* a groundbreaking success and led the way for new forms of theater. But if Thompson's show sweetened social commentary with female display, the *Black Crook,* which began an unprecedented sixteen-month run at New York City's family-friendly Niblo's Garden in 1866, was all leg. The can-can element of the performance that would have made the piece unsupportable before the war drew in audiences with its novelty and spectacle. Attitudes towards theater had so shifted that a respectable minister's daughter later remembered attending the *Black Crook* in the late 1860s as part of a child's birthday celebration.

Meanwhile, on the West Coast, although cities appeared to be outside of the war's realm, the ideological differences of the conflict were shaping theater as well. Within a year of the major gold discoveries in Sacramento, 10,000 people came from around the world to set up temporary camps. Due to its natural harbor and proximity to the Sacramento Valley, San Francisco urbanized virtually overnight and by the 1860s had become one of the nation's most colorful cities. Single men with money to burn made entertainment a central industry before buildings had even replaced tents. A demand for entertainment led to lucrative traveling shows that catered to the mining camps and managed to attract significant talent from the East. One of the most celebrated talents was June Booth, who honed his eastern training in western camps, but made his name in San Francisco as a theater manager. He opened the Jenny Lind Theatre in 1852 in San Francisco, with his father and brother playing lead roles. After a short time, the patriarch returned to New York, and the Booth brothers trouped, becoming proficient in jigs and reels to accompany their Shakespearean training.

Theater performance was immediately perceived as a way to get rich quickly—particularly for women and children. Most celebrated of these was Lotta Crabtree, the first star of the eastern stage to hail from the West. According to one settler's memories, when Crabtree's family arrived in 1851, an "inordinate number of the city's 40,000 people consisted of saloon keepers, gamblers, gold speculators, miners in from the camps on a spree, Chilean prostitutes, gangs of Australian criminals known as the Sydney Ducks, Chinese opium peddlers, fugitives from justice, adventurers, and sailors who had jumped ship" (Dempsey 96). The Crabtrees rented a home in the midst of San Francisco's theater elite, and Lotta began dance lessons at a local tavern. Crabtree developed her craft differently than most of those acting in California, who were traditionally trained on the eastern stage. In contrast, Lotta grew up performing "variety"—which in the mining camps meant low comedy, songs, and other entertainment wedged into the framework of a play. Child actors were extremely popular in the West, "where, in the smaller camps, the very presence of a child was cause for wonder, and where a child who could sing, dance, or recite might be a better investment than the average claimstake" (Dempsey 99). Miners were an appreciative lot, and it was not unusual for performers to be showered with nuggets or mine claims after a good performance.

San Franciscans had an eclectic attitude towards theater in which "both actors and audiences flitted from serious drama to spectacle, to variety, to minstrelsy, and back again, sometimes all in the same evening" (Dempsey 104). By 1859 the drama had almost vanished from the San Francisco stage, according to historian Constance Rourke, and "variety—not yet called vaudeville—had come into an overwhelming popularity" (Rourke 149). The basic formula of variety developed to include a "first and second 'part' with a grand olio and concluding farce" (Rourke 154). This provided the opportunity for performers to take on many types of roles, from Irish sketches to operatic burlesque, with many performances done in blackface. More traditional performers lost their popularity and serious actors, including June Booth, were relegated to minor roles despite being stars in the previous decade. Meanwhile, actors from the East curtailed their travels during the war.

But not all of them: in 1863 Adah Isaacs Menken arrived in San Francisco prepared to take over the city with a month of performances of *Mazeppa* at Tom Maguire's Opera House. With San Francisco conquered, she went on to the center of the Comstock Lode, where a wealth in silver had turned Virginia City, Nevada, into a city overnight. Befriending self-professed San Francisco Bohemians like Bret Harte, and their Nevada cohorts of Mark Twain and Dan

Dequille, Menken made her mark upon the culture and earned a fortune in gold, silver, and mining shares.

When Menken returned to New York in 1864, she took two of the city's stars with her, Lotta Crabtree and June Booth. Rourke asserts that Booth's return East "suggested a fundamental alteration to the scene" of San Francisco theater: "He had been one of its earliest players, had acted in nearly every important theater in San Francisco and in the interior, had been actor-manager in many of these, and in one way or another had been associated with nearly every leading actor who had come to the Coast" (187). Other popular performers, including the Worrell sisters and the San Francisco Minstrels, left to try their luck with eastern audiences. Piece by piece, the variety scene of the West Coast moved to eastern shores, and by 1865 drama had asserted a new hold on western theaters.

Elsewhere, another Booth brother was active in a different theater arena. In the late 1850s, the youngest of the Booth brothers entered the family business and made his home in Richmond. Appearing as simply J.B. Wilkes, he went south to earn a reputation outside of the shadow of his famous family. As the war approached, he also became an avid supporter of secession and the Confederacy, much to the disgust of his brother Edwin. John Wilkes' time in Richmond honed his skills and "secured for him a greater success than Edwin had at the same stage in Edwin's career" (Smith 71). Despite such success, the Richmond Theater expelled John Wilkes when he left without notice to join a city militia in 1859—a decision that put him at the scene of John Brown's hanging in Charles Town, Virginia. He left the militia shortly after to begin touring the country as John Wilkes Booth, before resettling in Washington, D.C., in 1863.

Actors were not the only ones affected by their Confederate sympathies. In his 1863 play *The Guerillas*, Confederate playwright James D. McCabe, Jr. charged: "Our enemies have discarded every feeling of pity and humanity and have carried death and desolation wherever they have been" (3). Most Confederate plays depicted Confederate soldiers triumphing over Union forces, who roamed the spectrum from impolite to barbaric. In this particular play, the most popular of its kind, Union soldiers attack and sexually assault the hero's wife and eventually burn down the house with the his entire family inside. In short, Confederate drama was violent propaganda, with artistry and entertainment as by-products at best, and as with burlesque, playwrights created flexible plots so that plays could be rewritten to include new battles faced by southern troops.

But if the Confederate theater style was consistent in its propagandistic overtones, the performers and audiences were less consistent throughout the war. As men left for the battlefield, there were too few left to fill the plays' male roles. So, just as southern white women stepped into the roles of men off stage—managing businesses and running plantations—they began to play them on stage as well. It was cross-dressing, but of a different sort than appeared in other parts of the country. In addition to the changing performers, the audience members themselves changed as injured soldiers came to Richmond to recover and returned to fighting when healed. Unlike New York, where the war had little effect on the fare or actors, the invasion of Union forces overwhelmed every aspect of Richmond life including its theater.

The Confederate theater scene in Richmond evolved to serve a population in constant fluctuation. A constant movement of troops turned Richmond into a place of convalescence, and men awaiting a doctor's approval to return to the warfront made up the bulk of most audiences. Richmond was not the only city in the Confederate States to boast a lively theater culture, but Richmond produced "the archetype of theatre in the Confederacy. Its story is the essence of Confederate theatrical history, and that essence is flavored with the determination of the Confederates to prove themselves independent" (Harwell 42). Before the war, theater in the South was centered in New Orleans, with traveling shows hitting major cities such as Mobile, Savannah, Richmond and other population centers. Richmond had long attracted northern stars and was an important stop for traveling actors who trouped about the country. Joseph Jefferson, later famous for his portrayal of Rip Van Winkle, managed a theater in Richmond in the late 1850s where Edwin Booth had performed. But now the war made Richmond, the capital of the new Confederacy, into "the Broadway of the South" (Watson 101).

Performances of the period often focused upon the war itself, unlike their counterparts in the North. Even before the outbreak of war, the Richmond Theatre presented a tableau that the *Richmond Daily Dispatch* described as a "patriotic allegory" for election week. The tableau featured Peter Ritchings as General George Washington, who "as founding father might be associated with Union or disunion," and Ritchings' daughter Caroline as the Goddess of Liberty performing the *Star Spangled Banner*, who "might liberate the South from potential Republicans or represent the hard won condition of post-revolutionary America" (Mullenix 37). Three days later, election results were announced from the stage of the Richmond Theatre throughout the performance. Ten days following the election, the tableau was performed again, but the song of the French Revolution, the Marseillaise, had replaced the national anthem.

With the onset of war, trouping across the Mason-Dixon line ceased, and acting companies and new plays no longer crossed the borders. Confederate theaters were forced to rely on native actors and traveling actors who found themselves stuck behind southern lines. As one reviewer wrote of Eloise Bridges in 1864, "Miss Bridges continues the 'reigning star,' but has thus far appeared to little or no advantage, and, we venture to remark, with no satisfaction to herself, she having been required to speak not only her own lines, but most of the others of each character in every play in which she has yet appeared" (Harwell 76). This was a common occurrence, when one actor with a modicum of talent would have to cover for the many other novices on stage.

Some performers did have a lifetime of experience to rely upon, like Mrs. Clementina DeBar. Former wife of June Booth, DeBar became a core member of John Hewitt Hill's company throughout the war. The most famous entertainer in the South was Harry Macarthy, who proclaimed his dedication to the southern cause in songs such as "The Bonnie Blue Flag," and the most prolific writer was Richmond native John Hill Hewitt, who as writer and composer produced over 40 plays in his career. Hewitt managed the Richmond Theatre from 1861 onward, and produced many of his plays there. His first notable play, *The Scouts; or, the Plains of Manassas*, ran for eight nights before the end of November 1861. It was one of the first to include battles of the war, and this soon became a popular device for Confederate playwrights. Other plays by Hewitt include *The Battle of Leesberg* and *The Vivandiere*, both focusing on war. He left Richmond for Augusta, Georgia, in the fall of 1862, where he continued to write contemporary plays, such as *King Linkum, The First*, described as "one of the earliest dramatic treatments of Lincoln, illustrating that the northern president provoked mockery more than hatred from the Confederate side" (Watson 107).

On December 22, 1862, James Dabney McCabe's play *The Guerrillas* premiered at the Richmond theater and went on to become the most popular plays of the Confederacy, performed throughout the South. Like many other works produced in the period, *The Guerrillas* is a melodrama focused upon soldiers in western Virginia and McCabe used it to condemn northern brutality. Later, in his editorial introduction, McCabe falsely claimed that *The Guerrillas* was the "first original drama to be produced in the Confederacy" (3), even though Hewitt's plays were performed as early as November 1861.

Pro-confederate plays, while prominent, were not the only dramas to be produced in the South during the war. Richmond hosted Shakespeare, melodramas, farces, and burlettas throughout the war. However, the new works produced in the Richmond Theatre, and later New Richmond Theatre, were mainly war-themed. The audience most likely shaped this penchant for combat plays, as many soldiers convalescing in the city spent their time in the theaters of Richmond. The constant pressure of war did not prevent the theater from running as usual, and benefits were even performed for the poor. The notes of the Richmond City Council show the city's gratitude on October 19, 1863:

> *Resolved,* That the thanks of the Council be tendered to the management of the Richmond Theatre for the substantial result of the entertainment given for the benefit of the poor of the City, and that the amount of $3,387 be placed to the credit of the Overseers of the Poor to be disposed of as they may think best.
>
> *(Manarin 387)*

The theater was an important and vital part of the struggling city, keeping spirits light and providing entertainment for a city sliding into ruin as the Confederacy came to an end.

As the Confederacy fell, so did its theater. By late 1864, only the theaters in Richmond and Wilmington remained in operation. But despite the decline of talent in the company, the New Richmond Theatre still attracted large audiences. Richmond was evacuated on April 2, 1865, with the approach of the Union forces, but by April 4 Richard D'Orsay Ogden planned to reopen the theater, advertising in the *Evening Whig* that "invitations [were] sent to President Lincoln, Gen. Weitzel, Gen. Shelpy and other officers of distinction" (Harwell 91). The theater would go on, despite the fall of the Confederacy and the submission of the South.

Officially the war ended on April 9, 1865, with Robert E. Lee's surrender at Appomattox Courthouse, Virginia. By then, American theater outside of the South had refashioned itself for a much wider middle class. It was now common for men, women, and children of all classes to partake in theater offerings on a regular basis. When Lincoln and his party decided to attend a performance of *Our American Cousin*, a well-known farce starring Laura Keene, they were participating in popular entertainment—celebrating a return to "ordinary" life. In hindsight, many consider that night, April 14, the true ending of the war. As Lincoln watched the stage, John Wilkes Booth crept up behind him and waited for the right line to produce laughter that would cover the sound of his bullet firing from short range. Then, Booth dropped to the stage crying the Latin motto for Virginia, *Sic semper tyrannus,* "Thus always to tyrants." Lincoln died several hours after the shooting. Laura Keene, meanwhile, cleaned off the blood and returned several nights later to the stage. Theater now catered to most of the population in one form or other, and the postbellum masses wanted their entertainment. The show had to go on.

## Further Reading

Allen, Robert C. *Horrible Prettiness: Burlesque and American Culture.* Chapel Hill: University of North Carolina Press, 1991.

"Amusements." *New York Sunday Mercury.* January 20, 1861.

Butsch, Richard. "Bowry B'hoys and Matinee Ladies: The Re-Gendering of Nineteenth Century American Theater Audiences." *American Quarterly* 46 (1994): 374–405.

Davis, Tracy C. *Actresses as Working Women: Their Social Identity in Victorian Culture.* New York: Routledge, 1991.

Dempsey, David. *The Triumphs and Trials of Lotta Crabtree,* New York: William Morrow and Co., 1968.

Harwell, Richard Barksdale. "Brief Candle: The Confederate Theatre." *Proceedings of the American Antiquarian Society* 81 (1971): 41–160.

Henderson, Mary C. *The City and the Theatre: The History of New York Playhouses—A 235 Year Journey from Bowling Green to Times Square,* Clifton: James T. White and Co., 1973.

Manarin, Louis H., ed. *Richmond at War: The Minutes of the City Council 1861–1865.* Chapel Hill: University of North Carolina Press, 1966.

McCabe, James D. *The Guerrillas.* Richmond: West & Johnson, 1863.

McKay, Ernest. *The Civil War and New York City.* Syracuse: Syracuse University Press, 1990.

Mullenix, Elizabeth Reitz. "Yankee Doodle Dixie: Performing Nationhood on the Eve of War." *Journal of American Drama and Theatre* 18.3 (2006): 33–54.

Rourke, Constance. *Troupers of the Gold Coast, or the Rise of Lotta Crabtree.* New York: Harcourt, Brace, and Co., 1928.

Sentilles, Renee M. *Performing Menken: Adah Isaacs Menken and the Birth of American Celebrity.* New York: Cambridge University Press, 2003.

Smith, Gene. *American Gothic: The Story of America's Legendary Theatrical Family—Junius, Edwin, and John Wilkes Booth.* New York: Simon and Schuster, 1992.

Watson, Charles S. "Confederate Drama: The Plays of John Hill Hewitt and James Dabney McCabe." *The Southern Literary Journal* 21 (1989): 100–112.

# 25

# BASEBALL

*Ryan Swanson*

Baseball did not begin during the Civil War. Determining the exact origins of the game has been a topic of much scholarly debate. In recent years David Block in *Baseball Before We Knew It* (2005) and John Thorn in *Baseball in the Garden of Eden* (2011) both made compelling cases that pinning down exactly where and when baseball began might be an impossible task. We do know, though, that the game began to take on its modern form, or at least a form that would be recognizable to the twenty-first-century baseball fan, during the 1840s and 1850s. The establishment of the New York Knickerbocker Base Ball club in 1845 marked a watershed moment for the sport. The Knickerbockers came up with by-laws, elected officers, designed uniforms, and played a regular schedule of games. The club also began the process of formalizing baseball's rules. Due to the efforts of the "Knicks" and other New York City-based clubs, baseball's popularity spread quickly. In October 1845, the *New York Morning News* reported that interclub competition had begun. On a cold fall day, a New York City ballclub defeated a rival from Brooklyn in a four inning, eight-against-eight contest.

By the time Civil War fighting broke out, knowledge of the game had permeated the American Northeast, trickled into the South, and eased out West. Soldiers and civilians alike played baseball during the war. Baseball activity took place mostly in the North during the conflict, this reality reflecting the fact that southern cities such as Richmond, Charleston, and Savannah suffered a higher toll during the conflict than those north of the Mason Dixon line. Baseball reveals, in a different way than most historical lenses, the stresses the war caused on American society. Some Americans used the game as a metaphor to explain the times, others to escape the tedium of military life, and still others to raise money for those off fighting. And, of course, some men simply kept playing ball because it had been part of their antebellum lives.

As the Civil War began, baseball activity reverberated from New York City. The farther a ballplayer traveled from this city, the less likely he would find a baseball organization or regular game. Urban areas had far more teams than rural hamlets. The cities, with their more regimented and typically less physically demanding jobs, created a need for sporting activity. New York City's main rival for baseball supremacy (then as now) was Boston. Philadelphia also emerged during the war itself as a near equal to New York City and Boston in terms of its baseball success and influence.

Baseball rules and customs varied by locality. While some consensus about rules had emerged—four bases, runs scored by crossing home, outs made by catching a hit ball—the ballplayers from New York and Massachusetts espoused slightly different games. In the "Massachusetts game," for example, teams played to twenty-five runs and needed to win three games to take a match. Massachusetts ballplayers could also "soak" a baserunner, hitting him with the ball, in order to record an out. The New York game, among other differences, generally frowned on "soaking" and used the inning system to determine the length of a contest.

Ballplayers had organized nationally just before the outbreak of the war. In 1859, leaders from baseball clubs located primarily along the eastern seaboard, but also in Chicago and St. Louis, formed the National Association of Base Ball Players (NABBP). In 1860, the NABBP convention drew sixty member clubs. The NABBP espoused gentlemanly play and demanded that its players resist the lure of professionalization. Before and during the Civil War, baseball's leaders, especially Henry Chadwick (the self-proclaimed "Father of Baseball"), touted amateurism. While the best players in New York City, Boston, Philadelphia, and other baseball-crazy cities undoubtedly received covert compensation, outright pay-for-play would not begin until the war was over. The Cincinnati Red Stockings became baseball's first openly professional team in 1869.

While the soon-to-be "Yankees" dominated antebellum baseball, the game had also spread to the South before the Confederacy made its move for independence. As in the North, the cities of the South fostered the region's first baseball clubs. New Orleans had nine ballclubs playing in 1860. Similarly, Louisville and St. Louis, and Galveston and Houston, each had several baseball clubs organize before the Civil War. There were, to be certain, far more baseball clubs in the North than South, but it is worth noting the sporting connections that did exist before the Civil War. While Southerners might have appreciated horse- and blood-sports (cock-fighting, etc.) more than baseball, the spread of baseball reiterates the fact that antebellum sectional differences were accompanied by shared experiences and national cultural trends.

Baseball also crossed the racial divide *before* the war started. The *New York Anglo-African* reported on December 10, 1859, on a game between the Henson

Base Ball Club of Jamaica, Long Island, and the Unknown of Weeksville, New York. During the war itself, black baseball would continue in New York. There is also some evidence to suggest that black baseball existed in other northern urban areas with large free-black populations, such as Baltimore, Boston, and Philadelphia, as well. The Civil War did not stop these black men from playing. The *Brooklyn Eagle* reported in 1862 on "Sambo as a Ball Player" and noted that not only the players, but the fans were "as black as the ace of spades" (Sullivan 34-36). Octavius Catto, a black educator from Philadelphia, would learn the game during the war, and organize the highly successful Philadelphia Pythians Base Ball Club when the war ended.

The question of how the war affected the development of baseball in the United States mirrors larger questions of the social and cultural legacies of the Civil War. Opinions vary widely. Albert Spalding set the benchmark for crediting the Civil War with changing everything in the baseball world. Spalding, who was among baseball's first professional stars and a man who made his fortune by selling sporting goods, claimed that the Civil War revolutionized baseball. The game had already existed, but, according to Spalding, the war spread knowledge of the game far beyond its New York City roots:

> No human mind may measure the blessings conferred by the game of Base Ball on the soldiers of our Civil War.... Base Ball had been born in the brain of the American soldier. It received its baptism in [the] bloody days of our Nation's direst danger.... It was during the Civil War, then, that the game of Base Ball became our national game.
>
> *(92–93)*

Spalding pointed out that prisoners of war played the game and, as a result, "Yanks" and "Johnnies" came into closer proximity than otherwise would have been possible.

Other analysts of the relationship between the Civil War and baseball have not been so sure. The game had existed before the start of the conflict. Knowledge of the game had already crossed the Mason-Dixon line. And certainly, it must be noted, the fighting had led to the dismantling of many teams and indeed to the dormancy of baseball activities altogether in some areas. With this in mind scholars such as George Kirsch, Benjamin Rader, and Harold Seymour have argued that the Civil War neither made nor significantly stunted the growth of baseball as a modern sport. "Baseball's spread was not stopped by the war; it was only temporarily slowed," Seymour clarified (40). The war did, however, help forge a codified version of the game. Out of the war, the New York game, with its use of the diamond-shaped field, innings, and more aggressive pitching rules, emerged as *the* game of baseball. The Civil War was a nationalizing agent—creating consensus out of regional variations.

Baseball also helped Civil War soldiers pass idle time. They played in prisoner of war camps, to celebrate holidays, and to commemorate significant wartime occurrences, merging the mundane with the realities of an ongoing military conflict. In 1864, for example, when New Yorkers were given a day off to focus on thanksgiving and fasting, New York City hosted more baseball club games than planned church services. They also played to combat boredom and because their higher-ups encouraged the game as a means of promoting health.

The U.S. Sanitary Commission took the lead in promoting the cause of health. In August 1861, as the fighting intensified and early notions of a quick conclusion to the war vanished, the Sanitary Commission issued its "Rules for Preserving the Health of the Soldier." The report left few issues uncovered. Soldiers should, the report preached, "eat at regular hours," dig trenches for "the calls of nature," and "sleep in their shirts and drawers." They should not be over-drilled. And, as a reprinting in *Harper's Weekly* made clear, men should be encouraged to exercise during free-time, partaking in "amusements, sports and gymnastic exercises should be favored among the men, such as running, leaping, wrestling, fencing, bayonet exercise, cricket, base-ball, foot-ball, quoits, etc" ("Rules" 542). The U.S. Sanitary Commission cared little whether the activity was baseball or "quoits," but the men gravitated towards those games that had been most popular before the war. Baseball had been on the upswing in the 1850s, and that trend continued even during the all-encompassing conflict.

With all the baseball activity swirling about, the press used the familiar game as a metaphor to describe the Civil War to its daily readers. That baseball was a commonly understood topic made this useful and practical. In 1863 for example, *Harper's Weekly* compared a baseball "invasion" to the invasion of Robert E. Lee's army, which was advancing quickly into Pennsylvania. "While Pennsylvania is invaded, Pennsylvania invades. While the balls of the rebels are base, it is with base-balls that the sons of the Keystone State advance upon New York," the reporter mused. But then just to be clear, the paper added: "Still there is a difference. It is play that the latter come for; it is in deadly earnest that the rebels ride" ("A Raid from Pennsylvania" 418). Using baseball to explain the war, or to lighten the day's news, was a common literary tactic throughout the conflict. Even as Lincoln had begun his ascent to the White House in 1860, reporters had linked activities on the diamond with political events. The *Chicago Press and Tribune* reported on a distinctly "political base ball match" in July 1860. With 1,200 spectators watching, a "Lincoln Nine" played a "Douglas Nine" in a spirited match. In this contest at least, Douglas won. Still, the reporter warned—again in baseball terms—that the election would turn out different: "Never mind, Lincoln boys, there's a victory in store where Douglas will make no 'runs.' He is a lame 'short stop,' and has been 'caught out'" ("The Political Base Ball Match" 1).

Holidays often meant baseball, among other leisure activities, for the enlisted man. Union troops in Port Royal, North Carolina, for example, rang in the New Year in 1863 with baseball games, as well as greased-pole climbing contests, wheelbarrow races, sack races, and target-shooting games. A.G.

Mills, later to become the President of baseball's National League, recalled a Christmas Day spent in Hilton Head, South Carolina, in 1862 punctuated by a ballgame. Members of a New York unit brashly decided to take on all comers; 40,000 soldiers watched the ensuing match. The game provided momentary relief for the men—from the war and homesickness during the holiday season. Albert Spalding speculated in his history of baseball that games even took place between Confederate and Union soldiers when there were breaks in the fighting. "I have not found any soldier of either army to corroborate these rumors or to deny," Spalding lamented, but he enjoyed the idea nonetheless (95–96).

One of the most celebrated episodes of Civil War baseball among the fighting men took place in a Salisbury, North Carolina, prison camp. Union soldiers held there, especially those from New York, passed some of their captivity hours by picking teams and playing baseball games. Otto Boetticher, an artist who served in the Union Army, preserved one such scene in a sketch before his release from the camp. And it was not just the Union soldiers playing. Will Irwin later explained that "New Orleans boys also carried baseballs in their knapsacks" and that Confederate prisoners from Georgia and South Carolina formed teams as well (12–13).

Soldiers did not need to rationalize their ballplaying ways. Whether they played during respites in the fighting or after being captured by the enemy, they had earned their recreation time. Newspapers did not condemn baseball in this context. Baseball on the home front, however, was not nearly as certain a subject. Baseball players were typically aged somewhere between their late teens and mid-30s—prime fighting age. So, the fact that these men were not at the frontlines, and that they had the time for and the physical health to engage in ballgames, was bound to raise a few eyebrows.

Perhaps the simplest explanation for baseball continuing in cities such as New York and Philadelphia amid the national crisis of a civil war was that recreation has always persisted. In defending the playing of baseball, one newspaper noted this reality: "Our people like those of every nation on earth will have amusement, and they will dance though Rome burns" (*Henry Chadwick Scrapbook* n.p.). Like in the encampments of the Union Army, baseball players on the home front in the North selected the game of baseball from dozens of leisure options. Reflecting this diversity, Beadle Publishers printed not only its popular *Beadle's Dime Base Ball Player* during the war, but also manuals for cricket, swimming, and singing, among other pastimes. The widely distributed and exhaustive *Games of Skill and Conjuring: Including Draughts, Dominoes, Chess, Morrice, Fox and Geese, Conjuring, Legerdemain, Tracks with Apparatus, Tricks with Cards, Boat-Building, Modeling, Deaf and Dumb Alphabet, Riddles, Acting Charades, Puzzles and Paradoxes, Useful Amusements, Shows, Model Stage, and Tinselling* demonstrated that capricious activity did not stop simply because of war.

More basically, baseball also survived during the Civil War because of the uneven enlistment and draft processes used to fill the Union Army. Volunteers

went first. Organized into state units, many of the early volunteers were looking as much for an adventure as a cause when they agreed to fight. When
volunteerism failed to meet the soldier-needs of the Union effort, President
Lincoln and the United States Congress passed the Conscription Act of 1863.
The draft brought tens of thousands more men into the Army. But for men
with means, such as many of the ballplayers who made up the upper-crust clubs
in New York City, Philadelphia, and Boston, fighting was hardly compulsory.
Men could arrange, through a substitutive payment or a plea to a high placed
official, to avoid military service. And so baseball survived.

In this context of some men going off to fight and others staying home,
many journalists argued that baseball was good for both the soldier and the
civilian male on the home front. "We hope to see the game fostered, even in
the midst of war, for it can do no harm, and may, indeed does [sic] do good,"
Henry Chadwick preached (*Henry Chadwick Scrapbook* n.p.). Chadwick extolled
baseball as the builder of good soldiers. "The Father of Baseball" carefully
clipped and placed in his meticulous baseball scrapbooks an article with the
following declaration:

> The practice of base ball is an admirable preliminary school for attain-
> ing many of the most important qualifications of a soldier, the endur-
> ance of bodily fatigue and the cultivation of activity of movement being
> two important elements. Add to these meritorious features of the game
> the fact by means of the exciting contests between first-class clubs ...
> thousands of our citizens are furnished with a gratuitous exhibition that
> affords them great pleasure.... For these reasons we hope to see the game
> fostered, even in the midst of war.
>
> (*Henry Chadwick Scrapbook* n.p.)

Chadwick's logic—that baseball somehow prepared men for the rigors of battle—points to a broader trend, especially during the first two years of the war,
of carefully rationalizing activities such as playing ball even as other men fought
and died.

Such rationalization was necessary because baseball did not receive the same
official "Green Light" during the Civil War that the Major Leagues did during
World War II. President Franklin D. Roosevelt had settled the issue of whether
it was proper to play baseball when the nation was at war during the 1940s. His
"Green Light Letter" stated that the continued playing of baseball would contribute to, not hinder, the war effort. In response to a letter from the baseball
commissioner at the time, Kennesaw Landis, Roosevelt replied: "I honestly
feel that it would be best for the country to keep baseball going" (n.p.). Without such a validation from Lincoln, baseball players and club administrators
proceeded with caution at the beginning of the Civil War. The 1861 NABBP
convention opened with a declaration of support for the Union war effort and
discussions about distributing any profits to support the soldiers.

This discussion lost steam when it became clear that the prospect of profits was limited. Attendance at the NABBP conventions steadily declined from sixty clubs in 1860 to thirty-four in 1861 and 1862. The treasurer's report at the 1862 meeting revealed that the association had only $314.97 in its coffers. Survival, rather than growth, was the NABBP's early war focus. At the nadir of participation, only twenty-eight clubs attended the 1863 convention. Baseball activity was tempered, it seemed, by the steady flow of bad news from the battle fronts. Looking back at the 1861 season, the *New York Clipper* explained the decline in baseball activity due to "the gloom and despondency that hung over the country as disaster after disaster attended the progress of the national arms in defense of the Union" ("The Ball Season of 1862" 1).

Baseball activity rebounded in late 1863. Union victories at Vicksburg and Gettysburg turned the fighting tide and helped Lincoln win reelection in 1864. During the last two years of the conflict, many baseball clubs returned to their antebellum customs of hosting elaborate banquets and taking expensive inter-city "tours." Among all teams, the Philadelphia Athletics emerged at the fore-front of this mid-war baseball renaissance. Mirroring the city's rising fortunes, the Athletics transitioned near the halfway point in the conflict from a strategy of quiet perseverance to one bent on capitalizing on wartime opportunities to vault to the head of the baseball class. Thus in August 1864, the club invited the Resolute Base Ball Club of Brooklyn for a visit. The Resolute was among baseball's best teams. The *New York Clipper* provided extensive coverage of the visit and noted the emergence of Philadelphia's baseball clubs:

> A Series of Grand Matches in Philadelphia. The Resolute of Brooklyn Against the Philadelphia Clubs: Base ball this season has flourished more than it has done since the war began, and especially has it thus far been lively in Philadelphia. The fact is the Philadelphians are rapidly taking high rank as practical illustrators of the attractive features of the game ... There are now five flourishing clubs in Philadelphia, besides others who will soon come up to the requisite standard.
>
> *("The Grand Matches" 3)*

It was not the first time that Philadelphia had played baseball host during the war. According to the *New York Clipper,* the Athletic Club was known, even during the war, to greet visiting clubs with "splendid bowls of claret punch," to provide accommodations at the tony Washington House and access to private a billiards club ("The Grand Matches" 3). The club even escorted one group of ballplayers to the city's Zoological Gardens.

Philadelphia baseball clubs flourished and the city's teams traveled and enter-tained with seemingly few wartime constraints, especially after 1863, because the city's economy was booming. Philadelphia had nearly mastered war time economics and politics. Calls for economic sacrifice had decreased; they were replaced by a widespread opinion that city life should return to normal. In June

1864, the city hosted the three week-long "Great Central Fair," which raised more than $1 million for the U.S. Sanitary Commission. Philadelphia's baseball success during the war mirrored the city's overall rising fortunes.

At the end of the 1864 season, with Union victory seeming more and more likely, baseball clubs in the North held their annual convention and resumed their pre-war practice of arguing over the rules of their game. Discussions over dedicating profits to soldiers or organizing charity games faded into the background. Instead, the NABBP convention held in December 1864 debated, not for the first time, the merits of the "fly" game of baseball versus the "bound" game. The *New York Times* had predicted that the convention of 1863 might resolve the debate, but a consensus over this "important revision of the rules" had not been reached ("Annual Convention" 2). Thus at the 1864 convention, the topic arose once again. The debate was over whether a player needed to catch a hit ball "on the fly" in order to make an out or if he could allow the ball to bounce first. During the 1850s, players had generally been credited with an out if they caught a ball after its first bounce.

This rule-debate revealed a changing tenor in the recreational norms of the United States. In light of the sobering milieu that came with the costly war, baseball leaders sought to make baseball suitably "manly," serious, and skillful—to emphasize technique over collegiality. Baseball became more competitive. Henry Chadwick led this masculine movement, one that he felt was imperative if baseball was to be America's national game. "Step by step, little by little, either directly or indirectly," Chadwick recalled in 1868 with the "fly game" having won out, "did I succeed in assisting to change the game from the almost simple field exercise it was some twenty years ago up to the manly, scientific game it is now" (11)

Baseball's popularity increased when the war ended. Men came home from the fight and began, or in many cases simply continued, playing baseball. The establishment of the National League in 1876 coincided with the end of Reconstruction. Of the relationship between baseball and the war, the *Brooklyn Eagle* concluded, "base ball has had to contend with obstacles, resulting from the war, that would have entirely destroyed any less objectionable or less popular sport.... We think the ordeal it has so successfully passed through has shown it to be possessed of characteristics that will insure its future existence as a permanent institution of the land" ("Sports and Pastimes: Base Ball" 2). Sure enough, baseball endured, persisting through several more wars since the United States' great sectional conflict.

## Further Reading

"Annual Convention of Base Ball Players." *The New York Times.* December 7, 1863: 2.
"A Raid from Pennsylvania." *Harper's Weekly.* July 4, 1863: 418.
Chadwick, Henry. *The Game of Base Ball: How to Learn It, How to Play It, and How to Teach It.* New York: George Monro and Co., Publishers, 1868.

*Henry Chadwick Scrapbook, 1860–1870.* Henry Chadwick Papers, Microform Reel 9, Albert G. Spalding Collection, New York Public Library.

Irwin, Will. "Baseball Before the Professionals Came." *Collier's Weekly.* May 8, 1909: 12–13.

Kirsch, George B. *Baseball in Blue and Gray: The National Pastime During the Civil War.* Princeton: Princeton University Press, 2003.

Roosevelt, Franklin D. "Letter to Kennesaw Landis." January 15, 1942, Franklin Delano Roosevelt Papers, President's Personal File, Document No. 227.

"Rules for Preserving the Health of the Soldier." *Harper's Weekly.* August 24, 1861: 542.

Seymour, Harold. *Baseball: The Early Years.* New York: Oxford University Press, 1960.

Spalding, Albert. *America's National Game: Historic Facts Concerning the Beginning, Evolution, Development and Popularity of Base Ball.* 1911, Lincoln: University of Nebraska Press, 1995.

"Sports and Pastimes: Base Ball." *Brooklyn Eagle.* March 17, 1864: 2.

Sullivan, Dean A. *Early Innings: Documentary History of Baseball, 1825–1908.* Lincoln: University of Nebraska Press, 1995.

"The Ball Season of 1862." *The New York Clipper.* March 15, 1862: 1.

"The Grand Matches in Philadelphia." *The New York Clipper.* August 6, 1864: 3.

"The Political Base Ball Match–The Score and Result." *Chicago Press and Tribune.* July 25, 1860: 1.

Tygiel, Jules. *Past Time: Baseball as History.* New York: Oxford University Press, 2001.

# 26

# SACRED AND SECULAR HOLIDAYS

*Suanna H. Davis*

Holiday celebrations during the Civil War were smaller and more restrained than today. Easter was not a major American holiday until the early twentieth century and was mostly celebrated during the Civil War by attending a church service. Halloween grew in popularity in the United States with the arrival of the Irish immigrants following the potato famine (1845–1852) but was still primarily viewed as a Catholic holiday during the Civil War. As well, there were no military remembrances in the 1860s, since Memorial Day was created to remember the Civil War dead in 1868 and Veteran's Day was created following World War I.

Other holidays and holy days that Americans celebrated regularly during the war have significantly changed or are now mostly ignored. The nineteenth-century practice of Maying, going out in early May to gather flowers and dance, is no longer a part of American life. Sundays during the Civil War were usually considered a time for church and quiet diversions, such as visiting and reading, rather than leisure time. Most people went to church and particular attire was expected for church attendance. An occupying soldier wrote about the church fashions in Madison, Virginia: "The ladies left the sermon decked out in their dresses of dazzling, though not always harmonious colors: silk, gauze, velour, muslin, plumes scintillating under the noonday sun" (Bandy 246). Even the poorer people dressed up. The understanding that people wore special clothing for Sunday is illustrated by the expression "Sunday best" in a *Harper's Weekly* article titled "The Parish Clerk's Story," published on March 23, 1861, that describes a woman getting dressed to make an impression at church. Then, after going to church, people relaxed on Sundays during the war. They visited friends, read, and wrote letters. In general, religious people did not play any games on Sunday, and sang no songs except hymns. They did not work, for Sundays were a "Sabbath time" of rest.

Laws governing the observance of Sunday were instituted within the United States almost as soon as the country began. These laws limited what was legally permissible activity on Sundays. But the limitations of these laws were tested during the Civil War, and in May 1861 the *New York Times* published an appeal by a Sabbath Committee: "If we would save our country we must hold fast to our Sabbath," the committee explained. "Never more than when extraordinary cares and excitements almost madden the brain, and the deepest passions of the soul surge like the ocean, are the still Sabbath hours needed to restore exhausted natures, calm the fevered pulse, and compose the perturbed spirit." The appeal also pointed to public reaction against any the loss of Sunday as a sacred day, claiming there was a "unanimity and strength of public sentiment" against "Sabbath desecration" ("The Sabbath in War" 2). The following year, Lincoln attempted to further enshrine Sunday as a holy day of rest, issuing a General Order that *Harper's Weekly* quoted in an article titled "About Thanksgiving" on November 29, 1862:

> The importance for man and beast of the prescribed weekly rest; the sacred rights of Christian soldiers and sailors; a becoming deference to the best sentiments of a Christian people, and a due regard for the Divine will, demand that Sunday labor in the army and navy be reduced to the measure of strict necessity. The discipline and character of the national forces should not suffer, nor the cause they defend be imperiled by the profanation of the day or the name of the Most High.
>
> *(755)*

But as even the Sabbath Committee had recognized, different standards must apply to the armed forces. Although there should be public outcry against working on Sunday, the appeal explained, most people recognized that troops were exempt: "No just interpretation of the law of the Sabbath would apply its provisions to the emergencies in individual or national life which involve vital interest.... All that is *necessary* to the public safety in the gathering of troops and the movement of armies, is innocent because of the necessity" ("The Sabbath in War" 2).

The war did intervene significantly with the ability of the soldiers to observe Sundays as a day of rest. As General Lee wrote to his daughter in December 1861, "one of the miseries of war is that there is no Sabbath, and the current of work and strife has no cessation" (56). Battles, drills, and troop movements were soon a regular part of Sunday activity, forcing religious observations into a lower priority. All manner of military necessity, including inspections and manual labor, took place on the Sabbath, and the first major battle of the Civil War, the Battle of Bull Run, took place on a Sunday. Nonetheless, leaders continued to try to minimize the desecration of the Sabbath by the war. In addition to Lincoln's General Order of November 1862, General Order No. 15 issued by Lee on February 7, 1864, insisted: "None but duties strictly necessary shall be required to be performed on Sunday.... Commanding officers will require the usual inspections on Sunday to be held at such time as not to interfere with the attendance of the men on divine service" (Jones 50).

One difficulty with providing a Sabbath experience for soldiers in the military was the limited number of chaplains. Prior to the Civil War, chaplains were not part of the military of the United States. But military leaders considered this a serious deficiency and created the position in both the Union and Confederate armies at the early stages of the war. Legislation announced on May 3, 1861, in the Confederate States provided for the appointment and pay of chaplains to regiments and brigades, while Lincoln authorized chaplains for volunteer and regular regiment the following day. Neither side was able to maintain enough chaplains, however. Although chaplains entered both armies as officers, their pay was cut throughout the war, and neither navy ever increased their number of chaplains, so there were not enough to go around. This meant there were fewer organized church services in the military, and soldiers were less likely to attend church than civilians. In addition, even when a chaplain *was* available, the simple fact of a chaplain being with a unit did not guarantee attendance at services by soldiers. Chaplains had to be recognized in their denominations, and denominational loyalty was strong. Some chaplains were Catholic priests, and the Protestant soldiers usually avoided their services.

When Sunday services were available, they were often held outdoors and were generally well attended; they consisted of much the same experience as civilian church. Soldiers would stand for hours at a time in order to celebrate the Sabbath, and Bibles were in heavy demand within the armies of both the North and the South. Reading clubs were formed in camps from both sides to study the Bible. Some soldiers ignored their religious options, however, even when church services were available. When payday fell on a Sunday, soldiers often preferred to gamble or purchase goods, rather than listen to sermons. Even when they were not paid that day, soldiers would sometimes skip church in order to catch up on sleep.

In addition to the regular holy day each week, Americans marked several annual holidays during the war. For example, George Washington's birthday was a major holiday prior to the Civil War and during the war's early years. It was celebrated each year following the American Revolution and that practice continued during the Civil War, before being declared an official holiday for Washington, D.C., in 1880 and for all federal employees in 1885. In 1862 the United States Senate began a tradition of celebrating Washington's birthday with a reading of his famous "Farewell Address" (1796). Though this did not become an annual event in the Senate until 1893, it was a popular decision. Individual cities celebrated the day as well. For example, in 1861 the Order of United Americans in New York celebrated with an oration. John Findlay gave a celebratory address to the General Assembly of Maryland in 1862, while the city of Boston conducted a reading of Washington's Farewell Address. Lt. Gov. Stanton addressed Ohio's Hall of Representatives in 1863, and national songs in honor of the past president were created and published in Boston that same year. The mayor of Cambridge, Massachusetts, gave a speech in 1865 during the observance of the holiday there.

St. Louis, Missouri, even created an 11-mile long procession to celebrate Washington's birthday in 1862. It started just after noon and included military regiments and military bands, for a total of 5,000 participants with 3,000 horses. The civilian portion of the parade also had bands, as well as 127 carriages of ladies, additional mercantile wagons, politicians in various conveyances, and regular citizens. One of the more famous personages was Tom Thumb, a little person who became an international celebrity under P.T. Barnum, accompanied by some Shetland ponies, and there was a float created to mimic Washington crossing the Delaware. Many companies were represented, including several railroad companies, a glass company, bakeries, and the American Express Company with seven wagons full of employees. Postal workers, police, and firefighters had a large representation in the parade, as did many of the schools. Entire ovens and printing presses were paraded on wagons as well. Coal miners stood atop coal heaped in wagons, while in other wagons molders filled molds, tinners worked, and coopers finished barrels. Gunboats, howitzers, and cannons were featured in the parade. By five o'clock, the parade was finished, and the celebration continued with a reading of Washington's Farewell Address and a choir performance of patriotic music.

Though other Civil War celebrations of Washington's birthday might not have matched the drama of St. Louis, they were widespread. Washington, D.C., held birthday parades during the war. In 1861, United States troops and the militia formed a parade, which included a thirty-four-gun salute, and many homes flew the flag. The next year, another parade took place and many people bought new flags in honor of the celebrations. On March 8, 1861, *Harper's Weekly* carried a sketch of a gala held to celebrate Washington's birthday, identified as taking place in the House of Representatives, that featured captured rebel flags. The celebrations did not continue unabated throughout the war, at least not in the capital. For Washington, D.C., residents, a snowstorm and the bad news of the war left little to celebrate in 1863, and in 1864 the holiday was generally ignored. But the city's lack of celebration during the later years of the war was not widespread. A news story about the "Capture of Wilmington," in the March 11, 1865, edition of *Harper's Weekly* mentioned that the event took place on Washington's birthday and the "later portion of the day was devoted by our sailors to the celebration of Washington's birthday" (145). It is possible that war fatigue was responsible for the diminishment of the popularity of Washington's birthday celebrations in the capital. Since many soldiers were staged through there and the city was often full of parading regiments, there seemed little reason to celebrate a hero from a previous war, when this current war had plenty of its own heroes to celebrate.

Other Civil War-era holidays included Valentine's Day, the Fourth of July, and Thanksgiving. Throughout the Civil War, Valentine's Day found many people separated from their loved ones. Letters and cards were a common means of communication and valentine cards were popular. Since valentines began to be mass produced during the 1840s, they had become more affordable to the general public and, during the Civil War the, cards could cost as little as a penny. The cards were both sentimental and comic. The sentimental cards, created to be purchased individually and only sent to someone special, were more expensive than the comic cards, which could be sent to anyone.

Valentine's Day cards were at their peak of popularity before and during the Civil War. Each of the *Harper's Weekly* editions for Valentine's Day week throughout the Civil War included advertisements for valentines and full-page illustrations. One illustration in the February 18, 1865, issue has at its center a young woman reading a missive, apparently a valentine letter. The top of the picture has envelopes being thrown from the skies by cherubs, while all around the bottom of the picture are people, primarily men, chasing letters, reading letters, and passing envelopes to other people.

Both sentimental and comic valentines referred to the war, and there were special valentines for soldiers. Some of the sentimental cards showed a couple separating, and others had an army tent that opened up to show a soldier inside. These sentimental cards contained verses referring to the war. For example, one card's rhyme read: "My country's cause to serve, / For her to do or die; / Thy love my arm to nerve, / Thy name my battle cry" ("Civil War Valentine Card"). Another read: "'To horse!' the bugle sounds the call, / The foemen rage like waves at sea; / If cruel fate should bid me fall, / My last fond thought shall be of thee" ("Civil War Valentines" 10). A lock of hair would often accompany these cards.

Comic valentine cards, however, managed to introduce humor about the war. For example, one with a verse called "An Aspiring Soldier" shows three soldiers, one significantly taller than the other and reads: "Gaunt and slim and bony baby, / You will be promoted—maybe; / Than your comrades two foot higher, / For what more can you aspire?" Another, with a verse called "Always Sleeping at Your Post," remonstrates with a soldier for drinking so much that he falls asleep and ends with the accusation: "You're enough to make a damsel sick." Sometimes cards combined both sentiment and comedy. A card titled "Bank of True Love," shaped and colored like a bank note, was decorated with couples walking. It read: "Secured by the Whole Stock of Truth, Honour, and Affection ... I promise to pay to [blank] on demand the homage and never failing devotion of Sincere Affection." It was sentimental yet it was comic, with a fill-in-the-blank romantic expression.

Like Valentine's Day, the Fourth of July was a holiday celebrated by both the North and South during the Civil War. Civilians managed to celebrate Independence Day each year of the war, and *Harper's Weekly* would publish full-page illustrations detailing a range of celebrations, including orations, fireworks, the raising of the flag, and celebratory drinking. However, soldiers' experiences of the Fourth of July depended upon where they were stationed on the holiday. For example, northern forces stationed in Union-occupied Louisiana in 1864 were able to spend the day eating—and drinking: "This is the anniversary of our independence," wrote one soldier in a letter home from the Louisiana barracks on July 4th 1864, "and we are going to celebrate the day, with our soil drenched in the best blood of the nation, mingled with the worst, and still drinking more and more" (Kinsley 155). But the war did not always pause for celebrations, and the Confederate army even launched the Battle of Helena on Independence Day in 1863.

One common facet of the celebrations in both the Union and the Confederacy, for both soldiers and civilians, was the commemorative speech—which often spoke directly about the war's purpose and progress. For example, on July 4th, 1864, Michael Hahn, the recently-elected governor of federally occupied Louisiana, addressed Union troops and told them to push forward to victory, while Sidney Dean gave a commemorative speech in Providence, Rhode Island, that focused on the cause and impact of the war. An equally widespread component of Independence Day celebrations was the firework display. In July 1863, the most famous fireworks of the Civil War were created in New York for the Fourth of July, with a pyrotechnic show demonstrating the battle between the ships *Monitor* and *Merrimac*. Revelers fired guns as well: *The New York Times* of July 6, 1863, printed two separate and long listings of various gunfire incidents, although adding that "with some ten or twelve exceptions they were not of a fatal character" ("Loyal League Celebration" 6). Most of the fatal gunfire incidents involved bullets, shot from guns by both children and adults, while the less drastic incidents involved cherry pits shot from guns.

As Americans continued to mark Independence Day, with adjustments to the speeches and events that acknowledged the war's victories and progress, they also created another federal holiday: Thanksgiving. Lincoln proclaimed Thanksgiving a federal holiday during the war's third year, in 1863. Although proclamations of Thanksgiving were declared during the first two years of the Civil War both in the United and Confederate States, these were single days dedicated to prayer and thankfulness to God. For example, in 1862, Confederate President Jefferson Davis declared September 18 as Thanksgiving. It was a Thursday, as was the eventual United States holiday, but it was a single, unique day celebrating battle victories rather than a date intended to be perpetuated. Similarly, Lincoln's proclamations of Thanksgiving in both April 1862 and July 1863 were also intended as singular days of thanks for victories in the war. In 1863, however, Thanksgiving became an official and ongoing part of the American calendar. Sarah Josepha Hale was able to persuade President Lincoln to declare it a national holiday. An influential writer and editor, Hale had campaigned for the national holiday since 1846. She finally succeeded on October 3, 1863, when Lincoln identified the fourth Thursday in November as the nation's day of Thanksgiving. This proclamation of a national holiday had no immediate effect on in the South, which did not mark the November day until after the war.

Despite the fact that Thanksgiving was not a national holiday in the United States until 1863, many states had celebrated it much earlier. Before Lincoln's national declaration of an official recurring holiday, each of the northern states had already independently established Thanksgiving as a yearly holiday. Charles Mackay, writing in 1859, described the Thanksgiving holiday as it was celebrated in Rhode Island:

> Thanksgiving-day is generally fixed in November, and corresponds in its festive character to the celebration of Christmas in England. The people shut up their stores and places of business; go to church, chapel, or conventicle in the forenoon or afternoon, or both, and devote the remainder of the day to such social pleasure and jollity as the custom of the place may sanction. The dinner, at which the piece de rigueur is roast turkey, is the great event of the day.
>
> *(65)*

Numerous other texts indicate that Thanksgiving was a major holiday for individual states before the Civil War. *Northwood: A Tale of New England,* written by Sarah Josepha Hale in 1827, describes the traditional feast of Thanksgiving as including turkey and pumpkin pies. Lydia Maria Child's poem "A Boy's Thanksgiving Day" (1844) also mentioned pumpkin pie as it celebrated childhood Thanksgiving celebrations, ending: "Hurrah for the fun! / Is the pudding done? / Hurrah for the pumpkin pie!" (Whittier 193).

The Civil War did not dampen Thanksgiving celebrations. In Washington D.C., during the first two Thanksgiving days of the war (1861 and 1862), government offices were closed and turkey was the meal of choice for families who could afford it. The Thanksgiving edition of *Harper's Weekly*, November 29, 1862, included a drawing of two turkeys on the street and detailed their discussion: Mrs. Gobbler said she would not eat to fatten herself for others' benefit, while Mr. Gobbler retorted that she was only injuring herself because she would still be sold, but because of her small size would grace only a boarding house table. In its December 3, 1864 edition, turkey continued to be the centerpiece of the Thanksgiving meal as represented by the holiday poem "Thanksgiving," which begins: "The feast of plenty comes once more / The turkey, king of birds" (770).

The holiday was also celebrated in the army camps, even before Lincoln's proclamation of a national holiday in 1863. The issue of *Harper's Weekly* published on November 29, 1862, included drawings of Civil War soldiers in camp at leisure on Thanksgiving Day. One illustration by Winslow Homer, titled "Thanksgiving at Camp," shows many soldiers gathered around the sutler's tent, which has signs describing the Thanksgiving meal: pie, herrings, and cider. A soldier holds a fish like a cigar as another soldier in a cavalry hat eats a half pie. A third drinks directly from a bottle. Six other soldiers are drawn in detail, sitting, standing, saluting, and hugging. Turkey is conspicuously absent, suggesting the limits on the amount of food available for consumption within the camps.

As a festival of peace, rather than a commemoration of revolution and military victory (like July Fourth and Washington's Birthday) or a chance to give thanks for war victories (like Thanksgiving), Christmas was harder to celebrate during the Civil War. The South continued to celebrate a version of Christmas involving a tree, presents for the children and feasting, along with religious celebrations, but the Northeast largely disavowed Christmas as a religious holiday to such an extent that December 25 was a school day. With many husbands and fathers away at war, the focus of families was simply bridging the distance. This involved sending Christmas care packages, as illustrated in Winslow Homer's drawing "Christmas Boxes in Camp-Christmas 1861," published in *Harper's Weekly* on January 4, 1862, which shows dozens of soldiers pulling socks out of a box and putting them on their bare feet, then eating the food and piling up the books that the box contained.

In spite of these attempts, however, numerous northern accounts depict Christmas during the Civil War as a sad and lonely time. Henry Wadsworth Longfellow wrote his poem "Christmas Bells" on Christmas Day 1864, while his Union army son was recovering from a severe bullet wound. Several stanzas focus on southern cannons and empty households, and Longfellow uses this imagery to express the meaninglessness of Christmas for a war-torn country:

Then from each black, accursed mouth
The cannon thundered in the South,
    And with the sound
    The carols drowned
Of peace on earth, good-will to men!

It was as if an earthquake rent
The hearth-stones of a continent,
    And made forlorn
    The households born
Of peace on earth, good-will to men!

And in despair I bowed my head;
"There is no peace on earth," I said;
    "For hate is strong,
    And mocks the song
Of peace on earth, good-will to men!" (133)

A Thomas Nast illustration titled "Christmas Eve 1862," published in *Harper's Weekly*, on January 3, 1863, evokes a similar despair. Each half of the illustration is a large circular frame. The left shows a mother, her children in bed behind her, kneeling and praying at the window; the right shows a soldier, sitting alone on guard duty and gazing at photographs of his family. Between the two is a smaller circle showing a row of newly filled graves.

Nast did create a jollier symbol of Christmas during the Civil War, however: the modern Santa Claus. His depiction of Santa drew on his native German tradition of Saint Nicholas, a fourth-century bishop, but inscribed a jolly, large man into the American perception of Christmas. Nast's illustration "Santa Claus in Camp," published on the cover of *Harper's Weekly* on January 3, 1863, shows a chubby Santa in a sleigh pulled by reindeer, wearing a dark jacket with white stars and pants of light and dark stripes, handing out Christmas presents at a Union camp. Even his mournful illustration "Christmas Eve 1862," published in the same issue, shows Santa Claus on top of the mother's house with his reindeer, about to climb into a chimney, in the upper left hand corner of the picture.

The following Christmas, his illustration "Christmas, 1863," published in *Harper's Weekly* on December 26, 1863, developed the figure of Santa Claus still further. The illustration has multiple frames within the page. The largest is in the center and shows a man in uniform home on furlough, hugging his wife. His young son has abandoned a toy on the ground in order to climbs his father's leg. The frame on the left is labeled "Eve" and shows a now-familiar Santa Claus with a bag full of goodies in the children's bedroom. The frame on the right is labeled "Morning" and shows the children opening their stockings. Far less visible are a small oval on the left that depicts the holy family in Bethlehem, and another small oval on the right that depicts a family attending church. The focus of the illustration is the soldier arriving home to a Christmas with his family and Santa Claus visiting the house, with the religious meaning of the holiday almost an afterthought. In this and his other Christmas illustrations, Nast created Santa as a secular symbol of gift giving removed from its Christian antecedents. Along with decorations, a tree and the stocking, it was this gift-giving Santa that endured in later authors' and artists' depictions of Christmas and became key to the modern American Christmas, especially after Congress proclaimed Christmas a federal holiday in 1870.

In fact, by end of the Civil War, the secularization of American holidays was complete. By 1865, Thanksgiving meant feasting, especially turkeys and pumpkin pie, and was an official national holiday. Independence Day continued to commemorate the Revolution of 1776. Valentine's Day had been a chance for sentimentality as soldiers and their loved ones exchanged cards, and an opportunity for some welcome humor in the form of comic cards; the original martyred Saint Valentine was long absent from the day's meaning. And the new main character of Christmas was Santa, rather than Christ. Only Sundays remained sacred within American society, and even the Sabbath had been challenged by the fact that war did not stop for rest. Though holidays began as holy days, during the Civil War they became, instead, a time to escape the conflict and simply be happy.

## Further Reading

"About Thanksgiving." *Harper's Weekly*. November 29, 1862: 755.

"Always Sleeping at Your Post." Circa 1861–65. McAllister Collection of Civil War Era Printed Ephemera, Graphics and Manuscripts. Library Company of Philadelphia.

"An Aspiring Soldier." Circa 1861–65. McAllister Collection of Civil War Era Printed Ephemera, Graphics and Manuscripts. Library Company of Philadelphia.

"Bank of True Love." Circa 1861–65. McAllister Collection of Civil War Era Printed Ephemera, Graphics and Manuscripts. Library Company of Philadelphia.

"Capture of Wilmington." *Harper's Weekly*. March 11, 1865: 145.

"Civil War Valentine Card." 1860s. The Warshaw Collection of Business Americana, National Museum of American History.

"Civil War Valentines." *Reflections* (Kansas State Historical Society) 5.1 (2011): 10–11.

Bandy, William Thomas. "Civil War Notes of a French Volunteer." *The Wisconsin Magazine of History* 45.4 (1962): 239–50.

"Fourth of July at Camp Hamilton, Near Fortress Monroe." *Harper's Weekly*. July 27, 1861: 470.

Homer, Winslow. "Thanksgiving in Camp." *Harper's Weekly*. November 29, 1862: 764.

Jones, J. William. *Christ in the Camp: Religion in Lee's Army*. Richmond: B.F. Johnson and Co., 1887.

Kinsley, Rufus. *Diary of a Christian Soldier: Rufus Kinsley and the Civil War*. Ed. David C. Rankin. Cambridge: Cambridge University Press, 2003.

Lee, Robert Edward. *Recollections and Letters of General Robert E. Lee*. New York: Doubleday, Page & Company, 1904.

Longfellow, Henry Wadsworth. *The Works of Henry Wadsworth Longfellow, Volume 3*. Boston: Houghton, Mifflin, 1910.

"Loyal League Celebration." *New York Times*. July 6, 1863: 6.

Mackay, Charles. *Life and Liberty in America; or, Sketches of a Tour of the United States and Canada, in 1857–8*. London: Smith, Elder, and Co., 1859.

"The Parish Clerk's Story." *Harper's Weekly*. March 23, 1861: 189–190.

"Rebel Flags in the Old House of Representatives at Washington." *Harper's Weekly*. March 8, 1862: 153.

"The Sabbath in War." *New York Times*. May 13, 1861: 2.

"Thanksgiving." *Harper's Weekly*. December 3, 1864: 770.

"Washington's Birthday in Saint Louis." *The Missouri Democrat*. February 23, 1862.

Whittier, John Greenleaf, ed. *Child Life: A Collection of Poems*. Boston: James R. Osgood and Company, 1872.

# PART VIII

# Death and Aftermath

# 27

# DEATH AND DYING

*Nicole Keller Day*

An estimated 360,000 Union soldiers and 260,000 Confederates died in the Civil War, together totaling 620,000 casualties. As death shrouded both nations, the physical and emotional traditions previously established by survivors in response to death came to an end and new customs ensued. The war made way for original symbolism, both political and religious, with which survivors would interpret both mass and individual death. The war demanded complex, innovative ways to explain the dead, physically and spiritually, and these new systems of belief came at enormous cost. As Drew Gilpin Faust explains, "Americans had not just lost the dead; they had lost their own lives as they had understood them before the war" (268). Loss was inscribed into the daily routines of those living in Civil War America.

Antebellum Americans were no strangers to mass death. Both northern and southern communities had experienced mortality on large scales during plagues and epidemics in Philadelphia in 1793, New York in 1849, and New Orleans in 1853. But while these events might have prepared Americans in methods of disposing of large numbers of dead bodies, none of these events could truly prepare them for the fratricide they were to experience. The nature of killing one's own countrymen required a more complicated way to interpret and realize death, as well as a concrete justification for such killing and dying. The only way to validate citizens murdering fellow citizens of a once-unified country, especially given the sheer number of fatalities required for victory, was to completely amend the symbolism that Americans had previously associated with death. For the new imagery to be effective, however, images could not be aligned as blatant political symbols; new systems for representing death politically would need to be couched in imaginative moral, religious, and social constructs.

The war had usurped the imagination for the purpose of political influence. Gary Laderman explains that for the North, "a landscape covered with mangled and broken bodies also symbolized the righteousness of the Union cause—the large numbers of young northern soldiers slaughtered on the fields of battle became evidence of Union patriotism and virtue" (98). Others in the North, specifically the Protestant population, saw the slaughter as necessary to repent for the sins of the nation: namely slavery and corruption. A widely accepted moral belief that made the deaths more tolerable was that Civil War soldiers believed their souls were immortal; if they bravely fulfilled their national duty, they would be spiritually rewarded and gain entrance to heaven. This encouraged soldiers to slaughter their former kinsmen and risk their own obliteration.

Looking at the total numbers of soldiers who died, including 225,000 Union and 194,000 Confederate soldiers who died from disease caused primarily by unsanitary conditions, made it easier for Americans to overlook the tragedy of the situation. As an entirety and as a social construct, the deaths could function as redemptive or nationalist symbols, whereas looking at the soldier's stories individually was heartbreaking and distracting from political objectives. *The Liberator* published an article in 1862 which emphasized the function of the army as a whole and how valorous it was to die for one's country: "A colossal army, at the waving of the emblem of native land, precipitating themselves into the deadly hell of battle, to conquer or die in a good cause, is the most dazzling embodiment of valor and self-sacrifice ever seen below the heavens" ("War" n.p.). It was crucial that the public imagination be focused on the larger issues, such as the future of the respective nations and power of military forces; it was the only way for citizens to tolerate the number of men that were dying. Ironically, men were dying to become the symbols that would ultimately perpetuate the war, leading to even more deaths.

Perhaps incongruously, death on the level of the individual Civil War fatality had much larger consequences than the death of masses, through a shift in the symbolic purpose of the dead body. Shortly before the war began, both rural and urban Americans were extremely intimate with death, through the participatory rituals of what has come to be known as the good death. To die a good death essentially meant to die a prepared death at home. For a man to be prepared to die, he should have accepted the fact that he was going to pass away, been surrounded by his family members, expressed his religious devotion to ensure his entrance to heaven, and perhaps helped his family members prepare for the actual death by making arrangements for the disposal of the body. It was imperative that family members be present for the moment of loss. Faust elaborates on this: "How one died thus epitomized a life already led and predicted the quality of life everlasting. The *hors mori*, the hour of death, had therefore to be witnessed, scrutinized, interpreted, narrated" (9). Witnessing death offered family members security that their relative would be accepted in the hereafter, and being unable to witness death left family members distraught as to the spiritual wellbeing of their loved one. Death and individual corpses had become a symbol of the eternal future.

After a person died, the surviving family members were responsible for making preparations at home for the burial of the corpse, transporting it to the gravesite, and, finally, interring or entombing it in the graveyard. Occasionally, there would be a small stop on the way to the gravesite for a last view of the body. One of Walt Whitman's biographers, Justin Kaplan, traces an important shift in the memorial vocabulary Whitman uses, which is representative of a shift in public attitudes prior to 1861: "The terms 'burial ground' and 'graveyard' gave way to the more consoling 'cemetery,' a sleeping place; the dead were no longer dead and gone but sweetly 'Asleep in Jesus'" (110-11). Also, before the war, neither cremation nor embalming was practiced, as survivors were appalled by the idea of destroying or altering the revered corpse. A wake was included in the first phase of this process, to watch the body until it was physically removed from the home, the purpose of which was to make sure that the deceased had in fact died; live burial was a serious concern at the time. In more urban settings, class and race divisions were apparent in these rituals. Wealthier families held more elaborate funeral ceremonies and helped to lay the foundation for a viable funeral industry, a market that was fully fledged by the end of the war.

To understand how drastically the war changed the ways in which individual deaths were realized, mourned, interpreted and finally symbolized, it is worth noting the degree to which some survivors were obsessed with the corpses of the departed. Prior to the outbreak of war, diary entries document young girls wishing to die that they might be buried next to siblings; mothers wanting to reopen their children's tombs for one last look; and spouses who cannot resist this urge, and actually open the tomb to find out whether the body has begun to decay. Laderman describes "a refusal to allow the dead to disappear from the living community, a fixation on the body of the deceased, and a demand that the integrity of the corpse be perpetuated in the grave as well as in collective memory" (73). Among other habits aimed at satisfying the needs that Laderman describes were posthumous mourning portraits, popular in America between 1830 and 1860. Mourning survivors commissioned artists to paint their beloved after they had died and before they were interred or entombed. But during the war, such intimacies and fixations would crumble when there were no bodies over which survivors could obsess.

Antebellum Americans saw corpses as symbols of the soul's immortality as they witnessed the body's literal transition from life to death. Once the war commenced, however, the good death and the way survivors mourned and healed were revolutionized in the absence of the deceased's body. Deaths no longer took place in the domestic safety of home; there was nothing families could do to prepare for the unfortunate and untimely event. The only option available to soldiers was to enter battle ready to die. Unexpected and abrupt death on the battlefield took with it the traditions that generations of

Americans had established to make the process of grieving serene and pain-less. Since most of the Civil War's battles occurred in the South, and means of bodily preservation and transportation had not progressed at the same rate at which men were being massacred in the war, soldiers were frequently left to deal with their own comrades' corpses.

The goal of living was reduced to merely ending up in a proper grave, and on his *Enlarged Devil's Dictionary*, conceived in 1869 although not published in its newspaper installments until 1881, the popular writer Ambrose Bierce even defined *dead* as "the golden goal / attained—and found to be a hole!" (87-88). The Civil War dead, in their seemingly limitless quantity, simply did not merit the time for reflection and treatment they would have received prior to the war. There were no coffins and certainly no religious ceremonies. There were more urgent priorities—a war to be fought and battles to be won—and therefore the physical remains of soldiers lost meaning. A corpse used to be a sign of immor-tality. By the 1860s, however, since it was no longer of use to the military, it was no longer significant. Death had become a symbol of the strength, or lack thereof, of the competing military forces.

Whereas preservation of corpses was frowned upon before the war, surviv-ing family members had a sudden change of heart if it meant that bodies would still be recognizable for one last look after making the journey home. But find-ing the bodies was nearly impossible. Some northern families had the financial means to travel and search for themselves, while others relied on writing letters to military officials requesting assistance and, later on in the war, employing the full range of search, preservation and transportation services offered by embalmers. On the other hand, southern officers were often found and brought home by the slaves who had accompanied them. For both northern and south-ern survivors, these scenarios were entirely dependent on a particular corpse being identifiable, and soldiers would pin their names to their uniforms so that they might be posthumously identified and returned home to be interred and mourned, following the rituals of the good death.

From survivors' perspectives, not witnessing the actual death robbed them of the security that their relative would be accepted in heaven. Part of a good death included, at the deathbed, reaffirmation of spiritual devotion and a wake where survivors could make sure the corpse was indeed dead. But the war meant there was often no physical proof for survivors to recognize and accept. Faust refers to Freud's research on the psychological consequences of this state of mind; he "contrasted mourning, a grief that understands that a loved object no longer exists, to melancholia, in which an individual 'cannot see clearly what it is that has been lost' and thus remains mired in 'profoundly painful dejection, cessation of interest in the outside world, loss of the capacity to love'" (144). If survivors could neither see nor understand what had been lost, they would be left in an emotional void and experience yet another of the Civil War's casualties: the ability to mourn.

Out of necessity, survivors began to rely heavily on their imaginations to help them move past this emptiness. Unlike before the war, when families were familiar with every aspect of death, they now knew next to nothing. Even if they were reunited with the corpse, after it was shipped home or found on the site of a bloody battle, there were gaps in both time and knowledge. What happened in this man's life between the time he left home and the time he died? The closest survivors came to having answering this question was a consolation letter. Letters usually came from one of three sources: a fellow soldier who witnessed the death on the battlefield; a nurse or hospital volunteer who could write on behalf of the soldier, either of his current living conditions or the circumstances surrounding his death; and finally, in the best possible case, from the loved one himself before death—wounded and hospitalized but still physically able to write. The objectives of the letter were the same as that of the good death. Letters often conveyed final messages to the people who would have usually surrounded the deathbed; messages that the deceased was ready to die and had reiterated his belief in God and general devotion to his religion. Authors of the letters chose to skip repugnant scenes in order to maintain an emphasis on the immortality of the spirit. These were not just letters of compassion; they served as replacements for the good death, insofar as they reassured families that the souls of their dead were absolutely bound for heaven. News of the good death replaced the actual good death. This practice of writing consolation letters was the best chance families stood of receiving news about their soldiers since formal reporting systems weren't in place and the Confederacy's postal service was defunct. Receiving a consolation letter was crucial in helping survivors realize death, and on a national level, these letters helped to create a new good death, one based on products of imagination.

Other forms of writing, including literature, had also become helpful to survivors as they grasped at new, more imaginative techniques to help them come to terms with death. Alice Fahs points out the dependency inherent in this relationship between readers and writers during the war: "If readers' perceived interest in the war helped to produce war literature, war literature in turn served to direct and shape readers' responses to the war" (8). This is especially true when it came to shaping readers' responses to the casualties of war. Readers purchased literature with imaginative representations of death that felt most suitable as a response to the national crisis and individual heartache; therefore the demand for and production of new literature specifically suited to the Civil War increased. The war period saw the development of a new genre of consolation literature, recognizable by its descriptions of heaven and long-awaited reunions with loved ones, and emphasis that relationships, like individual souls, are immortal.

Civil War authors produced great quantities of poetry and songs written in response to the war's slaughter. A majority of the poetry concentrated on what soldiers were thinking and feeling when they were dying on the battlefield.

Mark Schantz notes that the poets had something to teach their audience with their verse: "The poets taught that death itself—particularly the figure of the corpse—might be viewed as beautiful and aesthetically pleasing. Second, the death poems pointed to a life beyond the grave" (98). This second lesson of poetry contributed to filling the void left by the absence of a good death; if the imagined soldiers were thinking about heaven, they had clearly asked for salvation before dying and come to terms with their impending expiration. In contrast, before the war broke out, both northern and southern poetry celebrated the masculinity of the soldier. This literary shift aided in transforming melancholy into mourning through influences and products of the imagination.

Just as writers were responsible for influencing the imagination's intimate deathbed scene and notions of heaven, photographers influenced the grieving nation through their visual depictions of battlefield scenes. Like consolation letters and literature, photographs of war-torn landscapes helped Americans to recognize and realize death. Schantz explains that photographers "carefully manicured their battlefield scenes for public consumption. They assured citizens that men fell as whole beings even in the midst of horrific combat" (196). So whereas letter writers glossed over gory details, photographers "manicured" them, manipulating the American imagination. "Manicuring" meant featuring whole bodies, as opposed to corpses with missing limbs, and positioning bodies to remain anonymous, by angling heads away from the camera or turning them toward the shadows of the setting sun. This practice allowed survivors to come closer to the physical deathbed scene, as they had been in antebellum times, even as it portrayed an altered reality. This manipulation of the truth also supported political agendas, including Lincoln's re-election in 1864. The American public may not have continued to support the fratricidal war had they been shown the raw, unmanicured images of anonymous bodies blown to bits, a far cry from the sacred corpse of the good death.

One more party influenced individual and national imaginations: religious leaders. While they offered their congregations information about an afterlife of which they had no proof, some leaders also vacillated on whether it was morally permissible for their followers to use their imaginations. The crisis of the situation was not that some religious leaders wavered, but that in a time when all other systems of belief were in flux, people sought stability in at least one area of their lives—and spiritual guides could not adequately provide it. For example, the day after the war began in April 1861, *The Christian Recorder* explained that sins were products of the imagination. Only one year later in July 1862, the same publication referred to prayer as "a communication opened between earth and heaven," adding: "By this way the humble saint ... mingles in imagination with the glorious company that stand around the throne of God" ("Privilege" n.p.). According to the 1861 article, the human imagination was a place wrought with sin, a place that the devout should avoid as much as possible, while in 1862 the imagination is a physical place suitable for the meeting of saints and deities. The same journal also acknowledged that new forms of preaching were being used by 1862: a "pictorial kind seems to be coming into vogue" ("Different" n.p.). This "pictorial" preaching differed from the dry and expository oration formerly employed, and like the journal's own change of heart between 1861 and 1862, it reflected the fact that the imagination seemed increasingly less evil as Americans relied on it more and more to interpret the war's deaths.

This imagination and the art it produced, whether writing, photography, or posthumous portraits, cumulatively conveyed the Civil War's new symbolism for individual death: manifestation of the hero. Art forms helped survivors realize and comprehend the experience of death by filling in gaps in the good death experience, and a new symbolism for corpses and dying emerged. On some occasions, deceased soldiers were given religious representation and compared to Jesus, dying for the sins of others. Individual deaths could also be political symbols; if an officer died, his funeral procession through a town or city would be a ceremony that evoked feelings of patriotism. This symbolism was crucial to the revolutionized and more imaginative good death. Whereas previously death occurred within a group of tightly-knit family members at home, the war dispersed loved ones across the country and divided elements of the good death into individual responsibilities. Where possible, dying soldiers had to be ready to die and have confirmed their faith. Survivors were left with letters, stories and pictures to help them piece together the events of death, and relied on the imagination for reassurance that their heroes were on their way to heaven.

With this constructive use for the imagination and a modification of the good death, grieving survivors were pushed beyond traditional boundaries of mourning. Survivors were now encouraged to account for the dead by imagining them in heaven, where they would all reunite someday. The new emphasis on an imagined reunion led to the reinvention of heaven. Antebellum notions of heaven focused primarily on the relationship between the deceased and God; in this pre-war heaven, familial ties were considered earthly and for the living. But newer renditions of heaven took on a more tangible, earthly appearance and were more closely related to Emanuel Swedenborg's vision. This had four important characteristics: first, "only a thin veil divides heaven from earth," second, heaven "is seen as a continuation and fulfillment of material existence [of Earth]," third, heaven is not actually a place for rest as "saints are increasingly shown engaged in activities, experiencing spiritual progress," and finally, "social relationships, including love between a man and woman, are seen as fundamental to heavenly life" (McDannell and Lang 183). Fahs attests to the fact that Civil War novelists also depicted a heaven very similar to Swedenborg's hereafter, with a domestic emphasis that "moves the attention from the uniting couple to the reuniting family" (229).

In fact, literature had a definite impact on spiritual beliefs during the Civil War, infringing somewhat upon the territory of religious leaders. The popular literary adaptation of heaven emphasized that only a "thin veil" separated it from earth and emphasized death as a homecoming of sorts, which had a powerful influence on homesick soldiers. In addition, some perceptions of heaven "literally restored bodies to wholeness," as Schantz explains: "Civil War soldiers of all kinds wrote thoughtfully and extensively about heaven, seeing there a place that would reverse their earthly sufferings" (60). Wounded and dying soldiers imagined a heaven that would allow them to heal and return home to their wives and children.

But an increased interest in heaven accompanied a decreased faith in a benevolent God, and left soldiers in a spiritual quandary. To those soldiers for whom death had become a fixation, heaven was a possible exit from earthly pain and misery. But at the same time, they had seen enough slaughter to question whether God was benevolent. Another contributing factor to this loss in faith was the change in attitude toward the corpse. While the corpse was previously a sign of the soul's immortality, seeing piles of corpses in prisons and hospitals, and on battlefields, diminished the value of the remains for surviving soldiers. Even at home, survivors had, when necessary, adapted to new ways of mourning without the corpse. Many Americans were also adjusting to seeing photographs of dead bodies, which further diminished the religious and symbolic power of corpses. The medical profession was also responsible for devaluing remains: doctors began claiming the corpses of Civil War carnage to use as cadavers. The war had caused society to reprioritize the value of the corpse; it was more important to use the body for medicine than to view the corpse as a symbol of the soul's immortality—science seemed to triumph over religion and faith.

Summing up the spiritual state of Civil War America, Walt Whitman observed: "every man has a religion; has something in heaven or earth which he will give up everything else for—something which absorbs him, possesses itself of him, makes him over in its image—something" (Lowenfels 15). Man had *a* religion, but not necessarily *the* religion of the Christian church, and may even hold something on "earth" as a religion—including a political cause or the war itself. Sure enough, as the war progressed, both the North and the South demanded sacrifices of life for their respective cause, and each side also sacrificed the familiar modes and meanings of death, including grieving processes, understandings of heaven, and spiritual symbolism.

## Further Reading

Bierce, Ambrose. *The Enlarged Devil's Dictionary*. London: Penguin Books, 2001.

Burns, Stanley. *Sleeping Beauty: Memorial Photography in America*. Altadena: Twelvetree, 1991.

"Different Kinds of Preaching." *Christian Recorder*. March 1, 1862.

Eddy, Daniel C. *Angel Whispers; or, The Echo of Spirit Voices. Designed to Comfort Those Who Mourn*. Boston: Wentworth & Co., 1857.

Fahs, Alice. *The Imagined Civil War: Popular Literature of the North and South, 1861–1865*. Chapel Hill: University of North Carolina Press, 2001.

Farrell, James J. *Inventing the American Way of Death, 1830–1920*. Philadelphia: Temple University Press, 1980.

Faust, Drew Gilpin. *This Republic of Suffering: Death and the American Civil War*. New York: Knopf, 2008.

Isenberg, Nancy G., and Andrew Burnstein. *Mortal Remains: Death in Early America*. Philadelphia: University of Pennsylvania Press, 2002.

Kaplan, Justin. *Walt Whitman: A Life*. New York: Bantam Books, 1980.

Laderman, Gary. *The Sacred Remains: American Attitudes Toward Death, 1799–1883*. New Haven: Yale University Press, 1996.

Lowenfels, Walter, ed. *Walt Whitman's Civil War*. New York: Da Capo Press, 1989.

McDannell, Colleen, and Bernhard Lang. *Heaven: A History*. New Haven: Yale University Press, 2001.

Neely, Mark. *The Civil War and the Limits of Destruction*. Cambridge: Harvard University Press, 2007.

Pike, Martha V., and Janice Gray Armstrong. *A Time to Mourn: Expressions of Grief in Nineteenth Century America*. Stony Brook: Museums at Stony Brook, 1980.

"Privilege of Prayer." *Christian Recorder*. July 5, 1862.

Schantz, Mark S. *Awaiting the Heavenly Country: The Civil War and America's Culture of Death*. Ithaca: Cornell University Press, 2008.

"Vices of Imagination." *Christian Recorder*. April 13, 1861.

"War and Public Morals and Honor." *Liberator*. March 14, 1862.

# 28

# VETERANS

*John Casey*

Civil War soldiers coming home from the war experienced reintegration as a lengthy process that did not simply involve reuniting with their families and finding employment. Even those veterans who managed to avoid pauperism and disability still struggled with their sense of identity. They felt a subtle wall dividing them from the civilian populace that led to tension and persistent misunderstanding between civilians and former soldiers, although this tension has been largely masked by the more visible issues of race and regionalism that came to dominate the era.

The first stage of veteran reintegration in any war is demobilization: the official dismantling of the armies created to fight a war. As William Holberton notes, demobilization for the Union forces was "a well-organized and rapidly executed means of returning to civilian life just over a million volunteer soldiers" (143). Union soldiers about to be demobilized were first sent to one of nineteen field rendezvous sites that had been chosen by the army adjutant general's office during the last year of the war. These sites were typically close to the area of operations for a particular army unit, with most regiments fighting in Virginia reporting to field rendezvous sites near Washington, D.C. At the field rendezvous site, government property was returned and accounted for and the paperwork needed for discharge was filled out in multiple copies for processing. Once the necessary paperwork was completed, units were sent either by water or rail, and frequently a combination of both, to their state rendezvous sites. These were the locations in each state where a regiment had initially been mustered in to service, typically the state capital or a county seat. At the state rendezvous sites, a unit would wait for its back pay and any bounties due. Soldiers would typically receive copies of their discharge papers.

For most northern units, demobilization took anywhere from three to four weeks to complete. The 49th Ohio Regiment, which took part in Sherman's March to the Sea, camped at its field rendezvous site outside of Washington, D.C., for two weeks after taking part in the Grand Review. They were then placed on westbound trains headed for Columbus, Ohio, where they arrived in a little over ten days. Of course, there were exceptions when it came to the timetable of unit demobilization in the northern army. The 5th Connecticut, which fought alongside the 49th Ohio in Sherman's army, arrived at the same field rendezvous site as its sister regiment at about the same time, but they did not leave for home until nearly two months had passed. Part of the problem faced by the 5th Connecticut was the lack of adequate transportation for such large numbers of men, as moving people from one place to another on this scale was unprecedented at the time in the annals of American transport. What affected the speed of this particular unit's demobilization even more, however, was the fact that the 5th Connecticut was heading northeast into a heavily trafficked area. Edwin Marvin, a former captain in the regiment, notes that "as the summer dragged slowly along under a Washington sun in June and July of 1865, they [men of the unit] took French leave of their lousy encampment and returned to their homes" (391). Although their impatience was understandable, the actions of those men who went home without leave jeopardized their futures. Without the proper discharge papers, Union soldiers could not receive any back pay or be eligible for future veteran's benefits such as land grants and pensions. Knowledge of this encouraged many soldiers to wait, no matter how "lousy" conditions were in their demobilization camps and how impatient they were to go home.

Confederate demobilization, in contrast to the orderly and bureaucratic process established by the northern army, was ad hoc in nature. Little, if any, higher authorities remained by May of 1865 to direct the dismantling of the Confederate armies. State and local governments had been ravaged by Union attacks as well as the heavy demands for soldiers at the front that drained away men needed for administrative duties. Furthermore, the southern national government had officially collapsed with the capture of Jefferson Davis on May 10, 1865. The South was also one vast battleground with its infrastructure in ruins making travel of any kind difficult. Consequently, once southern units had surrendered and received their paroles from Union authorities, men simply headed home using whatever means of transport were available. Holberton notes that "the tendency was for men to travel in groups small enough to encourage local people to donate food and yet large enough to discourage any violence on the part of roving gangs" (146). George Henry Mills, a former Captain of the 16th North Carolina, recalled telling his men that "they had better get away from that crowd as soon as possible, as I had fears that they would suffer for food if they kept with it [and] that I expected to take the first road I saw leading to the right" (70). Captain Mills walked what he estimated to be a total of 310 miles from the site of his unit's surrender (Appomattox, Virginia) to his home town of Rutherfordton, North Carolina. For units fighting closer to their home states, getting home was relatively easy but so was the temptation to desert. Although desertion occurred in significant numbers in both armies, in the southern army it played a major role in the demobilization process. With fewer soldiers in the ranks, Confederate demobilization pressures were eased and there was less need for advanced planning.

The final commander of the 10th South Carolina, C.I. Walker noted that he and his men started for South Carolina on the January 19, 1865, adding: "It was to be our privilege to aid in the defence [sic] of the State against our old enemy, Sherman" (130). As Johnston's army, of which the 10th South Carolina was a part, began to retreat from South Carolina, it was harder for commanders like Walker to keep their men in the ranks. They were, after all, husbands, fathers, and brothers long before they were soldiers and Sherman was attacking their homes and families. In addition, many soldiers already sensed by January of 1865 that the end was near and decided not to wait for official discharge. Despite the fact that accurate statistics are hard to come by, anecdotal evidence indicates that desertion took a heavy toll on Confederate regiments in the last months of the war. Walker notes with some pride that members of his own regiment, the 10th South Carolina, did not succumb to the temptation to desert, but they did take the extraordinary measure of giving themselves five days leave without the approval of higher command. This unauthorized "leave of absence" was not strictly speaking desertion because the men came back and it was tacitly sanctioned by the officers who realized that most men "had not been home since they left South Carolina in 1862" (Walker 132). In the last year of the war, honor and duty to one's comrades were the primary forces that kept soldiers from permanently deserting. This was especially true when one's home was under assault. Once their paroles were signed, however, units rapidly melted away and the fabled armies of the Confederacy disappeared faster than they had been raised.

Contemporary observers in both the United States and in Europe marveled at the speed of army demobilization and the relatively peaceful manner in which it was taking place. Concerning northern demobilization, the New York *Herald* remarked that "a short time ago the thought of this disbandment and of the return of these soldiers to their Northern homes filled many persons with alarm. These were fears justified to some extent by the experience of other countries that had suddenly disbanded large armies. But our experience has been very different from that of any other country in this respect ("Coming Home from the Wars" 4). Although many civilians and a significant number of soldiers agreed with the *Herald* and saw the end of the army demobilization process as essentially marking the end of veteran reintegration, there was still a heightened sense of anxiety amongst the civilian populace about the return home of soldiers at the end of war. Newspapers across the nation but especially in the North spoke hysterically about everything from a potential coup d'état by former northern generals and the possibility of permanent guerilla warfare in the South to the fear of a post-war crime wave and acts of public drunkenness carried on by demoralized former soldiers. The men coming home from the armies did little to justify these fears, but the civilian anxiety of the early post-war years suggests an awareness that veteran reintegration would not be easy. Already in the months following the surrender there were intimations that it would take more than dismantling an army to turn a soldier back into a civilian.

Somewhat paradoxically, the presence of thousands of disabled veterans assisted in alleviating civilian anxiety regarding the return home of former soldiers. These men, commonly referred to by the phrase "the empty sleeve," suggested an avenue for civilian emotions and more importantly restored to the civilian populace a sense of agency that was lost during the war years. Rather than remain nervous about the fate of the nation following army demobilization and the end of the war, civilians could work to heal the wounds of war in its heroic victims. Former soldiers quickly came to resent this civilian attitude, which they saw as an attempt to turn them into helpless dependents by labeling all veterans as victims. In part, this emotion was responsible for the period of "hibernation" during the 1870s referred to by the historian Gerald Linderman in his book *Embattled Courage*. Linderman notes that "returned soldiers felt impelled to turn rapidly from the war ... they decided to say whatever would cause the least discomfort to themselves and others—little or nothing" (268). Rather than reminisce about the war, veterans largely ignored it in the years immediately following the conflict, seeking out jobs and peacetime careers as soon as they could after demobilization to prove both to themselves and others that they had not been negatively affected by the war. They viewed themselves first and foremost as civilians, having become soldiers only for the duration of the war. Like the hero of John William De Forest's Civil War novel *Miss Ravenel's Conversion from Secession to Loyalty* (1867), the Union Captain Edward Colburne, veterans wanted to believe that the same initiative that allowed them as amateur soldiers (i.e., citizen-soldier volunteers) to "face the flame of battle" would help them to "also earn [their] own living" (467) now that the war was over.

Veterans and civilians alike viewed economic achievement as the touchstone of successful re-entry into civil society. But the equation of economic achievement with successful veteran reintegration occurred at the worst possible time. The American economy was undergoing massive changes in the early years after the war. What had once been a predominantly rural and agricultural economy had industrialized seemingly overnight, making obsolete the older model of "artisanal manhood," which depended upon the dominance of small-scale business and family farms. As veterans struggled to find work in the post-war economy that fit within this older model of masculinity, they experienced a sense of culture shock that has been attributed by the historian Robert Wiebe to the "the death of the Island Community" (44). Wiebe notes that although "a majority of Americans would still reside in relatively small, personal centers for several decades more, the society that had been premised upon the community's effective sovereignty, upon its capacity to manage affairs within its boundaries, no longer functioned" (44). With small towns giving way to the urban industrial metropolis of the modern age, the values that were associated with these antebellum towns seemed to lack relevance, while at the same time they increasingly became subjects of idealization. Rather than accept these changes as permanent, there were increasing calls for a return to a better time in the nation's history, one that typically was associated with the island communities that had existed in the decades before the advent of the Civil War.

Veterans shared with the civilian populace this nostalgia for the simpler and seemingly more whole world that had supposedly preceded the war. In fact, many civilians saw veterans of the war as the embodiment of those supposedly better times. As David Blight argues, "former soldiers were the living reminders that the current society, however drab and materialistic, had evolved out of a more heroic time" (172). Civil War veterans thus offered to the nation an alternative to "the unheroic culture of the Gilded Age" (Blight 188). Together, civilians and soldiers mourned the death of the island communities of their youth, but former soldiers felt the gap between the ideals they carried with them into the war and the world they reentered at the war's end more acutely than the general populace. If the war had changed the nation irrevocably, the implication was that they had permanently been changed as well. These growing doubts and disillusionment that accompanied the economic struggles of veterans, and their related belief that the nation was heading in the wrong direction, served as a catalyst for the Civil War memoir boom of the 1880s. Former soldiers turned to the past as an antidote to the disappointments of the present. Their memoirs, however, were also meditations on the relationship between the pieces of their past and present selves. What reconciliation meant to the nation at large is well documented, having been called by contemporary historians such as David Blight and Nina Silber a "culture of conciliation" that sought to reunite whites in the North and South after the war at the expense of African Americans. The meaning of reconciliation to Civil War veterans, however, was more personal and urgent than the demands of nationalist nostalgia. In the writing of memoirs, veterans hoped to put to rest the painful memories of the past and reunite their increasingly fractured sense of self.

The urgency of the narrative reminiscences of Civil War veterans is well illustrated in the works of Ambrose Bierce, a former captain in the 9th Indiana, who wrote about the war in both fiction and non-fiction genres. Bierce was obsessed by the war and particularly with the haphazard nature of combat, which frequently brought with it sudden and un-heroic death. This haphazard quality is addressed in many of Bierce's works, but its significance becomes especially apparent in the biographical sketch "What I Saw of Shiloh." Published three times between the years 1874 and 1898, Bierce's retelling of the same story in print over a period of twenty-five years suggests that the need to piece together the fragments of the combat experience was just as important to him as the desire to prove that war is made up of a series of discrete sense perceptions rather than some grand strategic design. By creating a coherent portrait of battles like Shiloh, Bierce hoped to reconcile the events of the past to his life in the present, and position his current self in relation to the one that existed during the war. Bierce knew that he had been changed by the war and wanted desperately to understand those changes, but, ultimately, he was only capable of reliving through narrative the events that caused those changes rather than interpreting them. Like many other Civil War veterans in the closing years of the nineteenth century, Bierce was left with the sense that he was different from the general population without fully understanding what that difference meant.

Union veteran and future Supreme Court Justice Oliver Wendell Holmes articulated this dilemma poignantly in a Memorial Day speech given to the John Sedgwick Post No. 4 of the Grand Army of the Republic in May of 1884. In that speech, Holmes told his comrades that "the generation that carried on the war has been set apart by its experience. In our youth our hearts were touched with fire" (15). Borrowing from the biblical imagery of the Pentecost, Holmes explained the changes to his sense of self and that of his comrades in terms of belief. They had remained faithful to the pre-war vision of the nation for which they fought, and this faith is what made the changes to their sense of self positive. Chosen rather than chastened, Civil War veterans began to view themselves as superior to the general population. Although most veterans did not feel hostile toward civilians, they saw in them a different breed, a debased version of the American self that fit the diminished age they currently inhabited. Somewhat ironically, after decades of arguing that they were no different than anyone else, former soldiers finally embraced their difference and chose to interpret it as a sign of their indestructible tie to the true America that was rapidly passing away.

Historian James Marten notes the emergence of this rhetorical ploy on the part of Civil War veterans and christens it "veteranizing." Here, Marten suggests two things. First, that former soldiers of the Civil War were engaged in a timeless activity as old as war itself, telling anyone willing to listen about their battlefield prowess, and second, that their claims represented the harmless ramblings of old men desperately trying to hide from themselves their growing debility. He says that old soldiers chose to focus on "their wartime service as opposed to their need, their disabilities, and their age—qualities that highlighted their loss of manliness" (249). Even though there is evidence that focusing on their war service helped veterans to overlook post-war disappointments, Marten's view lessens the true power of what these former soldiers were claiming. Far from being an innocuous rant, their rhetoric set in motion lasting changes to the nation's understanding both of what it meant to be a veteran as well as a man. War became understood as a threshold that once crossed could never be undone. One would, despite outward appearance and circumstances, always be a "veteran," trapped in a no-man's land between the status of soldier and that of civilian. Yet at the same time, this no-man's land was romanticized as the pinnacle of masculinity. Real men were born in the crucible of war.

This rhetoric of veteran transcendence inspired a later generation of white men not to engage in the "holy" or just war envisioned by men like Holmes, but rather to search for any war—a war of their own to prove that they too were a breed set apart. Thereby, when the last of the Civil War generation soon passed away, the younger generation would prove worthy to take their place. The inter-generational struggle associated with this quest for "veteran-ness," as the older generation of warriors refused to die off at a rate acceptable to the younger, added yet another dimension to the already complex relationship between Civil War veterans and civilians. Signs of this struggle are visible throughout the Civil War writings of Stephen Crane as well as in the pension debate articles that flooded the newspapers during the late 1880s and 1890s. It reflected a shift in the nation's relationship both to the war and those who fought in its battles. Ironically, by the turn of the century, the veteran ethos constructed by the Civil War veteran gained in value while former soldiers themselves began to be viewed as a financial and cultural burden.

An awareness of the divide that existed between soldiers and civilians after the war changes how we understand the rhetoric of reconciliation that dominated the period following Reconstruction. It suggests that veterans in the North and South had more in common with each other than they did with the civilian authorities who used them as examples of post-war national harmony. This awareness also changes how we understand the issue of race relations in the years following the war. Because many of them were already confined to the margins of American society by direct and indirect forms of racism, African American veterans did not have the ability to write and publish their wartime experiences in the same quantities as did former white soldiers. White racism alone, however, is not sufficient to explain the curious absence of the African American soldier from the cultural discourse and imagery of the post-war nation. The concept of "racial uplift" or "improvement of the race" was highly influential within African American communities following the Civil War.

Seeking to address charges from the white community that they were part of an undeveloped race that was unprepared for full citizenship in a democracy, African Americans looked for exemplars both to prove their critics wrong and also offer role models for the rising generation. As "freedom's soldiers," African American veterans would seem to fit that role perfectly, but the way that these veterans chose to write about their experiences and the way their narratives were received within the African American community suggest that internal tensions as well as external ones may have contributed to the invisibility of former African American soldiers in the late-nineteenth century. Of the narratives that were written by African American veterans of the Civil War, those by William Wells Brown—*The Negro in the American Rebellion* (1867)—and George Washington Williams—*A History of the Negro Troops in the War of the Rebellion* (1887)—are the best known. Both are constructed as alternative histories that challenged existing interpretations of the war by reminding their readers about the centrality of "negro troops" in the struggle. Remembering that role, however, necessitated recalling the indignities as well as the honors connected with that military service. Denied equal pay, the opportunity to become officers, and, in many cases, used as laborers rather than combat troops, service as a Union soldier often bore little resemblance to freedom and even looked a little like slavery under a different name.

These indignities were a reminder that "black soldiers fought a different war" as they faced "enemies on two fronts, battling against the blue as well as the gray to achieve freedom and equality" (Berlin 26). Wells and Williams tried to prevent the memory of these humiliations from derailing the overall intent of their work by keeping their portrait of African American involvement in the war fairly distant and generic, not looking in any depth at the experience of particular soldiers. Nevertheless, the ambiguous status of the African American soldier, even as a generic figure, during the war remained to haunt his legacy and made him a dubious role model to the emerging generations of African American men after the war. Soldiering had initially been understood, especially by former slaves, "as a launching pad for political rights" (H.A. Williams 197). Presaging the disappointments that would follow the end of Reconstruction, the wartime indignities faced by African American soldiers soon made it clear that military service could not erase the problems faced by the African American community. New role models and other means would be needed to achieve the improvement of the race thought necessary for full citizenship and racial equality. The ambiguous social status of the African American soldier and the fact that it followed him into his post-war life helps explain why civilian authors within the African American community who were otherwise quick to praise exemplars of African American manhood, such as Frances Watkins Harper and Charles Chesnutt, would avoid portraying soldiers at all in favor of the civilian professional careers of ministers, doctors, lawyers, and teachers.

In the decades following the Civil War, veterans' issues (white and black, North and South) were gradually subsumed within larger social concerns involving race and regional reconciliation. This helped hide the growing rift between former soldiers and civilians that had developed in the decades following the war, which was signified by veterans' claims for a distinct and superior identity to the general populace. Fears that just such a rift would develop had surfaced not long after the war in civilian anxiety regarding army demobilization and the future role of soldiers once they had left the army. The emerging divide between former soldiers and civilians was primarily the result, however, of the growing disillusionment felt by many veterans as they struggled to match the ideals they carried into battle with the post-war world they now inhabited. Deep-rooted psychic scars only served to intensify this disillusionment, making veterans wonder about the value of their sacrifices and suffering, and increased the urgency of the demand to balance the unresolved past with the needs of the present. Veterans gradually came to believe that they had been chosen for

greatness as a way to achieve closure, to make sense of the otherwise meaning-
less events of the war and to justify the discrepancy between the world they
expected to emerge from the war and the one that actually did. Decades after
the war, veterans still did not see themselves as civilians. Instead, they understood themselves to be veterans, an identity that assured them of the meaning
and value of their sacrifice while it forced the nation to consider, for a brief
period of time, the exact nature of the relationship between the former soldier
and civil society.

## Further Reading

Berlin, Ira, Joseph P. Reidy, and Leslie S. Rowland, eds. *Freedom's Soldiers: The Black Military Experience in the Civil War.* New York: Cambridge University Press, 1998.

Bierce, Ambrose. *Phantoms of a Blood Stained Period: The Complete Civil War Writings of Ambrose Bierce.* Russell Duncan and David Klooster, eds. Amherst: University of Massachusetts Press, 2002.

Blight, David. *Race and Reunion: The Civil War in American Memory.* Cambridge: Harvard University Press, 2001.

Brown, William Wells. *The Negro in the American Rebellion: His Heroism and His Fidelity.* Boston: Lee & Shepard, 1867.

"Coming Home from the Wars: The Orderly Conduct of the Soldiers." *The New York Herald.* June 14, 1865: 4.

De Forest, John William. *Miss Ravenel's Conversion from Secession to Loyalty.* New York: Penguin Books, 2000.

Holberton, William. *Homeward Bound: The Demobilization of the Union and Confederate Armies, 1865–1866.* Mechanicsville: Stackpole Books, 2001.

Holmes, Oliver Wendell. *The Occasional Speeches of Justice Oliver Wendell Holmes.* Cambridge: Harvard University Press, 1962.

Linderman, Gerald. *Embattled Courage: The Experience of Combat in the American Civil War.* New York: The Free Press, 1987.

Marten, James. *Sing Not War: The Lives of Union and Confederate Veterans in Gilded Age America.* Chapel Hill: University of North Carolina Press, 2011.

Marvin, Edwin E. *The Fifth Regiment Connecticut Volunteers. A History Compiled from Diaries and Official Reports.* Hartford: Wiley, Waterman, and Eaton, 1889.

McClurken, Jeffrey W. *Take Care of the Living: Reconstructing Confederate Veteran Families in Virginia.* Charlottesville: University of Virginia Press, 2009.

Mills, George Henry. *History of the 16th North Carolina Regiment in the Civil War.* Hamilton: Edmonston Publishing, Inc., 1992.

Silber, Nina. *The Romance of Reunion: Northerners and the South, 1865–1900.* Chapel Hill: University of North Carolina Press, 1993.

Warren, Craig. *Scars to Prove It: the Civil War Soldier and American Fiction.* Kent: Kent State University Press, 2009.

Walker, C.I. *Rolls and Historical Sketch of the Tenth Regiment, South Carolina. Volunteers in the Army of the Confederate States.* Charleston: Walker, Evans, and Cogswell, 1881.

Wiebe, Robert H. *The Search For Order, 1877–1920.* New York: Hill and Wang, 1967.

Williams, George Washington. *A History of the Negro Troops in the War of the Rebellion, 1861–1865.* New York: Harper & Brothers, 1887.

Williams, Heather Andrea. "'Commenced to Think Like a Man': Literacy and Manhood in African American Civil War Regiments." In *Southern Manhood: Perspectives on Masculinity in the Old South.* Eds. Craig Thompson Friend and Lorri Glover. Athens: University of Georgia Press, 2004. 196–219.

# 29

# COMPETING MEMORIES

*James M. Gillispie*

In April 1865, the military phase of the Civil War effectively ended when the Confederacy's two principle armies, the Army of Northern Virginia and the Army of Tennessee surrendered to Generals Ulysses S. Grant and William T. Sherman, respectively. However, the result was not immediately accepted by everyone in the South. Jefferson Davis fled Virginia insisting that the Confederacy had not died at all and was still capable of achieving some manner of independence, until his own capture in Georgia a few weeks later. A few small units, mostly in the trans-Mississippi region, did not immediately give up the cause, but even for those die-hards the inevitable conclusion that they had lost their bid for independence was not long in coming as they stacked arms and rejoined the United States by the time summer arrived. The few desperate cries for a guerilla campaign fell on mostly deaf ears and were actively discouraged by Robert E. Lee and other realistic leaders. As the weather heated up in late spring of 1865, the reality was clear to all; the North had won and the South had lost the Civil War.

In many ways, the spring and summer of 1865 represented a conclusive end to the North–South conflict and settled many of the questions and issues that had spawned it in the first place. It represented the end of the South's attempt to establish itself as a separate nation. It ended the institution of slavery in the country, proving that Lincoln had been right about the country not being able to long endure half slave and half free. The end of the war also firmly established that the United States was an indivisible nation ultimately governed from Washington rather than a league of sovereign states with the right to do as they pleased. This new reality was even represented in language with the United States being transformed from a plural to a singular noun in the years following the Civil War.

If the spring of 1865 brought an end to the shooting war between North and South, it marked the beginning of a new cultural cold war between the regions. Northerners and Southerners understood that they had just lived through one of the great events, arguably the greatest, most important event, in American history and they wanted to make sure that it was properly interpreted and remembered. Of course, "properly" was defined very differently by Northerners and Southerners. Members of the war generation (along with many of their descendants) were not particularly interested in promoting an objective accounting of the Civil War's causes, events, and results. More often than not, the war was presented as the great epic American saga, the American *Iliad*. Both regions' inhabitants were determined to establish that their perspective on what the Civil War represented was the correct one and to assure that present and future generations of Americans looked most favorably on their respective cause.

The result was, in a very real sense, two Civil Wars. From the North's point of view, the war was to be remembered as one that was waged not only to preserve the United States from destruction but one that redeemed the nation by eradicating slavery. The Union cause had been the cause of democracy and freedom; Northerners had been the good guys in this version of the American *Iliad*. Confederates, on the other hand, had launched an immoral war to defend an immoral institution and had often fought dirty to achieve their traitorous ends; they were the bad guys. After the war, Southerners played down the slavery issue and presented the war as one to preserve the sacred principle of states' rights from the centralizing tyranny that had taken over the North. In the Confederate version of the American *Iliad*, Southerners had been the good guys, had always fought chivalrously, and were, ultimately, victimized by a numerically superior vandal horde that ignored all the rules of civilized warfare to subjugate the South. The regional cold war that began in 1865 for control of the war's popular memory was a vicious one that has influenced, and often clouded, our understanding of the Civil War.

For Northerners, victory in the war vindicated antebellum claims of moral and cultural superiority over the benighted South. As one historian has noted, "The final defeat of [the Confederacy] allowed the Yankees to ... proclaim again their superiority in matters of war, leadership, and culture" (Silber 18). Indeed, Northerners fully expected their defeated foemen to offer a complete repudiation of the Confederacy. White Northerners, like most Americans at the time, entered the war viewing it within a millennial framework—a sort of Old Testament style, or probably more accurately, an old Germanic trial by ordeal of good versus evil. The message emanating from Northern pulpits just prior and during the war had been loud and clear: the war was a holy crusade against heretics. Ministers such as Henry Ward Beecher told Unionist listeners not to fear the war because God would intervene on the North's behalf because its cause was the righteous one. Fighting against the sinful South was, according to Beecher and others, God's work. Mid-nineteenth century Americans saw the hand of

God in practically everything and their interpretations of events and history reflected that: the victory over the British during the Revolution had been part of God's plan to bring about a democratic republic on earth; westward expansion, America's "Manifest Destiny," was seen by many as a sort of holy mission for His special people; the suppression of the South and the preservation of the United States that God had established was something akin to a crusade, and the crusade's foes were enemies of God as well as the United States.

Of course, during wartime any and all negative propaganda about one's enemy is generally accepted at face value as unvarnished truth, while the actions of one's own government and soldiers are perceived and presented as above reproach or at least justifiable. This was certainly the case in the North after 1865 as Union veterans began writing and talking about their experiences of the greatest event in American history since the Revolution. For the next half-century veterans and their supporters churned out a massive amount of material about the Civil War. Accounts of battles were numerous, but many veterans also focused on other aspects of soldier life—camp life, marches, forms of recreation. One area that received close attention was how Union soldiers suffered in Confederate military prisons. Better than any other, this issue illustrated the Northern cause as a great world-battle wherein moral and patriotic Northerners had triumphed over a truly corrupt and inhumane society, thus cleansing and strengthening the nation. As historian William Marvel puts it, with reference to the South's notorious prison in Andersonville, Georgia, "Andersonville came to signify all that was evil in the hated Confederacy" (xi).

Having heard from Southerners for at least a generation how much more chivalrous, noble, Christian, and gentlemanly they were in comparison to selfish, money grubbing, amoral Yankees, Northerners seemed to enjoy attacking that image using Andersonville terror tales for their ammunition. One veteran said that the treatment he and his comrades received in Confederate hands were "defiant to the principles of Christianity," which he suggested did not exist in the South (Hamlin 150). Another ex-prisoner railed that the manner in which he was treated by the "chivalrous" gentlemen of the South "would disgrace the wild Arab of the Sahara" (Roach 62). In 1886 a former Andersonville inmate said the South "boasted of its chivalry, and yet no tribe of savages was ever guilty of greater barbarity" (Long 195). The way Confederate officials treated helpless Union prisoners, one wrote, was "revolting to every Christian civilization except that of the chivalrous slaveholding South" (Abbott 316). Northerners all agreed that Andersonville would forever stand as a monument "to the everlasting shame of ... the South, its chivalry and its humanity" (Spencer 108).

Far and away the most common specific charge made against the South's prison camps and officials after the war was that the guards routinely shot prisoners without provocation. Northern veterans frequently portrayed Confederate guards as trigger happy fiends who delighted in murdering Yankees for fun. One writer came to the conclusion that a "thirst for blood" was a basic character flaw Southerners suffered from and put many a Union prisoner in an early grave (Glazier 124). Another former prisoner claimed that, when the train for Andersonville stopped, he witnessed a prisoner get shot dead merely for stepping out of line to relieve himself. Yet another claimed that he frequently saw prisoners murdered for singing patriotic songs to keep their spirits up. For post-war Northerners, the evidence of pure, cold-blooded murder of helpless prisoners of war proved that good had triumphed over evil.

Post-war Northern accounts of life at places like Andersonville used alleged instances of guards murdering prisoners not as isolated events but rather to illustrate the depraved and immoral nature of the Confederacy. Guards mowed down prisoners and knew they would not be punished for it because it was not considered wrong to shoot an unarmed Yankee. In fact, not only did guards know they would not be punished for shooting prisoners for no reason, they could expect to be rewarded for doing so. Memoirs frequently claimed that homicidal Southern guards were rewarded with furloughs and even promotions for randomly killing prisoners. One ex-prisoner told readers that Confederate officials considered killing Northern prisoners a "very *virtuous deed*" and that he saw promotions and furloughs given out as rewards for successful shots (Kellogg 146).

Some Northern writers pointed out that to be murdered by a guard or a surgeon was at least a quick death. Lessel Long expressed the opinion that it "would have been doing many a poor boy a good service if they had ... drawn [the prisoners] up in a line and shot them, instead of torturing them by the slow process of starvation and exposure" (179). Another writer claimed that soldiers went mad because they were not given enough food to keep body and soul together. Confederate policy makers in Richmond were routinely charged in post-war narratives with formulating a fiendish plan to withhold rations not because the South was struggling to feed itself as the war progressed but as a means to systematically starve Union soldiers unlucky enough to become prisoners of war. As one Northern veteran argued, Richmond's policies "seemed to be to unfit us as much as possible for future service, [so] they cut down our scant half rations to one-half the usual quantity" (Hernbaker and Lynch 4).

Not only were Union prisoners allegedly denied medical care and adequate food as a matter of Confederate policy, cruel Southern officials, especially at Andersonville, apparently denied them shelter from the elements. At Andersonville, one survivor reported, all the trees that could have afforded some protection from the summer heat were cut down in order to increase prisoners' suffering. There were plenty of trees that could have been cut down and given to the prisoners to make shelter with, but having the inmates bake in the sizzling Georgia sun and shiver on cool, damp nights seemed part of the diabolical Confederate plot to weaken and kill prisoners of war. Thanks to a lack of protection from the extreme heat, one prisoner said that many inmates' bare feet became horribly and painfully blistered. To have refused to provide even rudimentary shelter at Andersonville, where plenty of materials existed and where, according to one ex-prisoner, the temperatures routinely reached between 120 and 140 degrees, signaled how barbaric, unchivalrous and unchristian the Old South culture had been.

In the decades following the surrender of Lee and Johnston in April 1865, northern writers accused southern officials of having purposefully chosen the most unhealthy sites imaginable for their prison pens. Belle Isle, an island in the James River near Richmond, "seemed to have been chosen for its capability of adding to the wretchedness to which our brave men were compelled to submit" (Sabre 23). Northerners often claimed that General John Winder, the Confederate official in charge of prison policies, picked Andersonville as a site because he knew of its horrible heat and tainted water supply. Writers argued that the stream running through the stockade at Andersonville, that was to provide the prisoners with their drinking water, was "well known in that country [to be] the prolific parent of disease and death" (Spencer 20). A more colorful writer described the stream as "a serpent, breathing death, its mouth full of corrosive poison" (Beard 184). These horrors were part of the plan, according to post-war writers, who maintained that Winder intended to kill more Yankees with Andersonville than died in battle. Winder apparently figured that he would be able to weaken the Northern cause as well as any of the armies in the field by exposing thousands of prisoners to extreme heat and forcing them to rely on a lone contaminated water source for cooking and drinking. Winder is often portrayed as being quite pleased with his ability to kill or at least debilitate the equivalent of entire Yankee divisions by cramming them into his pen in Georgia, and so symbolizes in post-war narratives the morally bankrupt Confederate cause.

Even Southern physicians did their part to kill as many Northerners as possible, claimed post-war accounts. According to an account entitled *The Demon of Andersonville*, which detailed numerous atrocities perpetrated on defenseless prisoners, surgeons poisoned inmates on the pretext of vaccinating them against smallpox. One 1870 narrative claimed that not only were prisoners poisoned, but many were injected with an hereditary disease so that survivors of captivity would return to the North to infect, weaken, and kill Yankees for generations. Another former prisoner claimed shortly after the war that Andersonville doctors ran a "dissecting house" where they performed "experiments" on human guinea pigs (Kellogg 256). No details about the "experiments" were provided, in order to allow Northern imaginations to supply gruesome images. Yet another account claimed that doctors at Andersonville performed amputations on fully conscious prisoners for fun.

Most of the Andersonville terror tales confine themselves to demonizing the Confederate cause and the society that supported it but many also take the extra time to remind (Northern) readers that the precarious and often terrifying ordeal Union prisoners endured for their sacred cause stood in stark contrast to Confederate prisoners' treatment in Union military prisons. A number of accounts portray Confederate prisoners as enjoying great kindness and care in Yankee prisons. With the war scarcely over, one commentator argued that while "our men in southern prisons were dying from starvation and exposure, the rebels in northern prisons fared sumptuously every day... and received the respect and civility due them as prisoners of war" (Roach 67). This same writer went so far as to compare the officers' prison at Johnson's Island, Ohio, to "a first class hotel" (Roach 67). A few years later, in the mid-1880s, a Union veteran claimed that Union prisons were entirely free from "any complaint of inhumanity such as disgraced the cause of the southern Confederacy" (Long 199). That Union prisoners did not receive the same magnanimity that Northerners supposedly showered upon lucky Confederate prisoners, made Southern policies, and through them the Southern cause and society, seem more repugnant in Northern minds. Exposing the "horrors" of Andersonville and juxtaposing them with pleasant prisons run by the Federals was a much-used method to control popular memory of the Civil War and assure that present and future generations of Americans knew exactly which cause had been wholly righteous.

Exaggerating and even fabricating tales of life in Southern prisons may have been fine for the North's veterans and the public, but white Southerners deeply resented Northerners' manipulation of the prisoner of war issue to brand them, their region, and their cause as immoral, barbaric, and dishonorable. While condescending and insulting attitudes from the North were nothing new, former Confederates felt their sting more acutely in the wake of defeat. White Southerners reacted to post-war insults as they had to the antebellum variety, by turning them on their heads. If Northerners would use the treatment of prisoners as the litmus test to prove which side embodied noble, Christian characteristics, Southerners would do the same.

Former Confederates did not want to be remembered as traitors or as members of a degraded society who had been defeated by a righteous foe. Many Southerners feared that the victors' version of history would become the official narrative of the Civil War. If the victors' version emerged triumphant, Richmond editor Edward A. Pollard worried that Southerners would feel ashamed of themselves and would want to abandon their traditional culture to become more like their Northern counterparts: "It would be immeasurably the worst consequence of defeat in this war," he wrote in 1866, "that the South should lose its moral and intellectual distinctiveness as a people, and cease to assert its well-known superiority in civilization ... and in all the standards of individual character over the people of the North" (751). Jefferson Davis expressed the concern of many Southerners, warning: "Men live in the estimation of posterity not by their deeds alone, but by their historians also" (United Daughters of the Confederacy 86). To make sure that the victors' history was not the only available narrative, Davis wrote his massive version of events, *The Rise and Fall of the Confederate Government* (1881). He made no claims about historical objectivity; this was going to be the pro-Confederate side of the war. By his own admission, the project was undertaken to celebrate the Confederate cause.

This attempt by Davis and other Southerners to portray the Confederacy as a romantic and glorious crusade countered the attempt by Northerners to portray Confederates as immoral and failures. An additional battle was over the divine meaning of the war. During the conflict, both sides had believed that God would grant victory to the righteous side. Southerners entered the war believing that the Confederate cause was the righteous one and therefore it was only a matter of when, not if, victory was achieved. Throughout the war, Southerners clung to the idea that they could not lose because God was a Confederate and would not permit the immoral Yankee vandals to prevail. The famous diarist Mary Chesnut recorded how she often heard women talk of how victory was inevitable because "God is on our side." Whenever she asked how they could be so sure that God was pro-South, she consistently received the answer: "Of course, He hates Yankees" (38). Even late in the war Confederate General Stephen Dodson Ramseur encouraged his brother to keep his spirits up, reminding him that they were "bound to succeed. The God of Justice will order all things for the good" (Gallagher 51).

When the South's two principle armies surrendered in 1865, Southerners faced an intellectual dilemma. On the one hand, there seemed to be evidence that God had not looked favorably on the South, and that the Richmond authorities had been brutal and unchristian towards helpless prisoners of war. On the other hand, ex-Confederates found it difficult to accept that God favored the hated Yankees or that Southern honor had been sullied by gross mistreatment of prisoners. Southerners resolved the intellectual crisis by creating a model for interpreting and remembering the Civil War era that came to be known as the Lost Cause. This interpretive model allowed Southerners to take pride in their Confederate past in part by denying that God had played a role in the military outcome and by arguing that the true story of how prisoners were treated showed the South had been humane and Christian (while Northerners had been the true demons). How each side prosecuted the war and conducted itself in battle became more important in the Lost Cause model than ultimate victory or defeat. The model taught, among other things, that losing carried no stigma and could even be called heroic and glorious if one fought nobly and chivalrously against a huge and unprincipled enemy who believed no barbarity was outside the boundaries of civilized warfare. In this way, Southerners of the war generation could hold their heads high. God had not forsaken them nor determined that there was some fatal flaw in Southern society. Rather defeat was the result of the North's overwhelming material and economic resources. "Your people whipped us," one former Confederate insisted, "because you had five times as many men as we had, and all the money and rations you wanted, and I don't think I ever heard that God gave one half-starved man the strength to whip five fully-fed men" (Foster 119). Such expressions were common in the region after the war and attempted to show that Northerners had won only because they had an unfair advantage.

The idea that defeat had been a sure sign of God's disapproval was tossed out in the Lost Cause model in favor of the idea that God often gives very difficult trials to those He most loves. "Defeat," a Richmond minister said in 1875 at the dedication of the monument there to Stonewall Jackson, "is the discipline which trains the truly heroic soul to further and better endeavors" (Wilson 23). As the South built an unapologetic pro-Southern memory of the Civil War era, Southerners were increasingly reminded that defeat, subjugation, and suffering at the hands of an enemy did not mean that their cause had been wrong in God's eyes. They also heard much about the North's dishonorable and immoral methods, especially Sherman's March to the Sea and Lee's Pennsylvania raid, and the South's honorable and moral conduct in battle. "To [Southerners'] everlasting honor," claimed one, "stands the fact that in their march through the enemy's country they left behind them no ruined homes, no private houses burned, no families cruelly robbed" (Foster 123). Post-war songs and poems depicted the South's leaders, including Lee and Jackson, not simply as gifted warriors but paragons of virtue and Christianity.

The prisoner of war issue figured prominently in this battle for how the Civil War would be remembered in the South, just as it was a major weapon in the North's arsenal. Andersonville atrocity stories potentially called Southern character and conduct during the war into serious question. Post-war Southerners were concerned and angry about Northern exploitation of Andersonville; losing the war had been bad enough, but portraying Southerners as fiendish, immoral, unchristian barbarians was too much salt for Southern wounds. Andersonville literature motivated a number of writers to counter the tales of Union veterans and other Northerners regarding Andersonville and other Confederate prisons. One former Tennessee Confederate admitted that there had been suffering at Andersonville, "but great as they were, they have been much exaggerated" (Clark 53). To provide a lasting and tangible reminder to future generations that Andersonville left no dishonorable stain upon the Confederate cause, a major effort was launched to erect a monument at the site of the former prison to Henry Wirz, a Confederate officer who commanded the Andersonville prison and was tried for conspiracy and murder between August and October 1865, then executed on November 10. Northern states' erection of markers to Andersonville victims played a role in these efforts. The desire to honor Wirz and declare in stone that he had been railroaded to the gallows was less about clearing Wirz's name than it was about clearing the Confederacy's name, and Lost Cause literature about Andersonville frequently tied Wirz's innocence to the South's.

But although Southerners did spend time and energy erasing the stain of Andersonville, far more was spent on hair-raising tales of unspeakable cruelty imposed on Confederate prisoners by their Yankee keepers. Showing that Union officials actively formulated and implemented policies to increase suffering and death offered solid proof that victory had not gone to the righteous or morally superior side in the Civil War. Hundreds of writers in the fifty years after Lee's surrender embarked on a mission to prove that Confederate prisoners were physically abused and denied adequate food, clothing, and shelter as a matter of policy throughout the war. A frequent theme was that Southerners were never given enough food to eat in Union prisons, even as the North was overflowing with food (unlike the blockaded and battle-scarred South). Yankees had the means to properly feed prisoners and keep them from starving to death but they *chose* to withhold food. Not coincidentally, this theme dovetailed nicely with the Lost Cause interpretation of Confederate defeat wherein the South was not beaten by a morally superior enemy but overwhelmed by a well-supplied and immoral foe.

Like Northern terror tales about Andersonville, Southern prisoner of war stories also contended that Confederate prisoners were routinely subjected to a variety of physical abuses. In these narratives Northerners beat and tortured helpless Southerners for pleasure. Guards were portrayed as regularly beating prisoners with sticks, belts, and fists, and prisoners attempting to defend themselves were certain to be shot. Northern prison guards would apparently suspend prisoners by the thumbs entirely off the ground until they died or their thumbs exploded, and often engage in cold-blooded murder. The most common way Union sentinels dispatched defenseless enemies was simply to shoot them down for no reason. One writer gave his opinion that "the practice of firing on our prisoners... appears to have been indulged in to a most brutal and atrocious extent" (Pollard 633). And just as in the Northern tales, Southern accounts accuse the authorities of rewarding murderous guards by promoting them and by granting furloughs. According to other accounts, a more insidious means of murdering Confederate prisoners, one that again mirrored Northern accusations, was a clumsy form of biological warfare: Union officials intentionally placed prisoners in camps where smallpox was raging. The more common germ warfare technique supposedly used was to inject Confederate prisoners with poison on the pretext of vaccinating them against smallpox. These accounts of torture and murder of Confederate prisoners of war demonstrated how truly cruel and immoral the Yankees had been during the war and reinforced the Lost Cause mantra that Northerners had refused to fight according the rules of civilized warfare.

In the final analysis, these prison narratives do not reveal what life was actually like in Civil War prisons. Narratives about Andersonville or the Union prisons Fort Delaware and Rock Island often do not match more objective wartime records. But by exploiting the explosive and emotional prisoner of war issue, both regions' citizens sought to prove that their prosecution of the Civil War, and therefore their cause, had been noble and honorable. These narratives demonstrate just how critical it was for Northerners and Southerners to exert control over the memory of the Civil War.

## Further Reading

Abbott, Allen O. *Prison Life in the South*. New York: Harper and Brothers, 1886.

Beard, Oliver Thomas. *Bristling With Thorns*. New York: Worthington Company, 1887.

Chesnut, Mary Boykin Miller. *A Diary from Dixie*. New York: D. Appleton and Company, 1905.

Clark, Reuben Grove. *Valleys of the Shadow: The Memoir of Confederate Captain Reuben G. Clark*. Knoxville: University of Tennessee Press, 1994.

Davis, Jefferson. *The Rise and Fall of the Confederate Government*. New York: D. Appleton and co., 1881.

Faust, Drew Gilpin. *The Creation of Confederate Nationalism: Ideology and Identity in the Civil War South*. Baton Rouge: Louisiana State University Press, 1988.

Foster, Gaines. *Ghosts of the Confederacy: Defeat, the Lost Cause, and the Emergence of the New South, 1865–1913*. New York: Oxford University Press, 1987.

Gallagher, Gary. *The Confederate War*. Cambridge: Harvard University Press, 1997.

Glazier, Willard W. *The Captive, the Prison Pen, and the Escape*. Hartford: H.E. Goodwin, 1868.

Hamlin, Augustus Choate. *Martyria; or Andersonville*. Boston: Lee and Shepard, 1866.

Hernbaker, Henry, and John Lynch. *True History: Jefferson Davis Answered. The Horrors of the Andersonville Prison Pen*. Philadelphia: Merrihew and Son, 1876.

Kellogg, Robert H. *Life and Death in Rebel Prisons: Giving a Complete History of the Inhuman and Barbarous Treatment of Our Brave Soldiers by Rebel Authorities*. Hartford: L. Stebbins, 1865.

Long, Lessel. *Twelve Months in Andersonville*. Huntington: Thad and Mark Butler, 1886.

Marvel, William. *Andersonville: The Last Depot*. Chapel Hill: University of North Carolina Press, 1994.

Pollard, Edward A. *The Lost Cause: A New Southern History of the War of the Confederates*. New York: E.B. Treat & Co, 1867.

Roach, Alva C. *The Prisoner of War and How Treated*. Indianapolis: Railroad City Publishing House, 1865.

Sabre, Gilbert E. *Nineteen Months a Prisoner of War*. New York: American News Co., 1865.

Silber, Nina. *The Romance of Reunion: Northerners and the South, 1865–1900*. Chapel Hill: University of North Carolina Press, 1993.

Spencer, Ambrose. *A Narrative of Andersonville*. New York: Harper and Brothers, 1866.

Sturgis, Thomas. *Prisoners of War, 1861–1865*. New York: Knickerbocker Press, 1912.

United Daughters of the Confederacy, North Carolina Division. *The Confederate Reveille, Memorial Edition*. Raleigh: Edwards & Broughton, 1898.

Wilson, Charles Reagan. *Baptized in Blood: The Religion of the Lost Cause, 1865–1920*. Athens: University of Georgia Press, 1980.

# ABOUT THE EDITORS

**Maggi M. Morehouse** is Professor of Southern History at Coastal Carolina University. She has a PhD in African Diaspora Studies from the University of California Berkeley. Her publications and films include *Fighting in the Jim Crow Army: Black Men and Women Remember World War II* (2000), *The African Diaspora: Using the Multivalent Theory to Understand Slave Autobiographies* (2007), *Smiling Faces, Beautiful Places: Stories of African Diaspora Relocation to the South* (2009), *Edgewood: Stage of Southern History* (2010), and *Military Service, Governance, and the African Diaspora* (2011).

**Zoe Trodd** is Professor and Chair of American Literature at the University of Nottingham in the Department of American and Canadian Studies. She has a PhD in The History of American Civilization from Harvard University and has taught at Columbia University and the University of North Carolina Chapel Hill. Her books include *Meteor of War* (2004), *American Protest Literature* (2006), *To Plead Our Own Cause* (2008), *Modern Slavery* (2009), and *The Tribunal: Responses to John Brown and the Harpers Ferry Raid* (2012).

# CONTRIBUTORS

**A.J. Angulo** is Associate Professor in the College of Education at Winthrop University. He received his doctorate from Harvard University where he was a Teaching Fellow in the history of education and the history of science. He is the author of *William Barton Rogers and the Idea of MIT*, which examines education, science, and technology in nineteenth-century America.

**Laura M. Ansley** is a graduate student in the History Department at The College of William & Mary.

**Shannon Smith Bennett** is a Future Faculty Teaching Fellow in the History Department at Indiana University-Purdue University Indianapolis, completing a PhD dissertation on rioting in the Lower Midwest during and after the Civil War.

**Lauren Brandt** is a lecturer in History and Literature and Allston Burr Resident Dean at Harvard University. She holds a PhD from Harvard's History of American Civilization program where she completed a dissertation entitled *Social Intercession: The Religious Nature of Public Activism among American Women Reformers in Boston, 1892 to 1930.*

**John Casey** holds a PhD in American literature from the University of Illinois at Chicago where he is currently a visiting lecturer. His dissertation, entitled *The Vanishing Civil War Veteran in Late Nineteenth-Century American Literature and Culture*, examined the veterans' experience during the post-Civil War era and how that experience shaped American culture after the war.

**Kimberly Cook** is an MA candidate in the College of Education at Winthrop University.

**Suanna H. Davis** received her PhD from Purdue University in Rhetoric and Composition. She teaches writing at all levels at Houston Baptist University.

**Nicole Keller Day** is a PhD candidate in the English Department at Northeastern University where she focuses on the history of science and nineteenth-century women's history and literature.

**W. Craig Gaines** is an independent scholar and the author of *The Confederate Cherokees; Civil War Gold and Other Lost Treasures;* and *Encyclopedia of Civil War Shipwrecks.*

**James M. Gillispie** is the division chair of Arts & Sciences at Sampson Community College in Clinton, North Carolina, where he has taught history since 1999. He earned a PhD in American History from the University of Mississippi, and is the author of *Andersonvilles of the North: The Myths and Realities of Northern Treatment of Civil War Confederate Prisoners,* and *Cape Fear Confederates: The 18th North Carolina Regiment in the Civil War.*

**Jack Hamilton** is a PhD candidate in Harvard University's History of American Civilization program where he is completing a dissertation on popular music and racial imagination in the 1960s. He has published articles on subjects ranging from bluegrass to professional basketball.

**Brayton Harris** is an independent scholar and the author of *War News: Blue & Gray in Black & White—Newspapers in the Civil War; Admiral Nimitz: The Commander of the Pacific Ocean Theater;* and *The Navy Times Book of Submarines: A Political, Social, and Military History.* He was also editor of *The Civil War: The Ironweed American Newspapers and Periodical Project.*

**Guy R. Hasegawa** is an independent scholar who works for the American Society of Health-System Pharmacists as an editor for the *American Journal of Health-System Pharmacy.* His books include *Years of Change and Suffering: Modern Perspectives on Civil War Medicine* and *Mending Broken Soldiers: The Union and Confederate Programs to Supply Artificial Limbs.*

**Sharon A. Roger Hepburn** is Professor of History and Chair of the History Department at Radford University. She received her doctorate in history at the University of Buffalo and is the author of *Crossing the Border: A Free Black Community in Canada.* She is working on a regimental history of the 102nd United States Colored Troops and its service in the Civil War.

**Mark A. Lause** is Professor of History at the University of Cincinnati. He is the author of *Race and Radicalism in the Union Army; Young America: Land, Labor, and the Republican Community*; and *The Civil War's Last Campaign: James B. Weaver, the Greenback-Labor Party and the Politics of Race and Section*, among several other books.

**Thomas Lawrence Long** is Associate Professor-in-Residence in the School of Nursing at the University of Connecticut. He holds a PhD from Indiana University of Pennsylvania and is the author of *AIDS and American Apocalypticism: The Cultural Semiotics of an Epidemic.*

**Megan Kate Nelson** is a lecturer in History and Literature at Harvard University. She has a PhD in American Studies from the University of Iowa and has taught at Texas Tech University and California State University, Fullerton. She is the author of *Trembling Earth: A Cultural History of the Okefenokee Swamp* and *Ruin Nation: Destruction and the American Civil War.*

**Jennifer Raab** is an Andrew W. Mellon Postdoctoral Fellow at New York University's Institute of Fine Arts where she is completing a book titled *The Art and Science of Detail: Frederic Church and Nineteenth-Century Landscape Painting.* She holds a PhD in the History of Art from Yale University.

**Daniel Rasmussen** is an independent scholar and the author of *American Uprising: The Untold Story of America's Largest Slave Revolt.*

**Rachel Redfern** is an independent scholar who has published articles on women's history and legal history.

**Mandy A. Reid** is Assistant Professor in the English Department at Indiana State University and received a PhD in English from Rice University. She has published articles on the covers of *Uncle Tom's Cabin*, photographing race in nineteenth-century America, and other topics.

**James R. Rohrer** is Associate Professor of History at the University of Nebraska, Kearney and the author of *Keepers of the Covenant: Frontier Missions and the Decline of Congregationalism, 1774–1818.*

**James M. Schmidt** is an independent scholar whose books include *Notre Dame and the Civil War: Marching Onward to Victory; Years of Change and Suffering: Modern Perspectives on Civil War Medicine*; and *Lincoln's Labels: America's Best Known Brands and the Civil War.*

**Renée M. Sentilles** is Associate Professor of History and Director of Undergraduate Studies in the History Department at Case Western Reserve University. She also serves on the faculty for the American Studies Program and

Women's Studies Program. She is the author of *Performing Menken: Adah Isaacs Menken and the Birth of American Celebrity.*

**John Stauffer** is a leading authority on antislavery, social protest movements and the Civil War era. He is a Harvard University professor of English and American Literature and African American Studies, and Chair of Harvard's History of American Civilization program. His eight books include *The Black Hearts of Men: Radical Abolitionists and the Transformation of Race* (2002) and *Giants: The Parallel Lives of Frederick Douglass and Abraham Lincoln* (2008), which both won numerous awards.

**Vanessa Steinroetter** is Assistant Professor of English at Washburn University and holds a PhD in English from the University of Nebraska-Lincoln. She has published articles in journals, including the *New England Quarterly*, and she is currently working on a book that examines representations of readers and reading in American literature of the Civil War.

**Jennifer A. Stollman** is Assistant Professor in the Department of History at Fort Lewis College, where she also teaches in the Gender and Women's Studies Program. She holds a PhD from Michigan State University, where she completed a dissertation on Jewish women in the antebellum and Civil War South.

**Ryan Swanson** is Assistant Professor of History at George Mason University and the author of *Jim Crow on Deck: Baseball During America's Reconstruction.*

**Phyllis Thompson** is the Departmental Teaching Fellow in Women, Gender and Sexuality at Harvard University, and a final year PhD candidate in Harvard's History of American Civilization program. She is completing a dissertation entitled *Domestic Pleasures: Fantasies of Joy and Fulfillment in American Home Life*, which focuses on the licit pleasures linked to the home in the nineteenth and twentieth centuries.

**David Williams** is a Professor of History at Valdosta State University at Valdosta State University. He is the author of *Bitterly Divided: The South's Inner Civil War; A People's History of the Civil War; Plain Folk in a Rich Man's War; Johnny Reb's War*; and *Rich Man's War.*

**Bradford A. Wineman** is Associate Professor of Military History at Marine Corps University. He has also been an Assistant Professor in the Department of Military History, U.S. Army Command and General Staff College, and is a member of the U.S. Marine Corps Reserve where he currently serves as an historian for the U.S. Marine Corps Historical Division. He holds a PhD in History from Texas A&M University, where he completed his dissertation on antebellum southern military education.

# INDEX

*abatis*, 71

abolitionism: and Hutchinson Family Singers, 236; Northern, 88, 90; and Oberlin College, 115; and photography, 214–15; and reform and welfare societies, 102–4; Southern, 86–87; and women's wartime roles, 35

abortion, 38–40

*The Absentee* (Edgeworth), 81

acoustic shadows, 68

Act to Encourage Immigration, 176

Adair, William Penn, 188

Adams, Isaac, 161

Adams, Victoria, 145

Adams, William, 158, 161

aesthetic appreciation of the environment, 67–68

African Americans: and Cincinnati riots, 3–5; and emancipation celebrations, 161–62; and medical care, 142; and minstrel songs, 235; and New York riots of 1863, 11; and spirituals, 239–41; veterans, 290–91; wartime writers, 210. *See also* blacks; black troops; slave emancipation

African religious traditions, 79

*After the Battle* (illustration), 223–24

Agricultural College of Pennsylvania, 118–19

agriculture: and farmland devastation, 69–70; and women's wartime roles, 39

aid societies: United States Sanitary Commission (USSC), 24–25; and women's wartime roles, 35–37

Alabama, 17

Alcott, Bronson, 101

Alcott, Louisa May, 35, 205, 207, 209

Alford, Barney, 158, 160, 161

Allen, Richard, 103

Allen, William Francis, 239, 241

allopathic medicine, 132–33, 136–37, 139

All Souls church, 93

alternative medical practices, 146–47, 149

American and Foreign Antislavery Society, 103

American Anti-Slavery Association (AAS), 102–3

American Board of Commissioners for Foreign Missionaries (ABCFM), 102

American Colonization Society, 105

American Literary, Scientific and Military Academy (ALSMA), 121, 125

American Medical Association, 148

American Missionary Association (AMA), 95–96

American Temperance Society, 100

Anderson, Robert, 217

Anderson, Willis, 158

Andersonville prison, 295–98, 300

Andrews, Eliza, 35, 39

Anglican Society for the Propagation of the Gospel in Foreign Parts, 79, 80

Antietam, 237

anti-Semitism, 178–79

apologists, Southern, 85–86

Appleton, Nathan, 59

Arkansas, 18

army camps, 73

*Army Life in a Black Regiment* (Higginson), 210, 239

*The Army of the Potomac–A Sharp-Shooter on Picket Duty* (print), 224–25

*The Army of the Potomac–Sleeping on their Arms* (engraving), 225

Arthur, T.S., 209

artisan republicanism, 46

Asbury, Francis, 86

Ashley, Sarah, 160

Ashton, Charles H., 73

Associated Press (AP), 194, 197

Asstogatogeh (Cherokee lieutenant), 183

*Atlantic Monthly*, 37, 80, 81, 91, 205, 209, 237, 239

*Augusta Chronicle and Sentinel*, 14

authority, local vs. national concepts of, 8

Averell, William W., 114


Baccus, Joesphine, 145

Bagby, George W., 201

ballads, 235, 238

Baptists, 84, 85

Barnard, Frederick A.P., 114

Barnard, George, 215, 220

Barnes, William H., 238

Barnum, P.T., 195, 236, 265

Barr, James, 67

Barrow, John, 86

barter of medical supplies, 134–35

baseball: black baseball players, 254–55; and conscription, 257–58; National Association of Base Ball Players (NABBP), 158–59, 254, 258–59, 260; and New York City, 254; origins of, 253; in Philadelphia, 259–60; popularity of, 260; in the South, 254; and the war, 255–58

*Baseball Before We Knew It* (Block), 253

*Baseball in the Garden of Eden* (Thorn), 253

Bates, John, 159

"The Battle Cry of Freedom" (song), 237, 238

battleground tactics and the environment, 68–69

"The Battle Hymn of the Republic" (song), 237, 238

Battle of Bull Run, 14, 74, 263

Battle of Caving Banks, 185

Battle of Honey Springs, 188

Battle of Pea Ridge, 186

Battle of Shiloh, 237, 288–89

Battle of the Wilderness, 225–26

*Battle-Pieces and Aspects of the War* (Melville), 203, 206

battle wounds and women soldiers, 27–28

Beauregard, P.G.T., 207

Beckett, Harrison, 162

Beecher, Catherine, 101, 104

Beecher, Henry Ward, 89, 294

Beecher, Lyman, 100

Beers, Ethel Lynn, 205, 206

Bell, Frank, 159

Bell, James M., 185

Bellew, Frank, 228

Bellows, Henry W., 93–94, 95, 105

Benjamin, Judah P., 82

Bennett, James Gordon, 194, 202

Berry, Carrie, 41

biblical texts: and slavery apologists, 85–86; and slave uprisings, 80, 81

Bierce, Ambrose, 278, 288–89

birding, 67–68

birthday rituals, 41–42

Bivens, Lige, 18

*Black Crook* leg show, 246

blackface theater, 244

blacks: activism and abolitionism, 103; black baseball players, 254–55; black dockworkers, 3; paintings and illustrations of, 228–29; and Southern dissent, 21

black troops: battle experiences of, 166–67; black women's support of, 169–70; and civil rights, 164; Confederate, 169; and "contraband" slaves, 165–66,

167–68; death toll of, 170; and the Emancipation Proclamation, 158, 167–68, 171; enlistment of, 163–65; and First and Second Confiscation Acts, 166; pay, commission, and duty disparities, 168–69; regimental organization of, 167, 170–71; and repatriation efforts, 165
Block, David, 253
Blunt, James C., 188
Boetticher, Otto, 257
Boker, George, 205
Boles, Elvira, 162
Bontecou, R.B., 217, 219
*Book of American Negro Spirituals* (Johnson), 240
Booth, Edwin, 243, 245, 248
Booth, John Wilkes, 243, 248, 251
Booth, June (son), 243, 247–48, 250
Booth, Junius, 243, 247
Boston Labor Reform Association, 55
Boudinot, Elias C., 185, 187
Bourne, George, 86
Bowery theater, 242, 244
Bowman, Alexander Hamilton, 123
Boyd, Belle, 207
Boyd, Issabella, 159
Bradshaw, Wesley, 207
Brady, Mathew, 214, 217, 218–19, 220
Bragg, Arial, 59
Bragg, Braxton, 68, 199
Breadbasket of the Confederacy, 70
bread riots, 6–7, 15, 40
Breckinridge, Lucy, 25
bridge building, 71–72
Bridges, Eloise, 249
Brisbane, William, 156
British Blondes, 246
British immigrants, 176, 179
Broadway theater, 242, 244
Broken Arm (Osage major), 188
Brooklyn Navy Yard, 51
Brooks, Preston, 112
Brotherhood of Locomotive Engineers, 51
Brown, Joe, 13
Brown, John, 81, 103, 123, 206, 207
Brown, William Wells, 86, 102, 210, 290

Browne, Junius Henry, 201
Bryant, William Cullen, 207
Buchan, William, 143
Buell, Don Carlos, 68
Bull Run battles, 14, 25, 74, 237, 263
Burbridge, Stephen G., 53
Bureau of Colored Troops, 168
Bureau of Indian Affairs, 184
burlesque theater, 244, 245, 246
Butler, Benjamin, 154, 198
Byrd, W.H., 14

Cades Cove, Tennessee, 18
cadet corps and southern universities, 112
Cajun parishes, 17–18
California Native Americans, 182
Cameron, Simon, 94
Camfield, Caleb, 21
Canal Era, 56
Capers, Francis W., 123
Caperton, George, 66, 72
*Capture of Jefferson Davis at Irwinsville, Ga.* (illustration), 228
Carolina Colony charter, 81
Carroll, John, 83
Carson, Kit, 187
Catholicism: Catholic immigrants, 173; and nativism, 174; in the North, 91; in the South, 83
cattle, 67
Catto, Octavius, 255
censorship of newspapers, 198
Chadwick, Edwin, 93
Chadwick, Henry, 254, 258, 260
chaplains, military, 92–93, 264
Charles Pfizer & Co., 134, 148
Charleston, South Carolina: and Catholicism, 83; College of Charleston, 111–12, 114; and Judaism, 81, 82; the *Mercury*, 198, 200, 201; South Carolina Military Academy (SCMA), 123, 124–25, 129; "The Charleston Ode", 211
Cheatam, Henry, 157
Cherokee Nation, 184–90
Cherokee soldiers, 183–85
Chesnut, Mary, 299
Chesnutt, Charles, 291

Chester, Thomas Morris, 199
*chevaux de frise*, 71
Chicago, 61
*Chicago Tribune*, 10
Child, Lydia Marie, 104, 268
childbirth in wartime, 38–40
children: effect of war on, 41–42; as song trope, 237–38
Children's Aid Society, 102
Chinese immigrants, 174–75
Chisolm, J.J., 136
Choctaw soldiers, 185
Christianity: Christian benevolent societies and education, 101–2; and Christian relief organizations, 93; and slavery, 80–81, 85
*Christian Reporter* (newspaper), 210
Christie, Smith, 188
Christmas, 269–70
Christy's Minstrels, 236
Church, Frederic Edwin, 226–27
church attendance, 262–63
Church of All Souls, 93
Cincinnati, 3–5, 61
"City on a Hill", 90
civil disobedience and religious abolitionists, 86–87
civilian healthcare: divisions and inequities of, 142; household medicines, 143; Mark Twain on, 142–43; patent medicines, 146–47, 148, 149; pharmaceutical industry, 147–48; self-care by slaves, 144–45; traditional vs. alternative medical practices, 146–47, 149; and veteran pensions, 148–49; war-related civilian deaths, 145–46; women as caregivers, 143–44, 145, 146
civil rights, 164, 171
*Clotelle* (Brown), 86, 210
cloth, 35, 38
clothing fashions, 37–38
coal and iron mining, 60
coal miner riots, 7–8
Cobb, Thomas R.R., 113
Coffin, Charles Carleton, 70
Coke, Thomas, 86
College of Charleston, 111–12, 114
College of the Holy Cross, 116

Columbia College, 116
Columbia University, 114, 115
commerce and industry: coal and iron mining, 60; cotton production, 56–58; effects of war on, 62; New England textile mills, 58–59; New York and industrialist wealth, 60–61; and slavery, 62; and transportation systems, 56; western economic growth, 61–62
commutation fees, 11, 14–15, 167, 168, 182
Confederacy: and black enlistment, 164–65, 169; and bread riots, 6–7; Confederate theater, 248–51; conscription and labor resistance, 51–52; demobilization of soldiers, 285–86; and draft resistance, 10, 13–14; drug supplies, 134–35; and immigrant soldiers, 176; Jewish soldiers and anti-Semitism, 178–79; and Native American soldiers, 183–87; political paintings and illustrations, 222–23; raids on northern cities, 4; and Southern dissent, 21–22; Southern Jewish support of, 82; and Southern memories of the war, 298–301
Congressional Medal of Honor, 49
conscription: and baseball, 257–58; and commutation fees, 11, 14–15, 167, 168; and draft resistance, 8–10; and the Emancipation Proclamation, 167; and immigrant soldiers, 178; and labor organizations, 7–8, 51–52; and southern military schools, 126; and southern students in combat, 114
Conscription Act, 8
Constitution, proposed Christian amendment to, 96
"contraband" camps and slaves, 95, 165–66, 167–68, 228
contraception, 38–40
Cook, George S., 215, 217–18
Cook, Joel, 69, 71, 72
Cooke, John Esten, 206–7
Cooke County, Texas draft resisters, 10
Cooper, Anna Julia, 107
Cooper, Douglas H., 185, 187, 188
Copperheads, 8–9, 10, 11, 52

corduroy roads, 72
corpse obsession, 277–78
cotton production: and American economy, 56–57; and food riots, 15; and slavery, 57–58; wartime effects on, 50
courtship and marriage in wartime, 36–37
coverture, 103–4
Crabtree, Lotta, 247, 248
Crane, Stephen, 290
Crasson, Hannah, 157
Creighton, William R., 49
Crittenden, John J., 154
Crittenden Compromise, 48, 153, 154
cross-dressing and the theater, 245, 246
Cummings, Amos Jay, 49
Cummings, Kate, 146
Cushman, Charlotte, 245
Cusick, Cornelius, 182
Cutting, James A., 216

Daguerre, Louis Jacques Mande, 213
*Dark Artillery* (political cartoon), 228
Dart, Anson, 147
Davidson College, 112, 113, 114
Davis, Jefferson: and Catholicism, 83, 91; and desertion, 16; and end of war, 293; and journalists, 199; as literary inspiration, 207; memoirs of war, 298–99; paintings and illustrations of, 223, 227–28; and southern students in combat, 114, 125; student opinions of, 116; and Thanksgiving, 267; and Virginia bread riots, 7
Davis, Rebecca Harding, 211
Dean, Sydney, 267
death and dying: antebellum plagues and epidemics, 275; corpse obsession, 277–78; and the good death, 276–77, 278, 281; and heaven, 281–82; hero symbolism, 281; and mourning, 278–80; paintings and illustrations of, 223–24; poetry and songs about, 279–80; and politics, 276; and religion, 280–81; wartime tolls, 275
DeBar, Clementina, 250
Declaration of Rights and Sentiments, 104

De Forest, John William, 211, 287
deforestation, 70–71, 72–74
Delaware Plan, 155
demobilization, 284–87
Democrats: Copperheads and draft resistance, 8–9, 10, 11, 52; and partisan newspapers, 196, 197; Peace Democrats and draft resistance, 11; and shoemakers' strike, 48; War Democrats, 52
desertion and Southern dissent, 15–17
"Destroying Angels", 17
Dickinson, Emily, 203, 204
disabled veterans, 287
disease: and military prisons, 297; and Native Americans, 181; and war-related civilian deaths, 145–46
*Dispatch* (newspaper), 197
dissent. *See* Southern dissent
"Dixie Doodle" (song), 237
dockworkers, Cincinnati riots, 3
Dodge, William E., 95
domesticated animals, 66–67
*Domestic Medicine* (Gunn), 143
domestic sphere: antebellum ideologies of womanhood, 33–34; courtship and marriage during war, 36–37; wartime effects on gender roles, 33, 35, 43; women's status and activism, 104–5; and women's wartime aid, 35–36. *See also* women
Douglass, Ambrose, 160
Douglass, Frederick: and abolition, 102, 103, 153; and black enlistment, 163–64, 167; on Christian hypocrisy, 80; and emancipation celebrations, 156; photographs of, 215
Downing, Lewis, 188
draft resistance and riots, 8–11, 244
Draper, Alonzo Granville, 48, 49
Drew, John, 184–85
Drowning Bear (Cherokee chief), 183
drug companies, 134
drummer boy song trope, 238
*Drum-Taps* (Whitman), 204
Du Bois, W.E.B., 57, 240
duty, local vs. national concepts of, 8
Dwight, Howard, 74

dying soldier trope, 208

Earlham College, 115
earthworks, 70–71
Easter, 262
ecumenical relations and religion in the
    North, 96–97
Edgeworth, Maria, 81
Edmonds, Sarah (Private Franklin
    Thompson), 28
education: and Freedmen's Bureau, 106;
    and goals of reform and welfare
    societies, 101–2. *See also* higher
    education; military schools
Educational Commission of Boston, 96
Edwards, Jay D., 217
Edwards, Justin, 100
Elliot, Samuel, 159
Elliott, Stephen, 84
Emancipation Proclamation, 90–91, 116,
    155–56. *See also* slave emancipation
Emanuel, Gabe, 157
*Embattled Courage* (Linderman), 287
Emerson, Ralph Waldo, 99
Emory College, 112, 114
the empty sleeve, 287
*Enlarged Devil's Dictionary* (Bierce), 278
enlistment: of black troops, 163–64, 167;
    and women soldiers, 25–26
the environment: aesthetic appreciation
    of, 67–68; battle effects on farmland,
    69–70; and battleground tactics,
    68–69; deforestation, 70–71, 72–74;
    and domesticated animals, 66–67;
    inclement weather, 65–66; resource
    degradation, 64–65, 69, 71, 73–74;
    and soldiers' log cabins, 72–73;
    transportation network impacts, 71–
    72; wartime use of, 64–65; and wild
    game, 67
Episcopalians, 84
Equal School Rights Committee, 103
Erlich, Paul, 147
ethnic consciousness of immigrants, 175,
    179–80
ethnic groups: and draft resistance, 11; and
    labor organization, 7–8; wage laborers
    and American working class, 46

European immigrants, 173, 175
Evans, Augusta Jane, 209
*Every Man His Own Doctor* (Buchan), 143
exemption fees and draft resistance, 11,
    14–15

families: and death, 276–78; and divided
    allegiances, 35; and mourning, 278–80
Farewell Address, 264–65
farmland, battle effects on, 69–70
Farquhar, John M., 49
federal government: and Folger Anti-
    Trade Union Strike Bill, 54; and New
    York riots of 1863, 11; and personal
    authority, 5–6, 9; and suppression of
    riots, 5, 7
feminism: effect of war on gender
    roles, 33, 35; and Southern views of
    womanhood, 34–35. *See also* women
Field, Dudley, 115
*The Field Hospital* (painting), 227
5th Connecticut Regiment, 285
54th Massachusetts Infantry, 167, 168,
    170, 229
fighting and women soldiers, 25–29
Fincher, Jonathan C., 47, 50
Findlay, John, 264
1st Kansas Colored Volunteers, 167
1st South Carolina Volunteers, 156, 158,
    167, 170
First Confiscation Act, 154, 166
*The First Flag of Independence* (lithograph),
    222–23
First Manassas, 14
Fisk Jubilee Singers, 240
Five Civilized Tribes, 181–82, 184
Folger Anti-Trade Union Strike Bill, 54
food quality and availability, 38
foreign missionary work, 102
Forrest, Nathan Bedford, 169
Forsyth, John, 199
Forten, James, 103
Fort Sumter, 88–89, 237
49th Ohio Regiment, 285
Foster, Stephen Collins, 233, 235, 238
the Fourth of July, 266–68
Fox, George, 84
*Frank Leslie's Illustrated Newspaper*, 195,

200, 214, 228
Franklin, Benjamin, 222
Franklin, William, 236
Franklin College, 112, 114, 115
Freedmen's Bureau, 106
freedmen's relief associations, 95–96
freedom: and black military service, 171; gradual spread of, 158–60; lack of guidelines for, 160–61
freedpeople: wage laborers and American working class, 45–46, 52–53; and white laborers' fears, 4–5, 9, 12
"free state of Jones", 17
Frelinghuysen, Theodore, 116
Fugitive Slave Law, 62

gabions, 70–71
*Games of Skill and Conjuring*, 257
Gardner, Alexander, 73, 217, 218, 219, 220
Garland, Landon C., 123
Garnet, Henry Highland, 156
Garrison, Lucy McKim, 239, 241
Garrison, William Lloyd, 102, 103, 153
*The Gates Ajar* (Phelps), 208
Gauss, Bryant, 26
Gauss, Lucy Thompson, 26
gender roles: effect of war on, 33, 35, 43; and the theater, 245–46, 248–49; and views of womanhood, 33–35; and women as caregivers, 143–44, 145, 146; women's status and activism, 103–4
Georgia and local militias, 20–21
Georgia Military Institute (GMI), 123, 129
German immigrants, 175, 176–77
"Get off The Track!" (song), 236
Gettysburg: and New York riots of 1863, 11; photographs of, 218, 219; and southern college students, 113
Gibbs, J.W., 116
Gladden, Washington, 97
"Glorious Cause", 35
Glover, Caroline Howard, 205
God: and Lost Cause ideology, 299–300; and Manifest Destiny, 295
the good death, 276–77, 278, 281
Grand Review, 285

Granger, Gordon, 159, 171
Grant, Ulysses S.: and battleground tactics, 68–69; and the Battle of the Wilderness, 225; on Elizabeth Van Lew, 25; and Ely Samuel Parker, 89, 182; and farmland devastation, 70; graduation from West Point, 125; Jewish soldiers and anti-Semitism, 179; and journalists, 199
Gray, T.R., 81
Greeley, Horace, 155, 165, 196
Greene, William B., 49
Green Light Letter, 258
Gregory, Russell, 18
grief: national grief and Reconstruction, 210–11; as wartime literature theme, 207–8
Grimké, Angelina, 86–87, 104
*The Guerillas* (play), 248, 250
Gunn, John C., 139, 143

Hadley, Sylvester, 72–73
Hahn, Michael, 267
Hale, Sarah Josepha, 267–68
Hall, Thomas, 156
Halleck, Henry, 154, 198
Halloween, 262
Hamilton, Gail, 33
Hamilton, James, 16–17
Hammond, William, 133
Hardinge, Emma, 54
Harney, William S., 154
Harper, Frances Watkins, 103, 211, 291
Harper's Ferry, 103
*Harper's Weekly*, 195, 200, 207, 208, 210, 211, 218, 219, 228, 256, 262, 266
Harrison, Constance Cary, 205
Hartford Female Seminary, 101
Harvard University, 117, 119
*A Harvest of Death* (photograph), 229
Hayne, Paul Hamilton, 205
Hayward, Albert Morton, 131
Haywood, Felix, 171
healthcare. *See* civilian healthcare
heaven, 281–82
heavy goods industry, 59–60
Henry, Judith, 74
hero symbolism, 281

Hewitt, John Hill, 250
Hewitt, John Till, 206
Higginson, Thomas Wentworth, 80, 81, 156, 204, 205, 209–10, 239, 240, 241
higher education: and Land-Grant Act, 118–19; northern campuses, 115, 117–18; northern faculty, 115–16; northern students, 116–17; southern campus damage and closures, 114; southern campuses used as hospitals, 115; southern faculty, 111–12; southern students, 112–13, 114; southern university officials, 113–14
*A History of the Negro Troops in the War of the Rebellion* (Williams), 290
history paintings, 221
Hitchcock, Watson, 66, 68
Hoge, Jane, 106
holidays: and baseball games, 256–57; Christmas, 269–70; Easter, 262; effects of war on, 41, 262, 263, 267, 268–69; the Fourth of July, 266–68; George Washington's birthday, 264–65; Halloween, 262; and Sabbath observances, 262–64, 270–71; Thanksgiving, 268–69; Valentine's Day, 266
Holmes, Oliver Wendell, 204, 216, 218, 289
Holmes County, Ohio draft resisters, 10
"Holy Joe's", 92
homefront disorder and violence, 4–6
home missionaries, 93
homeopathic medicine, 132–33
Homer, Winslow, 207, 224–26, 229, 230, 269
homespun cloth, 35
Homestead Act, 46, 175
Hooker, Joseph, 199, 201
horses, 66–67
*hors mori*, 276–77
hospitality, 37
*Hospital Sketches* (Alcott), 207
hospital stewards, 138
household medicines, 143
households, wartime ransacking of, 42–43
housework during wartime, 38–40
Howe, Julia Ward, 91–92, 209, 237

Huff, Charles "Captain", 20
Hugo, Victor, 209
hunting, 67
Hutchinson Family Singers, 236
hydrology and battleground tactics, 68–69
hypocrisy of Christian slaveowners, 80–81

"I Am Fighting for the Nigger" (song), 235
identity: and veterans, 288–90; and women soldiers, 26–29
immigrants: and anti-Semitism, 178–79; British, 176, 179; Chinese, 174–75; economic and military laborers, 175–76; and ethnic consciousness, 175, 179–80; European, 173, 175; German, 175, 176–77; and military service, 176, 177–79; and nativism, 174, 178; and patriotism, 173; and temperance movements, 174; views on slavery, 176–77; working-class fears of, 173–74
Independence Day, 266–68
Independents, 196
Indian Territory, 182
individual worthiness, 100, 101
industrialization, 58, 60
industry. *See* commerce and industry
*Inviting a Shot Before Petersburg, Virginia* (painting), 225
Irish dockworkers, Cincinnati riots, 3
Irish immigrants, 174, 175, 177–78, 262
Iroquois Confederacy, 181
Island Community death, 287–88

*J. R. Williams* (steamship), 188
Jackson, Martin, 169
Jackson, Patrick T., 59
Jackson, Thomas J. "Stonewall", 125, 129, 206
Jacobs, Harriet, 103
James, William, 107–8
*Jeff Davis Reaping the Harvest* (political cartoon), 223
Jefferson, Joseph, 249
Jefferson, Thomas, 81, 86, 111, 115
Johehouse, Charles, 28
"John Brown's Body" (song), 237

Johns, Edward W., 134, 136

Johnson, Eastman, 227

Johnson, Gus, 162

Johnson, James Weldon, 240

Johnson, Joseph E., 189

Johnson, Nancy, 159

John Wyeth and Brother, 134, 148

Jones, Thomas, 69

Jones County, Mississippi, 17

journalism as a profession, 193–94

Judaism: Jewish soldiers and anti-Semitism, 178–79; and slavery apologists, 85; Southern, 81–82

Jumper, John, 188

Junkin, George, 113–14

Kansas Indian Home Guard, 186, 187, 188, 190

Keene, Laura, 243, 245, 246, 251

Keetoowah Society, 185

Knickerbockers, 253

Knight, Newton, 17

Knight, Samuel, 13

Knights of Father Mathew, 100–101

Know Nothing party, 174

labor: Cincinnati riots, 3–5; immigrant laborers, 175–76

labor organizations: and conscription, 7–8, 51–52; national craft organizations, 47; National Typographical Union (NTU), 49–50; and naval shipyard workers' strike, 51; new industries and manufacturing, 50–51; and partisan politics, 52, 54–55; railroad network and unionization, 51; and secession, 48–49; and shoemakers' strike, 48; and solidarity, 45, 55; and trade unionism, 47–48, 53–54; wage laborers and American working class, 45–46, 52–53; and workers' rights, 46–47

Land-Grant Act of 1862, 118–19, 129

Landis, Kenneth, 258

landscape. See the environment

laundry and manual labor, 38–39

layout gangs, 16–17

LeConte, Emma, 39, 41–42

Lee, Mattie, 157

Lee, Robert E.: and the Battle of the Wilderness, 225; and Catholicism, 91; and food for soldiers, 70; graduation from West Point, 125; and Jewish soldiers, 82; as literary inspiration, 207, 211; paintings and illustrations of, 227–28; and the Sabbath, 263, 264; surrender of, 189, 251, 293

leg shows, 244, 246

Leland, John, 86

Les Misérables (Hugo), 209

Letcher, John, 7

letter writing: and death and mourning, 279; and evolution of newspapers, 193–94; and military chaplains, 92; and news of household health, 143; and Valentine's Day, 266; and wartime literature, 208–9; and women's wartime roles, 36

The Liberator (newspaper), 153, 276

Lilly, Eli, 148

Lincoln, Abraham: Act to Encourage Immigration, 176; assassination of, 251; black criticism of, 156; black praise of, 157; and black soldier enlistment, 164, 165, 166; and the Emancipation Proclamation, 90–91, 116, 154, 155, 156–57, 166; Jewish soldiers and anti-Semitism, 179; and journalists, 199; as literary inspiration, 207; and military chaplains, 92; and military recruiting, 8; naval blockade and medical supplies, 134; and naval shipyard workers' strike, 51; on religion, 79, 90; and the Sabbath, 263; on slavery and cause of civil war, 153; on strikes and free labor, 48; and Thanksgiving, 267–68; and U.S. Sanitary Commission, 24, 94

Lind, Jenny, 236, 243

Linderman, Gerald, 287

Lindley, Martha Parks, 26

literature: African American writers, 210; battle themes, 206; black women writers and activism, 103; and death, 279; dying soldier theme, 208; effects of war on writers, 203–4; and letter writing, 208–9; and military figures, 206–7; and political figures, 207;

literature (*continued*): Reconstruction and national grief, 204, 210–11; veterans' memoirs, 288–89, 295–98, 298–99; and wartime poetry, 204, 205–6; and wartime politics, 206–7, 209–10; wartime popularity of newspapers and magazines, 204–5; and wartime roles of women, 207–8
*Little Women* (Alcott), 207
Livermore, Mary, 106–7
Locke, Alain, 240
Locke, John, 81
log cabins, 72–73
Long, Thomas, 158
Longfellow, Henry Wadsworth, 203, 269
looting and bread riots, 6–7
Lost Cause ideology, 83, 87, 299–300
Louisiana, 17–18, 82
Louisiana Native Guards, 167
Louisiana Seminary of Learning, 113
Louisiana State Seminary and Military Academy, 129
Love, James R., 189
love letters, 36
Lowell, Francis Cabot, 59
Lowell, Massachusetts, 59
Lowell Mill Girls, 59
lumber, 61
Lumpkin, Joseph Henry, 112
Lunt, Dolly, 41, 42–43
Lynch, William Bigham, 112
Lynn, Ethel, 209

*Macaria* (Evans), 209
Macarthy, Harry, 250
Mackay, Charles, 268
Macready, James, 244
Madigan, William, 49
Madison, James, 84
*Magnolia Weekly*, 205
*A Man Knows a Man* (illustration), 228
man's relationship to the divine, 99–100
manufactured goods, 56
marching and seasoning of soldiers, 66
Marks, James Julius, 71
Mark Twain on civilian healthcare, 142–43
marriage during wartime, 36–37

Marrs, Elijah, 157
Marsh, O.C., 116
Martin, James G., 189
Marvin, Edwin, 285
Mason, Lowell, 234
Massachusetts Institute of Technology (MIT), 117–18, 119
Maying, 262
*Mazeppa* theater performance, 245–46
McCabe, James D., Jr., 248, 250
McCarty, Eli, 10
McClellan, George B., 114, 218, 233, 236
McCrady, John, 111–12
McIntosh, Chilly, 185, 188
McIntosh, Daniel "Dode", 185, 188
Mead, Hiram, 115
media, portrayal of women in bread riots, 7
medical care: wartime effects on gender roles, 40–41. *See also* civilian healthcare; military medicines
medicinal plants, 135–36, 145
*Medicine and Slavery* (Savitt), 144
medicines. *See* civilian healthcare; military medicines
melodramas, 244, 250
Melville, Herman, 90, 203–4, 206
memoirs', veteran, 288–89, 295–98, 298–99
Memorial Day, 262, 289
memories of war: Andersonville prison, 295–98, 300; Northern, 294–98; Southern, 298–301
Menken, Adah Isaacs, 243, 245–46, 247–48
Methodists, 84–85
Midwest, 9
Miles, Josh, 162
military chaplains, 92–93, 264
military medicines: and allopathic medicine, 132–33, 136–37, 139; Confederate drug supplies, 134–35; drug companies, 134; drug quality, 133, 135; drugs as commodities, 133; and knowledge of illness causation, 137; medicinal plants, 135–36; military medical laboratories, 136; pharmacies, 133–34; physicians' status, 138–39;

treatment of symptoms, 137–38, 140; wartime-era drugs, 131–32

military schools: alumni enlistment and wartime leadership, 124–25; antebellum popularity of, 121–22; closure during war, 125–26; curriculums of, 127–28; enrollment and operations during war, 126–27; and pre-war sectional tensions, 122–23; and soldier training, 123–24; southern tradition of, 121–22, 129; and students in combat, 128–29; wartime effects on graduation, 124

Militia Act, 8

Militia Law of 1792, 164

militias, state vs. federal control, 8

Mills, A. G., 256–57

Mills, George Henry, 285

mining, 51, 60

*Minnie's Sacrifice* (Harper), 211

minstrel songs and theater, 235, 244

missionaries, 93

Mississippi, 16–17

*Miss Ravenel's Conversion from Secession to Loyalty* (De Forest), 211, 287

Mitchell, Maggie, 242

money: and enlistment of women soldiers, 26; payments to soldiers' wives, 40

Moody, Dwight L., 97

Moore, Josiah, 65

Moore, Samuel Preston, 135

morality plays, 244

Moran, Thomas, 226

Mordecai, Rachel, 81

Morgan, John Hunt, 4

Morgan, Sarah, 25, 39

Morrill, Justin, 118–19

Morse, Charles, 67

Moses, Charlie, 157

mother song trope, 237, 238

Mount Holyoke, 102, 115

mules, 66–67

music: African American spirituals, 239–41; diversity of, 233; and George F. Root, 233, 237, 238–39; parlor songs, 234–36; war songs, 236–39

*Narrative of the Life of Frederick Douglass* (Douglass), 80

Nast, Thomas, 223–24, 228, 270

National Association of Base Ball Players (NABBP), 158–59, 254, 258–59, 260

national craft organizations, 47

nationalism and daguerreotypes, 213

National Labor Union, 54

National Trades' Union, 46

National Typographical Union (NTU), 47, 49–50

National Union of Iron Moulders, 47–48

National Union of Machinists and Blacksmiths, 47

National Women's Suffrage Association, 107

Native Americans: and disease, 181, 182; effects of war on, 184–85; and the Five Civilized Tribes, 181–82; medical traditions of, 143; and military service, 182–90; religious conversion of, 79, 80, 181; removal from land and resettlement on reservations, 181–82

nativism, 174–75, 178

*Nature* (essay), 100

naval shipyard workers' strike, 51

naval warfare, 51

*The Negro in the American Rebellion* (Brown), 210, 290

New England Freedmen's Aid Association, 96

New England textile mills and industrialization, 58–60

new industries and manufacturing, 50–51

*The New Negro* (Locke), 240

New Richmond Theater, 251

newspapers: as American time capsule, 193; and civilian war correspondents, 197–201; and journalism as profession, 193–94; and labor organizations, 54; military censorship of, 198; and paper production, 202; partisan nature of, 195–97, 201; and printing technology, 194, 195; and telegraphy, 194; wartime popularity of, 204

New York City: and baseball, 254; and industrialist wealth, 60–61; and theater, 242, 243–44

New York City Industrial Congress (NYCIC), 47

*New York Clipper*, 259

*New York Herald*, 194, 196, 200

New York Knickerbockers Base Ball club, 253

*New York Times*, 196, 198, 218–19, 263, 267

*New York Tribune*, 11, 196, 198–99, 201

the North: and draft resistance, 9–10; religion in the North, 88–97

North Carolina: and anti-Confederate militias, 18–19; and Unionist militias, 19

*Northwood* (Hale), 268

nostalgia, 288

nurses, 25

Oberklein, Fred, 48–49

Oberlin College, 115, 116–17

O'Connor, Arthur, 66

Ogden, Richard D'Orsay, 251

Oglethorpe, James, 84

Olmstead, Frederick Law, 94

opium, 135

Opothleyahola (Creek chief), 185

"Order No., 11", 179

Osgood, Samuel, 207

O'Sullivan, Timothy, 217, 229

*Our American Cousin* (play), 251

*Our Banner in the Sky* (painting), 226–27

pacifism, 88–90, 115

paintings and illustrations: of blacks, 228–29; by Frederic Edwin Church, 226–27; images of death, 223–24; of Lee and Davis, 227–28; political cartoons, 222–23, 227, 228; and realism, 221, 224; of reconciliation, 228; by Thomas Moran, 226; by Thomas Nast, 223–24, 228, 270; by Winslow Homer, 224–26, 229, 230; of women, 224, 227

Panic of 1857, 47, 48

parades, 265

*Pardon/Franchise* (engraving), 228

Park, William T., 136

Parker, Ely Samuel, 182, 189

parlor songs, 234–36

patent medicines, 146–47, 148, 149

patriotism: and artists, 227; and enlistment of women soldiers, 26; and hero symbolism, 281; and homespun cloth, 35; and immigrants, 173; local vs. national concepts of, 8; and views of womanhood, 33, 43; and wartime love letters, 36

Peck, George, 90

Pegg, Thomas, 186

Pember, Phoebe Yates, 81

Pennsylvania, 7–8

pensions, veteran, 148–49

personal moral codes, 5–6

Petermen, Rebecca "Georgianna", 28

*Peterson's Ladies Magazine*, 205, 208

Petty, J.W., 217

Phares, Joseph, 20

pharmaceutical industry, 147–48

Phelps, Elizabeth Stuart, 208

Philadelphia: and baseball, 259–60; and early U.S. labor organizations, 46

philanthropy, 101–2, 107–8

Phillips, William A., 187, 188

*The Photographic Sketchbook of the Civil War* (Gardner), 220, 229

*Photographic Views of Sherman's Campaign* (Barnard), 220

photography: and Alexander Gardner, 73, 217, 218, 219, 220; and ambrotypes, 215–16; and *cartes-de-visite*, 216–17; and daguerreotypes, 213, 214, 215; and death and grieving, 280; and George S. Cook, 215, 217–18; and Mathew Brady, 214, 217, 218–19, 220; and panoramas, 215; and portraits, 214–15; and stereoviews, 217; and tintypes, 216; and wartime photographers, 217; and wartime photojournalism, 214

physical examinations and enlistment of women soldiers, 26

pianos, 234

Piatt, Sarah Morgan Bryan, 211

Piggot, A. Snowden, 136

Pike, Albert, 184, 186

Pittman, Isaac, 193

Pius IX, Pope, 83

plantations, 57

*Planter* (steamship), 167
plants, medicinal, 135–36, 144
poetry, 204, 205–6, 268, 269, 279–80
politics: and baseball metaphor, 256; and
    death, 276; and labor organizations,
    52, 54–55; and partisan newspapers,
    195–97, 201; political cartoons, 222–
    23, 227, 228; political parties and labor
    organizations, 54–55; and theater, 242,
    243, 248–51; and wartime literature,
    206–7, 209–10; and women's wartime
    roles, 35–36
Polk, Leonidas, 84
Pollard, Edward A., 298
polygenesis, 86
the poor and draft resistance, 8, 11
poppies, 135
"Porkopolis", 61
pregnancy and women soldiers, 28–29
Presbyterianism, 84, 85
Princeton University, 117
printing technology, 194, 195
Prioleau, William H., 134, 136
prisons, Confederate military, 295–98
propaganda, post-war, 295
Prosser, Gabriel, 81
prostitution and the theater, 244
Protestantism: and death, 276; and
    nativism, 174; in the North, 90, 94; in
    the South, 84
provost marshals and draft resistance, 10
"Prowling Brigades", 17
public opinion, influence of paintings and
    illustrations on, 222–23

Quakers (Society of Friends): Earlham
    College, 115; John Greenleaf Whittier,
    88; in the South, 84, 86–87
quinine, 133, 135, 137, 140

race riots in New York, 11
railroads, 51, 56, 174
Ramseur, Stephen Dodson, 299
Randall, James Ryder, 209
Raymond, Henry J., 196–97
realism in paintings and illustrations, 221,
    224
Rebel Bishop, 83

Reconstruction: illustrations of
    reconciliation, 228; and literature
    themes, 210–11; and veterans, 290,
    291–92
reform and welfare societies: and
    abolitionism, 102–4; Christian
    benevolent societies and education,
    101–2; Christian relief organizations,
    93; and civilian medical care, 146;
    Freedmen's Bureau, 106; goals of,
    100–101; and individual worthiness,
    100, 101; legacy of, 107–8; and
    man's relationship to the divine,
    99–100; Sabbatarians, 101; temperance
    movements, 100–101; U.S. Christian
    Commission, 94–95; U.S. Sanitary
    Commission, 24–25, 93–94, 105–6;
    women and activism, 103–5, 105–6,
    106–7
regional identity: and enlistment of
    women soldiers, 26; and religion in
    the South, 79; and southern military
    schools, 122
Reid, Whitlaw "Agate", 201
religion: African American spirituals, 239–
    41; African religious traditions, 79; and
    death, 280–81; and the Hutchinson
    Family Singers, 236
religion in the North: and the American
    Missionary Association (AMA),
    95–96; and Catholicism, 91; clerical
    pacifism vs. support for war, 88–90;
    and ecumenical relations, 96–97;
    Lincoln's covenant with his Maker,
    91; military chaplains, 92–93; post-
    war piety vs. secularism, 97; proposed
    Christian amendment to Constitution,
    96; and Protestantism, 90, 94; relief
    organizations, 93; and transcendent
    meaning of war, 91–92; U.S. Christian
    Commission, 94–95; U.S. Sanitary
    Commission, 93–94
religion in the South: abolitionists,
    86–87; apologists, 85–86; Catholicism,
    83; Christianity and slavery, 80–81;
    diversity of, 79; Episcopalian split
    over secession, 84; Judaism, 81–82;
    Protestantism, 84; and secession, 84–85

Reno, Ella, 27
repatriation efforts, 165
Republicans, 196
resource degradation, 64–65, 69, 71, 73–74
Reynolds, L. M., 188
Rice, David, 86
Richardson, Albert Dean, 200–201
"rich man's war, poor man's fight", 8, 11, 14–15
Richmond, Virginia: bread riots, 6–7, 40; the *Dispatch*, 197; and theater, 243, 248, 249, 250–51
Ridge, Frank and Jasper, 17
rights: women's rights, 35; workers' rights, 46–47
riots: Cincinnati riots, 3–5; coal miners, 7–8; and draft resistance, 8–11, 244; federal suppression of, 5, 7; food riots, 6–7, 15; New York race riots, 11
*The Rise and Fall of the Confederate Government* (Davis), 298–99
Ritchings, Caroline, 249
Ritchings, Peter, 249
rivers and battleground tactics, 69
road building, 72
Rogers, William Barton, 118
romantic ballads, 235
Roosevelt, Franklin D., 258
Root, George F., 233, 237, 238–39
Rosecrans, William S., 53
Ross, John, 184, 186
Ross, William Potter, 185, 186
Rowson, Susanna, 245
Russell, A.J., 217
Russell, William Howard, 197, 198
Rutgers University, 115, 116, 118
Ryan, Abram Joseph, 83, 210–11

Sabbatarians, 101
Sabbath observances, 262–64, 270–71
sacred holidays: Christmas, 269–70; Easter, 262; and Sabbath observances, 262–64, 270–71
Salomon, Frederick, 187
San Francisco and the theater, 242–43, 246–48
Santa Claus, 270

Savage, James, Jr., 117
Savannah, Georgia: and Judaism, 81, 82; and secession, 222–23
*Savannah Morning News*, 15
Savitt, Todd, 144
Schreiner, Herman L., 238
*Scientific American*, 147
Scott, Winfield, 198
Scraper, George W., 188
secession: and labor organizations, 48–49; and religion in the South, 84–85; southern opposition to, 14
2nd Kansas Indian Home Guard, 186, 187, 188
Second Battle of Bull Run, 25, 237
Second Confiscation Act, 154–55, 166
Second Great Awakening, 81
secularism in post-war America, 97
segregation of military units, 171
self-reliance of women, 38–41
Seton, Elizabeth Ann Bayley, 83
*The Seven Sisters* (play), 246
sewing bees and wartime aid efforts, 35–36
shadow dance, 242
Shakespeare performances, 245, 250
*Sharpshooter* (painting), 224–25
Shaw, Mary, 159
Shaw, Robert Gould, 168–69
*Shaw Memorial* (monument), 229
sheet music, 234
Shelton, Julia, 205
Shenandoah Valley, 70
Shepherd, Oliver, 11
Sheridan, Phil, 70
Sherman, Thomas W., 165
Sherman, William T., 113, 114, 125, 285, 286
shoemakers' strike, 48
Shpperson, William G., 205
Sibley, John, 18
Siegel, Franz, 129
Siegling Music Publisher, 234
Simms, William Gilmore, 203, 205
singing school movement, 234
*Skirmish in the Wilderness* (painting), 225–26
skull imagery in political illustrations, 223

slave emancipation: annual celebration of, 161–62; black criticism of Lincoln, 156; and black military service, 158; black praise of Lincoln, 157; and cause of civil War, 153; and the Emancipation Proclamation, 155–56, 157–58; gradual nature of freedom, 158–60; and labor organizations, 52; Lincoln's death and martyrdom, 157; Lincoln's views on emancipation, 155; military policy on escaped slaves, 154–55; newly freed slaves, 160–61; and slave escapes during war, 153–54; white response to Emancipation Proclamation, 158, 159–60, 161. *See also* black troops

*Slave Hunt* (painting), 226

slavery: and Chinese immigrants, 175; and Christianity, 80–81, 88–90; and cotton production, 57–58; immigrant views on, 176–77; and industrialization, 62; medical self-care by slaves, 144–45; and relief organizations, 95–96

*Slave Songs of the United States*, 80, 233, 239–40, 241

Smalley, George W., 199

Smalls, Robert, 167

Smith, Francis H., 123, 124

Smith, Kirby, 189

Smith, Thomas Southwood, 93

smuggling of medical supplies, 135

snake imagery in political illustrations, 222–23

Snow, Susan, 157

social contract and workers' rights, 46

social reform. *See* reform and welfare societies

social rituals during wartime, 37

Society of Friends (Quakers): Earlham College, 115; John Greenleaf Whittier, 88; in the South, 84, 86–87

soldiers: and baseball, 255–58; and battleground tactics, 68–69; dying soldier trope, 208; faith and concepts of heaven, 282; and hero symbolism, 281; immigrant soldiers, 176; and inclement weather, 65–66; paintings and illustrations of, 223–27; payments to soldiers wives, 40; photographs of dead soldiers, 218–19; ransacking of households, 42–43; and transcendent meaning of war, 91–92; and white response to Emancipation Proclamation, 158–60; women soldiers, 24–29. *See also* veterans

solidarity, 45, 55

sorrow songs, 80

the South: and notions of womanhood, 34–35; religion in the South, 79–87; Southern women and social reform, 105. *See also* Southern dissent

South Carolina: and desertion, 19–20; South Carolina College, 114; South Carolina Volunteers, 239

South Carolina Military Academy (SCMA), 123, 124–25, 129

Southern dissent: county secessions, 17–18; and desertion, 15–17; and draft resistance, 13–15; and food riots, 15; and local militias, 17–21; planters and the Confederacy, 13, 15; and Union secession, 14

*Southern Illustrated News*, 195, 222

*Southern Literary Messenger*, 205

Spalding, Albert, 255, 257

spirituals, 239–41

Spooner, Henry, 64–65, 66, 68

sports. *See* baseball

Squibb, Edward R., 132, 133, 134, 148

St. Joseph's College, 117

St. Louis, Missouri, 265

Stand Watie (Cherokee soldier), 184, 185, 187, 188, 189

Stanton, Edwin, 133, 188

Stanton, Elizabeth Cady, 104

starvation, and food riots, 6–7, 15

Steele, Frederick, 188

Steinway and Sons, 234

Stephens, Alexander H., 21–22

stevedores, Cincinnati riots, 3

Stiles, E.B., 116

Stone, Lucy, 104

Stowe, Harriet Beecher, 35

Stuart, J.E.B., 207

suffrage, women's, 107

Sumner, Charles, 112

Sumner, William Graham, 116
Sunderland, Byron, 90
surgeons: Mary Edwards Walker, 25. *See also* military medicines
Swedenborg, Emanuel, 281
Sylvis, William H., 47

tableau theater, 249
Talbot, William Henry Fox, 215
Tappan, Lewis, 95
Taylor, Susie King, 170
telegraphy, 194
temperance movements, 100–101, 107, 174, 236
Temple School, 101
Tennessee, 18, 19
Terrell, Mary Church, 107
Texas: and anti-Confederate militias, 18; delayed news of emancipation in, 159; and German immigrants, 177
textile mills, 58–59
Thanksgiving, 268–69
Thayer, Sylvanus, Col., 121
theater: and Adah Isaacs Menken, 243, 245–46, 247–48; and the Booth brothers, 243, 246–47, 248; burlesque, 244, 245, 246; Confederate theater, 248–51; and cross-dressing, 245, 246; dramas, 245; and Maggie Mitchell, 242; melodramas, 244, 250; minstrel theater, 244; and New York, 242, 243–44; in Richmond, 243, 248, 249, 250–51; and San Francisco, 242–43, 246–48; on the West Coast, 246–48
37th Wisconsin Regiment, 183
Thomas, William Holland, 183, 184, 189, 190
Thomas' Legion, 183–84
Thompson, Franklin (Sarah Edmonds), 28
Thompson, Lydia, 246
Thomson, Methvin, 136
Thoreau, Henry David, 86–87, 103
Thorn, John, 253
Thornwell, James Henley, 86
Thumb, Tom, 265
*Time on the Cross* (Engerman and Fogel), 58–59
Timrod, Henry, 205, 209, 211

tobacco production and food riots, 15
Tobin, John M., 49
topography and battleground tactics, 68–69
tory gangs, 16, 20–21
Towne, Laura, 157
trade. *See* commerce and industry
trade unionism and labor organizations, 47–48, 53–54
traditional vs. alternative medical practices, civilian healthcare, 146–47, 149
Trail of Tears, 182
transcendent meaning of war: and religion in the North, 91–92; and veterans, 288–90
transformation, goals of reform and welfare societies, 99–101
transportation systems: described, 56; and environmental impacts, 71–72; and western economic growth, 61–62
Trinity College, 112, 113
Tripler, Charles S., 132
Trowbridge, John T., 74
Truth, Sojourner, 169
truth and photography, 213
*Turel* (steamboat), 69
turkey, 268
Turner, Emery, 158
Turner, Henry McNeil, 156
Turner, Nat, 81
twenty-slave law, draft exemption, 14–15

U.S. Army Surgeons, 25
U.S. Christian Commission, 94–95
U.S. Constitution, proposed Christian amendment to, 96
U.S. economy diversification and growth, 61–62
U.S. Sanitary Commission, 24–25, 93–94, 105–6, 256, 260
uniforms, women's manufacture of, 35–36
Union: conscription and labor resistance, 51–52; control of art centers and publishing houses, 222; demobilization of soldiers, 284–85, 286–87; and draft resistance, 8–10; and enlistment of black troops, 163–65; and immigrant

soldiers, 176, 177–78, 179; and Native American soldiers, 182–90; and Northern memories of the war, 294–98; political paintings and illustrations, 223; Unionist threats to North Carolina plantations, 19; and white laborers' fears of freedpeople, 4–5
United States Colored Troops (USCT), 168, 210
United States Military Academy (West Point), 121, 123, 124, 125, 127
University of Alabama, 122, 129
University of Maryland, 116
University of Massachusetts, 119
University of Michigan, 117, 118
University of Mississippi, 112, 113, 114, 115
University of North Carolina, 112, 113
University of Virginia, 112, 117
upright pianos, 234

Valentine's Day, 266
Van Dorn, Earl, 186
Van Lew, Elizabeth, 25
variety theater shows, 247
Vassar, 118
Vaughan, Mary C., 209
Verot, Jean-Pierre Augustine, 83
Vesey, Denmark, 81
The Veteran in a New Field (painting), 229
veterans: African American, 290–91; and demobilization, 284–87; disabled veterans, 287; memoirs of, 288–89, 295–98; and nostalgia, 288; and postwar economic achievement, 287–88; and Reconstruction, 290, 291–92; sense of self and transcendence, 288–90; veteran pensions, 148–49
Veteran's Day, 262
Vickery, John, 21
Vicksburg, Mississippi, 68–69
Virginia Military Institute (VMI), 114, 119, 121, 122–23, 124, 125, 126, 129
voting and labor organizations, 54

Wade, Benjamin, 82
wage laborers and American working class, 45–46, 52–53

Waggoner, Sarah, 157
Waiting for the Verdict (Davis), 211
Wakeman, Rosetta, 27
Walker, C. I., 286
Walker, Mary Edwards, 25
Walker, Tandy, 188
Wallack, James W., 245
Waltham, Massachusetts, 59
Ward, John, 21
Ware, Charles Pickard, 239, 241
Warner, Lucien, 116
war-related civilian deaths, 145–46
war songs, 236–39
War Songs of the South (Shepperson, ed.), 205
Washington, George, 264–65
Washington, Indiana, 10
Washington College, 113
Washingtonian Movement, 100–101
waterways and battleground tactics, 68–69
Watie's Regiment, 184, 185
Watkins, Sam, 14–15
wealth: and conscription exemptions, 8; and industrialization, 58–59
The Wearing of the Gray (Cooke), 206–7
weather, inclement, 65–66
Weer, William, 187
Weir, Margaret, 237
Wells, James Madison, 17
Wesley, Charles, 84
Wesley, John, 84
West Coast theater, 246–48
western economic growth, 61–62
West Point (United States Military Academy), 121, 123, 124, 125, 127
"We Wait Beneath the Furnace Blast" (poem/song), 236
Whelan, Peter, 83
"When Johnny Comes Marching Home" (song), 236–37
"When the Swallows Homeward Fly" (song), 235
white laborers, 3–5, 9, 12
Whitman, Walt, 203, 204, 207, 277, 282
Whitney, Eli, 59
Whittier, John Greenleaf, 88, 236
wild game, 67

Wilkes County, North Carolina, 18–19
Wilkie, Frank "Galway", 201
Williams, George Washington, 290
Williams, Isaac, 158–59
Williams, Nellie, 27
Williams College, 115, 118
Wilson, Edmund B., 89
Winder, John, 297
Winston County, Alabama, 17
Winthrop, John, 90
Wirz, Henry, 300
Wisconsin Oneidas, 183
Wise, Henry, 123
women: black women's support of black troops, 169–70; as caregivers, 143–44, 145, 146; and food riots, 6–7, 15, 40; literary treatment of women's roles, 207; paintings and illustrations of, 224, 227; reform and welfare society activism, 103–5, 105–6, 106–7; and wartime poetry, 205–6; women soldiers and aid societies, 24–25; and women spies, 25; women's rights, 35, 236
Women's Central Association for Relief, 24
Women's Central Association of Relief, 94
Women's Christian Temperance Union, 107
Wood, Fernando, 243
Woodbury Bridge, 72
wool production, 50
Work, Henry Clay, 233
workers' rights and early U.S. labor organizations, 46–47
working-class fears of immigrants, 173–74
Working Women's Protective Association, 53
wounded reader trope, 207–8

xenophobia, 173–74, 177

Yale University, 116